Lecture Notes in Computer Science 9882

Commenced Publication in 1973
Founding and Former Series Editors:
Gerhard Goos, Juris Hartmanis, and Jan van Leeuwen

Editorial Board

More information about this series at http://www.springer.com/series/7407

Marco Dorigo · Mauro Birattari
Xiaodong Li · Manuel López-Ibáñez
Kazuhiro Ohkura · Carlo Pinciroli
Thomas Stützle (Eds.)

Swarm Intelligence

10th International Conference, ANTS 2016
Brussels, Belgium, September 7–9, 2016
Proceedings

 Springer

Editors
Marco Dorigo
Université Libre de Bruxelles
Brussels
Belgium

Mauro Birattari
Université Libre de Bruxelles
Brussels
Belgium

Xiaodong Li
RMIT University
Melbourne, VIC
Australia

Manuel López-Ibáñez
University of Manchester
Manchester
UK

Kazuhiro Ohkura
Hiroshima University
Hiroshima
Japan

Carlo Pinciroli
École Polytechnique de Montréal
Montréal, QC
Canada

Thomas Stützle
Université Libre de Bruxelles
Brussels
Belgium

ISSN 0302-9743   ISSN 1611-3349 (electronic)
Lecture Notes in Computer Science
ISBN 978-3-319-44426-0   ISBN 978-3-319-44427-7 (eBook)
DOI 10.1007/978-3-319-44427-7

Library of Congress Control Number: 2016947393

LNCS Sublibrary: SL1 – Theoretical Computer Science and General Issues

Printed on acid-free paper

This Springer imprint is published by Springer Nature
The registered company is Springer International Publishing AG Switzerland

Preface

These proceedings contain the papers presented at ANTS 2016, the 10th International Conference on Swarm Intelligence, held at IRIDIA, Université Libre de Bruxelles, Brussels, Belgium, during September 7–9, 2016. The ANTS series started in 1998 with the First International Workshop on Ant Colony Optimization (ANTS 1998). Since then ANTS, which is held bi-annually, has gradually become an international forum for researchers in the wider field of swarm intelligence. In 2004, this development was acknowledged by the inclusion of the term "Swarm Intelligence" (next to "Ant Colony Optimization") in the conference title. Since 2010, the ANTS conference has been officially devoted to the field of swarm intelligence as a whole, without any bias toward specific research directions. This is reflected in the title of the conference: "International Conference on Swarm Intelligence."

This volume contains the best papers selected out of 47 submissions. Of these, 18 were accepted as full-length papers, while seven were accepted as short papers. This corresponds to an overall acceptance rate of 53%. Also included in this volume are eight extended abstracts.

All the contributions were presented as posters. The full-length papers were also presented orally in a plenary session. Extended versions of the best papers presented at the conference will be published in a special issue of the *Swarm Intelligence* journal.

We take this opportunity to thank the large number of people that were involved in making this conference a success. We express our gratitude to the authors who contributed their work, to the members of the international Program Committee, to the additional referees for their qualified and detailed reviews, and to the staff at IRIDIA for helping with organizational matters.

We hope the reader will find this volume useful both as a reference to current research in swarm intelligence and as a starting point for future work.

July 2016

Marco Dorigo
Mauro Birattari
Xiaodong Li
Manuel López-Ibáñez
Kazuhiro Ohkura
Carlo Pinciroli
Thomas Stützle

Organization

General Chair

Marco Dorigo   Université Libre de Bruxelles, Belgium

Co-chairs

Mauro Birattari   Université Libre de Bruxelles, Belgium
Thomas Stützle   Université Libre de Bruxelles, Belgium

Technical Chairs

Xiaodong Li   RMIT University, Australia
Manuel López-Ibáñez   University of Manchester, UK
Kazuhiro Ohkura   Hiroshima University, Japan

Publication Chair

Carlo Pinciroli   École Polytechnique de Montréal, Canada

Liaison Chair for Africa

Andries Engelbrecht   University of Pretoria, South Africa

Liaison Chair for Asia

Fumitoshi Matsuno   Kyoto University, Japan

Liaison Chair for North America

Magnus Egerstedt   Georgia Institute of Technology, USA

Program Committee

Afnizanfaizal Abdullah   Universiti Teknologi Malaysia, Malaysia
Andrea Perna   Université Libre de Bruxelles, Belgium
Andy Adamatzky   University of the West of England, UK
Ann Nowe   Vrije Universiteit Brussel, Belgium
Daniel Angus   The University of Queensland, Australia
Prasanna Balaprakash   Argonne National Laboratory, USA
Jacob Beal   BBN Technologies, USA

Giovanni Beltrame	École Polytechnique de Montréal, Canada
Gerardo Beni	University of California, USA
Spring Berman	Arizona State University, USA
Tim Blackwell	Goldsmiths, University of London, UK
Maria J. Blesa	Universitat Politècnica de Catalunya, Spain
Christian Blum	University of the Basque Country, Spain
Mohammad Reza Bonyadi	The University of Adelaide, Australia
Alexandre Campo	Université Libre de Bruxelles, Belgium
Stephen Chen	York University, Canada
Ran Cheng	University of Surrey, UK
Marco Chiarandini	University of Southern Denmark, Denmark
Anders Lyhne Christensen	Lisbon University Institute, Portugal
Maurice Clerc	Independent Consultant on Optimisation
Carlos Coello Coello	CINVESTAV-IPN, Mexico
Oscar Cordon	University of Granada, Spain
Nikolaus Correll	University of Colorado at Boulder, USA
Ana Luisa Custodio	Universidade Nova de Lisboa, Portugal
Swagatam Das	Indian Statistical Institute, India
Gianni Di Caro	Istituto Dalle Molle di Studi sull'Intelligenza Artificiale, Switzerland
Luca Di Gaspero	Università di Udine, Italy
Karl Doerner	Johannes Kepler University Linz, Austria
Haibin Duan	Beihang University, China
Mohammed El-Abd	American University of Kuwait, Kuwait
Andries Engelbrecht	University of Pretoria, South Africa
Hugo Jair Escalante	Instituto Nacional de Astrofísica, Óptica y Electrónica, Mexico
Susana Esquivel	Universidad Nacional de San Luis, Argentina
Nazim Fates	Laboratoire Lorraine de Recherche en Informatique et Ses Applications, France
Eliseo Ferrante	Katholieke Universiteit Leuven, Belgium
Ryusuke Fujisawa	Hachinohe Institute of Technology, Japan
Luca Gambardella	Istituto Dalle Molle di Studi sull'Intelligenza Artificiale, Switzerland
José García-Nieto	University of Málaga, Spain
Roderich Groß	The University of Sheffield, UK
Frédéric Guinand	Université du Havre, France
Walter Gutjahr	University of Vienna, Austria
Julia Handl	Manchester Business School, UK
Kiyohiko Hattori	National Institute of Information and Communications Technology, Japan
Tim Hendtlass	Swinburne University of Technology, Australia
Michael Hsiao	Virginia Tech, USA
Thomas Jansen	Aberystwyth University, UK
Mark Jelasity	University of Szeged, Hungary
Guillermo Leguizamón	Universidad Nacional de San Luis, Argentina

Simone Ludwig	North Dakota State University, USA
Stephen Majercik	Bowdoin College, USA
Vittorio Maniezzo	Università di Bologna, Italy
Antonio David Masegosa Arredondo	University of Granada, Spain
Massimo Mastrangeli	Max Planck Institut for Intelligent Systems, Germany
Michalis Mavrovouniotis	De Montfort University, UK
Yi Mei	Victoria University of Wellington, New Zealand
Ronaldo Menezes	Florida Institute of Technology, USA
Bernd Meyer	University of Hamburg, Germany
Martin Middendorf	University of Leipzig, Germany
Seyedali Mirjalili	Griffith University, Australia
Roberto Montemanni	Istituto Dalle Molle di Studi sull'Intelligenza Artificiale, Switzerland
Melanie Moses	University of New Mexico, USA
Frank Neumann	The University of Adelaide, Australia
Randal Olson	Michigan State University, USA
Koichi Osuka	Osaka University, Japan
Ender Ozcan	University of Nottingham, UK
Konstantinos Parsopoulos	University of Ioannina, Greece
Paola Pellegrini	Institut Français des Sciences et Technologies des Transports, de l'Aménagement et des Réseaux, France
Jorge Peña	Max Planck Institute for Evolutionary Biology, Germany
Günther Raidl	Vienna University of Technology, Austria
Andrea Roli	Università di Bologna, Italy
Mike Rubenstein	Harvard University, USA
Erol Sahin	Middle East Technical University, Turkey
Thomas Schmickl	University of Graz, Austria
Kevin Seppi	Brigham Young University, USA
Jurij Šilc	Jožef Stefan Institute, Slovenia
Christine Solnon	LIRIS, Centre National de la Recherche Scientifique, France
Dirk Sudholt	University of Sheffield, UK
Jon Timmis	University of York, UK
Colin Torney	University of Exeter, UK
Vito Trianni	ISTC, Centro Nazionale delle Ricerche, Italy
Elio Tuci	Aberystwyth University, UK
Richard Vaughan	Simon Fraser University, Canada
Michael Vrahatis	University of Patras, Greece
Justin Werfel	Harvard University, USA
Alan Winfield	University of the West of England, UK
Masahito Yamamoto	Hokkaido University, Japan
Yanjun Yan	Western Carolina University, USA

Contents

Extended Abstracts

Full Papers

A Bearing-Only Pattern Formation Algorithm for Swarm Robotics

Nicholi Shiell[1](✉) and Andrew Vardy[1,2]

[1] Faculty of Science, Department of Computer Science,
Memorial University of Newfoundland, St. John's, Canada
{nsm152,av}@mun.ca
[2] Faculty of Engineering and Applied Science,
Department of Electrical and Computer Engineering,
Memorial University of Newfoundland, St. John's, Canada

Abstract. Pattern formation is a useful behaviour for a swarm of robots in order to maximize their efficiency at tasks such as surveying. Previous pattern formation algorithms have relied upon various combinations of measurements (bearing, distance, heading, unique identity) of swarm mates as inputs. The ability to measure distance, heading, and identity requires significant sensory and computational capabilities which may be beyond those of a swarm of simple robots. Furthermore, the use of unique identities reduces the scalability, flexibility and robustness of the algorithm. This paper introduces a decentralized pattern formation algorithm using bearing-only measurements to anonymous neighbours as input. Initial results indicate the proposed algorithm improves upon the performance, scalability, flexibility, and robustness when compared to a benchmark algorithm.

Keywords: Bearing-only control · Pattern formation · Behaviour-based robotics · Swarm robotics

1 Introduction

This paper introduces a decentralized behaviour-based pattern formation algorithm which uses a neighbour-referenced approach [1], and bearing-only measurements to nearby swarm mates as input. The bearings are measured with respect to a common reference direction (i.e. North). The proposed algorithm differs from similar bearing-only techniques, for example [12], in two important ways; the definition of the desired formation, and the lack of statically defined reference neighbours. The pattern formation algorithm proposed in this paper will be referred to as the Dynamic Neighbour Selection (DNS) algorithm.

The DNS algorithm is intended for use with a swarm of simple robots with limited sensory and communication abilities. These limitations are imposed to keep the robots cheap and expendable, allowing the DNS algorithm to be used in dangerous applications.

© Springer International Publishing Switzerland 2016
M. Dorigo et al. (Eds.): ANTS 2016, LNCS 9882, pp. 3–14, 2016.
DOI: 10.1007/978-3-319-44427-7_1

Behaviour-based formation control techniques have a long history in the literature [1,8,10]. The techniques presented in these papers make use of bearing, distance, and heading information about neighbours. Acquiring this information requires significant sensory capabilities. However, bearing can be measured using more limited sensors. Lately there has been a significant amount of work in the study of bearing-only pattern formation algorithms [2–4,9,12]. The DNS algorithm is intended to improve upon the scalability, flexibility, robustness, and performance of similar bearing-only algorithms. The cost for these improvements however, is a reduced set of possible formations.

The pattern formation algorithm presented in [12] shares many traits with the DNS algorithm. Both algorithms use bearing-only measurements as inputs, are intended for use with a swarm of simple robots, and are meant for a human operator to dictate formation parameters. For these reasons the algorithm from [12] will be used as a benchmark for evaluating the DNS algorithm. The evaluation will be based on the range of formations which can be constructed, and the scalability, flexibility, robustness, and performance of the algorithms. The pattern formation algorithm from [12] will be referred to as the Static Neighbour Selection (SNS) algorithm. Note that neither algorithm controls the spacing between adjacent robots. As a result robots will not be uniformly distributed along the formation's edges, and the relative lengths of edges may differ. For example, a square formation will actually result in the convex hull of a rectangle.

The performance of the DNS and SNS algorithms will be evaluated using a discrete time simulation. The simulated robots will be controlled by behaviour-based controllers incorporating pattern formation and simple obstacle avoidance. The controller implementing the DNS algorithm will be used in a second simulation meant to test the algorithm's performance under more realistic conditions in preparation for live trials on a group of BuPiGo robots [15]. The first set of simulations will be referred to as the evaluation simulations, and the second will be called the proof-of-concept simulations.

This work is the first step in the development of a behaviour-based solution to the sweep coverage problem [5]. In this problem robots are equipped with a payload sensor (for example an optical camera) in addition to other non payload sensors, and cooperate to collectively survey a given area. This is a task for which pattern formation is quite useful. The DNS algorithm was developed to construct formations which maximize sensor coverage (line or wedge), however, other formations were also found to be possible. In order to effectively cover an entire region the spacing between robots must be controlled. This can not be done with bearing-only data. Future work will explore how environmental cues can be used to determine when adjacent robots are "close enough". This type of indirect communication is known as stigmergy [6]. For example, to conduct optical surveys of the sea floor external lighting must be supplied by the robots. Adjacent robots could sense when they are "close enough" to a neighbour when the illuminated region of their payload camera's field of view has been maximized. This would have the added effect of constricting spacing when visibility worsens, and expanding spacing when it improves.

The structure of the paper follows. First the technique used to define formations in both the DNS, and SNS algorithms will be explained. The range of formations, scalability, flexibility, and robustness of the two formation definitions will then be examined. Next the implementation of the algorithms as behaviours and their incorporation into a behaviour-based controller will be described, Next a series of numerical simulations which evaluate the performance of the algorithms will be described, and their results discussed. Finally, the paper will conclude with a summary of the results, and description of future work.

2 Formation Definitions

2.1 Static Neighbour Selection

The SNS algorithm [12] defines the desired formation by specifying bearing constraints between a robot and a subset of its swarm mates. Each robot must be uniquely identifiable in order to converge to the desired formation. Figure 1(a) illustrates how these constraints are defined by the SNS algorithm using the example of 4 robots forming a square. Each robot has a unique identification number (1 to 4), and a set of constraints (target ID and bearing). The bearing constraint is used to construct a unit vector f which the algorithm uses to calculate a control signal.

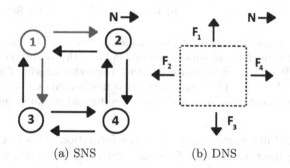

(a) SNS   (b) DNS

Fig. 1. Defining a square formation using the SNS and DNS algorithms. Each arrow in the figures represents a constraint or edge normal required by the formation definition. In (a) robot 1 has bearing constraints 0 and $-\pi/2$ with robots 2 and 3 respectively. Similar constraints exist for the remaining 3 robots. In (b) the formation definition is given by only 4 values ($\pi/2$, π, $-\pi/2$,0) regardless of the number of robots. All bearings are measured counter clockwise from North as indicated in the top right corner each figure.

2.2 Dynamic Neighbour Selection

The DNS algorithm defines the desired formation by specifying a set of unit vectors, $\{F_i\}$, perpendicular to the formation's edges. Note, for the remainder of the paper perpendicular refers to a 90 degree rotation counter clockwise (CCW). The swarm of robots is divided into teams and each team assigned one vector from the set. During the operation of the algorithm the robots do not need to identify the individual or team ID of another robot. Figure 1(b) illustrates how a square formation is defined by the DNS algorithm.

2.3   Comparison of Formation Definitions

Variety of Formations. The SNS algorithm is able to form any parallel rigid formation [12]. This includes shapes with internal structure (e.g. filled polygons). Based on the formations tested in simulation, the DNS algorithm is limited to line segments and the convex hulls of polygons. Although limited, the formations available to the DNS algorithm are useful in the context of the sweep coverage problem and others [1,13]. Example formations are shown in Fig. 2.

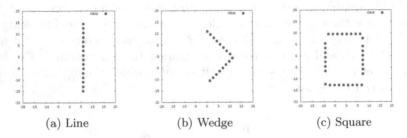

(a) Line   (b) Wedge   (c) Square

Fig. 2. Examples of the formations studied in simulation. (a) The line maximizes the cumulative field of view (FoV) of sensors perpendicular to the formation. (b) The wedge formation has similar FoV benefits as the line with the added benefit of increased visual contact between robots. (c) The square formation has benefits outside the context of the sweep coverage problem such as perimeter keeping and containment.

Neither algorithm controls the scale of the formation. This is a result of having only bearing information to define the formation. However, with the inclusion of an obstacle avoidance behaviour, which treats other robots as obstacles, a minimum scale is maintained.

Scalability, Flexibility, and Robustness. The advantages of a swarm robotic system as identified by [7] are scalability, flexibility, and robustness. The DNS and SNS algorithms will be evaluated based on these attributes.

Scalability, as defined by [7], in a swarm robotic system means the same control algorithm can be used regardless of swarm size. Both DNS and SNS are decentralized algorithms, and so both scale in this sense. However, both algorithms were developed with human interaction in mind. In order for a human operator to manipulate the formation new information must be transmitted to the swarm (i.e. sets of formation normals, or target IDs and bearing values for DNS and SNS respectively). In order for communication with the swarm to be scalable, it must be independent of group size [4]. Figure 1 shows how the information require to define a formation in the SNS algorithm depends linearly on the group size. Therefore, communication with the swarm is not scalable when using the SNS algorithm. The definition of a formation in the DNS algorithm is independent of group size, and therefore communication with the swarm is scalable with respect to group size. However, communication would scale linearly with the complexity of the formation (i.e. number of edges).

Flexibility of a swarm robotic system is the ability to handle changes to group size [7]. The SNS algorithm requires changes to the bearing constraints of neighbours of a lost or added swarm member. The DNS algorithm requires no changes to the information stored by the swarm when members are added or removed.

A source of robustness in swarm robotic systems comes from unit redundancy [7]. That is any member of the swarm can take on the role of another member of the swarm (assuming homogeneous robots). The DNS algorithm maintains unit redundancy by not requiring neighbours to be uniquely identifiable. The SNS algorithm requires robots to be uniquely identifiable and so lacks unit redundancy.

3 Methods

This section will describe the methods used to compare the DNS and SNS algorithms. The model of the robot used in the simulations will be described first. Next the behaviour-based controller used to implement the algorithms, as well as a definition of the behaviours will be given. Finally, the simulations used to evaluate the algorithms will be described.

3.1 Robot Sensors and Drive System

The robot model can be broken into two parts, the sensors, and the drive system. The sensor modalities of the robots are the same in both the evaluation and proof of concept simulations. However, the range, and effects of line of sight differ. Robots will be given their heading with respect to a common direction (compass measurement), the bearing to all visible robots, and the bearing to any robots in physical contact. The drive systems will differ between the simulations. In the evaluation simulations the robots are assumed to be holonomic, and able to change their velocities instantly. In preparation for future live trials the robots in the proof-of-concept simulations will use a differential drive system. A simple proportional control law will convert desired velocities into right and left wheel speeds.

3.2 Behaviour-Based Controller

The simulated robots are controlled by a behaviour-based controller composed of a set of behaviours, $\{\beta_1...\beta_n\}$. Each behaviour responds to sensor stimuli with a desired velocity vector. The controller sums these vectors, Eq. 1, to produce the final velocity command.

$$v_{cmd} = \sum_i v_i \qquad (1)$$

where v_{cmd} is the velocity command, and v_i is the ith behaviour's velocity vector with magnitude bounded between [0,1]. Details of the behaviours' stimuli, and responses are given in the following sections.

Two different controllers were defined for the evaluation simulation, controller D (dynamic), and controller S (static). In addition to a pattern formation behaviour, a simple obstacle avoidance behaviour is included in each controller's behaviour set. The behaviour sets for Controller D and S are $\{\beta_{obst}, \beta_{DNS}\}$, and $\{\beta_{obst}, \beta_{SNS}, \beta_{SNS}\}$, respectively. Controller S contains two β_{SNS} behaviours, one for each constraint used to define the formation [12]. Controller D was also used by the proof of concept simulations.

Obstacle Avoidance Behaviour (β_{obst}). The input for the obstacle avoidance behaviour is a vector, r, in the direction of the detected obstacle. If there is no obstacle in physical contact then the response is $v_{obst} = 0$. The behaviour response in the presents of an obstacle, v_{obst} is given by Eq. 2,

$$v_{obst} = \left(\gamma r^{\perp} - r\right) \qquad (2)$$

where γ is a random uniformly distributed number between [0,1], and $r^{\perp}$ is perpendicular to r. The random vector was used to break robots apart which previously became stuck in cyclic behaviours. These stuck robots resulted in the DNS algorithm diverging from the desired formation.

SNS Algorithm Behaviour (β_{sns}). The input for the SNS behaviour is a unit vector, r, in the direction of the target robot specified by the bearing constraint. (Sect. 2.1). The behaviour response, v_{sns} is given by Eq. 3,

$$v_{sns} = (r \cdot f^{\perp})r^{\perp} \qquad (3)$$

where $f^{\perp}$ is perpendicular to the target bearing, f, associated with the target robot, and $r^{\perp}$ is the vector perpendicular to input r. This behaviour causes the robot to travel along a circular arc centred on the target robot until the target bearing is achieved.

DNS Algorithm Behaviour (β_{dns}). The input for the DNS behaviour is the set of unit vectors, $\{r_i\}$, encoding the bearings to all visible swarm mates. The field of view of the robot's bearing sensor is divided into three sensing regions; dead ahead, forward, and rear (See Fig. 3). Note that the dead ahead region is a subset of the forward region. If a robot is detected in a region the corresponding boolean flag (B_{da}, B_{fw}, B_{re}) is set to true. The value of these flags determines the response of the DNS behaviour. The response and its dependence on the boolean flags, is shown in Eq. 4.

$$
v_{dns} = \begin{cases} -F & B_{re} \cdot (!B_{fw}) \\ F^{\perp} & R_{\text{..}} \\ (r \cdot F)F & B_{fw} \end{cases} \tag{4}
$$

where $r \in \{r_i\}$ is the bearing vector with the largest projection on to the formation normal, F. The DNS behaviour causes the robot to move in the direction of F until one of two conditions are met. The first condition is if a swarm mate is detected in the dead ahead visual region. In this case the direction of travel is rotated by $\pi/2$ radians (CCW). The other condition is if the robot has no swarm mates ahead of it. In this case the behaviour responds by moving backward along F. This backward motion is meant to stabilize the edge in the presence of noise.

The parameter, ω_{width}, controls the angular width of the dead ahead visual region (See Fig. 3). Two different values of ω_{width} were used depending on the formation being constructed. A value of 18° was used for line formations. This value should realistically depend on physical dimensions of the robot since it is intend to help the robot find an empty space along its edge, however the above

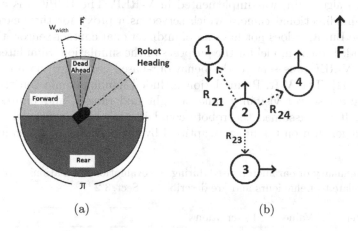

(a)   (b)

Fig. 3. (a) The sensing regions are defined with respect to the formation normal, F, and not the orientation of the robot. The width of the dead ahead region is controlled by the ω_{width} parameter. (b) An illustrated example of the DNS behaviour responses of 4 robots with the same F. The formation normal F is shown in the upper right corner. Robot 1 only senses swarm mates to the rear, and response with $-F$. Robots 2 and 4 sense neighbours ahead (outside of the dead ahead region), and in their rear sensing region and response with F. Lastly, robot 3 senses a neighbour in its dead ahead region, and so travels along $F^{\perp}$. The vectors R_{21}, R_{23}, R_{24} encode the bearings measured by robot 2 of its neighbours. Vector R_{21}, the bearing measured by robot 2 of robot 1, has the largest projection on the F, and is used by robot 2 in the calculation of its DNS behaviour's response (see Sect. 3.2).

value was found to be adequate for the simulations. It was found that using the dead ahead visual zone for non-linear formations caused the algorithm to diverge from the desired formation.

3.3 Simulation Software

The performance of both algorithms was compared using a single integrator simulation written in C++ by the author (available for download from GitHub[1]). Performance was evaluated based on the average integrated path length of all robots in the swarm. The robots were modelled as hard disks with radius r_{robot} and mass m_{robot}. Collisions between robots were approximated using 2d kinematics. Each robot has direct control over its instantaneous velocity. Control was provided by either controller S or D. Once a time step, robots were updated with sensor data (Sect. 3.1). The simulation then waited for a velocity response from all robots, and then updated the robot positions. This loop was repeated until a maximum number of times steps was reached. The simulation parameters used are summarized in Table 1. The simulation assumed the robots were always visible to each other regardless of range or line of sight. To initialize the simulation robots were randomly distributed in a circle of radius r_{deploy}.

The proof of concept simulations for the DNS algorithm were conducted in V-REP [14]. A model of the BuPiGo robot [15], which will be used for live trails of the DNS algorithm, was implemented in V-REP. The BuPiGo is equipped with an omnidirectional camera which served as a proxy for the bearing-only sensor. The BuPiGo does not have an omnidirectional contact sensor, therefore one was added to the model for the purposes of the simulation. Simulated sensor data from V-REP was sent to the behaviour-based controller via an interface with ROS [11]. The V-REP simulation included nonholonomic constraints, as well as limited sensor visibility (line of sight and range), and limited sensor resolution. It was assumed the robots could identify each other using a blob detection algorithm on the images captured by the omnidirectional camera.

Table 1. Summary of parameters used during the evaluation simulations. Note ω_{width}, and r_{max} relate to behaviours and are described in Sect. 3.2

Parameter	Value	Description
Δt	0.05	Length of time step
maxTimeSteps	100000	Max number of time steps
r_{deploy}	50	Radius of initial deployment
ω_{width}	$18°$ or $0°$	Angular width of dead ahead visual region (Sect. 3.2)
r_{robot}	5.0	Robot radius
m_{robot}	1.0	Robot mass

---

[1] https://github.com/nicholishiell/DiskSimulation.

4   Experimental Results

The performance of the algorithms was evaluated when constructing line, wedge, and square formations with various group sizes (8, 16, 20 and 32 robots). Each set of evaluation parameters (algorithm, formation, group size) was simulated 100 times and the metric values recorded for each run. The average metric values and standard deviation over all runs were calculated, and the results shown graphically in Fig. 4.

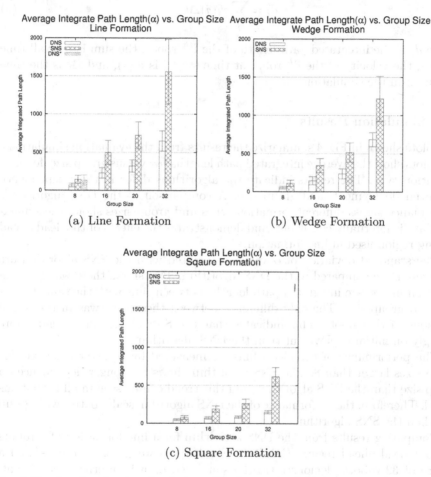

(a) Line Formation   (b) Wedge Formation

(c) Square Formation

Fig. 4. Results of evaluation simulations. The bar in plot (a) labelled DNS* is the result of running the DNS algorithm for a line formation without the dead ahead region.

4.1   Performance Metric

The performance metric, α, is the average integrated path length of robots in the swarm. A distance based metric was used to evaluate the performance of the algorithms as an analogy for energy use, which is a limiting factor in mobile robotic systems. The performance metric is defined in Eq. 5,

$$\alpha = \frac{\sum_i d_i}{N} \tag{5}$$

where d_i is the integrated path length of the ith robot, and N is the total number of robots in the swarm. The integrated path length of each robot is defined by Eq. 6.

$$d_i = \sum_j v_i(j)\Delta t \tag{6}$$

where d_i is the integrated path length of the ith robot, the sum is over all time steps j, the velocity of the ith robot at time step j is $v_i(j)$, and Δt is the time step used in the simulation.

4.2 Simulation Results

The plots shown in Fig. 4 summarize the results from the evaluation simulations. The plots show the average integrated path lengths (α) versus group size, for each formation type. The results indicate the algorithms differ in their dependence on initial deployment, and group size. A comparison of the DNS algorithm's performance across different formation types and group sizes shows the simulation data is internally consistent, and demonstrates the effects of the dead ahead sensing region used in line formation.

The standard deviation of α values associated with the SNS algorithm are relatively large compared to the DNS algorithm. This shows there was a strong variation in average integrated path lengths between runs with the same formation and group size. The only difference between these runs was in the initial positions of the robots. This indicates that the SNS algorithm depends more strongly on initial deployment than the DNS algorithm.

The performance of the algorithms, as measured by α, diverge quickly for group sizes larger than 8. The SNS algorithm shows a stronger dependence on group size than the DNS algorithm, and this trend can be seen in all formations tested. Therefore, the performance of the DNS algorithm scales better with group size than the SNS algorithm.

Comparing results from the DNS algorithm for a line formation of 8 robots without dead ahead region, (DNS* in Fig. 4(a)), a wedge of 16 robots, and a square of 32 robots, demonstrates the simulated data is internally consistent. The formation of a wedge of 16 robots involves forming 2 lines of 8. Similarly a square of 32 robots involves the construction of 4 lines of 8. The average α in these three cases should be similar. This similarity is seen in the plots shown in Fig. 4. Differences in these values can be attributed to robots colliding, and avoiding each other.

Comparing the results of the DNS algorithm when constructing a line formation, with (DNS) and without (DNS*) dead ahead regions shows the regions utility. Using the dead ahead region decreased α by a factor of approximately 2.

Unfortunately, the use of this sensing region in more complex formations (wedge and square) caused the algorithm to diverge.

A video showing the proof of concept simulations in V-REP is available online[2]. The video shows the DNS algorithm constructing line, wedge, and square formations with a group size of 12 robots

5 Conclusion

This paper introduced a decentralized bearing-only pattern formation algorithm, known as the Dynamic Neighbour Selection algorithm. The DNS algorithm was compared to a similar algorithm presented in [12] using a single integrator simulation, and by comparing the impact of their differing formation definitions. The DNS algorithm was further tested in a more realistic V-REP simulation. A cooperative behaviour-based controller was used in both simulations which integrated each pattern algorithm with a basic obstacle avoidance behaviour. The formation definition comparison shows the DNS algorithm improves upon the scalability, flexibility, and robustness of the SNS algorithm. Furthermore, the simulation shows the DNS algorithm to be more efficient than the SNS algorithm for group sizes greater than 8. The simulations also showed the DNS algorithm to be less dependent on group size, and initial deployment than the SNS algorithm.

Although the DNS algorithm has improved upon some aspects of bearing-only pattern formation algorithms, it still has limitations similar to all bearing-only algorithms. The relative lengths of polygon segments are not controlled, and the density of robots along a segment of the formation is not uniform. In the context of a solution to the sweep coverage problem these limitations are significant and will need to be addressed.

Before the DNS algorithm can be integrated into a behaviour-based solution to the sweep coverage problem a number of tasks remain. A theoretical proof of convergence and shape limitations of the DNS algorithms would strengthen the case for the robustness of the algorithm. Another task is the development of a behaviour to space the robots at "effective" intervals using environmental cues. Lastly, the control software developed in ROS for the V-REP simulation must be ported to the BuPiGo robots and live trials of the DNS algorithm conducted to confirm the results reported in this paper.

Acknowledgements. The authors of this paper would like to thank the anonymous reviewers for their helpful comments and insights.

References

1. Balch, T., Arkin, R.C.: Behavior-based formation control for multirobot teams. IEEE Trans. Robot. Autom. **14**(6), 926–939 (1998)
2. Bishop, A.N., Basiri, M.: Bearing-only triangular formation control on the plane and the sphere. In: 2010 18th Mediterranean Conference on Control & Automation (MED), pp. 790–795. IEEE (2010)

---

[2] https://youtu.be/D7ZB4lNxJsE.

3. Bishop, A.N., Shames, I., Anderson, B.: Stabilization of rigid formations with direction-only constraints. In: 2011 50th IEEE Conference on Decision and Control and European Control Conference (CDC-ECC), pp. 746–752. IEEE (2011)
4. Franchi, A., Giordano, P.R.: Decentralized control of parallel rigid formations with direction constraints and bearing measurements. In: 2012 IEEE 51st Annual Conference on Decision and Control (CDC), pp. 5310–5317. IEEE (2012)
5. Gage, D.W.: Command control for many-robot systems. Technical report, DTIC Document (1992)
6. Grassé, P.P.: La reconstruction du nid et les coordinations interindividuelles chezbellicositermes natalensis etcubitermes sp. la théorie de la stigmergie: Essai d'interprétation du comportement des termites constructeurs. Insectes Soc. 6(1), 41–80 (1959)
7. Martinoli, A.: Collective complexity out of individual simplicity. Artif. Life 7(3), 315–319 (2001)
8. Monteiro, S., Bicho, E.: A dynamical systems approach to behavior-based formation control. In: Proceedings of IEEE International Conference on Robotics and Automation, ICRA 2002, vol. 3, pp. 2606–2611. IEEE (2002)
9. Moshtagh, N., Michael, N., Jadbabaie, A., Daniilidis, K.: Vision-based, distributed control laws for motion coordination of nonholonomic robots. IEEE Trans. Robot. 4(25), 851–860 (2009)
10. Reynolds, C.W.: Flocks, herds and schools: a distributed behavioral model. Comput. Graph. 21(4), 25–34 (1987)
11. ROS: Robot Operating System. http://www.ros.org
12. Schoof, E., Chapman, A., Mesbahi, M.: Bearing-compass formation control: a human-swarm interaction perspective. In: American Control Conference (ACC), pp. 3881–3886. IEEE (2014)
13. Sousselier, T., Dreo, J., Sevaux, M.: Line formation algorithm in a swarm of reactive robots constrained by underwater environment. Expert Syst. Appl. 42(12), 5117–5127 (2015)
14. V-REP: Virtual Robot Experimentation Platform. http://www.coppeliarobotics.com/
15. Vardy, A., Shiell, N.: Bupigo: an open and extensible platform for visually-guided swarm robots (2015)

A Macroscopic Privacy Model for Heterogeneous Robot Swarms

Amanda Prorok[✉] and Vijay Kumar

University of Pennsylvania, Philadelphia, PA, USA
{prorok,kumar}@seas.upenn.edu

Abstract. To date, the issues of privacy and security remain poorly addressed within robotics at large. In this work, we provide a foundation for analyzing the privacy of swarms of heterogeneous robots. Our premise is that information pertaining to individual robot types must be kept *private* in order to preserve the security and resilience of the swarm system at large. A main contribution is the development of a macroscopic privacy model that can be applied to swarms. Our privacy model draws from the notion of *differential privacy* that stems from the database literature, and that provides a stringent statistical interpretation of information leakage. We combine the privacy model with a macroscopic abstraction of the swarm system, and show how this enables an analysis of the privacy trends as swarm parameters vary.

1 Introduction

To date, the issues of privacy and security remain poorly addressed within robotics at large. These issues are particularly important in large-scale multi-robot systems, where individual robots must share data to coordinate their actions and communicate with human operators. In this work, we frame the problem of privacy within the context of heterogenous robot swarms. Indeed, while much research in the domain of distributed robotics and multi-robot systems explores how to develop strategies for coordinating robots of the same type (i.e., homogeneous robot teams), it is generally acknowledged that exploiting *heterogeneity* by design leads to more robust, versatile, and efficient systems — especially when functional, temporal, spatial, and behavioral heterogeneity are explicitly sought after [3,12]. However, by introducing heterogeneity by design, we impose a certain degree of uniqueness and specialization. As a consequence, any given robot type may be critical to securing the system's ability to operate without failure. Hence, we must find ways of protecting the heterogeneous swarm to avoid threats that arise when the various roles within the swarm can be determined by adversaries.

A class of applications for swarm robotic systems is based on an architecture that exploits a centralized component (e.g., cloud connectivity). This type of architecture has been shown to be a very efficient and practical means for coordinating robotic swarms, because it enables a form of feedback control based on abstract information of the swarm's state, permitting high-level interaction

© Springer International Publishing Switzerland 2016
M. Dorigo et al. (Eds.): ANTS 2016, LNCS 9882, pp. 15–27, 2016.
DOI: 10.1007/978-3-319-44427-7_2

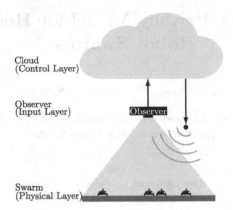

Fig. 1. The swarm of robots is supported by additional infrastructure in the cloud: observable system-level information is gathered by some sensor modality (e.g., camera), and forwarded to remote processing entities that reside in the cloud. Optionally, processed information (such as control feedback) may be relayed back to the swarm.

between the swarm and a supervisory agent [1,10]. In addition, this structure is beneficial as it facilitates *(i)* access to big data, *(ii)* access to parallel computing facilities, *(iii)* access to collective learning structures, and *(iv)* access to human support [8]. Figure 1 schematizes the architecture. The robot swarm operates on a physical layer. On a subsequent layer, *observable system-level* state information is gathered by means of some sensory data stream (camera, radio, etc.). This data stream is public, and is observable by one or several observers that are physically co-located with the swarm itself. Finally, the state information is forwarded to the cloud, where it is used for purposes such as monitoring, data processing, or machine learning. The data may also be used as input to a controller, which, based on this stream and potentially other information available in the cloud, computes a control feedback that is relayed back to the swarm. In this scheme, there are two points where privacy matters. The first point is at the level of the physical observer(s), who may not be allowed to determine private data (e.g., identify the different types of robots operating in a given space). The second point is within the cloud, where entities (such as the controller) are not allowed to act upon private information. In the following, we will formalize the notion of privacy with respect to system-level information.

Definition 1 (Private Robot Swarm). *A private robot swarm is a swarm of heterogeneous robots where any individual robot cannot be attributed to a particular robot type (or species), due to a lack of outstanding observable features.*

The current paper presents a technique that allows us to analyze the privacy of heterogeneous robot swarms by quantifying the amount of information leaked when an external observer is able to gather high-level information on the swarm's behavior. We demonstrate our technique through a case-study of collaborative task solving. Specifically, we make the following contributions:

(1) Heterogeneous Swarm Model: We begin by formalizing a framework that allows us to capture the essential behavioral characteristics of a heterogeneous swarm. We are interested in the dynamics that arise in systems where robots of different species (or types) must collaborate to achieve high-level goals. We show how our model facilitates the design of the swarm based on a definition of *inter specific interactions* [2], i.e., states that depend on the interactions of multiple species. Finally, we introduce the notion of *observable system-level* information, i.e., information that can be observed by an outsider, and show how it is embedded in our model.

(2) Privacy Model: The definition of privacy (or anonymity) is a difficult task, and a significant amount of research in the database literature is dedicated to this subject. A recent successful definition is that of *differential privacy* [4], which provides strong anonymity guarantees in the presence of arbitrary side information. One of our main contributions in this work is the development of an equivalent notion of privacy that can be applied to dynamic robot swarms.

(3) Method of Analysis: Finally, we present a technique that employs the swarm model and privacy model jointly to produce a quantitative analysis of privacy. The method is based on computational tools that can be applied to a wide variety of swarm dynamics. We demonstrate this application in a case-study of collaborative task-solving.

2   Model of Robot System

Heterogeneity and diversity are core concepts of this work. To develop our formalism, we borrow terminology from biodiversity literature [2]. We define a system of robots, where each robot belongs to a *species*. The system is composed of N_S species $\mathcal{S} = \{1, \ldots, N_S\}$, with a total number of robots N, and $N^{(s)}$ robots per species such that $\sum_{s \in \mathcal{S}} N^{(s)} = N$. At the individual level, the robots are governed by stochastic control policies [1,12]. A finite-state-machine (FSM) accounts for interspecific states. We denote these states as $a_{(\cdot)}^{\mathcal{I}}$, where the subscript denotes the state activity (e.g., search, navigate, etc.), and the superscript $\mathcal{I}$ is the set of all species that are involved in this state. For example, $a_{(\mathrm{grip})}^{\{1,2\}}$ is a state where species 1 and 2 collaborate to grip an object. Note that $\mathcal{I}$ may also be an empty set, which indicates that the state is unrelated to any particular species (we call such states byproducts, as they can relate to performance metrics or environmental conditions).

Since we focus on designing interspecific interaction mechanisms, we choose a modeling framework that implicitly accounts for system-level state transitions. We build our formalism on the theory of Chemical Reaction Networks (CRN) [5], because it allows us to define interaction mechanisms efficiently, while capturing essential system dynamics that depend on robot-to-robot interactions. CRNs are a powerful means of representing complex systems — though not a new field of research, many recent research findings that simplify the calculations are accelerating the adoption of CRNs into domains other than biology and chemistry [5,11].

We define our CRN as a triplet $\mathcal{N} = (\mathcal{A}, \mathcal{C}, \mathcal{R})$, where $\mathcal{A}$ is the set of states, $\mathcal{C}$ is the set of complexes, and $\mathcal{R}$ is the set of reactions.

State set $\mathcal{A}$: The state set encompasses all states that arise in the system, with $\mathcal{A} = \{A_1, \ldots, A_{N_A}\}$ where N_A is the number of states. States relating to a specific species s are denoted by $\mathcal{A}^{(s)}$. The set of all states includes both species-specific states as well as byproduct states $a^{\emptyset}_{(\cdot)}$. We have

$$\mathcal{A}^{(s)} = \bigcup_{s \in \mathcal{I}} a^{\mathcal{I}}_{(\cdot)} \text{ and } \mathcal{A} = \bigcup_{s=0}^{N_S} \mathcal{A}^{(s)} \text{ where } \mathcal{A}^{(0)} = \{a^{\emptyset}_{(\cdot)}\} \tag{1}$$

We can identify the interactive (interspecific) states of an arbitrary subset of species $\tilde{S} \subset S$ by considering the intersection of sets $\cap_{i \in \tilde{s}} \mathcal{A}^{(i)}$. Trivially, if $\cap_{i \in \tilde{s}} \mathcal{A}^{(i)} = \emptyset$, then the species in $\tilde{S}$ do not interact.

The CRN is a population model, and allows us to keep track of the number of robots in each of the states in $\mathcal{A}$. Hence, we define a population vector $\mathbf{x} = [x_1, \ldots, x_{N_A}] \in \mathbb{N}^{N_A}_{\geq 0}$, where x_i corresponds to the population present in state A_i. We refer to the population vector $\mathbf{x}$ as the system-level state. In order to simplify the formulation of our case studies later on, we will also use the notation $x^{\mathcal{I}}_{(\cdot)}$ to refer explicitly to the population in state $a^{\mathcal{I}}_{(\cdot)}$.

Complex set $\mathcal{C}$: The complex set is defined as $\mathcal{C} = \{C_1, \ldots, C_{N_C}\}$ where $C_j = \sum_{i=1}^{N_A} \rho_{ij} A_i$ for $j = 1, \ldots, N_C$, with vector $\boldsymbol{\rho}_j = [\rho_{1j}, \ldots, \rho_{N_A j}]^\top \in \mathbb{N}^{N_A}_{\geq 0}$. A complex is a linear combination of states, and denotes the net input or output of a reaction. In other words, a complex denotes either *(i)* the states that are required for a certain reaction to take place, or *(ii)* the states that occur as an outcome of a certain reaction that took place. The non-negative integer terms ρ_{ij} are coefficients that represent the multiplicity of the states in the complexes.

Reaction set $\mathcal{R}$: We use complexes to formulate reactions $R_l : C_j \xrightarrow{r_l} C_k$. The reaction set is defined as $\mathcal{R} = \{R_1, \ldots, R_{N_R}\}$, with N_R the number of reactions, such that $R_l \in \{(C_j, C_k) | \exists\, C_j, C_k \text{ with } C_j \to C_k\}$ for $j, k = 1, \ldots, N_C$, and where r_l is the propensity function $r_l(\mathbf{x}; \kappa_l) : \mathbb{N}^{N_A}_{\geq 0} \mapsto \mathbb{R}_{\geq 0}$ parameterized by κ_l. In this work, we use mass-action propensity functions, and $r_l(\mathbf{x}; \kappa_l) = \kappa_l \prod_{i=1}^{N_A} x_i^{\rho_{ij}}$ for all $R_l = (C_j, \cdot)$. The net loss and gain of each reaction is summarized in a $N_A \times N_R$ stoichiometry matrix Γ, the columns of which encode the change of population per reaction. In particular, the i-th column of Γ corresponds to the i-th reaction $R_i = (C_j, C_k)$ and thus, the column is equal to $\boldsymbol{\rho_k} - \boldsymbol{\rho_j}$. The elements Γ_{ji} are the so-called stoichiometric coefficients of the j-th state in the i-th reaction. Positive and negative coefficients denote products and reactants of the reaction, respectively.

Finally, we describe the dynamics of our system with help of two functions: an execution function $f_\mathcal{N}$, and a query function q:

$$f_\mathcal{N}(\mathbf{x_0}, t) : \mathbb{N}^{N_A}_{\geq 0} \times \mathbb{R}_{\geq 0} \mapsto \mathbb{N}^{N_A}_{\geq 0}$$

$$q(\mathbf{x}) : \mathbb{N}^{N_A}_{\geq 0} \mapsto \mathbb{N}^{N_O}, N_O \in \mathbb{N}_{>0} \tag{2}$$

The execution function $f_\mathcal{N}$ is a stochastic process that formulates the system's evolution over time, and that is governed by the states and reactions defined in $\mathcal{N}$. It is based on an initial population $\mathbf{x_0}$ of the swarm in states A_i, and returns the population vector $\mathbf{x}(t)$, evaluated at a fixed time t. The query function q allows us to formalize the notion of an observable, system-level state, as introduced in Sect. 1. It takes the population vector $\mathbf{x}$ as input, and returns a vector of observable values $\mathbf{y}^1$. In its most basic form, the query function is the identity function, meaning that an observer is able to capture the exact system-level state, and $\mathbf{x} = \mathbf{y}$. In this work, we show a more involved analysis by assuming that the observed values take the form of simple summations over the population vector. This assumption is well motivated when individual states are physically not distinguishable from an outside vantage point, and thus, only aggregated values can be observed. I.e., $y_i = \sum_{j \in \Omega_i} x_j$ with $\Omega_i \subset \{1, \ldots, N_A\}$, $\cup_{i \in \{1, \ldots, N_O\}} \Omega_i = \{1, \ldots, N_A\}$, and all Ω_i disjoint. We revisit these notions in our case-study, presented in Sect. 4.

3 Definition of Differentially Private Swarm

In this section, we develop our analogy to a formal definition of privacy that stems from the database literature, and that is referred to as differential privacy (formerly known as indistinguishability) [4]. This concept considers two key components: a *database* that holds sensitive information pertaining to individuals, and a *query* that releases information obtained from the database via a mechanism. The goal of differential privacy is to develop mechanisms that are able to provide information in response to database queries, while preserving the privacy of the individuals recorded therein, even in the presence of arbitrary side information[2]. Side information can be understood as a prior probability distribution over the database, and hence, privacy is preserved if no additional information about this distribution is obtained through the query. It is important to note that the condition of differential privacy is made with respect to the release mechanism (i.e., query), and does not depend on the database itself, nor on the side information. In particular, if an individual's presence or absence in the database does not alter the distribution of the output of the query by a significant amount, regardless of the side information, then the privacy of that individual's information is assured.

---

[1] The modeling framework (CRN) can encompass any measurable state that is associated to the swarm (beyond physical robot states). As a consequence, there are no limitations to what the observable state can represent. This choice can be made by the designer as a function of what may be exposed in a given system.

[2] In our context of a robotic swarm, an example of side information could be the number of manufacturing parts ordered to build the swarm. If different robot species are made of different parts, such information can be used to construct an initial guess about the number of robots per species. Thus, one would be able to derive the probability of a robot belonging to a given species.

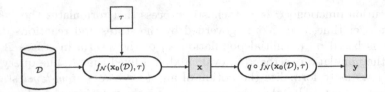

Fig. 2. The composition of the robot swarm is recorded in a database $\mathcal{D}$. The function $f_\mathcal{N}$ is a stochastic process that executes the swarm and returns a system-level state output $\mathbf{x}$. Query function q reads the (internal) system-level state, and returns the observable output $\mathbf{y}$. Parameter τ denotes the time at which the system is observed.

Our analogy applies the concepts of database and query to the context of heterogeneous swarms. We consider a database that represents the composition of our robot swarm, and that records the species of each of the robots. Also, we consider an observer who is capable of observing the swarm during its operation, and who can query the system by retrieving information about the system-level state (i.e., observable system-level state). Then, our analogous definition of privacy is the notion that the observer cannot obtain private information about individual robots by querying the system (i.e., it remains private to which species the robots belong, cf. Definition 1). The composition of our robot swarm is recorded in a database $\mathcal{D} \in \mathcal{S}^N$ that consists of N entries, where each entry $\mathcal{D}_i$ denotes the species of robot i. We define an *adjacency* set $\mathrm{Adj}(\mathcal{D})$ that encompasses all databases $\mathcal{D}$' adjacent to $\mathcal{D}$. Two databases $\mathcal{D}$ and $\mathcal{D}$' are adjacent if they differ by one single entry. In other words, two robot swarms (represented by $\mathcal{D}$ and $\mathcal{D}$') are adjacent if they differ by one robot i, meaning that robot i belongs to s_i in $\mathcal{D}$ (i.e., $\mathcal{D}_i = s_i$), and to a different species $s_i' \neq s_i$ in $\mathcal{D}$' (i.e., $\mathcal{D}_i \neq s_i$). As previously described, the behavior of the robot swarm can be described by tracking the states that compose the FSM. If we let the system run, it produces a trajectory that can be evaluated at a given time τ, resulting in a snapshot of the population vector $\mathbf{x}$[3]. Our query/response model consists of a user who is able to observe this system-level state (at time τ). Hence, the query $q \circ f_\mathcal{N}(\mathbf{x_0}(\mathcal{D}), \tau)$ depends on the swarm composition $\mathcal{D}$, and the time at which the system is observed τ. The function $\mathbf{x_0}(\mathcal{D}) : \mathcal{S}^N \mapsto \mathbb{N}_{\geq 0}^{N_A}$ distributes the robots in $\mathcal{D}$ to their initial states. A schema of this system is shown in Fig. 2. Our aim is to analyze the differential privacy of the observed system output. To this end, we propose a definition of differential privacy that applies to dynamic swarms.

Definition 2 (ϵ–indistinguishable heterogeneous swarm). *A heterogeneous swarm with dynamics defined by a system $\mathcal{N}$ is ϵ-indistinguishable (and gives ϵ-differential privacy) if for all possible swarm compositions recorded in databases $\mathcal{D}$, we have*

---

[3] We assume a snapshot adversary that gains system-level information at a specific time. This system-level information is a design variable, called the *observable* state.

$$\mathcal{L}(\mathcal{D}) = \max_{\mathcal{D}' \in \mathrm{Adj}(\mathcal{D})} \left| \ln \frac{\mathbb{P}[q \circ f_{\mathcal{N}}(\mathbf{x_0}(\mathcal{D}), \tau)]}{\mathbb{P}[q \circ f_{\mathcal{N}}(\mathbf{x_0}(\mathcal{D}'), \tau)]} \right| \leq \epsilon. \tag{3}$$

where $\mathbb{P}[\mathbf{y}]$ denotes the probability of the output $\mathbf{y}$, obtained through query q of the system-level state given by $f_{\mathcal{N}}$.

The value ϵ is referred to as the leakage. Intuitively, this definition states that if two swarm systems are close, in order to preserve privacy they should correspond to close distributions on their observable outputs. As noted by Dwork et al. [4], the definition of differential privacy is stringent: for a pair of distributions whose statistical difference is arbitrarily small, the ratio may still result in an infinite value when a point in one distribution assigns probability zero and the other non-zero. Later, in our evaluations, we use a smooth version of the leakage formula above, by adding an arbitrary, negligibly small value ν, uniformly over the support of the probability distributions. This allows us to differentiate between large and small mismatches of the output when one point of a probability distribution returns zero. Due to this addition, we are able to show continuous privacy trends as a function of the underlying parameters.

4   Analysis of Privacy

The formula in Eq. (3) provides strong privacy guarantees. Yet, it requires that we have a way of specifying the probability distribution over the swarm's observable output. For certain classes of swarm dynamics (e.g., when the behavior can be described by complex-balanced CRNs [13]), we can formulate the stationary probability distribution analytically, and hence, plug this formula into our privacy model. Yet, in the general case, we may not be able to derive a stationary probability distribution. Also, we may explicitly need to analyze privacy during transient, non-steady-state, behavior. In this section, we detail a method that enables the analysis of privacy for heterogeneous swarms with arbitrary dynamics.

4.1   Methodology

The most widely-used computational method for obtaining the time-dependent behavior of the state of a CRN is the Stochastic Simulation Algorithm (SSA) [6]. The basic idea behind this algorithm is to use the propensity rates to evaluate which reaction is most likely to happen within a given time interval. The result of the algorithm is a sample state trajectory. To obtain meaningful statistical information, the algorithm needs to be repeated a large number of times, which is computationally expensive overall. An alternative approach consists of evaluating the Chemical Master Equation (CME) [9]. The CME describes the temporal evolution of the probability mass function over all possible population vectors, and is described by a set of ordinary differential equations associated to a continuous-time, discrete-state Markov Chain. Since approaches based on the evaluation of the CME tend to be more precise than those based on SSA (when they are computationally tractable), we adopt a solution that builds on the former approach.

The CME is given by the linear ordinary differential equation

$$\dot{\boldsymbol{\pi}}(t) = K\boldsymbol{\pi}(t) \tag{4}$$

with $\boldsymbol{\pi} = [\pi_{\mathbf{x}_i} | \mathbf{x}_i \in \mathcal{X}_\mathcal{N}(\mathcal{D})]$ and where is $\mathcal{X}_\mathcal{N}(\mathcal{D})$ is the set of all possible population vectors $\mathbf{x}$ that can arise from the CRN $\mathcal{N}$ and robot species specified by $\mathcal{D}$. The entries of $\mathbf{K} \in \mathbb{R}^{|\mathcal{X}_\mathcal{N}(\mathcal{D})| \times |\mathcal{X}_\mathcal{N}(\mathcal{D})|}$, are given by

$$\mathbf{K}_{ij} = \begin{cases} -\sum_{m=1}^{N_R} r_m(\mathbf{x}_i; \kappa_m), & \text{if } i = j \\ r_m(\mathbf{x}_i; \kappa_m), & \forall j : \mathbf{x}_j = \mathbf{x}_i + \boldsymbol{\rho}_l - \boldsymbol{\rho}_k \\ & \text{with } R_m = (C_k, C_l) \\ 0, & \text{otherwise} \end{cases} \tag{5}$$

When the number of possible system-level states $|\mathcal{X}_\mathcal{N}(\mathcal{D})|$ is small, it is possible to obtain a closed-form solution to Eq. (4). However, when $|\mathcal{X}_\mathcal{N}(\mathcal{D})|$ is large or even infinite, it may become computationally intractable to solve the system. In such cases, we can resort to Finite State Projection (FSP) methods [11] that approximate the solution by compressing the number of possible states (and, hence, also the size of $\mathbf{K}$). The idea of FSP is to expand the number of states dynamically, according their probabilities. States with low probabilities are pruned, and, hence, only statistically relevant states are added to the domain of the solver. Finally, we compute the probability of the observable state $\mathbf{y}$ for a given time τ, which we can then plug into our formula for differential privacy, Eq. (3). This is straightforward since $\pi_{\mathbf{x}}(\tau)$ is equivalent to $\mathbb{P}[\mathbf{x}(\tau)]$, and thus, $\mathbb{P}[q \circ f_\mathcal{N}(\mathbf{x}_0(\mathcal{D}), \tau)]$ is equivalent to $\pi_{\mathbf{y}}(\tau)$, where $\pi_{\mathbf{y}}(\tau) = \sum_{\forall \mathbf{x} \text{ s.t. } \mathbf{y} = q(\mathbf{x})} \pi_{\mathbf{x}}(\tau)$.

4.2   Case Study

This case study considers the general problem of collaborative task solving, where robot species have distinct capabilities, and hence, depend on each other in order to complete tasks. Our system is composed of three species, $\mathcal{S} = \{1, 2, 3\}$. For any given task to be completed successfully, one robot of each species must be present at the respective task. There are a number of realistic scenarios that relate to this setting. A well-known work considers a setting where a homogeneous swarm of robots is tasked to pull sticks out of the ground [7] — because the length of a single robot's arm is limited, a successful manipulation requires two robots to collaborate. Our current case study can be formulated analogously by expanding the original statement to a heterogeneous setting. By default, all robots are in exploration mode, searching for tasks that need to be completed. A robot encounters tasks at a certain rate. Once it has encountered a task that is either unattended, or that is occupied by one of the other two species, it will wait at the task. The robot may abandon the task (with a given rate) before it is completed, or wait until all other robots from the other species join the task. If the robot abandons the task, it returns to exploration mode. If a robot

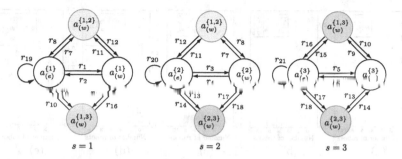

Fig. 3. Finite state machines of the three species in the case study presented in Sect. 4. The reactions correspond to the system detailed in Eq. (6). The interspecific states are colored.

encounters a task where both other species are already present, the three robots are able to collaborate and successfully complete the task. All three robots then return to exploration mode. We formalize this behavior with the following CRN:

$$a_{(e)}^{\{1\}} \underset{r_2}{\overset{r_1}{\rightleftharpoons}} a_{(w)}^{\{1\}} \qquad a_{(e)}^{\{2\}} + a_{(w)}^{\{3\}} \underset{r_{14}}{\overset{r_{13}}{\rightleftharpoons}} a_{(w)}^{\{2,3\}}$$

$$a_{(e)}^{\{2\}} \underset{r_4}{\overset{r_3}{\rightleftharpoons}} a_{(w)}^{\{2\}} \qquad a_{(e)}^{\{3\}} + a_{(w)}^{\{1\}} \underset{r_{16}}{\overset{r_{15}}{\rightleftharpoons}} a_{(w)}^{\{1,3\}}$$

$$a_{(e)}^{\{3\}} \underset{r_6}{\overset{r_5}{\rightleftharpoons}} a_{(w)}^{\{3\}} \qquad a_{(e)}^{\{3\}} + a_{(w)}^{\{2\}} \underset{r_{18}}{\overset{r_{17}}{\rightleftharpoons}} a_{(w)}^{\{2,3\}}$$

$$a_{(e)}^{\{1\}} + a_{(w)}^{\{2\}} \underset{r_8}{\overset{r_7}{\rightleftharpoons}} a_{(w)}^{\{1,2\}} \qquad a_{(e)}^{\{1\}} + a_{(w)}^{\{2,3\}} \xrightarrow{r_{19}} a_{(e)}^{\{1\}} + a_{(e)}^{\{2\}} + a_{(e)}^{\{3\}}$$

$$a_{(e)}^{\{1\}} + a_{(w)}^{\{3\}} \underset{r_{10}}{\overset{r_9}{\rightleftharpoons}} a_{(w)}^{\{1,3\}} \qquad a_{(e)}^{\{2\}} + a_{(w)}^{\{1,3\}} \xrightarrow{r_{20}} a_{(e)}^{\{1\}} + a_{(e)}^{\{2\}} + a_{(e)}^{\{3\}} \qquad (6)$$

$$a_{(e)}^{\{2\}} + a_{(w)}^{\{1\}} \underset{r_{12}}{\overset{r_{11}}{\rightleftharpoons}} a_{(w)}^{\{1,2\}} \qquad a_{(e)}^{\{3\}} + a_{(w)}^{\{1,2\}} \xrightarrow{r_{21}} a_{(e)}^{\{1\}} + a_{(e)}^{\{2\}} + a_{(e)}^{\{3\}}$$

The states of this system are

$$\mathcal{A}^{(0)} = \emptyset \qquad\qquad \mathcal{A}^{(2)} = \{a_{(e)}^{\{2\}}, a_{(w)}^{\{2\}}, a_{(w)}^{\{1,2\}}, a_{(w)}^{\{2,3\}}\}$$

$$\mathcal{A}^{(1)} = \{a_{(e)}^{\{1\}}, a_{(w)}^{\{1\}}, a_{(w)}^{\{1,2\}}, a_{(w)}^{\{1,3\}}\} \quad \mathcal{A}^{(3)} = \{a_{(e)}^{\{3\}}, a_{(w)}^{\{3\}}, a_{(w)}^{\{1,3\}}, a_{(w)}^{\{2,3\}}\}$$

with $\mathcal{A} = \cup_{s=\{0,1,2,3\}} \mathcal{A}^{(s)}$, and where $a_{(e)}^{\mathcal{I}}$ corresponds to the exploration state and $a_{(w)}^{\mathcal{I}}$ to the waiting state (e.g., $a_{(w)}^{\{1,3\}}$ corresponds to the state where one robot of species 1 and one robots of species 3 are waiting at a task for a robot of species 2). From the reaction equations above, we see that robots interact when two robots are waiting for the remaining robot. The interspecific states are:

$$\mathcal{A}^{(1)} \cap \mathcal{A}^{(2)} = \{a_{(w)}^{\{1,2\}}\}, \quad \mathcal{A}^{(1)} \cap \mathcal{A}^{(3)} = \{a_{(w)}^{\{1,3\}}\}, \quad \mathcal{A}^{(2)} \cap \mathcal{A}^{(3)} = \{a_{(w)}^{\{2,3\}}\} \quad (7)$$

Our population vector keeps track of the number of robots per state, and is:

$$\mathbf{x} = [x_{(e)}^{\{1\}}, x_{(e)}^{\{2\}}, x_{(e)}^{\{3\}}, x_{(w)}^{\{1\}}, x_{(w)}^{\{2\}}, x_{(w)}^{\{3\}}, x_{(w)}^{\{1,2\}}, x_{(w)}^{\{1,3\}}, x_{(w)}^{\{2,3\}}]. \quad (8)$$

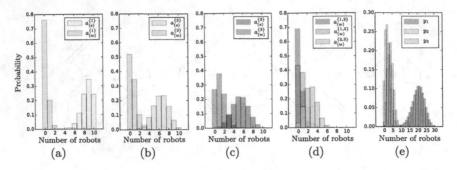

Fig. 4. Panels (a)–(d) show the marginal probability distributions resulting from $\pi_{\mathbf{x}}(\tau)$, for $\tau = 10$, for all nine components x_i of $\mathbf{x}$. Similarly, panel (e) shows the marginal distribution of $\pi_{\mathbf{y}}(\tau)$ over the components y_i of the observation data $\mathbf{y}$. The data is obtained for encountering rates $\kappa_1, \kappa_9, \kappa_{19} = 0.2$, $\kappa_3, \kappa_{13}, \kappa_{20} = 0.5$ and $\kappa_5, \kappa_{15}, \kappa_{21} = 0.8$, and abandoning rates $\kappa_2, \kappa_8, \kappa_{10} = 0.8$, $\kappa_4, \kappa_{12}, \kappa_{14} = 0.5$, and $\kappa_6, \kappa_{16}, \kappa_{18} = 0.2$, for species 1, 2, 3, respectively.

We consider an adversary who is able to observe the number of robots that are in exploration mode, the number of robots that are waiting alone, and the number of robots that are waiting in twos. Hence, we formulate the observable data as $\mathbf{y} = [y_1, y_2, y_3]$ and

$$y_1 = x_{(e)}^{\{1\}} + x_{(e)}^{\{2\}} + x_{(e)}^{\{3\}}, \ y_2 = x_{(w)}^{\{1\}} + x_{(w)}^{\{2\}} + x_{(w)}^{\{3\}}, \ y_3 = x_{(w)}^{\{1,2\}} + x_{(w)}^{\{2,3\}} + x_{(w)}^{\{1,3\}} \quad (9)$$

To illustrate this system, we depict the FSM of all species in Fig. 3. We note that the structure of the species' FSMs are equivalent, yet, by definition, the distinct species own distinct capabilities, and hence, their roles in the respective states are complementary (and distinct). The reactions' propensity rates can be attributed to the individual species. For instance, reaction R_7 is defined by the rate κ_7 at which species 1 encounters tasks at which species 2 is waiting. Hence, κ_7 is attributed to species 1. We define these values as $\boldsymbol{\kappa}^{(s)}$, and summarize them as $\boldsymbol{\kappa}^{(1)} = [\kappa_1, \kappa_2, \kappa_7, \kappa_8, \kappa_9, \kappa_{10}, \kappa_{19}]$, $\boldsymbol{\kappa}^{(2)} = [\kappa_3, \kappa_4, \kappa_{11}, \kappa_{12}, \kappa_{13}, \kappa_{14}, \kappa_{20}]$, and $\boldsymbol{\kappa}^{(3)} = [\kappa_5, \kappa_6, \kappa_{15}, \kappa_{16}, \kappa_{17}, \kappa_{18}, \kappa_{21}]$. As an example of the resulting dynamics, Fig. 4 shows the marginal distributions resulting from $\pi_{\mathbf{x}}(\tau)$, for all nine components x_i of $\mathbf{x}$, and $\pi_{\mathbf{y}}(\tau)$, for all three components y_i of $\mathbf{y}$.

4.3   Evaluation

A query that maintains a high level of privacy ensures that no individual can be isolated when information pertaining to that individual is changed (i.e., one element in the database is changed). Our query is defined by the observable state of the system. Hence, evaluating the privacy of a heterogeneous swarm with Eq. (3) is analogous to answering the following question: *'How much information is given to an observer when the species of one robot is switched?'*. Since our query is a function of the system-level state, it is defined by the number of robots per

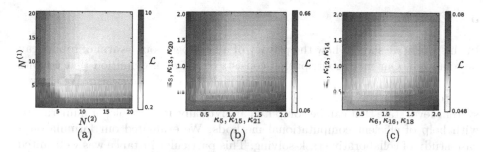

Fig. 5. Differential privacy of the collaboration case study. The colorbar shows the leakage. In (a), we vary the population of robots in species 2 and 3 while keeping species 1 fixed. In (b), we vary the task encountering rates of species 2 and 3, and in (c), we vary the task abandoning rates of species 2 and 3, while keeping the rates of species 1 fixed.

species $N^{(s)}$, and by propensity rates κ. By varying these values, we can show how swarm composition and behavior affect privacy.

We evaluate the leakage of the system for the three different settings. First, we fix the propensity rates $\kappa = 1$, and we vary the population $N^{(2)}$ and $N^{(3)}$ in the range $[1, \ldots, 20]$ with $N^{(3)} = 10$. Figure 5(a) shows reduced leakage along the diagonal $N^{(1)} = N^{(2)}$. The minimum leakage occurs at $N^{(1)} = N^{(2)} = N^{(3)} = 10$. This indicates that species with equivalent observable behaviors should have a similar number of robots in order to maximize privacy. In other words, since species 1, 2, and 3 have equivalent FSMs with identical interspecific states (see Fig. 3), larger differences in the number of robots per species will produce more easily identifiable changes in the observable system-level state distributions. The plot also reveals that increasing the total number of robots increases privacy, as shown by the low leakage values in the upper right corner. Evidently, a system composed of many robots is more opaque (to an external observer): probability distributions spread over larger population ranges, and, thus, small differences in the initial population creates smaller differences in observable state distributions. In the second and third settings, we fix the population $N^{(1)} = N^{(2)} = N^{(3)} = 10$ and vary the propensity rates in the range $[0.2, 2]$. Figure 5(b) shows the leakage when we vary the rates at which species 2 ($\kappa_3, \kappa_{13}, \kappa_{20}$) and species 3 ($\kappa_5, \kappa_{15}, \kappa_{21}$) encounter tasks. Figure 5(c) shows the leakage when we vary the rates at which species 2 ($\kappa_4, \kappa_{12}, \kappa_{14}$) and species 3 ($\kappa_6, \kappa_{16}, \kappa_{18}$) abandon tasks. If we program the species with the same rates, we obtain indiscernible behaviors, and hence, increase privacy. This is exemplified in the plots, where off-diagonal values exhibit higher leakage, and the minimum leakage value is situated at the cell corresponding to rate uniformity. Finally, we also note that for the considered parameter ranges, varying the number of robots per species has a much larger impact on privacy than varying the behavior.

5   Conclusion

In this work, we showed how the privacy of a heterogeneous swarm of robots can be analyzed. Our main contribution consists of a formal definition that couples the notion of differential privacy with a model of the robotic swarm. We showed how to evaluate the formula by considering a macroscopic description of the system-level state that can be computed analytically, if tractable, or numerically, with help of efficient computational methods. We evaluated our formula on a case-study of collaborative task-solving. This particular instance was well suited for demonstrative purposes (due to its very general and representative form). Our results show that we are able to determine how privacy levels vary as we vary the design parameters of the underlying swarm system. Privacy is an urgent and important topic — systems that are capable of maintaining high levels of privacy are more secure and resilient. We intend to further this line of work by developing active privacy mechanisms that are able control the amount of information leaked, while maintaining overall system performance.

Acknowledgments. We gratefully acknowledge the support of ONR grants N00014-15-1-2115 and N00014-14-1-0510, ARL grant W911NF-08-2-0004, NSF grant IIS-1426840, and TerraSwarm, one of six centers of STARnet, a Semiconductor Research Corporation program sponsored by MARCO and DARPA.

References

1. Berman, S., Halasz, Á., Hsieh, M.A., Kumar, V.: Optimized stochastic policies for task allocation in swarms of robots. IEEE Trans. Robot. **25**, 927–937 (2009)
2. Cardinale, B.J., Palmer, M.A., Collins, S.L.: Species diversity enhances ecosystem functioning through interspecific facilitation. Nature **415**(6870), 426–429 (2002)
3. Dorigo, M., Floreano, D., Gambardella, L.M., Mondada, F., Nolfi, S., et al.: Swarmanoid: a novel concept for the study of heterogeneous robotic swarms. IEEE Robot. Autom. Mag. **20**(4), 60–71 (2013)
4. Dwork, C.: Differential Privacy. Encyclopedia of Cryptography and Security, pp. 338–340. Springer, New york (2011)
5. Feinberg, M.: Some recent results in chemical reaction network theory. In: Aris, R., Aronson, D.G., Swinney, H.L. (eds.) Patterns and Dynamics in Reactive Media, pp. 43–70. Springer, New York (1991)
6. Gillespie, D.T.: Exact stochastic simulation of coupled chemical reactions. J. Phys. Chem. A **25**, 2340–2361 (1977)
7. Ijspeert, A.J., Martinoli, A., Billard, A., Gambardella, L.M.: Collaboration through the exploitation of local interactions in autonomous collective robotics: the stick pulling experiment. Auton. Robots **11**, 149–171 (2001)
8. Kehoe, B., Patil, S., Abbeel, P., Goldberg, K.: A survey of research on cloud robotics and automation. IEEE Trans. Autom. Sci. Eng. **12**(2), 398–409 (2015)
9. López-Caamal, F., Marquez-Lago, T.T.: Exact probability distributions of selected species in stochastic chemical reaction networks. Bull. Math. Biol. **76**(9), 2334–2361 (2014)

10. Michael, N., Fink, J., Loizou, S., Kumar, V.: Architecture, abstractions, and algorithms for controlling large teams of robots: experimental testbed and results. In: Kaneko, M., Nakamura, Y. (eds.) Robotics Research. Springer Tracts in Advanced Robotics, vol. 66, pp. 409–419. Springer, Berlin (2011)
11. Munsky, B., Khammash, M.: The finite state projection algorithm for the solution of the chemical master equation. J. Chem. Phys. 124(4), 044104 (2006)
12. Prorok, A., Hsieh, A.M., Kumar, V.: Formalizing the impact of diversity on performance in a heterogeneous swarm of robots. In: IEEE International Conference on Robotics and Automation (ICRA) (2016)
13. Siegel, D., MacLean, D.: Global stability of complex balanced mechanisms. J. Math. Chem. 27, 89–110 (2000)

A New Continuous Model for Segregation Implemented and Analyzed on Swarm Robots

Benjamin Reh[✉], Felix Aller, and Katja Mombaur

Optimization in Robotics and Biomechanics,
Interdisciplinary Center for Scientific Computing,
Heidelberg University, Heidelberg, Germany
orb@uni-hd.de

Abstract. T.C. Schelling's Dynamic Model of Segregation might be one of the most known agent based models. Macroscopic segregation is caused by microscopic preference for a specific feature in the local neighborhood. Based on Schelling's original work we derive a spatiotemporal continuous segregation model which is implemented on a swarm of thirty Elisa-3 robots. To define the neighborhood between the entities we use the density-based spatial clustering algorithm DBSCAN. Furthermore we expand the binary decision criterion to a probabilistic approach to produce a more realistic behavior. The evaluation of our extensive experiments with the swarm of robots show that a segregation effect can be reproduced with our model similar to the observations Schelling made in his work.

Keywords: Segregation · Schelling · Swarm robotics · Elisa-3

1   Introduction

After in the mid-1960 the legal foundations for racial discrimination in the U.S. were abolished, the tendency to segregate the population in U.S. cities by race or economical factors kept on going. Thomas C. Schelling studied the question whether this effect was a result of a general intolerance inside the population or if it might be an emerging pattern caused by a system of agents with only a small preference to group with its own kind [6–8].

To examine this phenomenon, Schelling developed a model of agents with two distinguishable features on a regular grid [8]. For practical reasons he chose to use two kinds of coins on a chessboard as a form of visual representation.

The neighbourhood of an agent can be defined as the eight closest surrounding squares. Looking at this neighbourhood, one can calculate the ratio r of agents having the same feature divided by total number of agents in the neighbourhood:

$$r = \frac{n_{same}}{n_{total}} \tag{1}$$

This ratio also includes the agent itself. Depending on a threshold th common to all agents, each agent decides based on this ratio whether it is satisfied ($r \geq th$)

M. Dorigo et al. (Eds.): ANTS 2016, LNCS 9882, pp. 28–39, 2016.
DOI: 10.1007/978-3-319-44427-7_3

or not ($r < th$). In the first case the agent stays in its current position whereas in the second case it moves to another square that meets its requirements. Schelling states that with a threshold $th \geq 30\%$ one can observe a total segregation into regions of a high purity.

Since the publication of the original work a lot of research followed up on different aspects of Schelling's model. We name only a few that influenced the work presented in this paper.

Brandt et al. examine the dynamics of randomly chosen unhappy agents on a one dimensional ring [1]. The role of randomness is examined by us as well in our probabilistic approach.

Laurie and Jaggi introduce a distance inside which an agent is able to see its neighbours. They study the role of this distance with respect to the stability of the system [4].

Pancs and Vriend discuss the stability of the system and show that even if agents have a preference for integration rather than for their own characteristic, a segregation still can be observed [5].

The work presented in this paper aims on adapting Schelling's time and spatio discrete model to an algorithm that can be implemented on Eliza-3 swarm robots. We are interested in the question to what extend the effect of segregation can be reproduced.

In the introduction we shortly presented Schelling's original model. Following the principles of this model we present our own segregation model in Sect. 2. The implementation of the algorithm onto Elisa-3 swarm robots is described in Sect. 3. Section 4 outlines the setup used for the experiments we conducted in order to analyze the resulting behavior of our model. The data obtained hereby is then interpreted in Sect. 5. We conclude our findings in Sect. 6 and give an outlook on future research options enabled by our setup.

2 Development of a New Continuous Segregation Model

The objective of this work is to examine to which extent the observations Schelling made on his model can be reproduced by an adapted model implemented on real swarm robots.

The original model works with spatio-discrete squares arranged as a two dimensional grid. The agents' moves are round based and not limited in the distance they can travel within one discrete time step. To transform this model into a continuous one which respects the properties of real physical swarm robots several adaptations have to be made which are presented in this section.

2.1 Redefining the Neighbourhood

In the original discrete case the neighbourhood of an agent is defined as the agents in the eight squares surrounding this agent. This method works well on a grid in which only discrete positions are allowed. In the case of spatial continuity a different approach to define a neighbourhood is needed.

Instead of considering agents within a certain range as a neighbourhood, we chose a density based algorithm to form clusters of agents. To be able to recognize interdependent groups of different shapes we defined groups as clusters using the *Density-Based Spatial Clustering of Applications with Noise* - algorithm (DBSCAN) [2].

This algorithm is used to form clusters based on the position of each agent at a given time step. Information on the cluster an agent is affiliated with is passed on to it.

2.2 The Two Basic States of Agents

Similar to Schelling's model each agent knows two states: *satisfied* in which the robot is stationary and *searching* in which it is moving. The decision making process is based solely on four variables determined by the clustering algorithm. The first two variables are the number of agents of the same feature n_{same} and the number of agents in total n_{total}. These values respect only stationary agents. The so called extended cluster consists also of agents in motion that in this instant also are to be considered inside the cluster. The number of moving entities in the extended cluster are named $n_{same,moving}$ and $n_{total,moving}$. Clusters can also consist only of moving entities. This case is needed to form new clusters later in condition (5).

We define a function $S(r)$ to determine if an agent is satisfied depending on the given ratio r as defined in (1). In accordance with the original model by Schelling we define:

$$S(r) := \begin{cases} true & r \geq th \\ false & r < th \end{cases} \tag{2}$$

Satisfied. In this state the agent is stationary but constantly checking the conditions of the cluster it is affiliated to. The decision of an agent to leave the cluster, i.e. changing from *satisfied* to *searching* and to start moving, is made as soon as the ratio of agents having the same feature compared to total number of agents in the cluster drops below the threshold:

$$\neg S\left(\frac{n_{same}}{n_{total}}\right) \Rightarrow \text{leave cluster} \tag{3}$$

This can occur if for example agents of the other kind join the cluster or agents with the same feature leave the group.

Searching. In this state the agent is moving linear inside the available plane, changing direction only to avoid collision with other agents or with the border. As soon as an agent reaches the proximity of an existing cluster, i.e. is a member of the extended cluster, it decides on joining it. This decision is based on whether the agent would feel satisfied if it would join the cluster. This condition is expressed as follows:

$$S\left(\frac{n_{same}+1}{n_{total}+1}\right) \Rightarrow \text{join cluster} \tag{4}$$

So far an agent can only join an existing cluster. To form new clusters, we decided that a minimum of three agents is needed in order not to form too many small groups. This is expressed as:

$$n_{total,moving} > 2 \wedge S\left(\frac{n_{same,moving}}{n_{total,moving}}\right) \Rightarrow \text{new cluster} \tag{5}$$

2.3   Probabilistic Approach to State Changes

So far the threshold th is a fixed constant common to every agent. In order to make the scenario more dynamic and also more realistic we allow the decision function $S(r)$ to be probabilistic.

We introduce a uniform distributed random variable $x \in [0,1]$ and a probabilistic function P_k

$$P_k(r) = \frac{1}{e^{k \cdot (r-th)} + 1} \tag{6}$$

$P_k(r)$ describes an agent's probability of being satisfied with a given ratio r and threshold th. The parameter k defines slope of the distribution as shown

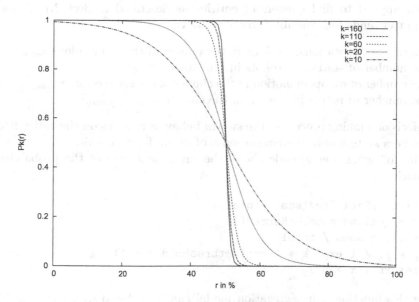

Fig. 1. Plot for different parameters k in the distribution $P_k(r)$ (6) for $th = 0.5$

in Fig. 1. For the case $k \to \infty$ the distribution behaves like a binary decision function similar to (2). We can then redefine $S(r)$ as

$$S(r,x) := \begin{cases} true & x \geq P(r) \\ false & x < P(r) \end{cases} \tag{7}$$

3 Implementation on Swarm Robots

We chose Elisa-3 robots produced by GCTronic [3] as a platform to implement our segregation model. They have a differential drive with magnetic wheels to improve the adhesion to a metal surface. This allows for controlled motions up to a velocity of 60 cm/s while at the same time having a diameter of only 5 cm. This is an advantage over the systems driven by vibration motors as they tend to move slower leading to a longer duration of the experiments.

Our segregation model as described by Eqs. (6) and (7) is implemented directly in C on the Atmega 2560 microcontroller of each Elisa-3 unit. In case of a dissatisfied, i.e. moving robot we make use of the collision-free driving behaviour provided along with the Elisa-3 software. This function uses the eight infrared proximity sensors around the robot to prevent collisions by adjusting the speed and direction of the wheels sophisticatedly. This results in a linear movement when possible and a deflection from obstacles such as the borders or other Elisa-3 units.

The onboard RGB LED indicates the affiliation to a group by showing either a green or blue color. A video stream taken from a camera overlooking the experiment is analyzed to trace each individual robot. The DBSCAN algorithm is then applied to find clusters of entities as described in Sect. 2.1. A radio transmitter sends four variables to each entity:

– The number of stationary robots in the cluster of the same color (n_{same})
– The number of stationary robots in the cluster (n_{total})
– The number of robots in motion in the cluster of the same color ($n_{same,moving}$)
– The number of robots in motion in the cluster ($n_{total,moving}$)

The decision making process of the swarm behavior remains on the entity itself, the camera system only emulates a sense of vision for each unit.

The following pseudo code shows the implementation of the probabilistic approach

```
function isSatisfied(same, total):
    x = getRandomNumberNormed()
    ratio = same / total
    p = 1. / ( exp( k * ( ratio-threshold)) + 1)
    return ( x > p )
```

Using this function, our segregation model can be reduced to a state machine with two basic states:

```
loop:
  if state == SEARCHING:
    if isSatisfied(sameCluster + 1, totalCluster + 1) or
    (totalMoving > 2 and isSatisfied(sameMoving, totalMoving)):
      driveStop()
      waitSeconds(2)
      state=INCLUSTER
  if state == INCLUSTER:
    if not isSatisfied(sameCluster, totalCluster) or
        totalCluster == 0:
      driveForward()
      waitSeconds(2)
      state=SEARCHING
```

The conditions for a state change are explained in Sect. 2.2. The waiting time of 2 s between the state changes is needed especially for the probabilistic behaviour to achieve stable decisions which are not reverted in the following iteration.

The following section describes how this algorithm's effects are measured.

4 Experiments

4.1 Setup

For the experiments a plane of 118 cm × 88 cm is used. Borders prevent the 30 Elisa-3 robots from leaving the area. Figure 2 shows the setup with robots forming clusters during an experiment.

The image recognition system described in the previous section is also used to log the number of units respective to their colors in each cluster. This information is available for every image frame of the camera resulting in a sample frequency of 15 Hz.

Fig. 2. Elisa-3 units forming clusters during an experiment

Prior to an experiment the robots move for 30 s on the plane without forming any clusters. This assures a random and homogeneous distribution at the starting point of each experiment.

A transition period between this random initial state and a behavior that is characteristic is to be expected. Several measurements each over a length of 5 min were performed to determine the end of this transition phase in order to prevent sampling non-characteristic behavior. The results show that starting after one minute for the duration of another minute is an adequate time frame for sampling data in an experiment.

4.2   Variations

Experiments were performed for a threshold of

$$th \in \{1\,\%, 10\,\%, 20\,\%, 30\,\%, 40\,\%, 50\,\%, 60\,\%, 70\,\%, 80\,\%, 90\,\%, 100\,\%\}$$

and a distribution parameter of

$$k \in \{10, 20, 60, 110, 160\}$$

Each experiment was repeated three times resulting in 165 experiments with a total of 148500 data sets. There is a fixed number of 15 blue and 15 green robots in each experiment, each having the same value for th and k.

5   Results

5.1   Microscopic Effects

We can observe the following 5 basic effects that determine the swarm behavior on a microscopic level which are shown in Fig. 3.

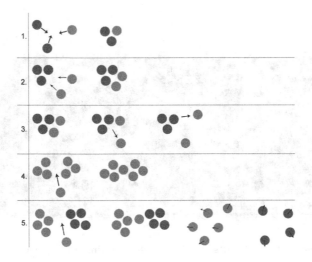

Fig. 3. Forms of microscopic effects

1. Formation of a new cluster by three robots.
2. The simultaneous arrival of two robots to a cluster with a different dominant color leads to a satisfactory condition for both entities. This might not be the case if only one would have arrived depending on the threshold.
3. One robot leaving a cluster worsens the ratio for other robots of the same color. If as a result the remaining robots of that color decide to leave the cluster as well this effect is called reaching a *tipping point*. A completely segregated (pure) cluster is the result.
4. An arriving robot leads to a merge of two clusters of the same dominant color.
5. An arriving robot connects two clusters of different dominant colors, which results in the cluster breaking up.

These effects on a microscopic level lead to phenomena on system level which will be analyzed in the next section.

5.2 Macroscopic Effects

Graphical Representation. To analyze the overall behavior of the system, a graphical representation of the data obtained by the large sets of experiments is needed. We developed a diagram that combines several aspects needed in order to draw conclusion from the measurements.

Each diagram shows all experiments for one value of k. Each column in this diagram represents the results obtained with one threshold th. Each box in this column represents a specific cluster size indicated on the x-axis.

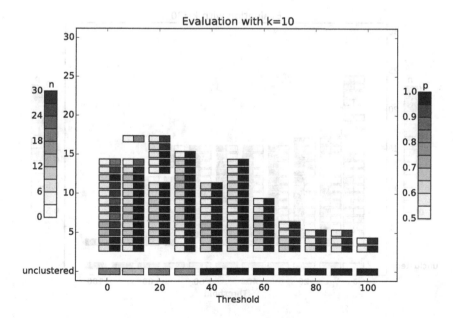

Fig. 4. Diagram with k=10

For example the box in the bottom left corner in Fig. 4 shows that for the experiments with $th = 1\%$ about half of the robots were unclustered. This can be determined by comparing the shade of the box to the scale on the left of the diagram. The box above represents a cluster size of 3 robots. The shade on the left half shows that in average only a few robots can be found in a cluster of that size. The shade on the right half shows that the average purity p of that cluster is very high. The purity is defined as

$$p = \frac{n_{dominant\ color}}{n_{total}} \tag{8}$$

The next box in top direction represents clusters with the size of 4 and so on. One column of boxes to the right the results of the experiments with a threshold of $th = 10\%$ can be seen.

With the help of these diagrams we interpret the data obtained from our experiments.

Interpretation. Looking at the experiments with $k = 160$ (Fig. 8) which is the case of a sharp binary decision criterion the following observations can be made: The number of unclustered and therefore unsatisfied robots increases with the threshold. For $th < 30\%$ the overall cluster purity is very low compared to the cases with $th \geq 30\%$. This means a segregation takes place starting with a threshold of $th \approx 30\%$ Furthermore the number of large clusters decreases for higher thresholds.

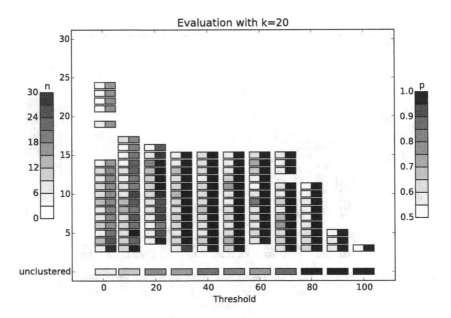

Fig. 5. Diagram with k=20

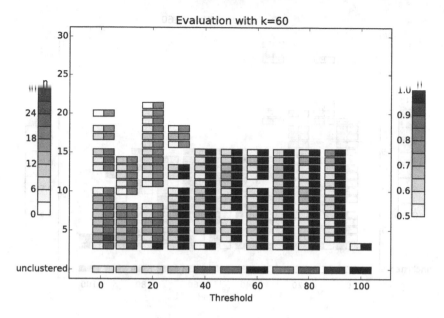

Fig. 6. Diagram with k=60

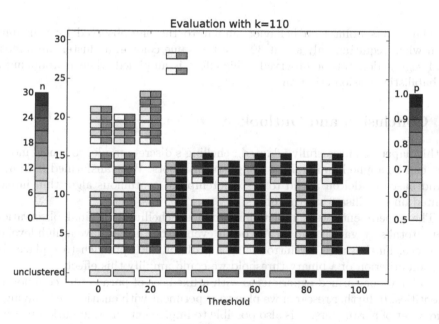

Fig. 7. Diagram with k=110

Smaller values for k (see Figs. 4, 5, 6, 7 and 8), which equals a softer, more probabilistic decision making process, lead to a higher purity even for thresholds smaller than 30 %. Figure 4 also shows that smaller k produces more unclustered robots for $k > 30$ %.

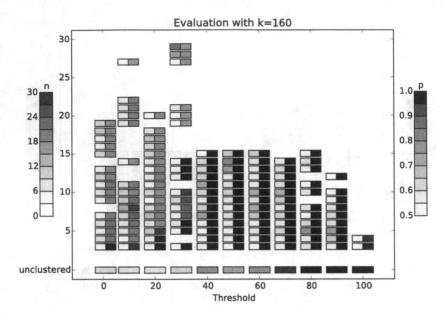

Fig. 8. Diagram with k=160

The results point to a behavior similar to the one observed by Schelling. Even when requiring only about 30 % of the same color in a cluster, an almost total segregation can be observed. This effect is amplified when introducing a probabilistic decision criterion.

6   Conclusion and Outlook

In this paper we successfully adapted Schelling's discrete model to a new model that can be applied and studied using swarm robots. We transformed it from a round based model on a grid to a spatiotemporal continuous algorithm implemented on the Elisa-3 swarm robots.

The experiments we conducted reproduce Schelling's original observation that a total segregation can already occur even if the entities have a high level of tolerance. Furthermore, by introducing a probabilistic approach to replace the decision criterion of a binary threshold we could amplify this effect.

So far we performed experiments with a fixed set of parameters common to all entities. In further research we plan to experiment with entities each having a unique set of parameters. It is also possible to implement an assimilation process so that entities can change their characteristic to adapt to the dominant feature. Also an equal distribution of 15 blue to 15 green robots have been analyzed so far. The effects of having a dominant majority seems also worth to study.

It can be concluded that the model we presented in this paper successfully reproduces Schelling's original study on a swarm robot platform. Our setup can serve as a platform for further experiments.

References

1. Brandt, I., Kamath, K.: An analysis of one-dimensional Schelling segregation. In: Proceedings of the Forty-fourth Annual ACM Symposium on Theory of Computing, STOC 2012, pp. 789–804. ACM, New York (2012) http://doi.acm.org/10.1145/2213977.2214048

2. Ester, K., Sander, X.: A density-based algorithm fordiscovering clustersin large spatial databases with noise. In: Proceedings of the Second International Conference on Knowledge Discovery and Data Mining (KDD-96), Portland, Oregon, USA, pp. 226–231 (1996). http://www.aaai.org/Library/KDD/1996/kdd96-037.php

3. GCtronic: Elisa-3. http://www.gctronic.com/doc/index.php/Elisa-3. Accessed 3 Oct 2016

4. Laurie, J.: Role of 'vision' in neighbourhood racial segregation: a variant of the Schelling segregation model. Urban Stud. **40**(13), 2687–2704 (2003). http://usj.sage pub.com/content/40/13/2687.abstract

5. Pancs, V.: Schelling's spatial proximity model of segregationrevisited. J. Public Econ. **91**(12), 1–24 (2007). http://www.sciencedirect.com/science/article/pii/S00 47272706001228

6. Schelling, T.C.: Dynamic models of segregation. J. Math. Sociol. **1**(2), 143–186 (1971)

7. Schelling, T.: Micromotives and Macrobehavior. W. W. Norton, New York (2006). https://books.google.de/books?id=DenWKRgqzWMC

8. Schelling, T.C.: Models of segregation. Am. Econ. Rev. **59**(2), 488–493 (1969). http://www.jstor.org/stable/1823701

A Study of Archiving Strategies
in Multi-objective PSO for Molecular Docking

José García-Nieto[1]($\boxtimes$), Esteban López-Camacho[1]($\boxtimes$),
María Jesús García Godoy[1]($\boxtimes$), Antonio J. Nebro[1]($\boxtimes$), Juan J. Durillo[2]($\boxtimes$),
and José F. Aldana-Montes[1]($\boxtimes$)

[1] Khaos Research Group, Department of Computer Sciences,
University of Málaga, ETSI Informática, Campus de Teatinos, Málaga, Spain
{jnieto,esteban,mjgarciag,antonio,jfam}@lcc.uma.es
[2] Distributed and Parallel Systems Group, University of Innsbruck,
Innsbruck, Austria
juan@dps.uibk.ac.at

Abstract. Molecular docking is a complex optimization problem aimed at predicting the position of a ligand molecule in the active site of a receptor with the lowest binding energy. This problem can be formulated as a bi-objective optimization problem by minimizing the binding energy and the Root Mean Square Deviation (RMSD) difference in the coordinates of ligands. In this context, the SMPSO multi-objective swarm-intelligence algorithm has shown a remarkable performance. SMPSO is characterized by having an external archive used to store the non-dominated solutions and also as the basis of the leader selection strategy. In this paper, we analyze several SMPSO variants based on different archiving strategies in the scope of a benchmark of molecular docking instances. Our study reveals that the SMPSOhv, which uses an hypervolume contribution based archive, shows the overall best performance.

Keywords: Multi-objective optimization · Particle Swarm Optimization · Molecular docking · Archiving strategies · Algorithm comparison

1 Introduction

Molecular docking is a complex optimization problem found in biology, which consists in predicting the position of a small molecule (ligand) in the active site of a receptor (macromolecule) that registers the minimum binding energy. Molecular docking is traditionally faced by means of metaheuristics [4,8] as a continuous optimization problem, since it requires to adjust position variables corresponding to coordinates of translation and torsion movements of molecules.

In the last decade, a number of studies have centered on the application of single- and multi-objective metaheuristics [4–6,8,15] to the molecular docking problem, showing successful results for a number of molecular compounds. In these previous works, different objective formulations were proposed that focused on energy scoring functions. Recently, a new multi-objective approach has been

© Springer International Publishing Switzerland 2016
M. Dorigo et al. (Eds.): ANTS 2016, LNCS 9882, pp. 40–52, 2016.
DOI: 10.1007/978-3-319-44427-7_4

proposed [9] in which two different objectives are to be minimized: the binding energy (the unbound and bound energy terms of the ligand/receptor complex) and the Root-Mean-Square-Deviation (RMSD) score. The latter objective leads the algorithms to guide the search when the co-crystallized ligand is known, which complements the traditional energy function.

Among these optimization techniques, a multi-objective swarm-intelligence approach, namely SMPSO [11], has emerged as one of the most prominent optimizers for molecular docking [4,9]. This technique performs a limitation mechanism of particle's velocity to avoid the movement of particles in search regions out of the problem ranges. SMPSO uses an external archive to store non-dominated solutions according to the crowding distance [2]. This archive is also used in the leader selection mechanism. Here, our motivation is to go one step beyond by evaluating, in the scope of a benchmark of molecular instances, new versions of SMPSO using different archiving strategies (hypervolume, cosine distance, and aggregation) and, consequently, different strategies for the selection of the leaders.

With this aim, we compare and analyze the proposed versions of SMPSO when solving 11 flexible ligand-receptor docking complexes taken from the Auto-Dock 4.2 benchmark [10]. This dataset includes flexible ligands with different sizes and flexible side-chains of HIV-protease receptors. The performance of the algorithms has been assessed by applying two main quality indicators intended to measure convergence and diversity of the computed Pareto front approximations.

The remainder of this article is organized as follows: Sect. 2 describes the molecular docking problem from a multi-objective formulation. Studied algorithms are described in Sect. 3. Section 4 reports the experimentation methodology and Sect. 5 analyzes the obtained results. Finally, Sect. 6 reports conclusions and future lines of research.

2   Molecular Docking

From a biological point of view, the main objective in the molecular docking problem is to find an optimized conformation between the ligand (L) and the receptor (R) that results in a minimum binding energy. The interaction between L and R can be described by an energy function calculated from three components representing degrees of freedom: (1) the translation of the ligand molecule, involving the three axis values (x, y, z) in cartesian coordinate space; (2) the ligand orientation, modeled as a four variables quaternion including the angle slope (θ); and (3) the flexibilities, represented by the free rotation of torsion (dihedral angles) of the ligand and sidechains of the receptor.

- *Solution Encoding:* Each problem solution is then encoded by a real-value vector of $7 + n$ variables (as illustrated in Fig. 1), in which the first three values correspond to the ligand translation, the next four values correspond to the ligand and/or receptor orientation, and the remaining n values are the ligand torsion dihedral angles.

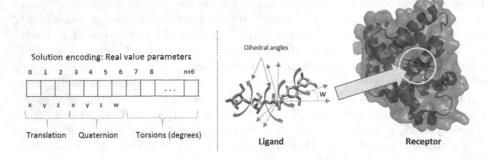

Fig. 1. Solution encoding. The first three values (translation) are the coordinates of the center of rotation of the ligand. The next four values correspond to quaternion and (θ). The rest of the values hold the torsion angles in degrees.

The range of translation variables (x, y, z) is $[0 \cdots 120]$, which has been delimited between the limits of the coordinates of a grid space previously set for each problem. Orientation (quaternion) and torsion variables are measured in radians and encoded in the range of $[-\pi, \pi]$.

- **Fitness Functions:** the bi-objective formulation used here consists of: the $E_{binding}$ and the RMSD score. The $E_{binding}$ is the energy function as used in Autodock, which is calculated as follows:

$$E_{binding} = Q_{bound}^{R-L} + Q_{unbound}^{R-L} \tag{1}$$

$$Q = W_{vdw} \sum_{i,j} (\frac{A_{ij}}{r_{ij}^{12}} - \frac{B_{ij}}{r_{ij}^{6}}) + W_{hbond} \sum_{i,j} E(t) \left(\frac{C_{ij}}{r_{ij}^{12}} - \frac{D_{ij}}{r_{ij}^{10}} \right)$$
$$+ W_{elec} \sum_{i,j} \frac{q_i q_j}{\varepsilon(r_{ij}) r_{ij}} + W_{sol} \sum_{i,j} (S_i V_j + S_j V_i) e^{(-r_{ij}^2/2\sigma^2)} \tag{2}$$

Q_{bound}^{R-L} and Q_{bound}^{R-L} are the states of bound and unbound of the ligand-receptor complex, respectively. Each pair of energetic evaluation terms includes evaluations (Q) of dispersion/repulsion (vdw), hydrogen bonds $(hbond)$, electrostatics $(elec)$ and desolvation (sol). Weights W_{vdw}, W_{hbond}, W_{conf}, W_{elec}, and W_{sol} of Eq. 2 are constants for Van der Waals, hydrogen bonds, torsional forces, electrostatic interactions and desolvation, respectively. An extended explanation of all these variables can be found in [10].

The RMSD is a measure of similarity between the real ligand position in the receptor and the computed position of the docking ligand. The lower RMSD score the better the solution is. A ligand-receptor docking solution with an RMSD score below 2Å is considered as a solution with high docking accuracy.

The RMSD score for two identical structures a and b is defined as follows:

$$RMSD_{ab} = max(RMSD'_{ab}, RMSD'_{ba}), \ with \ RMSD'_{ab} = \sqrt{\frac{1}{N}\sum_i \min_j r_2^{ij}}$$

(3)

The sum is over all N heavy atoms in structure a, the minimum is over all atoms in structure a with the same element type as atom i in structure b.

3   Algorithms

In this section, we describe the SMPSO variants we are going to study. We start with the original algorithm and then we give details of the considered variants.

SMPSO is a Multi-Objective Particle Swarm Optimization (MOPSO) characterized by two features: a velocity constraint mechanism and an external bounded archive to store the non-dominated solutions found during the search [11]. A perturbation, implemented as a mutation operator, is also incorporated. Its pseudocode is included in Algorithm 1. The archive contains the current Pareto front approximation found by the algorithm, and it applies the crowding distance density estimator [2] to decide which particle to remove when it is full. The archive is also used in the leader strategy selection, consisting on binary tournament based on randomly selecting two solutions from it and taking the one with the highest crowding distance value (i.e., the one located in less crowded region of the front composed by all archived solutions). The local best position of a particle i is obtained by applying a dominance test with the rest of particles in the swarm, in such a way that the current best particle (which initially is particle i) is updated when it is dominated by another one.

In [12], a study of different leader selection mechanisms on SMPSO was conducted. In that work, the most salient variant consisted in replacing the crowding distance by the degree of contribution of the solutions in the external archive according to the hypervolume indicator [18]. This way, the leader selection is based on a binary tournament that chooses the particle having the largest hypervolume contribution value. This version was named as SMPSO$_{hv}$ and it is the second selected algorithm to be compared in our study.

We introduce in this paper a new variant of SMPSO. The cosine similarity is a measure of similarity between two vectors that measures the cosine of the angle between them. This way, two vectors in the same direction have a cosine similarity value equals to zero, while two perpendicular vectors have a cosine similarity value of 1. As all the solutions in an external archive are non-dominated, we can define a density estimator by fixing a reference point and computing the cosine similarity among the vectors conformed by the archive solutions with regards to that reference point. The studied problem in this paper has two objectives, so we can sort the solutions in the archive by the first objective and compute, for each solution, a density value by summing up the cosine similarity of each point to their previous and next points; extreme points have a similarity distance equals to 0. This way, points having a largest cosine density value are in

---

Algorithm 1. Pseudocode of SMPSO

```
1:  initializeSwarm()
2:  initializeLeadersArchive()
3:  generation = 0
4:  while generation < maxGenerations do
5:      computeSpeed()
6:      updatePosition()
7:      mutation() // perturbation
8:      evaluation()
9:      updateLeadersArchive()
10:     updateParticlesMemory()
11:     generation ++
12: end while
13: returnLeadersArchive()
```

---

the most densely populated region. The resulting algorithm is called SMPSOC. An important issue in this technique is to select the proper reference point. Our previous study [9] indicated that the fronts have a convex shape, so we choose an approximation to the nadir point by taking the highest objective values of the solutions in the archive.

The fourth SMPSO version in our study, also presented in this paper for the first time, is an archive-less approach and it is called SMPSOD. To leave out the archive, we take the strategy of designing an aggregative version of SMPSO inspired by MOEA/D [17], where a multi-objective problem can be decomposed into a set of single-objective problems that can be optimized at the same time. This way, a set of evenly spread weight vectors $\lambda^1, \lambda^2, \ldots, \lambda^N$ are defined, being N the size of the swarm. Then, each particle i has associated the vector λ^i and a neighborhood defined as a set of its several closest weight vectors in $\lambda^1, \lambda^2, \ldots, \lambda^N$. The scalarizing strategy follows the Tchebycheff scheme. The strategy for getting the local best of a particle i is the same procedure as used by MOEA/D to update a neighborhood. The leader updating strategy consists in finding the best solution in the neighborhood by considering the scalar values of the particles taking into account their weight vectors.

SMPSO was inspired in the OMOPSO algorithm proposed by Reyes and Coello in [14], so we decided to also include it in our comparisons as a reference multi-objective particle swarm optimizer in the state of the art.

In summary, in our study we include OMOPSO and four SMPSO variants with different archiving strategies: crowding distance based (original SMPSO), hypervolume contribution based (SMPSO$_{hv}$), cosine distance based (SMPSOC), and archive-less (SMPSOD), being the last two ones proposed in this paper.

4   Experimentation

For the experiments, we have considered a benchmark of 11 molecular instances with receptor and ligand flexibility. These complexes are actually difficult dock-

Table 1. The accession codes, the X-ray crystal structure and resolution taken from PDB database are presented.

PDB code	Protein-ligand complexes	Resolution (Å)
1AJV	HIV-1 protease/AHA006	2.00
1AJX	HIV-1 protease/AHA001	2.00
1BV9	HIV-1 protease/α-D-glucose	2.20
1D4K	HIV-1 protease/Macrocyclic peptidomimetic inhibitor 8	1.85
1G2K	HIV-1 protease/AHA047	1.95
1HIV	HIV-1 protease/U75875	2.00
1HPX	HIV-1 protease/KNI-272	2.00
1HTF	HIV-1 protease/GR126045	2.20
1HTG	HIV-1 protease/GR137615	2.00
1HVH	HIV-1 protease/Q8261	1.80
2UPJ	HIV-1 protease/U100313	3.00

ing problems containing a wide range of ligand sizes (from small to large inhibitors). The docking studies performed with these instances in [10] to test the energy function of AutoDock 4.2 demonstrated that the most difficult problems are those involving smaller ligands. This is due to the flexibility added to the receptor side-chains (ARG-8) that increases the space of ligand interactions. These instances have been taken from the PDB database[1].

Table 1 summarizes the set of problems selected showing the PDB accession code, the X-ray crystal structures names and the structure resolution (Å). For all instances, the torsional degrees of freedom for ligands and receptors are 10 and 6, respectively, selecting those torsions that allow the fewest number of atoms to move around the ligand core. Therefore, the solution vector contains: 3 variables for translation, 4 variables for rotation quaternion, and 16 variables for torsional degrees, summing up a total number (n) of 23 variables.

4.1 Methodology

The followed methodology consists in running each combination of algorithm and molecular instance 30 independent times. From these executions, we have calculated the median and interquartile range (IQR) as measures of central tendency and statistical dispersion, respectively. We have considered two quality indicators to assess the algorithm performance: Hypervolume (I_{HV}) [18] and Unary Additive Epsilon Indicator ($I_{\epsilon+}$) [19]. The former takes into account both convergence and diversity, whereas the later gives a measure of the convergence degree of the obtained Pareto front approximations. It is worth noting that we are dealing with a real-world optimization problem, and therefore the Pareto

---

[1] In URL: http://www.rcsb.org/pdb/home/home.do.

Table 2. Parameter settings.

Common parameters	
Swarm size	150 Particles
Iterations	10,000
SMPSO [3] & SMPSO$_{hv}$ & SMPSOD & SMPSOC	
Archive size	100
C_1, C_2	1.5
w	0.9
Mutation	polynomial mutation
Mutation probability	1.66
Mutation distribution index η_m	20
Selection method	Rounds
OMOPSO [1]	
Archive size	100
C_1, C_2	$rand(1.5, 2.0)$
w	$rand(0.1, 0.5)$
Mutation	uniform + non-uniform + no mutation
Mutation probability	Each mutation is applied to 1/3 of the swarm

fronts to calculate these two metrics are not known. To cope with this issue, we have generated a reference Pareto front for each instance by combining all the non-dominated solutions computed in all the executions of all the algorithms.

We have used the implementation of the five studied algorithms provided in the jMetalCpp framework [7], in combination with AutoDock 4.2 to evaluate the new generated solutions. To cope with the high computational requirements needed to carry out all the experiments, we have used the Condor[2] system, a middleware platform acting a distributed task scheduler of up to 400 cores.

The parameter settings are summarized in Table 2. We set a common subset of parameters which are the same for all the evaluated algorithms. The size of the swarm is 150 and the stopping condition is reached when 1,500,000 function evaluations are performed. These values were chosen as they are the default settings in AutoDock and they have been used in previous studies [13]. The archive size, when applicable, is set to 100.

All SMPSO versions use the polynomial mutation with distribution index $\eta_m = 20$, which is applied to one sixth of the particles in the swarm. The acceleration coefficients C_1 and C_2 are set to 1.5 and the inertia weight is $w = 0.9$. With these parameters setting, our approach has been to use common settings in order to make a fair comparison, keeping the rest of the parameters of SMPSO and OMOPSO according to the papers where they were originally described.

---

[2] In URL: http://research.cs.wisc.edu/htcondor/.

Table 3. Median and interquartile range of I_{HV} for each algorithm and instance. Best and second best median results have dark and light gray backgrounds, respectively.

	SMPSO	SMPSO$_{hv}$	SMPSOD	SMPSOC	OMOPSO
1AJV	$3.65e-01_{5.1e-02}$	$4.33e-01_{4.0e-02}$	$3.63e-01_{4.6e-02}$	$3.55e-01_{4.8e-02}$	$0.00e+00_{0.0e+00}$
1AJX	1.91 01	$5.06e-01$	$4.74e-01$	$4.43e-01$	$0.00e+00$
1D4K	$6.67e-01_{8.1e-02}$	$8.48e-01_{1.1e-01}$	$7.11e-01_{9.4e-02}$	$7.05e-01_{...}$	$0.00e$
1G2K	$3.84e-01_{5.3e-02}$	$4.58e-01_{5.9e-02}$	$3.82e-01_{4.1e-02}$	$3.52e-01_{5.2e-02}$	$0.00e+00_{0.0e+00}$
1HIV	$4.86e-01_{2.0e-01}$	$6.74e-01_{2.9e-02}$	$5.87e-01_{7.1e-02}$	$4.66e-01_{2.4e-01}$	$0.00e+00_{0.0e+00}$
1HPX	$3.60e-01_{1.8e-01}$	$6.30e-01_{9.7e-02}$	$4.77e-01_{1.0e-01}$	$4.63e-01_{1.4e-01}$	$0.00e+00_{0.0e+00}$
1HTF	$2.61e-01_{3.3e-01}$	$4.17e-01_{2.4e-01}$	$3.96e-01_{7.9e-02}$	$2.77e-01_{3.1e-01}$	$0.00e+00_{0.0e+00}$
1HTG	$8.33e-02_{1.3e-01}$	$1.46e-01_{9.6e-02}$	$1.03e-01_{8.2e-02}$	$7.13e-02_{1.3e-01}$	$0.00e+00_{0.0e+00}$
1HVH	$7.78e-01_{4.7e-02}$	$8.69e-01_{9.3e-03}$	$7.70e-01_{2.4e-02}$	$7.85e-01_{2.9e-02}$	$0.00e+00_{0.0e+00}$
1VB9	$4.10e-01_{1.2e-01}$	$5.09e-01_{5.6e-02}$	$4.12e-01_{1.1e-01}$	$4.38e-01_{9.1e-02}$	$0.00e+00_{0.0e+00}$
2UPJ	$5.82e-01_{9.6e-02}$	$6.96e-01_{5.1e-02}$	$6.27e-01_{7.4e-02}$	$6.20e-01_{6.8e-02}$	$1.99e-01_{6.4e-01}$

Table 4. Median and interquartile range of $I_{\epsilon+}$ for each algorithm and instance. Best and second best median results have dark and light gray backgrounds, respectively.

	SMPSO	SMPSO$_{hv}$	SMPSOD	SMPSOC	OMOPSO
1AJV	$5.12e-01_{1.0e-01}$	$3.94e-01_{6.7e-02}$	$5.35e-01_{1.0e-01}$	$5.46e-01_{1.0e-01}$	$5.31e+00_{2.0e+00}$
1AJX	$2.31e-01_{1.1e-01}$	$1.32e-01_{4.3e-02}$	$1.94e-01_{6.1e-02}$	$2.57e-01_{9.4e-02}$	$2.54e+00_{3.2e+00}$
1D4K	$2.06e-01_{8.6e-02}$	$4.41e-02_{1.2e-01}$	$1.54e-01_{7.3e-02}$	$1.57e-01_{8.1e-02}$	$8.81e+00_{4.1e+00}$
1G2K	$4.29e-01_{1.7e-01}$	$2.81e-01_{2.0e-01}$	$4.75e-01_{9.7e-02}$	$5.15e-01_{1.1e-01}$	$6.01e+00_{2.3e+00}$
1HIV	$3.95e-01_{3.6e-01}$	$9.03e-02_{6.4e-02}$	$2.66e-01_{1.2e-01}$	$4.36e-01_{3.2e-01}$	$4.91e+00_{1.1e+00}$
1HPX	$4.25e-01_{2.8e-01}$	$1.30e-01_{9.2e-02}$	$2.95e-01_{1.2e-01}$	$3.17e-01_{1.7e-01}$	$1.13e+01_{5.7e+00}$
1HTF	$6.60e-01_{1.5e+00}$	$5.46e-01_{3.7e-01}$	$5.64e-01_{1.1e-01}$	$6.85e-01_{4.3e-01}$	$1.49e+00_{6.2e-01}$
1HTG	$9.07e-01_{1.4e-01}$	$8.35e-01_{9.3e-02}$	$8.84e-01_{8.8e-02}$	$9.23e-01_{2.1e-01}$	$1.21e+01_{7.7e+00}$
1HVH	$1.46e-01_{4.4e-01}$	$6.12e-02_{4.8e-03}$	$1.47e-01_{3.9e-02}$	$1.52e-01_{3.1e-02}$	$5.11e+00_{2.4e+00}$
1VB9	$3.34e-01_{2.2e-01}$	$1.96e-01_{7.7e-02}$	$3.44e-01_{1.8e-01}$	$2.97e-01_{1.3e-01}$	$9.31e+00_{1.6e+00}$
2UPJ	$2.86e-01_{7.9e-02}$	$1.76e-01_{9.2e-02}$	$2.25e-01_{1.4e-01}$	$2.70e-01_{5.1e-02}$	$7.74e-01_{4.0e+00}$

5   Results and Analysis

A first analysis in our experimentation corresponds to the of results in terms of the hypervolume indicator I_{HV}. This indicator computes the sum of the contributed volume of each point in the Pareto front (non-dominated solutions) with regards to a reference point. Therefore, the higher the convergence and diversity degree of a front, the higher (better) the resulting I_{HV} value is.

Table 3 shows the median and interquartile range of the computed distributions (out of 30 independent runs) of I_{HV}, for the set of 11 docking instances and for the five compared algorithms. As we can observe, SMPSO$_{hv}$ obtains the best median values of I_{HV} for all the molecular instances and SMPSOD is the second best performing technique. We have to mention that some results of OMOPSO have a I_{HV} equal to zero. This happens when all the points of the produced fronts are dominated by the reference point. In contrast, all the SMPSO versions obtained I_{HV} values higher than zero, which indicates that they are all able to produce solutions within the limits of the reference point.

In the case of $I_{\epsilon+}$, a similar observation can be extracted from Table 4. That is, SMPSO$_{hv}$ shows the best results for all instances, followed by SMPSOD and SMPSO (the lower $I_{\epsilon+}$ value, the better the result is). For this indicator, SMPSOC obtains a second best median value only for instance 1VB9.

These results are assessed with statistical confidence (in this study p-value = 0.05) by focusing on the entire distribution of each of the two studied metrics. In

Table 5. Average Friedman's rankings with Holm's Adjusted p-values (0.05) of compared algorithms for the test set of 11 docking instances. Symbol * indicates the control algorithm and column at right contains the overall ranking of positions with regards to I_{HV} and $I_{\epsilon+}$.

Hypervolume (I_{HV})			Epsilon ($I_{\epsilon+}$)			Overall	
Algorithm	Fri_{Rank}	$Holm_{Ap}$	Algorithm	Fri_{Rank}	$Holm_{Ap}$	Algorithm	Rank
*SMPSO$_{hv}$	1.01	-	*SMPSO$_{hv}$	1.00	-	SMPSO$_{hv}$	2
SMPSOD	2.54	$2.18e-02$	SMPSOD	2.45	$3.09e-02$	SMPSOD	4
SMPSOC	3.09	$3.85e-03$	SMPSO	2.99	$6.02e-03$	SMPSOC	5
SMPSO	3.36	$1.36e-03$	SMPSOC	3.54	$4.79e-04$	SMPSO	5
OMOPSO	4.99	$1.19e-08$	OMOPSO	4.98	$1.19e-08$	OMOPSO	10

concrete, we have applied Friedman's ranking and Holm's post-hoc multicompare tests [16] to know which algorithms are statistically worse than the control one (i.e., the one ranking the best).

This way, as shown in Table 5, SMPSO$_{hv}$ is the best ranked variant according to Friedman test for the two indicators (I_{HV} and $I_{\epsilon+}$), and it is followed by SMP-SOD. Therefore, SMPSO$_{hv}$ is established as the control algorithm in the post-hoc Holm tests, which is compared with the rest of algorithms. The adjusted p-values ($Holm_{Ap}$ in Table 5) resulting from these comparisons are, for the remaining variants (SMPSO, SMPSOD, SMPSO, and OMOPSO), lower than the confidence level (0.05), meaning that SMPSO$_{hv}$ is statistically better than these algorithms. SMPSO and SMPSOC obtained similar overall performances, although showing SMPSOC better ranking than SMPSO in terms of I_{HV}.

Figure 2 shows the boxplots of the distributions of results concerning the I_{HV} values, for each compared algorithm and molecular instance. In this figure, we can check that SMPSO$_{hv}$ variant obtains the best distributions for all the instances. An interesting observation can be made regarding OMOPSO, whose distributions denote poor results, although it produces outlier solutions with the best indicator values for some instances: 1AJV, 1AJX, 1HPX, and 1HTF. These outliers lead OMOPSO to contribute with many solutions to the reference Pareto fronts. An example of this can be observed in Fig. 3, where the fronts with best I_{HV} values of all compared algorithms are plotted for instance 1AJX. However, the overall results (in boxplots) of OMOPSO indicate that it behaves irregular (non-robust) for all the molecular instances.

Following with Fig. 3, another interesting observation lies in the ability of SMPSOD to obtain non-dominated solutions in the region of the reference Pareto front with low energy and high RMSD values (top-left in plots of Fig. 3). In contrast with the other compared algorithms, SMPSOD is able to properly cover this area, as well as other areas with low RMSD. Therefore, as suggested in our previous study [9], a hybrid implementation of SMPSO using an aggregative (archive-less) strategy as done in MOEA/D, would cover the reference front with non-dominated solutions in the two objective ends. This assumption is now tested with SMPSOD in this study.

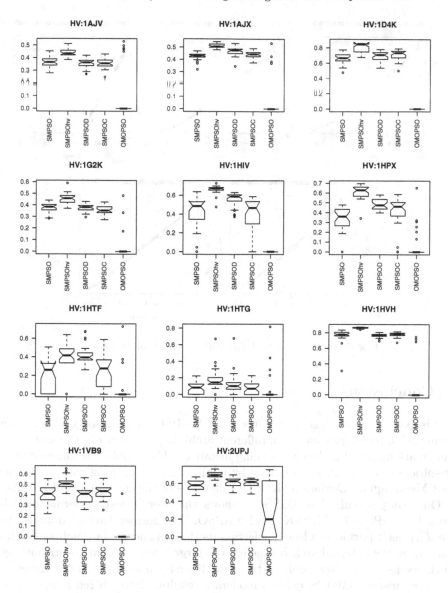

Fig. 2. Resulting boxplots of each compared algorithm and instance for I_{HV}

In summary, SMPSO$_{hv}$ shows the overall best behaviour followed by SMP-SOD. Intuitively, the former obtains the best I_{HV} as it performs a leader selection method of non-dominated solutions (from the external archive) with largest hypervolume contributions. That is, the particles in the swarm are guided by leaders with large hypervolume contributions, which would enable SMPSO$_{hv}$ to obtain, not only high values of I_{HV}, but also accurate results in terms of $I_{\epsilon+}$.

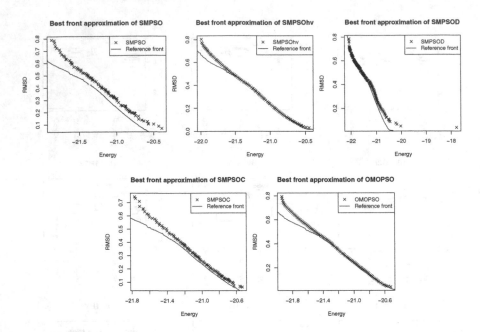

Fig. 3. Fronts with best I_{HV} values on problem 1AJX.

6 Conclusions

In this paper, we analyze new variants of SMPSO, a multi-objective swarm optimization technique, based on different archiving strategies in the scope of a benchmarking set of molecular docking instances. The problem is formulated as a bi-objective optimization problem, by minimizing the binding energy and the Root Mean Square Deviation (RMSD) difference in the coordinates of ligands.

Our study reveals that SMPSO$_{hv}$ shows the overall best performance, followed by SMPSOD, SMPSOC, and SMPSO. The former variant obtains the best I_{HV} as it performs a leader selection method of those non-dominated solutions (from the external archive) having the largest hypervolume contributions, which seems to be responsible of the best diversity and convergence values in this comparison. OMOPSO shows moderate results, although reaching outperforming outlier solutions for some instances: 1AJV, 1AJX, 1HPX, and 1HTF. Interestingly, SMPSOD variant is able to cover the reference front with non-dominated solutions in the two objective extremes, i.e., with low energy and RMDS values. In this regard, as suggested in our previous study [9], a hybrid implementation of SMPSO using an aggregative (archive-less) strategy as done in MOEA/D, would cover the reference front with non-dominated solutions in the two objective ends. This assumption is now tested with SMPSOD in this study. Ideally, this SMPSO variant would contribute to discover other different (unknown) active sites in the receptor molecule with low energy, but far from the known active site (that is, with low RMSD).

This last open a future line of research for us on the selection and study of interesting solutions to be evaluated from a biological point of view. In addition, a natural extension of this work would be to test these conclusions on a greater number of molecular instances and using other quality indicators.

Acknowledgments. This work is partially funded by Grants TIN2011-25840 (Ministerio de Ciencia e Innovación) and P11-TIC-7529 and P12-TIC-1519 (Plan Andaluz I+D+I). This article is based upon work from COST Action CA15140, supported by COST (European Cooperation in Science and Technology).

References

1. Coello, C.A., Toscano, G., Lechuga, M.S.: Handling Multiple objectives with Particle Swarm Optimization. IEEE Trans. Evol. Comp. **8**(3), 3 (2004)
2. Deb, K., Pratap, A., Agarwal, S., Meyarivan, T.: A fast and elitist multiobjective genetic algorithm: NSGA-II. IEEE Trans. Evol. Comput. **6**(2), 182–197 (2002)
3. Durillo, J.J., García-Nieto, J., Nebro, A.J., Coello, C.A.C., Luna, F., Alba, E.: Multi-objective particle swarm optimizers: an experimental comparison. In: Ehrgott, M., Fonseca, C.M., Gandibleux, X., Hao, J.-K., Sevaux, M. (eds.) EMO 2009. LNCS, vol. 5467, pp. 495–509. Springer, Heidelberg (2009)
4. García-Godoy, M.J., López-Camacho, E., García Nieto, J., Nebro, A.J., Aldana-Montes, J.F.: Solving molecular docking problems with multi-objective metaheuristics. Molecules **20**(6), 10154–10183 (2015)
5. Gu, J., Yang, X., Kang, L., Wu, J., Wang, X.: MoDock: a multi-objective strategy improves the accuracy for molecular docking. Algs. Mol. Bio. **10**, 8 (2015)
6. Janson, S., Merkle, D., Middendorf, M.: Molecular docking with multi-objective particle swarm optimization. Appl. Soft Comput. **8**(1), 666–675 (2008)
7. López-Camacho, E., García-Godoy, M.J., Nebro, A.J., Aldana-Montes, J.F.: jMetalCpp: optimizing molecular docking problems with a C++ metaheuristic framework. Bioinformatics **30**(3), 437–438 (2014)
8. López-Camacho, E., García-Godoy, M.J., García-Nieto, J., Nebro, A.J., Aldana-Montes, J.F.: Solving molecular flexible docking problems with metaheuristics: a comparative study. Appl. Soft Comput. **28**, 379–393 (2015)
9. López-Camacho, E., García-Godoy, M.J., García-Nieto, J., Nebro, A.J., Aldana-Montes, J.F.: A new multi-objective approach for molecular docking based on RMSD and binding energy. In: 3rd International Conference on Algorithm for Computational Biology (2016, in-Press)
10. Morris, G.M., Huey, R., Lindstrom, W., Sanner, M.F., Belew, R.K., Goodsell, D.S., Olson, A.J.: AutoDock4 and AutoDockTools4: automated docking with selective receptor flexibility. J. Comput. Chem. **30**(16), 2785–2791 (2009)
11. Nebro, A., Durillo, J., Garcia-Nieto, J., Coello Coello, C.A., Luna, F., Alba, E.: SMPSO: a new PSO-based metaheuristic for multi-objective optimization. In: IEEE Symposium on Computational Intelligence in Multi-criteria Decision-Making, pp. 66–73 (2009)
12. Nebro, A., Durillo, J., Coello Coello, C.A.: Analysis of leader selection strategies in a MOPSO. In: Proceedings of IEEE Congress on Evolutionary Computation (CEC), pp. 3153–3160, June 2013
13. Norgan, A.P., Coffman, P.K., Kocher, J.P.A., Katzmann, D.J., Sosa, C.P.: Multilevel parallelization of AutoDock 4.2. J. Cheminform. **3**(1), 12 (2011)

14. Sierra, M.R., Coello Coello, C.A.: Improving PSO-based multi-objective optimization using crowding, mutation and ε-dominance. In: Coello Coello, C.A., Hernández Aguirre, A., Zitzler, E. (eds.) EMO 2005. LNCS, vol. 3410, pp. 505–519. Springer, Heidelberg (2005)
15. Sandoval-Perez, A., Becerra, D., Vanegas, D., Restrepo-Montoya, D., Nino, F.: A multi-objective optimization energy approach to predict the ligand conformation in a docking process. In: Krawiec, K., Moraglio, A., Hu, T., Etaner-Uyar, A.Ş., Hu, B. (eds.) EuroGP 2013. LNCS, vol. 7831, pp. 181–192. Springer, Heidelberg (2013)
16. Sheskin, D.J.: Handbook of Parametric and Nonparametric Statistical Procedures. Chapman & Hall/CRC, Boca Raton (2007)
17. Zhang, Q., Li, H.: MOEA/D: a multiobjective evolutionary algorithm based on decomposition. IEEE Trans. Evol. Comp. $11(6)$, 712–731 (2007)
18. Zitzler, E., Thiele, L.: Multiobjective evolutionary algorithms: a comparative case study and the strength pareto approach. IEEE Trans. Evol. Comp. $3(4)$, 257–271 (1999)
19. Zitzler, E., Thiele, L., Laumanns, M., Fonseca, C.M., da Fonseca, V.G.: Performance assessment of multiobjective optimizers: an analysis and review. IEEE Trans. Evol. Comp. $7(2)$, 117–132 (2003)

Ant Colony Optimisation-Based Classification Using Two-Dimensional Polygons

Morten Goodwin[1](✉) and Anis Yazidi[2](✉)

[1] Deptartment of ICT, Institute for Technology and Sciences,
University of Agder, Agder, Norway
morten.goodwin@uia.no
[2] Department of Computer Science,
Akershus University College of Applied Sciences, Oslo, Norway
anis.yazidi@hioa.no

Abstract. The application of Ant Colony Optimization to the field of classification has mostly been limited to *hybrid approaches* which attempt at boosting the performance of existing classifiers (such as Decision Trees and Support Vector Machines (SVM)) — often through guided feature reductions or parameter optimizations.

In this paper we introduce PolyACO: A novel Ant Colony based classifier operating in two dimensional space that utilizes ray casting. To the best of our knowledge, our work is the first reported Ant Colony based classifier which is *non-hybrid*, in the sense, that it does not build on any legacy classifiers. The essence of the scheme is to create a separator in the feature space by imposing ant-guided random walks in a grid system. The walks are self-enclosing so that the ants return back to the starting node forming a closed classification path yielding a many edged polygon. Experimental results on both synthetic and real-life data show that our scheme is able to perfectly separate both simple and complex patterns, without utilizing "kernel tricks" and outperforming existing classifiers, such as polynomial and linear SVM. The results are impressive given the simplicity of PolyACO compared to other approaches such as SVM.

1 Introduction

Supervised Learning is one of the most central tasks in Machine Learning and Pattern Recognition. However, it becomes intrinsically challenging whenever the data to be classified is not easily separable in the feature space. A myriad of classification algorithms have been proposed in the literature with a variety of behaviors and limitations [11]. Examples of these algorithms include Neural Networks, SVM and Decision trees.

Common trends in research is to apply Ant Colony Optimization (ACO) as rule based variants or as a way to enhance some of the state-of-the-art classifiers. The latter work as optimisers for classifiers such as decision trees or neural networks [3,12]. To the best of our knowledge, there is no similar work on non-hybrid Ant Colony based classifiers that solely resorts to ACO without the aid of any other legacy classifier.

© Springer International Publishing Switzerland 2016
M. Dorigo et al. (Eds.): ANTS 2016, LNCS 9882, pp. 53–64, 2016.
DOI: 10.1007/978-3-319-44427-7_5

A broad class of classification algorithms such as SVM and perception rely upon defining mathematical functions with weights that efficiently can separate two or more classes of data where unknown weights are learned based the training data. Often, the "best" hyperplane[1] to separate classes does not follow the mathematical properties of a function. The "best" line can for example be a polygon encircling certain data points, which is not a function and therefore cannot straightforward be outputted by SVM or similar classifiers.

Figure 1 shows an example of labeled data where it is not possible to perfectly separate the data with one function simply because any line separating the data perfectly will have multiple $y-$values of some of the $x-$values — which defies the definition of mathematical functions. SVM deals with this by projecting the data in high dimensional space or using the "kernel trick".

Many kernels are available for SVM as a way to provide a "shape" of the separator which is not limited to linear or polynomial functions. The kernel yields an equivalent functionality as to transposing the data to many dimensions. However, the accuracy of the SVM is dependent on the right choice of the kernel function, as well as several other parameters, which is not an easy task given the unlimited number of available kernels. It is often based on trial and error.

This paper introduces PolyACO, a novel classification scheme operating in two dimensions using ACO that does not involve a "kernel trick" whenever the data is not easily separable. The presented approach deals with classification problems in two-dimensional Euclidean space by building separators with many-sided polygons. The polygons are extrapolated from pheromone trails of ants walking with a preference towards encapsulating of all items from one class and excluding any items from other classes from the encapsulation. This way, emerging polygons encapsulate each class in such a way that they can be used as classifiers. The clas-

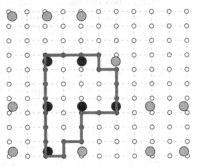

Fig. 1. Example of simple two class classification scenario with the classes Black (T_1) and Gray (T_2) (Color figure online)

sification takes place by resorting to ray casting unknown items which identifies whether an item is part of a polygon, and each item is labeled accordingly.

Classification of unknown items based on labeled data is a supervised learning problem. Hence, in line with common practice, the problem is divided into two phases, namely (1) training and (2) classification:

1. **Training phase:** The aim is to create a polygon that encircles classes of items so that the polygons separate the training classes from each other.
2. **Classification phase:** In this phase, we use the polygon as a basis to determine which class a new unknown item to be classified belongs to.

---

[1] The hyperplane is a line in a two-dimensional space.

The overall aim of the training phase can therefore be stated as to find a polygon $s*$, consisting of vertices and edges, that minimises $f(s*)$ where $f(s*)$ tells how well the polygon $s*$ separate the items in the training. Thus, formally, we aim to find an $s* \subset \mathbf{S}$ so that $f(s*) \leq f(s) \in \mathbf{S}$. For this we use ACO explained in Sect. 2. In turn, the classification determining whether the item to be classified is within or outside of the polygon $s*$.

The paper is organised as follows. Section 2 reviews the-state-of-the-art in the area of swarm intelligence based classifiers with special focus on ACO. Section 3 continues with introducing our solution: PolyACO as a method for creating polygons for classification with two classes and corresponding results. Finally, in Sect. 4, we draw conclusions and gives insights into future work.

2   Ant Colony Optimisation (ACO)

For completeness of the paper, we will briefly discuss variants of ACO. Details of ACO, including updating rules, are presented in many other papers [4]. We therefore include elements relevant to PolyACO are included.

2.1   Standard ACO

Swarm intelligence denotes a set of nature-inspired paradigms that have received a lot of attention in computer science due to its simplicity and adaptability [20]. ACO figures among the most popular swarm intelligence algorithms due to its ability to solve many optimization problems. ACO involves artificial ants operating a reinforced random walk over a graph. The ants release pheromones in favorable paths which subsequent ant members follow creating a reinforcement learning based behavior. The colony of ants will thus concentrate its walk on the most favorable paths and in consequence iteratively optimize the solution [4].

Finding the shortest path in a bidirectional graph with vertices and edges $G(V, E)$ using ACO in its simplest form works as follows. Artificial ants move from vertex to vertex. An ant that finds a route s from the source v_s to the sink v_t will release pheromones $\tau_{i,j}$ corresponding to all edges $e_{i,j} \in s$, and $\Delta\tau_{i,j}^k$ corresponds to the change in pheromones for ant k . The pheromones for all ants m is defined as:

$$\tau_{i,j} \leftarrow (1 - p)\tau_{i,j} + \sum_{k=1}^{m} \Delta\tau_{i,j}^k \tag{1}$$

2.2 $\mathcal{MAX} - \mathcal{MIN}$ ACO

In order to improve the convergence performance of ACO a special greedier variant called $\mathcal{MAX} - \mathcal{MIN}$ ACO was introduced [18,19]. Another variant referred to as $\mathcal{MMAS}$ was reported in [13]. These variants are greedier in the sense that they only spread out pheromones for the best solutions, and in this way subsequent ants will converge faster than with the traditional variants. Certain setups even have theoretically guaranteed convergence [5].

The improvement is summarized as follows [19]: (1) Only the global best ant is allowed to release pheromones. (2) The pheromones on each edge are limited to an interval $[\tau_{min}, \tau_{max}]$ to avoid stagnation. (3) All edges are initiated with τ_{max}. This is to achieve high exploration in the beginning of the search.

It follows that the pheromone trails are updated according to the function 2 (an update of Eq. 1):

$$\tau_{i,j} \leftarrow (1 - p)\tau_{i,j} + \Delta\tau_{i,j}^{best} \qquad (2)$$

$\mathcal{MAX} - \mathcal{MIN}$ ACO is shown to be a good alternative to existing algorithms when solving NP-hard combinatorial optimization problems such as Traveling Salesman where it performs at the same level as comparative algorithms. In the asymmetric variants, it outperforms other known approaches [1].

2.3   ACO for Classification

A considerable amount of work for Swarm Intelligence classification tasks, including ACO, is reported in the literature. The existing approaches fall into three main categories: (1) Rule based extractors, and (2) Hybrid approaches involving ACO that attempt to enhance the quality of existing classifiers, (3) Clustering based approaches using Swarm Intelligence.

The rule based classifiers [10, 12, 14] construct graphs by letting the ants walk with preference towards common occurring examples so that strong pheromone trails are used as rules in the classifier, or a set of IF-THEN rules. Probably, the most notable rule based ACO classifiers are the AntMiner series [7] including: AntMiner [14], AntMiner2, AntMiner3, AntMiner+ [12] and new variantssuch as MAnt-Miner [6]. All the aforementioned AntMiner variants rely on the idea of letting the ant walk "on" examples so that the pheromone trails can yield usable rules.

The hybrid approaches use ACO to improve the performance of legacy classifiers, for example in feed forward neural networks [16]. In the latter case, this is achieved by letting the ants minimize a function consisting of a set of decision variables corresponding to the neuron parameter weights. Furthermore, there is a multitude of hybrid ACO variants for Bayesian networks [3], multi-net classifiers [17], and rule pruning [2].

The clustering based swarm intelligence rely techniques such as Particle Swarm and Artificial Bee Colony to cluster data in an unsupervised manner [8]. Even though these have similarities with PolyACO, they cannot be directly applied for supervised learning such as classification.

3   PolyACO

This section presents the novel algorithm PolyACO. For the training phase, it maps the $\mathcal{MAX} - \mathcal{MIN}$ ACO to the problem area by formally specifying an appropriate cost function that encircles one class. PolyACO trains the classifier by defining a polygon s. Subsequently, it uses s with ray casting to find if an item is part of the s.

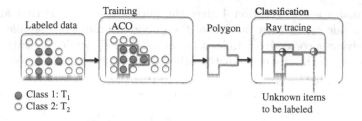

Fig. 2. Overview of PolyACO

Figure 2 presents an overview of the approach. The data is separated using ACO yielding a polygon. Next, the polygon is used in the classification with ray casting. In this example, the first item to be labeled will be classified as a T_1 ("Class 1") since it is shown to be inside the polygon, while the second item will be classified as T_2 ("Class 2") since it is outside the polygon.

In order to use ACO for encircling points into polygons, we extend the ACO $\mathcal{MAX} - \mathcal{MIN}$ update function (Eq. 2) with a cost function that measures the quality of PolyAco solution. In order to find whether a point is within a polygon we use ray casting.

3.1 Ray Casting

Vertical ray casting is used to consider whether an item is within or outside a many edged polygon [15]. Ray casting is a simple algorithm that determines where a virtual ray enters and exits a given solid.

In a two-dimensional XY-plane, a ray is sent with a $y-$coordinate and a bit starting at 0 and is increased by one very time an edged is passed. When the ray hits the item to be labelled, whether it is inside or outside the polygon is determined by reading the bit. An even number means outside while an odd number means inside. Formally, for node t_i and a polygon s, we get $h(t_i, s)$ representing to what extent it is inside or outside of the polygon as follows:

$$h(t_i, s) = \begin{cases} 1 \; if \; t_i \in T_1 \; and \; is \; inside \; of \; s. \\ 0 \; otherwise \end{cases} \tag{3}$$

$h(t_i, s)$ gives 1 if t_i is correctly inside of the polygon, 0 otherwise. Note that the cost function $f(s)$ in Eq. 4 handles both items correctly inside and correctly outside of polygons.

3.2 Cost Function

Equation 4 presents the cost function. The cost function takes into account the information about whether an item t_i is inside or outside of a polygon s. It measures how good a polygon s is at encircling and isolating one class in the training data and is defined as:

$$f(s) = \frac{\sum_{t_i \in T_1} h(t_i, s) + \sum_{t_j \notin T_1}(1 - h(t_j, s))}{|T|}. \tag{4}$$

In layman's terms; function 4 gives the percentage of items that are either correctly inside or correctly outside of the polygon. From the example in Fig. 1 the red polygon s correctly encircles all items of class T_1, while correctly avoiding to encircle any other items from the other class T_2. Since s is a polygon that perfectly separates the two classes, it gives $f(s) = 1$.[2]

Hence, the pheromones update obeys the following function, combining Eqs. 2 and 4.

$$\Delta\tau_{i,j} = \frac{f(s)}{|s|} \tag{5}$$

The problem reduces to optimising $f(s)$, given the training data T, subject to the search space $\mathbf{S}$ — which is equivalent to finding an $s* \in \mathbf{S}$ so that $f(s*) \leq f(s) \in \mathbf{S}$.

3.3 Training Phase

The classifier is trained using a guided walk with $\mathcal{MAX} - \mathcal{MIN}$ ACO optimising for the score function $f(s)$ in order to create a polygon. Since new ants released walk with a preference towards high pheromone areas, the ant will converge towards a polygon that is a good separator. This polygon is the key to the classification. Hence, the pheromones on the path are deposited directly in accordance with a score function over the length of the path.

Note that the classifier, implicitly, performs optimization according to two properties of the data: the score function $f(s)$ and the length of the path, $|s|$. A shorter path will give larger amounts of pheromones per edge than a longer path because a shorter path gives pheromones over fewer edges.

The classifier can therefore be considered as a many-edged polygon with only vertical or horizontal edges. The ants are not allowed to walk on nodes that has previously been selected, except for the initial starting node.

Convergence. Figure 3 shows an example for optimisation over time, i, during the training phase. The figure clearly depicts that in the beginning of the optimisation, after 50 ants, $i = 50$, PolyACO has already found an acceptable but imperfect solution that gives a score function $f(s) = 0.830$. The polygon s is continuously improved according to two ways: (1) The result from the score function increases and reaches close to 1 at $i = 850$. It reaches 1 at $i = 2000$. (2) The polygon becomes shorter over time. Consequently, the polygon is increasingly better fitting the data as i increases in this example.

The algorithm includes some off-the-shelf features to aid the convergence of the training, namely: graph pruning to help stuck ants, random start, and pheromone evaporation.

Pruning: To improve the performance, the graph is after each iteration pruned for indisputable simplifications. An example is a solution that goes directly from

---

[2] Note that s is one of the possible polygons with the shortest circumference that is able to perfectly separate the data. The reason for this is explained in Sect. 3.3.

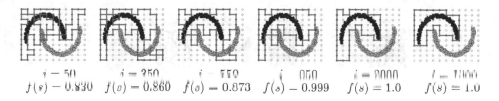

$i = 50$ $i = 350$ $i = 550$ $i = 650$ $i = 8000$ $i = 1000$
$f(s) = 0.830$ $f(s) = 0.860$ $f(s) = 0.873$ $f(s) = 0.999$ $f(s) = 1.0$ $f(s) = 1.0$

Fig. 3. Example of best known polygon, $s*$ over training periods.

node v_i to v_j, and directly back to v_i. Such a solution is automatically pruned by removing v_i from the solution s.

Stuck ants: Since the ants cannot walk on previously visited nodes, they can easily get stuck. Any solution with stuck ants are simply ignored since the solution is obviously not correct.

Random starts: The ants start at random positions in the grid. A natural strategy would have been to always start the ants from the same node, say v_1. Nevertheless, the "best" polygon $s*$ harvesting the highest output from the score function may not include v_1. Accordingly, the ants start at a random node.

Pheromone evaporation: Pheromones are evaporated with 1% probability. This means that 1% of the pheromones are after each iteration dropped to avoid too early convergence and at the same time enable exploration. This is a balance between exploration and convergence in line with the literature [19].

3.4 Classification Phase

The training phase produces a polygon $s*$ that separates the training data in two sets. For any new unknown item t_i, the ray casting function from Eq. 3 is used. If $h(t_i, s) = 1$, t_i is classified as T_1, otherwise it is classified as T_2. This section presents results from various scenarios ranging from simple solutions with easily separable data to more complex settings with noisy data both real-life and synthetic. For each generated scenario, 1000 data points per class are generated or extracted. For the real scenarios, all data is used. In all cases, half of the data is used for training and the other half for classification as cross validation. All scenarios are run with 10000 ants unless otherwise explicitly specified. Table 1 presents a summary of the results.[3]

Simple Environments. We shall present a simple experimental settings as proof of concept of PolyACO. This section empirically shows that the approach works in a simple environment with two easily separable sets of data. The data is composed of two blocks of data: T_1 and T_2. Figure 4(a) shows the pheromone trails after the training phase in this environment. The pheromones have built

---

[3] Many more data sets where tested, but due to the limited space in the paper only the most interesting results are included.

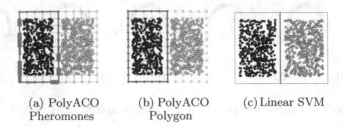

(a) PolyACO   (b) PolyACO   (c) Linear SVM
Pheromones   Polygon

Fig. 4. Example of solutions based on easily separable items with the classes Black (T_1) and Gray (T_2).

a rectangular polygon encircling all items in T_1, but none of the items in T_2. Figure 4(b) presents the best known polygon s based on the pheromone trail. Since this is a polygon that perfectly separates the classes, it yields $f(s) = 1$. The mapping from pheromones to polygon in this example is quite straight forward. Lastly, for comparison purposes, Fig. 4(c) depicts the corresponding linear SVM. It is interesting to observe that PolyACO and SVM find the same boundaries.

This example strongly indicates that, for this particular example with easily separable data, the result of the PolyACO is equivalent to that of a linear SVM — both can be interpreted as perfect classifiers. Table 1 shows an overview of the classification results. Both PolyACO and SVM reach an accuracy of 1.0 — which is not surprising given the simplicity of the classification task.

Overlapping Data. In the above scenario, the data is organized so that it is perfectly separable. In contrast, the data in Fig. 5 is more challenging because it is overlapping — no line or polygon can perfectly separate the data sets.

Figure 5(a) shows the pheromones after the training phase. For the left- and lower part of the polygon, the pheromone trail is strong — the lines are thick. In contrast, where the data is overlapping in the diagonal where there are both items from T_1 and T_2, the scheme is less confident the trail is less strong. This indicates that when the confidence of the classifier is strong, PolyACO provides heavy pheromone trails. Figure 5(b) shows the corresponding polygon, and Fig. 5(c) and (d) show corresponding boundaries of linear and polynomial SVM.

From Table 1, we observe that PolyACO reaches an accuracy of 0.852, while linear SVM reaches 0.837, and polynomial SVM reaches 0.842. A conclusion to be drawn from this example is that PolyACO finds a slightly better boundary than the SVM lines, presumably because the rigged lines better fits the data than the straight and polynomial lines. Note that for this example, PolyACO even outperforms SVM with Gaussian kernel.

Circular. Classification in a circular environment is particularly difficult because there does not exist one mathematical function that separate the data

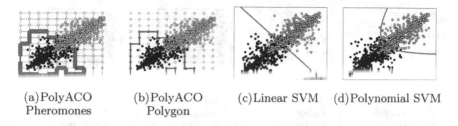

(a) PolyACO
Pheromones

(b) PolyACO
Polygon

(c) Linear SVM

(d) Polynomial SVM

Fig. 5. Example of solutions based on overlapping data with the classes Black (T_1) and Gray (T_2).

without mapping it to multiple dimensions. The data is generated by a Gaussian distribution from two circles with the same center but with two different radius.

Figure 6(a) shows that the polygon is able to perfectly encircle class T_1, which is only matched by SVM with and Gaussian kernel in Fig. 6(c). The linear SVM in Fig. 6(b) and polynomial SVM (not presented as a figure) do not find any viable solution.

By adding 5 % noise to the data, meaning that 5 % of the data is intentionally wrongly labelled, Fig. 6(d) shows that PolyACO is still able to a close to perfect solution despite this discrepancy.

Table 1 shows that PolyACO gets an accuracy of 1 compared to 0.538 for linear SVM and 0.892 for polynomial SVM. The PolyACO accuracy is only matched by Gaussian SVM — which relies upon high dimension space. In the noisy environment, the PolyACO algorithm has only marginally reduced accuracy to 0.948. Correspondingly, the polynomial SVM dropped from 0.892 to 0.778.

Real Data Sets. Figure 7 shows the results from two real data sets from the UC Irvine Machine Learning Repository[4]; namely the Iris Plant Database and the Wine Quality Database. The intention is to show that the proposed scheme works not only in synthetic environments, but with real data.

Figure 7(a) and (b) show the pheromone trail and corresponding polygon for the Iris Plan Database. It is interesting to observe that there is evenly spread

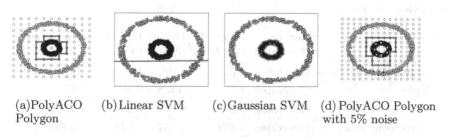

(a) PolyACO
Polygon

(b) Linear SVM

(c) Gaussian SVM

(d) PolyACO Polygon
with 5% noise

Fig. 6. Example of solutions based on circles with the classes Black (T_1) and Gray (T_2).

---

[4] http://archive.ics.uci.edu/ml/.

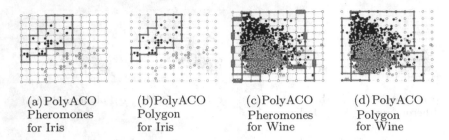

(a) PolyACO
Pheromones
for Iris

(b) PolyACO
Polygon
for Iris

(c) PolyACO
Pheromones
for Wine

(d) PolyACO
Polygon
for Wine

Fig. 7. Example of solutions with the classes Black (T_1) and Gray (T_2) for the real data sets: Iris and Wine tasting.

out pheromones resulting in a solid polygon. Similarly, Fig. 7(c) and (d) show the pheromone trail and corresponding polygon for the Wine Quality Database. In this scenario, the data is more chaotic giving polygons with seemingly odd edges. This demonstrates that PolyACO is able to find rather odd and complex patterns. For both scenarios, the accuracy in Table 1 is very close to all variants of SVM. For the Iris Plant Dataset the accuracy for PolyACO is 0.960 compared to 0.980 for all SVM variants. For the Wine Quality Database, PolyACO reaches an accuracy of 0.690 compared to 0.685,0.683, and 0.690 for linear, polynomial and Gaussian SVM. Hence, assuming that SVM is able to classify the data well, so is arguably the PolyACO algorithm.

3.5 Comparisons

Table 1 presents the classification accuracy of PolyACO on the problems introduced in this paper. For comparison purpose SVM (with linear, polynomial and Gaussian kernel) is presented with exactly the same data. To avoid side effects due to the randomness of the data, all results are averages of 1000 runs. This is true even for the real data where the only randomness is which data is used for training and classification.

Table 1. Comparisons of the behaviour of various algorithms through classification for Real or Generated data.

Problem	Real or Generated	PolyACO PolyACO	Linear SVM	Polinomial SVM	Gaussian SVM
Easily separable items	Generated	1.0	1.0	1.0	1.0
Circles	Generated	1.0	0.538	0.892	1.0
Noisy circles	Generated	0.980	0.538	0.892	0.959
Overlapping data	Generated	0.852	0.837	0.842	0.840
Iris	Real	0.960	0.980	0.980	0.980
Wine tasting	Real	0.690	0.685	0.683	0.690

4   Conclusion

In this paper, we introduced PolyACO, a *non-hybrid* Ant Colony Optimisation (ACO) based classifier. To the best of our knowledge, PolyACO is the first *non-hybrid* ACO based classifier reported in the literature. It uses a combination of $\mathcal{MAX} - \mathcal{MIN}$ ACO and Ray Casting. PolyACO is a classification algorithm for data in two dimensions which relies upon encircling items with ant pheromones so that the pheromone trails can be used as polygons in a classification scheme.

We demonstrate that PolyACO gives impressive performance by applying it in many simulated and real environments. In all situations, PolyACO is able to perform equally well or better than state-of-the-art algorithms such as Support Vector Machine with linear, polynomial, and Gaussian kernel. PolyACO does this without relaying upon high dimensional space or the "kernel trick".

Even though PolyACO shows very promising classification performance, several areas need further exploration. As a future work, we aim to extend the current approach to work with more than two classes, potentially as a combination of multiple polygons similar to multiple functions separate many classes in an SVM. Additional exploration when data are represented by more than two features presumably means examining the behavior of PolyACO in more than two dimensions, or as an intelligent combination of several two-dimensional approaches. Furthermore, we plan to examine the fact some areas in the grid could benefit from additional fine tuned resolution while other areas do not, for example using multi-level ACO approach [9].

References

1. Asmar, D., Elshamli, A., Areibi, S.: A comparative assessment of ACO algorithms within a TSP environment. Dyn. Continous Discrete Impulsive Syst.-Ser. B-Appl. Algorithms **1**, 462–467 (2005)
2. Chan, A., Freitas, A.A.: A new classification-rule pruning procedure for an ant colony algorithm. In: Talbi, E.-G., Liardet, P., Collet, P., Lutton, E., Schoenauer, M. (eds.) EA 2005. LNCS, vol. 3871, pp. 25–36. Springer, Heidelberg (2006)
3. Daly, R., Shen, Q.: Learning Bayesian Network Equivalence Classes with Ant Colony Optimization (2014). arXiv preprint arXiv:1401.3464
4. Dorigo, M., Birattari, M., Stutzle, T.: Ant colony optimization. IEEE Comput. Intell. Mag. **1**(4), 28–39 (2006)
5. Gutjahr, W.J.: ACO algorithms with guaranteed convergence to the optimal solution. Inf. Process. Lett. **82**(3), 145–153 (2002)
6. Hota, S., Satapathy, P., Jagadev, A.K.: Modified ant colony optimization algorithm (MAnt-Miner) for classification rule mining. In: Jain, L.C., Patnaik, S., Ichalkaranje, N. (eds.) Intelligent Computing, Communication and Devices, pp. 267–275. Springer, New Delhi (2015)
7. Junior, I.C.: Data mining with ant colony algorithms. In: Huang, D.-S., Jo, K.-H., Zhou, Y.-Q., Han, K. (eds.) ICIC 2013. LNCS, vol. 7996, pp. 30–38. Springer, Heidelberg (2013)
8. Karaboga, D., Ozturk, C.: A novel clustering approach: Artificial Bee Colony (ABC) algorithm. Appl. Soft Comput. **11**(1), 652–657 (2011)

9. Lian, T.A., Llave, M.R., Goodwin, M., Bouhmala, N.: Towards multilevel ant colony optimisation for the Euclidean symmetric traveling salesman problem. In: Ali, M., Kwon, Y.S., Lee, C.-H., Kim, J., Kim, Y. (eds.) IEA/AIE 2015. LNCS, vol. 9101, pp. 222–231. Springer, Heidelberg (2015)

10. Liu, B., Abbas, H., McKay, B.: Classification rule discovery with ant colony optimization. In: IEEE/WIC International Conference on Intelligent Agent Technology, IAT 2003, pp. 83–88. IEEE (2003)

11. Madjarov, G., Kocev, D., Gjorgjevikj, D., Džeroski, S.: An extensive experimental comparison of methods for multi-label learning. Pattern Recogn. 45(9), 3084–3104 (2012)

12. Martens, D., De Backer, M., Haesen, R., Vanthienen, J., Snoeck, M., Baesens, B.: Classification with ant colony optimization. IEEE Trans. Evol. Comput. 11(5), 651–665 (2007)

13. Neumann, F., Sudholt, D., Witt, C.: Analysis of different MMAS ACO algorithms on unimodal functions and plateaus. Swarm Intell. 3(1), 35–68 (2009)

14. Parpinelli, R.S., Lopes, H.S., Freitas, A., et al.: Data mining with an ant colony optimization algorithm. IEEE Trans. Evol. Comput. 6(4), 321–332 (2002)

15. Roth, S.D.: Ray casting for modeling solids. Comput. Graph. Image Process. 18(2), 109–144 (1982)

16. Salama, K.M., Abdelbar, A.M.: Learning neural network structures with ant colony algorithms. Swarm Intell. 1–37, 229–265 (2015)

17. Salama, K.M., Freitas, A.A.: Ant colony algorithms for constructing Bayesian multi-net classifiers. Intell. Data Anal. 19(2), 233–257 (2015)

18. Stützle, T., Hoos, H.: MAX-MIN Ant System and local search for the traveling salesman problem. In: IEEE International Conference on Evolutionary Computation, 1997, pp. 309–314. IEEE (1997)

19. Stützle, T., Hoos, H.H.: MAX-MIN ant system. Future Gener. Comput. Syst. 16(8), 889–914 (2000)

20. Stützle, T., López-Ibáñez, M., Dorigo, M.: A concise overview of applications of ant colony optimization. Wiley Encycl. Oper. Res. Manage. Sci. 26(2), 25–27 (2011)

Collective Perception of Environmental Features in a Robot Swarm

Gabriele Valentini[1](✉), Davide Brambilla[2], Heiko Hamann[3],
and Marco Dorigo[1](✉)

[1] IRIDIA, Université Libre de Bruxelles, Brussels, Belgium
{gvalenti,mdorigo}@ulb.ac.be
[2] Department of Computer Science, Politecnico di Milano, Milan, Italy
davide14.brambilla@mail.polimi.it
[3] Heinz Nixdorf Institute, University of Paderborn, Paderborn, Germany
heiko.hamann@uni-paderborn.de

Abstract. In order to be effective, collective decision-making strategies need to be not only fast and accurate, but sufficiently general to be ported and reused across different problem domains. In this paper, we propose a novel problem scenario, *collective perception*, and use it to compare three different strategies: the DMMD, DMVD, and DC strategies. The robots are required to explore their environment, estimate the frequency of certain features, and collectively perceive which feature is the most frequent. We implemented the collective perception scenario in a swarm robotics system composed of 20 e-pucks and performed robot experiments with all considered strategies. Additionally, we also deepened our study by means of physics-based simulations. The results of our performance comparison in the collective perception scenario are in agreement with previous results for a different problem domain and support the generality of the considered strategies.

1 Introduction

When a distributed system is composed of a large number of relatively incapable and poorly informed components, which is generally the case for robot swarms [2], the limitations of single individuals can be overcome by aggregating and processing the information collectively; in fact, by making collective decisions [1,5,9]. In addition to its accuracy and to the time it takes to make a decision [14], the success of a collective decision-making strategy can also be measured by the extent at which it can be generalized across different problem scenarios. The generality of a strategy allows the designer to reuse its high-level control logic in different problem scenarios and, while doing so, to focus only on the implementation of domain-specific, low-level control routines.

In this paper, we propose a novel decision-making scenario referred to as the *collective perception* problem and use this scenario to investigate the generality of two previously proposed strategies—the *Direct Modulation of*

M. Dorigo et al. (Eds.): ANTS 2016, LNCS 9882, pp. 65–76, 2016.
DOI: 10.1007/978-3-319-44427-7_6

Majority-based Decisions (DMMD) [13,14] and the *Direct Modulation of Voter-based Decisions* (DMVD)[1] [15]. In the collective perception scenario, a swarm of robots is required to explore an environment and evaluate the frequency of certain features that are scattered across it (e.g., the availability of precious metals, the presence of pollutants or cancer cells) with the objective to determine which feature is the most frequent. In our performance comparison, we also consider a third non-self-organizing decision-making strategy that we called *Direct Comparison* (DC). In this strategy, we allow robots to share a larger amount of information (i.e., quality estimates) and, based on this information, to modify their opinions by comparing their quality estimate with those of their neighbors. The DC strategy is representative of a class of more informed strategies which are generally expected to outperform self-organized approaches. Our aim is to use the DC strategy as a reference to highlight the benefits of self-organized approaches.

Previous studies focused on providing robots with the means to determine features of individual objects or specific regions in the environment. In [6], the authors develop a strategy that allows robots to individually and locally evaluate the shape of an object using their IR sensors and then to perform distributed sensor fusion with the aim of achieving collective perception. Schmickl et al. [11] propose two strategies, a hop-count strategy and a Trophallaxis-inspired strategy, that allow a swarm of robots to collectively perceive which area in the environment is the largest. Tarapore et al. [12] propose instead a control strategy that is inspired by the adaptive immune system of vertebrates; this strategy allows a swarm of agents to collectively discriminate between dangerous and non-dangerous objects and to adopt appropriate actions (e.g., tolerate or clear out the objects). Finally, Mermoud et al. [7] develop an aggregation-based strategy that allows robots to collectively perceive the type of a spot (i.e., good or bad) and to destroy the spots that have been perceived by the swarm as bad.

The DMMD and DMVD strategies were originally proposed for a site-selection scenario. The goal of the swarm in the site-selection scenario is to select the best location of the environment where to nest [14,15]. In this paper, we support the generality of these strategies by implementing them for the collective perception scenario and comparing their performance by means of robot experiments and physics-based simulations. We use a swarm of $N = 20$ e-pucks [8] and study the performance of each strategy over two different problem setups representing a simple and a difficult decision-making problem. After successfully demonstrating the generality of the DMMD and DMVD strategies through robot experiments, we deepen our analysis using physics-based simulations. We implement the collective perception scenario using the ARGoS simulator [10] and use this setup to show that the self-organized mechanisms of the DMMD and DMVD strategies allow these strategies to sustain high levels of noise that would instead prevent the use of the more informed DC strategy.

2   Robotic Platform and Experimental Setup

We performed experiments using the e-puck robotic platform [8]. The e-puck, shown in Fig. 1a, is a popular robotic platform within the community of swarm

---

[1] The DMVD strategy was originally named the *weighted voter model*.

robotics and has been been adopted in a large number of experimental studies. It is a commercially available robot designed for research and education with a diameter of 7 cm and a battery autonomy of up to 45 min. The e-puck is a differential drive robot that can move with a maximum speed of 16 cm/s. In its basic configuration, the robot is equipped with RGB LEDs, a low-resolution camera, an accelerometer, a sound sensor, and 8 proximity sensors. Figure 1a shows the e-puck configuration used in our experiments where the robot is extended with the range & bearing IR communication module [4], the ground sensor, the Overo Gumstick module, and the omnidirectional turret (not used in these experiments). In our experiments, the robots use the range & bearing module to share their information locally with their neighbors (e.g., internal state, quality estimate). This module consists of 12 IR transceivers positioned around the circumference of the robot that allow it to send and receive messages up to a distance of approximately 70 cm. Additionally, the e-puck mounts 8 IR proximity sensors that are used to detect the presence and measure the distance of nearby obstacles. The e-puck has 3 ground sensors that allow it to measure gray-scale values of the surface. Finally, the Overo Gumstick module provides the e-puck with the capabilities to run Linux and with a Wi-Fi connection.

We consider a collective perception scenario characterized by an environment with $n = 2$ features (see Fig. 1b). The robots are positioned in a square arena with a total area of $200 \times 200 \, cm^2$. The environment is approximately three orders of magnitude larger than a single robot footprint. It is bounded by four walls that can be detected by the proximity sensors of the robots. The surface of the environment is characterized by a grid consisting of $10 \times 10 \, cm^2$ cells. The color of each cell is used as an abstraction to represent a particular feature of

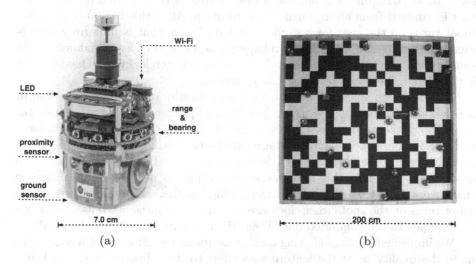

(a)   (b)

Fig. 1. Illustration of the robotic platform and the experimental setup. (a) the e-puck robot with details of its hardware. (b) top-view picture of the collective perception scenario with two features represented by the black and white colors.

the environment. Robots always have an opinion about which feature they currently believe to be the most frequent. In particular, the color black represents the feature of the environment associated to opinion a while the color white represents the feature of the environment associated to opinion b. Without loss of generality, we always have the black feature as the most frequent in the environment and, as a consequence, the goal of the swarm is to make a collective decision favoring opinion a. Each robot of the swarm uses its LEDs to show its current opinion: LEDs are lighted up in red when the robot favors opinion a and in blue when the robot favors opinion b. The robots use their ground sensors to perceive the brightness of the underlying surface, determine its color, and estimate the quality of the corresponding option.

3　Robot Control Algorithm

In this section, we describe the three collective decision-making strategies used in our performance comparison (i.e., the DMMD, DMVD, and DC strategies). All three strategies rely on common low-level control routines (i.e., random walk, obstacle avoidance, and quality estimation) that are described in Sect. 3.1. In Sect. 3.2, we describe the DMMD strategy and the DMVD strategy. Section 3.3 provides instead the description of the DC strategy.

3.1　Low-Level Motion Routines

We implemented a random walk routine as follows. A robot performing random walk alternates between straight motion and rotation on the spot. The robot moves straight for a random period of time with a mean duration of 40 s that is sampled from an exponential distribution. After this period of time, the robot turns on the spot for a random period of time that is uniformly distributed between 0 s and 4.5 s. The turning direction is also chosen randomly. With equal probability, the robot turns clockwise or counterclockwise. Once turning is completed, the robot resumes straight motion.

　　The detection by a robot of one or more nearby obstacles (i.e., a wall or a neighboring robot at a distance less than approximately 30 cm) causes the execution of the random walk to be paused and triggers the obstacle avoidance routine. We implemented the obstacle avoidance routine as follows. The robot uses its proximity sensors to detect the distance and the bearing of each perceived obstacle. It then uses this information to compute a new direction of motion that is opposite to the obstacles. Depending on the computed direction, the robot turns on the spot either clockwise or counterclockwise until its orientation corresponds to the computed one. Then, the robot resumes its random walk.

　　We implemented the following quality estimation routine to let a robot estimate the quality ρ_i of the feature associated to its opinion $i \in \{a, b\}$. When executing the quality estimation routine, the robot uses its ground sensors to sample the color of the surface while moving randomly in the environment. During the entire execution of the quality estimation routine, the robot keeps track of the amount of time τ_i during which it perceived the color associated to its current opinion i. Finally, the robot computes a quality estimate $\hat{\rho}_i$ which is the ratio of τ_i to the overall duration of the quality estimation routine.

3.2 DMMD and DMVD Strategies

The DMMD strategy and the DMVD strategy are characterized by a common structure of the robot controller that is implemented as a probabilistic finite-state machine (PFSM) and differ only in the individual decision-making mechanism used by robots to reconsider their current opinions[2]. The DMMD strategy uses the majority rule whereby a robot takes the opinion that is favored by the majority of its neighbors (including its own current opinion). On the other hand, the DMVD strategy uses the voter model whereby a robot adopts the opinion of a random neighbor. The PFSM of these strategies consists of two control states, the *dissemination* state D_i and the *exploration* state E_i, that are replicated for both options of the decision-making problem (i.e., a total of four control states).

In the exploration states E_i, $i \in \{a, b\}$, a robot with opinion i explores the environment by performing the random walk routine and, when necessary, the obstacle avoidance routine. Meanwhile, the robot samples the environment locally and estimates the option quality ρ_i by executing the quality estimation routine. The duration of the exploration state is random and exponentially distributed with a mean duration of σ s (see [14] for details). After this period of time, the robot switches to the dissemination state D_i.

In the dissemination states D_i, $i \in \{a, b\}$, a robot with opinion i broadcasts its opinion locally to its neighbors. Meanwhile, the robot performs the same random walk and obstacle avoidance routines as in the exploration states. The aim of this motion pattern, however, is not to explore the environment but to mix the positions of robots of different opinions in the environment which eases the decision-making process. The robot uses its current quality estimate $\hat{\rho}_i$ to amplify or inhibit the duration of the dissemination state D_i in a way that this duration is proportional to its estimated quality. This modulation promotes the spread of the best opinion. To do so, the duration of the dissemination state is exponentially distributed with mean $\hat{\rho}_i g$ sec, where g is a design parameter that defines the unbiased dissemination time. This modulation allows robots with better opinions (i.e., with higher quality estimates $\hat{\rho}_i$) to increase their chances to influence other robots. Finally, the robot collects the opinions broadcast by its neighbors and applies the individual decision-making mechanism (either the majority rule in the DMMD strategy or the voter model in the DMVD strategy) to determine its new opinion $j \in \{a, b\}$. Then, the robot switches to the exploration state E_j to collect a new estimate $\hat{\rho}_j$ of the option quality.

3.3 Direct Comparison of Option Quality

We define a third decision-making strategy, the direct comparison (DC) of option quality, by using the same PFSM of the DMMD and DMVD strategies but letting

---

[2] Refer to [14, 15] for a detailed description of the DMMD and DMVD strategies.

robots compare their quality estimates directly to modify their opinion. When executing the DC strategy, robots alternate periods of exploration to periods of dissemination. In contrast to the DMVD and DMMD strategies, the DC strategy does not make use of a mechanism for the modulation of positive feedback and the mean duration of the dissemination state D_i, $i \in \{a, b\}$, is g, independently of the option quality ρ_i. During the dissemination period, the robot broadcasts also its current estimate $\hat{\rho}_i$ in addition to its opinion i. This additional information is used by robots to modify their opinions. At the end of the dissemination state, a robot with opinion i compares its opinion with that of a random neighbor with opinion $j \in \{a, b\}$. If the neighbor's estimate $\hat{\rho}_j$ is greater than the considered robot's estimate $\hat{\rho}_i$, then robot modifies its current opinion to j. Next, the robot switches to the exploration state E_j which is implemented identically to that of the DMMD and DMVD strategies. Our aim is to use the DC strategy to show the benefits of a self-organized approach. Indeed, the ability of the DMMD and DMVD strategies to discriminate different options is based on the self-organized processing of a multitude of individual quality estimates by the swarm [3]. These quality estimates are processed by modulating positive feedback in combination with a decision-making mechanism that operates on opinions of neighbors only.

4 Experiments

Given the collective perception scenario described in Sect. 2, we perform experiments using the DMVD, DMMD, and DC strategies. We look at the number D_i, $i \in \{a, b\}$, of robots in the dissemination state D_i and at the number E_i, $i \in \{a, b\}$, of robots in the exploration state E_i and define consensus as $D_i + E_i = N$ for any $i \in \{a, b\}$. We measure the strategies' speed using the average time T_N necessary for the swarm to reach consensus on any opinion, and the strategies' accuracy using the exit probability E_N, that is, the probability to make the best decision, computed as the proportion of runs that converge to consensus on opinion a. We first perform experiments using a swarm of $N = 20$ e-pucks in two different setups representing a simple and a more difficult decision-making problem[3]. Then, we deepen our experimental analysis by means of physics-based simulations implemented using the ARGoS simulator [10]. In both robot experiments and physics-based simulations, we set robots to start the execution of their controllers in the exploration state. Additionally, we set the mean duration of the exploration state to $\sigma = 10\,\mathrm{s}$ and the unbiased duration of the dissemination state to $g = 10\,\mathrm{s}$.

4.1 Robot Experiments

We considered two different experimental setups for the collective perception problem. The first setup represents a simple decision-making problem where the proportion of resource a (i.e., color black) in the environment is approximately

---

[3] See http://iridia.ulb.ac.be/supp/IridiaSupp2016-002/ for videos of the experiments.

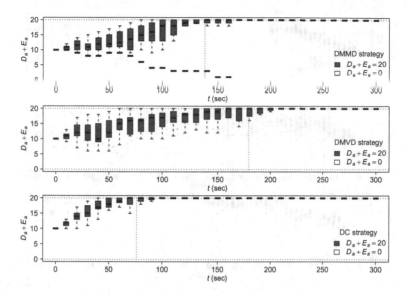

Fig. 2. The figure shows the evolution over time of the number of robots with opinion a (i.e., $D_a + E_a$) for the DMMD strategy (top), the DMVD strategy (middle), and the DC strategy (bottom). Gray and white box-plots show the distribution of the experimental runs converging to consensus on opinion a and consensus on opinion b. When white box-plots are not plotted, all runs converged on opinion a. The vertical lines show the average time necessary to reach consensus on any opinion. Parameters: $\rho_a^\star = 1$, $\rho_b^\star = 0.515$.

twice that of resource b (i.e., color white). Specifically, the surface of the environment is $\rho_a = 66\%$ black and $\rho_b = 34\%$ white and the problem difficulty is defined by the normalized option qualities $\rho_a^\star = 1$ and $\rho_b^\star = \rho_b/\rho_a = 0.515$. The second setup consists of a more difficult collective perception problem where the surface of the environment is $\rho_a = 52\%$ black and $\rho_b = 48\%$ white (i.e., $\rho_a^\star = 1$ and $\rho_b^\star = 0.923$). For each combination of the problem setup and strategy, we performed 15 repetitions of the robot experiment. In all experiments, the swarm is initially unbiased with 10 robots in state E_a and 10 robots in state E_b.

Figure 2 shows the results of the robot experiments for the simple collective perception scenario using the DMMD strategy (top), the DMVD strategy (middle), and the DC strategy (bottom). The box-plots provide the evolution over time of the number $D_a + E_a$ of robots with opinion a. The vertical lines indicate the average time T_N to reach consensus. When executing the DMMD strategy (see Fig. 2, top), the swarm of e-pucks requires on average $T_N = 138$ s to converge on a consensus decision and has an accuracy of $E_N = 0.933$ (i.e., 1 out of 15 repetitions converges to a wrong consensus on opinion b). In contrast, when executing the DMVD strategy or the DC strategy, the swarm of e-pucks is always able to identify the most frequent feature in the environment correctly (i.e., decision accuracy $E_N = 1.0$). However, the DMVD strategy converges to consensus after $T_N = 179.3$ s while the DC strategy is faster and requires only $T_N = 76$ s. In agreement with the results

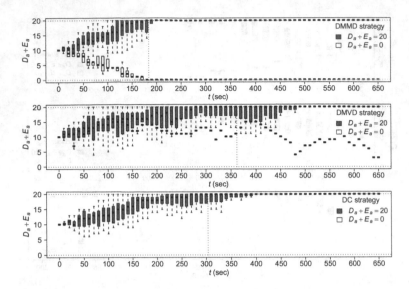

Fig. 3. The figure shows the evolution over time of the number of robots with opinion a (i.e., $D_a + E_a$) for the DMMD strategy (top), the DMVD strategy (middle), and the DC strategy (bottom). Gray and white box-plots show the distribution of the experimental runs converging to consensus on opinion a and consensus on opinion b. The vertical lines show the average time necessary to reach consensus on any opinion. Parameters: $\rho_a = 1$, $\rho_b = 0.923$.

in [14], we observe that the DMMD strategy is faster but also less accurate than the DMVD strategy. For the simple experimental setup, the DC strategy benefits from using more information in the form of robots exchanging their quality estimates; it is faster than the DMMD and DMVD strategies and has the same accuracy as the DMVD strategy.

Figure 3 shows the results of the robot experiments in the difficult collective perception scenario in which the normalized option qualities are given by $\rho_a^\star = 1$ and $\rho_b^\star = 0.923$. The increased difficulty of the decision-making problem overturns the results obtained by the simple experimental setup. The DMMD strategy based on the majority rule is the fastest strategy in the comparison and with an average consensus time of $T_N = 184\,\mathrm{s}$. The DMVD strategy based on the voter model is still the slowest strategy with an average consensus time of $T_N = 362\,\mathrm{s}$ while the DC strategy has a consensus time of $T_N = 303.3\,\mathrm{s}$. In contrast, the DMMD strategy has the lowest accuracy, $E_N = 0.667$, reaching consensus on opinion a 10 times out of 15 repetitions (cf. [14]). The DMVD strategy, with a decision accuracy of $E_N = 0.933$, performs similarly to the DC strategy whose decision accuracy is still maximal, $E_N = 1.0$. In this more difficult collective perception scenario there is no strategy that outperforms all others in both speed and accuracy.

The communication overhead underlying the DC strategy seems to provide stronger benefits than those of the modulation of positive feedback used by the

DMMD and DMVD strategies. However, a comparison of the results obtained with the simple and difficult experimental setups reveals an interesting performance trend. The increase in the difficulty of the decision-making problem resulted in a relative little slowdown of the DMMD strategy which is 1.33 times slower when compared to the simple experimental setup; the DMVD strategy is 2.02 times slower; while the DC strategy has a more pronounced slow down of 3.99 times. The DMMD strategy, with an accuracy 28.5 % less than the simple setup, is preferable when consensus time is the most critical constraints. The DMVD strategy loses only 6.7 % of its accuracy and its consensus time increases much less than that of the DC strategy. This trend suggests that the DMVD strategy could be the choice of reference for the designer when favoring the accuracy of the collective decision. The results of our robot experiments provide us with useful indications; however, since such experiments are particularly time-consuming, we could collect a limited amount of data (i.e., only 15 repetitions for each parameter configurations). In the next section, we deepen the results of our analysis by means of physics-based simulations.

4.2   Physics-Based Simulations

We performed physics-based simulations using the ARGoS simulator [10] and compared the performance of the DMMD, DMVD, and DC strategies over a wider region of the parameter space than what we did in the robot experiments. We varied the initial number $E_a(0)$ of robots favoring opinion a, the difficulty $\rho_b^\star$ of the collective perception scenario, and the swarm size N. For each parameter configuration, we performed 1000 repetitions of the simulated experiment.

We set $N = 20$ and study the simple and difficult scenarios defined above as a function of the initial number $E_a(0)$ of robots with opinion a (see Fig. 4). For the simple scenario, the exit probability E_N of the three strategies corresponds to that obtained in the robot experiments (cf. $E_a(0) = 10$ in Fig. 4a). For all strategies, E_N increases with increasing values of the initial number $E_a(0)$ of robots with opinion a; the DC strategy has the highest accuracy while the DMMD strategy has the lowest. However, for all three decision-making strategies, the consensus time T_N shown in Fig. 4b is considerably shorter than that obtained with robot experiments. Additionally, the DMMD strategy is now the fastest strategy and it outperforms the DC strategy for all initial conditions $E_a(0)$. For the difficult scenario, we observe similar differences in the speed and accuracy of the three decision-making strategies. Both the DMVD and DC strategies are considerably less accurate than in the robot experiments (see Fig. 4c). In addition, the decision accuracy of the DMMD strategy decreases more slowly than that of the DMVD and DC strategies when decreasing the value of $E_a(0)$. As for the simple scenario, all strategies converge faster to consensus (see Fig. 4d). The DC strategy is the slowest strategy in the comparison.

The results of physics-based simulations reproduce only partially the performance obtained with robot experiments. We conjecture that the observed discrepancies are a result of differences in the level of noise between simulation

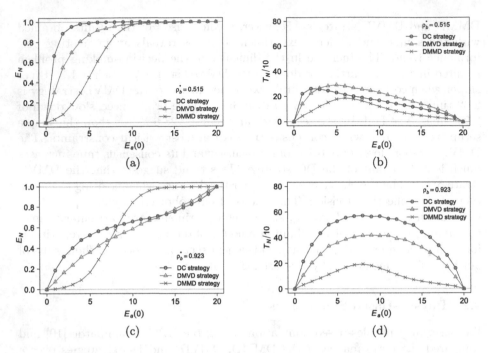

Fig. 4. Illustration of (a) the exit probability and (b) the consensus time as a function of initial number $E_a(0)$ of robots with opinion a for the simple experimental setup. Figures (c) and (d) show the same metrics but for the difficult experimental setup. Parameters: $\rho_a = 1.0$, $\rho_b \in \{0.515, 0.923\}$, $N = 20$.

and reality. For example, a few robots used during the experiments have particularly noisy proximity sensors; as a result they often collide with other robots or with the walls. Additionally, the uneven surface of the experimental arena caused robots to remain temporarily stuck over the same cell resulting in erratic quality estimates. The influence of these factors is increased by the limited number of runs performed with real robots as shown by the high variance of the consensus time characterizing the results in Figs. 2 and 3. Nonetheless, the physics-based simulations confirm a poor scalability of the DC strategy as previously shown by the robot experiments.

We deepen our comparison by analyzing the speed of the DMMD, DMVD, and DC strategies when varying the swarm size N and the difficulty $\rho_b^\star$ of the collective perception scenario (see Fig. 5). For swarms of size $N = 20$ and $N = 100$, we observe that the DC strategy is the strategy that suffers the largest loss of performance as a result of increasing problem difficulty. Additionally, by comparing Fig. 5a with Fig. 5b, we also observe that the consensus time of the DC strategy increases much faster than that of the other strategies when the size of the swarm is $N = 100$; therefore, the DC strategy does not scale with the swarm size. In contrast, the DMMD and DMVD strategies are only slightly affected by the larger swarm size.

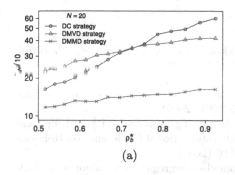 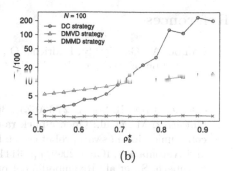

(a)   (b)

Fig. 5. Illustration of the consensus time T_N as a function of the difficulty of the decision-making problem (i.e., option quality $\rho_b \to \rho_a$) for a swarm of (a) $N = 20$ robots and (b) $N = 100$ robots. Parameters: $\rho_a = 1.0$, $\rho_b \in [0.515; 0.923]$, $N \in \{20, 100\}$, $E_a(0) = N/2$, $E_b(0) = N/2$. The vertical axis is in log-scale.

5 Conclusion

We considered a novel decision-making scenario, collective perception, that requires a swarm of robots to explore a certain environment, perceive the presence of certain features, and determine which feature is the most frequent. We investigated the generality of the direct modulation of majority-based decision (DMMD) strategy and that of the direct modulation of voter-based decision (DMVD) strategy—two collective decision-making strategies previously proposed for the site-selection problem [14,15]. DMMD and DMVD are modular strategies that combine a direct modulation mechanism of positive feedback (i.e., modulation of opinion dissemination) with an individual decision-making mechanism (respectively, the majority rule and the voter model). We investigated the benefit of these modules by considering a third strategy, the direct comparison of option quality (DC), that has no modulation mechanism and whose decision mechanism relies on a larger amount of information (i.e., quality estimates). Using both robot experiments and physics-based simulations, we performed an extensive comparison of the DMMD, DMVD, and DC strategies under realistic working conditions. Our results are twofold. On the one hand, we have shown that the DMMD and DMVD strategies provided us with off-the-shelf solutions to a decision-making scenario different from their original context of site-selection. These design solutions maintained their speed and accuracy performance and showed a promising level of generality. On the other hand, we have shown the benefits of a self-organized approach by highlighting the scalability problems of the consensus time of the DC strategy. It is more robust to noise, although it relies on less information. Clearly, there are problem setups for which the DC strategy outperforms both the DMMD and DMVD strategies. However, the communication overhead of this strategy requires sufficiently capable robots.

Acknowledgments. The authors would like to thank A. Reina, L. Garattoni, and A. Antoun for their assistance during the development of this study.

References

1. Campo, A., Garnier, S., Dédriche, O., Zekkri, M., Dorigo, M.: Self-organized discrimination of resources. PLoS ONE **6**(5), e19888 (2010)
2. Dorigo, M., et al.: Swarm robotics. Scholarpedia **9**(1), 1463 (2014)
3. Edwards, S.C., Pratt, S.C.: Rationality in collective decision-making by ant colonies. Proc. R. Soc. B **276**(1673), 3655–3661 (2009)
4. Gutiérrez, M., et al.: Open e-puck range & bearing miniaturized board for local communication in swarm robotics. In: IEEE International Conference on Robotics and Automation, ICRA 2009, pp. 3111–3116 (2009)
5. Kernbach, S., et al.: Re-embodiment of honeybee aggregation behavior in an artificial micro-robotic system. Adapt. Behav. **17**(3), 237–259 (2009)
6. Kornienko, S., et al.: Cognitive micro-agents: individual and collective perception in microrobotic swarm. In: Proceedings of the IJCAI 2005 Workshop on Agents in Real-Time and Dynamic Environments, Edinburgh, UK, pp. 33–42 (2005)
7. Mermoud, G., et al.: Aggregation-mediated collective perception and action in a group of miniature robots. In: Proceedings of the 9th International Conference on Autonomous Agents and Multiagent Systems, AAMAS 2010, pp. 599–606. IFAAMAS (2010)
8. Mondada, F., et al.: The e-puck, a robot designed for education in engineering. In: Proceedings of the 9th Conference on Autonomous Robot Systems and Competitions, vol. 1, pp. 59–65. IPCB (2009)
9. Montes de Oca, M., et al.: Majority-rule opinion dynamics with differential latency: a mechanism for self-organized collective decision-making. Swarm Intell. **5**, 305–327 (2011)
10. Pinciroli, C., et al.: ARGoS: a modular, parallel, multi-engine simulator for multi-robot systems. Swarm Intell. **6**(4), 271–295 (2012)
11. Schmickl, T., Möslinger, C., Crailsheim, K.: Collective perception in a robot swarm. In: Şahin, E., Spears, W.M., Winfield, A.F.T. (eds.) SAB 2006 Ws 2007. LNCS, vol. 4433, pp. 144–157. Springer, Heidelberg (2007)
12. Tarapore, D., et al.: Abnormality detection in multiagent systems inspired by the adaptive immune system. In: Proceedings of the 12th International Conference on Autonomous Agents and Multiagent Systems, AAMAS 2013, pp. 23–30. IFAAMAS (2013)
13. Valentini, G., et al.: Efficient decision-making in a self-organizing robot swarm: on the speed versus accuracy trade-off. In: Proceedings of the 14th International Conference on Autonomous Agents and Multiagent Systems, AAMAS 2015, pp. 1305–1314. IFAAMAS (2015)
14. Valentini, G., Ferrante, E., Hamann, H., Dorigo, M.: Collective decision with 100 Kilobots: speed versus accuracy in binary discrimination problems. Auton. Agent. Multi-Agent Syst. **30**(3), 553–580 (2016)
15. Valentini, G., Hamann, H., Dorigo, M.: Self-organized collective decision making: the weighted voter model. In: Proceedings of the 13th International Conference on Autonomous Agents and Multiagent Systems, AAMAS 2014, pp. 45–52. IFAAMAS (2014)

Communication Diversity in Particle Swarm Optimizers

Marcos Oliveira[1]($\boxtimes$), Diego Pinheiro[1]($\boxtimes$), Bruno Andrade[2],
Carmelo Bastos-Filho[3]($\boxtimes$), and Ronaldo Menezes[1]($\boxtimes$)

[1] BioComplex Laboratory, Florida Institute of Technology, Melbourne, USA
{moliveira,dsilva,rmenezes}@biocomplexlab.org
[2] Universidade Federal de Goiàs, Goiàs, Brazil
brunoandrade@inf.ufg.br
[3] Universidade de Pernambuco, Recife, Brazil
carmelo.filho@upe.br

Abstract. Since they were introduced, Particle Swarm Optimizers have suffered from early stagnation due to premature convergence. Assessing swarm spatial diversity might help to mitigate early stagnation but swarm spatial diversity itself emerges from the main property that essentially drives swarm optimizers towards convergence and distinctively distinguishes PSO from other optimization techniques: *the social interaction between the particles*. The swarm *influence graph* captures the structure of particle interactions by monitoring the information exchanges during the search process; such graph has been shown to provide a rich overall structure of the swarm information flow. In this paper, we define swarm *communication diversity* based on the component analysis of the swarm influence graph. We show how communication diversity relates to other measures of swarm spatial diversity as well as how each swarm topology leads to different communication signatures. Moreover, we argue that swarm *communication diversity* might potentially be a better way to understand early stagnation since it takes into account the (social) interactions between the particles instead of properties associated with individual particles.

Keywords: PSO · Swarm assessment · Premature convergence · Early stagnation analysis · Component graph analysis

1 Introduction

Particle Swarm Optimization (PSO) is a computational intelligence technique inspired by the social behavior of bird flocks and used to solve optimization problems [4]. The technique consists of a population (swarm) of simple reactive agents (particles) interacting among themselves while exploring the search space by seeking the best solutions. The communication between the particles plays an important role on the swarm behavior [8]. Such aspect may be seen, for

© Springer International Publishing Switzerland 2016
M. Dorigo et al. (Eds.): ANTS 2016, LNCS 9882, pp. 77–88, 2016.
DOI: 10.1007/978-3-319-44427-7_7

instance, when the swarm topology is analyzed. The topology defines the neighborhood of each particle thus impacting how the information is shared within the swarm. Less connected topologies slow down the information flow since information is transmitted indirectly through intermediary particles [5]. Conversely, highly-connected topologies decrease the number of these intermediaries creating a tendency for the swarm to move quickly towards local optima. These different behaviors are also intimately related to the exploration-exploitation balance in the swarm [6].

Although communication among particles is an essential aspect of swarm behavior, many researchers only focus on the final result of the interactions between them such as using the particles properties (*e.g.* their positions, velocities, etc.) to assess the swarm behavior [13,16]. These approaches bring interesting findings but they are actually analyzing the final results of the particles interactions and not the *information flow* of the swarm execution. Some of the few works addressing information flow introduced the concept of swarm influence graph that captures the actual flow of information between the particles [9,10].

The analyses performed with these approaches allow a better understanding of the swarm search mode. However, they do not capture the *dynamics* in the information flow during the algorithm execution, but only analyze a snapshot from a given iteration. The analysis of swarm dynamics can promote the comprehension of its behavior which leads, for example, to swarm stagnation.

In this work we define swarm *communication diversity* using component analysis of the influence graph. We show how our definition relates to swarm behavior and how each swarm topology leads to different communication signatures. We argue that swarm communication diversity is a more suitable analysis of the swarm because the social interactions of the particles are included, instead of only properties associated with individual particles.

2   PSO, Diversity and Particle Interactions

Particle Swarm Optimization is a stochastic, population-based optimization technique inspired by the social behavior of bird flocks and is composed by particles that move around the search space [4]. The equations that control the swarm are not included in this paper but an interested reader should refer to the standard PSO paper [1]. The particles can only share information with the ones in their neighborhood defined by the swarm topology consisting of a graph in which two nodes (particles) are linked if they are allowed to share information to each other. The topology influences the flow of information between particles. For instance, when the average distance between nodes is too short, the swarm tends to move quickly towards the best solution found in earlier iterations which usually leads to a fast convergence to the global optimum in unimodal problems, but with the caveat of the possibility to prematurely reach a local optimum, specially in multimodal problems [1,5]. In this sense, communication topologies with fewer connections may yield better results. Since the information spreads slowly, the swarm has a better chance of exploring different regions of the search space.

In a global topology, the swarm shares the same (social) memory because particles are directly connected and any particle can be the information spreader to all the other particles. Conversely, the particles have different neighbors in local topologies and hence their social memories are different [1]. For instance, in a ring topology, the particles can only communicate with two other particles and although it prevents premature attraction of the whole swarm to a single location due to slow spread of information, it brings the inconvenience of a slow convergence time [1]. These extreme behaviors motivate considering topologies that balance their strengths and weaknesses such as the von Neumann topology [1,5].

2.1   Early Stagnation and Swarm Diversity

Convergence and stagnation are closely related terms often referred interchangeably although they subtly differ from each other. Convergence towards global optima tightly links to objective function improvement and is an appealing feature for any optimizer. Particularly in the case of PSO, premature convergence means that the swarm attained an equilibrium state which is often a local optima. Clearly, this is not desired since we would like the swarm to converge while effectively working in order to find better candidate solutions. In fact, many mechanisms to prevent premature convergence have been proposed [2,14,17].

Stagnation is often the result of an exploration-exploitation imbalance that causes the search space not to be explored adequately. This imbalance led researchers to believe early stagnation strongly relates to swarm spatial diversity and that consequently the assessment of such diversity is a way prevent undesired stagnation [14]. In this sense, PSO would ideally start the optimization process in exploration mode with a high diversity and, as the search space is adequately explored, it would initiate the exploitation mode focusing its efforts on smaller areas of the search space with a lower diversity.

Metrics for assessing swarm diversity are mostly spatial in nature and quantify swarm diversity as the degree of dispersion of particles around a given swarm center [12]. We enumerate the main diversity metrics as hereafter described. Let $|S|$ be the size of swarm S, x_i the position of particle i, $f[\cdot]$ the fitness function, $x_{best}(t)$ the position of the best particle at iteration t, $\bar{f}(t)$ the average fitness at iteration t, and $d(p, q)$ the euclidean distance between p and q.

1. Aggregation degree:

$$AD(t) = \frac{f(x_{best}(t))}{\bar{f}(t)}. \tag{1}$$

2. Normalized average distance around the swarm center using the swarm diameter or radius:

$$\mathcal{D}_{\bar{x}}^{D}(t) = \frac{\mathcal{D}_{\bar{x}}(t)}{D(t)}, \quad \mathcal{D}_{\bar{x}}^{R}(t) = \frac{\mathcal{D}_{\bar{x}}(t)}{R(t)}. \tag{2}$$

3. Average distance around the swarm center $\bar{\boldsymbol{x}}$ [7]:

$$\mathcal{D}_{\bar{\boldsymbol{x}}}(t) = \frac{1}{|S|}\sum_{i=1}^{|S|}d\big(\boldsymbol{x_i}(t),\bar{\boldsymbol{x}}(t)\big). \tag{3}$$

4. Average of the average distance around all particles in the swarm:

$$\mathcal{D}_{all}(t) = \frac{1}{|S|}\sum_{i=1}^{|S|}\mathcal{D}_{\boldsymbol{x_i}}(t). \tag{4}$$

5. Diameter, the maximum distance between the positions of any two particles i and j in the swarm:

$$D(t) = \max_{i \neq j \in [1,|S|]} d\big(\boldsymbol{x_i}(t),\boldsymbol{x_j}(t)\big). \tag{5}$$

6. Radius, the maximum distance between the swarm center $\bar{\boldsymbol{x}}$ and any particle i in the swarm:

$$R(t) = \max_{i \in [1,|S|]} d\big(\boldsymbol{x_i}(t),\bar{\boldsymbol{x}}(t)\big). \tag{6}$$

These metrics attempt to quantify swarm diversity as the amount of swarm expansion and dispersion. Both diameter, D, and radius, R, are highly sensitive to outliers since one single particle can greatly influence the result. Since they are employed as normalization factors, the same applies for the normalized average distance around the swarm center ($\mathcal{D}_{\bar{\boldsymbol{x}}}^{D}$ or $\mathcal{D}_{\bar{\boldsymbol{x}}}^{R}$). The average distance around the swarm center, $\mathcal{D}_{\bar{\boldsymbol{x}}}$, as well as the average of the average distance around all particles in the swarm, $\mathcal{D}_{all}$, are less sensitive to outliers and while $\mathcal{D}_{\bar{\boldsymbol{x}}}$ considers a swarm center $\bar{\boldsymbol{x}}$, $\mathcal{D}_{all}$ takes the average of each particle as the center. The aggregation degree, AD, measures how close the best fitness $f(\boldsymbol{x}_{best}(t))$ found at iteration t is from the average swarm fitness $\bar{f}(t)$ at iteration t. This supposedly approximates the degree of divergence among the new found candidate solutions thus measuring swarm diversity under the fitness perspective.

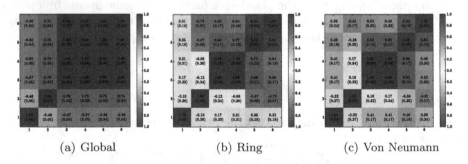

(a) Global   (b) Ring   (c) Von Neumann

Fig. 1. Correlations between Swarm Diversity Metrics using the Pearson Correlation Coefficient for Global (a), Ring (b) and (c) Von Neumann topologies. All simulations were repeated 30 times and the averages were considered.

The relationship between these swarm spatial diversity measures changes depending on the topology and some may not be appropriate for local topologies. The idea of a swarm center $\bar{x}$ might make sense for a global topology but not for a ring topology where more than one attractor might exist. Figure 1 depicts the correlations between those metrics regarding some main topologies and the only correlation which remains strong in all topologies are $\mathcal{D}_{\bar{x}}$ and $\mathcal{D}_{all}$.

This consistent disagreement between swarm diversity metrics based on particles' properties poses the question of what they are really measuring and if they can be applied to topologies other than the global topology. Indeed, although local topologies are less vulnerable to get trapped in local optima, the majority of research neglects them and focus their studies in the global topology only.

2.2 The Influence Graph

In the simple version of the PSO, at a given iteration t, each particle i solely gets information from its best neighbor $n_i(t)$. Since the swarm topology defines the neighborhood of each particle, this structure only bounds the range of such communication. On the other hand, the actual information exchange among the particles is described by the influence graph whose elements are defined as:

$$I_{t_{ij}} = \begin{cases} 1, & \text{if } n_i(t) = j \quad \text{or} \quad n_j(t) = i, \\ 0, & \text{otherwise.} \end{cases} \tag{7}$$

This graph represents the structure of the particles that shared information between them at a given iteration t and differs from the swarm topology (aka communication graph) which is just a static graph determining the neighborhood of each particle [10,11]. I_t is a snapshot of the swarm communication at iteration t, thus the interactions occurred in past iterations are not present in this graph. The information exchanges between the particles during the whole algorithm execution until iteration t can be conveniently defined as:

$$I_t^w = \sum_{i=1}^{t} I_i. \tag{8}$$

The result of this sum is a weighted graph in which the weights of the edges $I_{t_{ij}}^w$ are equal to the number of the times two particles i and j exchanged information during the algorithm execution [9]. The influence of each particle on each other during the whole history of the swarm until t is represented in I_t^w. In order to understand a more recent history of the swarm, an useful weighted influence graph at iteration t within a time window t_w is defined as follows:

$$I_t^{t_w} = \sum_{i=t-t_w+1}^{t} I_i, \quad \text{with} \quad t \geq t_w > 0. \tag{9}$$

In other words, $I_t^{t_w}$ is the communication structure of particles that communicated among themselves at most t_w iterations before the iteration t. The value

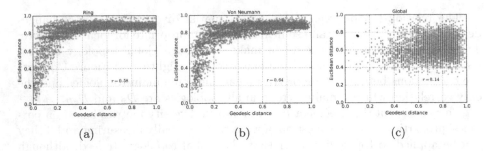

Fig. 2. The monitoring of the exchange of information in the swarm is enough to assess properties of the particles. The more distant two particles are in the influence graph, the farther they are from each other in the search space. The plot is the 1000th iteration of a run of the PSO algorithm optimizing the F_6 function [15].

of t_w changes the analysis of $I_t^{t_w}$ in such way that the lower t_w is, the shorter is the social memory being analyzed.

The influence graph provides insightful information about the intricate behavior of the swarm [9]. Even with the lack of details from the particles, the analysis of this graph allows one to examine the relationship between them. A simple supporting example of this is the distance between the particles in the search space. Figure 2 depicts the correlation between the geodesic distance among particles in the influence graph and the Euclidean distance between the particles in the search space. For a swarm with von Neumann or ring topologies, the more distant two particles are in the influence graph, the more certain we are that the two particles are far away of each other in the search space. This pattern is not as evident in the global topology due to the fact that the swarm, in this case, is condensed somewhere in the search space and the particles are nearer to each other than in the other topologies.

In fact, some analyses have been carried out with regards to the well-connected components in the influence graph [9]. Figure 3 exemplifies this kind of analysis, the edges are removed gradually according their weight in such way that components start to appear during the process. The speed that these components emerge as the destruction of the graph occurs is related to the search mode present in the swarm. For instance, an exploration mode is characterized by a slow increase in the number of components due to the different information flows present in the swarm [9]. On the other hand, this graph is rapidly destroyed in a swarm depending only on a small set of particles, a behavior related to an exploitation search mode.

3   Communication Diversity

The *structure* of the way information flows within the swarm can be assessed by the analysis of the well-connected components in the influence graph. The patterns found in this analysis are related to the diversity in the *communication* of the particles, *i.e.* the capacity of the swarm to have different information

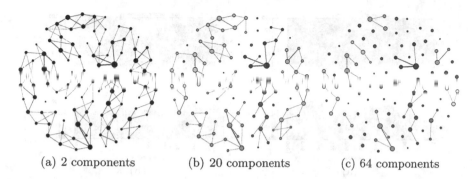

| (a) 2 components | (b) 20 components | (c) 64 components |

Fig. 3. The velocity components emerge while edges are removed from the influence graph is related to the search mode of the swarm. The edges are removed gradually depending on a threshold: below (*a*) 50 % of the highest edge weight, (*b*) 65 % and (*c*) 75 %. The different colors represent distinct components with more than one node. This is the 1000th iteration of a run of a PSO algorithm with the swarm using a von Neumann topology.

flows among its individuals. Figures 4(a)-(d) represent the communication diversity of the swarm. These plots depict the increasing number of components that emerge when edges are gradually removed from the influence graph with different time windows at the 1000th iteration of a run of a PSO algorithm on a ring/2-regular (Fig. 4(a)), von Neumann/4-regular (Fig. 4(b)), 30-regular (Fig. 4(c)) and global/100-regular (Fig. 4(d)) topologies. The gradual change in the number of components depends on the time window and represents the speed of the destruction occurring on the influence graph. A sharp behavior in the increase of the number of components, as seen in Figs. 4(c) and (d), is associated to lack of diversity in the communication, while a more gradual increase relates to more diversity, as depicted in Figs. 4(a) and (b).

The interactions between particles during the execution of a PSO algorithm might lead to variations in the communication diversity. For example, Fig. 4(e) shows how the number of components (y-axis) varies while applying different filters of weight removal on the influence graph with $t_w = 100$. For fixed topologies such as ring and von Neunmann, the number of components presents a consistently stationary behavior and reflects the static nature of these topologies. For a dynamic topology, the number of components could present an increasing or decreasing trend depending on how the communication structure changes towards the desired search mode. Besides, the variations in these curves along iterations (x-axis) suggest that an analysis of communication diversity needs to be performed also regarding time dimension. In order to carry out such analysis, we need to assess the *communication diversity*.

3.1   Assessing the Communication Diversity

Any column in the plots depicted in Figs. 4(a)-(d) represents the destruction of the influence graph with a certain t_w. A separate example of this curve is shown

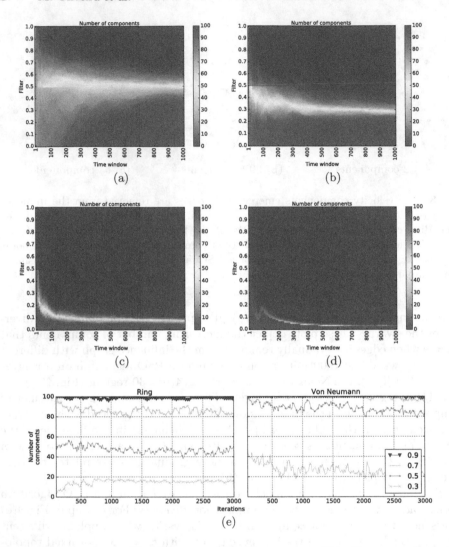

Fig. 4. The structure with which communication occurs within the swarm leads to distinct swarm behaviors. Each topology has its own communication diversity signature described by the number of components emerging (color intensity) as edges are removed (y-axis) of the influence graph with different time windows (x-axis). The edges are removed from the graph based on their weight and $2t_w$, *i.e.* the maximum weight possible in an influence graph with time window t_w. For a given filter, the number of components consistently varies within a well defined range through the iterations (e).

in Fig. 5 with $t_w = 100$ and $t_w = 1000$ for swarms with different topologies. Since such curves are always monotonically increasing, a simple way to have a characterization of them is to calculate the normalized area under the curve, namely $A_{t_w=t}$. Such procedure can be analogously performed with the snapshots

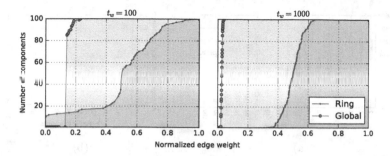

Fig. 5. The area under the curve of number of components that appear as the influence graph is destroyed can be used to compare swarm behaviors. The greater is the area, the less diverse is the communication of the swarm. For instance, a swarm with Global topology presents more exploitation than a swarm using the Ring topology.

of the communication diversity in Figs. 4(a)-(d) by taking into account all time windows. However, this approach can be computationally expensive given the great number of possible time windows. An approach to circumvent the computational cost is to use only a small set of time windows T in a such way that communication diversity (cd) can be assessed by:

$$cd = 1 - \frac{1}{|T||S|} \sum_{t \in T} A_{t_w = t}. \tag{10}$$

3.2 Communication Diversity and Stagnation

An implementation of the PSO algorithm with 100 particles was used to optimize the Ackley's F_6 *function* which is a shifted, single-group m-rotated, m-nonseparable and has many local minima. In all experiments, the number of dimensions was set to 1000 and m to 50, $c_1 = 2.05$, $c_2 = 2.05$, guaranteeing the algorithm to converge [3].

The experiments were performed with the swarm using connected k-regular graphs (*i.e.* graphs in which each node has k neighbors) as communication topology with $k = 2, 4, 5, 6, 7, 8, 9, 10, 20, 30, 40, 50, 60, 70, 80, 90, 100$ (special cases are: $k = 2$, ring topology; $k = 4$, von Neumann topology; and $k = 100$, global topology). The PSO was executed 30 times for each topology and the influence graph was retrieved from the information exchange between the particles in each iteration of each execution. In order to analyze stagnation, we defined that the swarm stagnated at iteration t if the global best fitness did not improve by at least ρ between consecutive iterations until $t + \delta$ with $\rho = 1.02$ and $\delta = 500$.

Our results demonstrated the capability of *communication diversity* to explain the stagnation phenomenon for different communication topologies of Particle Swarm Optimizers using an unified approach based on graph component analysis. For instance, *communication diversity* (Fig. 6(b)) appear to firmly constrain the iteration PSO stagnates (Fig. 6(a)). In fact, by closely analyzing

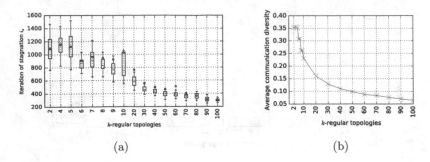

(a)   (b)

Fig. 6. The stagnation occurs earlier in swarms with k-regular topology as k increases (a), a tendency associated to the decrease of communication diversity (b). The boxplot (a) contains the value of the iteration the swarm stagnated in each of the 30 runs of the PSO algorithm, and the curve (b) depicts the average communication diversity until the iteration of stagnation.

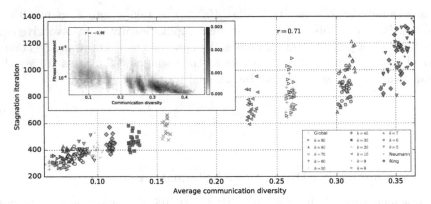

Fig. 7. The communication diversity of the swarm is associated to the iteration that stagnation occurs in the swarm. Each topology presents its range of communication diversity with some topologies sharing such range as well as iteration of stagnation. Each point is an execution of the 30 for each topology considered. Inset: Communication diversity is associated to the speed the global fitness f of the swarm changes between iterations t and $t+1$. The plot contains all the iterations until the swarm gets stagnated from 30 executions of PSO for each topology considered. The fitness improvement here is defined as $\frac{f_t - f_{t+1}}{f_{t+1}}$.

each execution (Fig. 7), different topologies can be clustered based on their *communication diversity*. These clusters captures the signatures associated with the communication diversity of each topology which plausibly explains, for instance, why the ring topology tends to consistently stagnate later when compared with the global topology. Surprisingly, *communication diversity* also relates to fitness improvement with a higher correlation (Fig. 7, inset) when compared with the other swarm spatial diversity measures albeit it only takes into account the component analysis of the *influence graph* and disregards properties related to individual particles such as fitness, position or velocity.

The results suggest that swarm stagnation may be more related to how information flows through the swarm social structure than to the way specific particle properties arc spread across the search space. For instance, simply restarting the swarm in order to highly disperse the particles might make sense considering the viewpoint of swarm spatial diversity but it does not make sense under the perspective of *communication diversity* for which this restarted swarm would be stagnated after the restart and still fated to consistently stagnate. Nevertheless, this also need to be confirmed in other problems and PSO variants.

4 Conclusions and Future Works

Early stagnation poses a barrier for Particle Swarm Optimizers and has only been tackled based on the assessment of the swarm spatial diversity. We advocate that our *communication diversity* based on component graph analysis of the *influence graph* is a good step towards an unified approach that can potentially better characterize early stagnation for different topologies.

Therefore, the design of stagnation prevention techniques should start concerning about *communication diversity* since it accounts for the social interactions among the individuals and not just properties associated with individual particles as the swarm spatial diversity. Approaches to control the communication diversity may be a fruitful way to control the execution of swarms in PSO and maybe other optimization approaches where an influence graph can be defined.

For future works, we will assess our *communication diversity* using other PSO variants in a panel of different problems, design a PSO variant with a stagnation prevention mechanism based on our *communication diversity* and extend the influence graph to other algorithms such as Ant Colony Optimization (ACO).

Acknowledgments. Marcos Oliveira, Diego Pinheiro and Bruno Andrade would like to thank the Science Without Borders program (CAPES, Brazil) for financial support under grants 1032/13-5, 0624/14-4 and 88888.067201/2013-00.

References

1. Bratton, D., Kennedy, J.: Defining a standard for particle swarm optimization. In: 2007 Swarm Intelligence Symposium, SIS 2007, pp. 120–127. IEEE, April 2007
2. Cheng, S., Shi, Y.: Diversity control in particle swarm optimization. In: 2011 IEEE Symposium on Swarm Intelligence (SIS), pp. 1–9, April 2011
3. Clerc, M., Kennedy, J.: The particle swarm - explosion, stability, and convergence in a multidimensional complex space. IEEE Trans. Evol. Comput. **6**(1), 58–73 (2002)
4. Kennedy, J., Eberhart, R.: Particle swarm optimization, vol. 4, pp. 1942–1948 (1995)

5. Kennedy, J., Mendes, R.: Population structure and particle swarm performance. In: Proceedings of the 2002 Congress on Evolutionary Computation, CEC 2002, vol. 2, pp. 1671–1676 (2002)
6. Kennedy, J., Eberhart, R.C.: Swarm Intelligence. Morgan Kaufmann Publishers Inc., San Francisco (2001)
7. Krink, T., Vesterstrom, J., Riget, J.: Particle swarm optimisation with spatial particle extension. In: Proceedings of the World on Congress on Computational Intelligence, vol. 2, pp. 1474–1479 (2002)
8. Mendes, R., Kennedy, J., Neves, J.: The fully informed particle swarm: simpler, maybe better. IEEE Trans. Evol. Comput. 8(3), 204–210 (2004)
9. Oliveira, M., Bastos-Filho, C.J.A., Menezes, R.: Towards a network-based approach to analyze particle swarm optimizers. In: 2014 IEEE Symposium on Swarm Intelligence (SIS), pp. 1–8, December 2014
10. Oliveira, M., Bastos-Filho, C.J.A., Menezes, R.: Using network science to assess particle swarm optimizers. Soc. Netw. Anal. Min. 5(1), 1–13 (2015)
11. Oliveira-Júnior, M.A.C., Bastos-Filho, C.J.A., Menezes, R.: Assessing particle swarm optimizers using network science metrics. In: Ghoshal, G., Poncela-Casasnovas, J., Tolksdorf, R. (eds.) Complex Networks IV. SCI, vol. 476, pp. 173–184. Springer, Heidelberg (2013)
12. Olorunda, O., Engelbrecht, A.P.: Measuring exploration/exploitation in particle swarms using swarm diversity. In: 2008 IEEE Congress on Evolutionary Computation (IEEE World Congress on Computational Intelligence), pp. 1128–1134. IEEE, June 2008
13. Pontes, M.R., Neto, F.B.L., Bastos-Filho, C.J.: Adaptive clan particle swarm optimization. In: 2011 IEEE Symposium on Swarm Intelligence (SIS), pp. 1–6. IEEE (2011)
14. Shi, Y., Eberhart, R.: Monitoring of particle swarm optimization. Front. Comput. Sci. China 3(1), 31–37 (2009)
15. Tang, K., Li, X., Suganthan, P.N., Yang, Z., Weise, T.: Benchmark functions for the CEC 2010 special session and competition on large-scale global optimization. Technical report, University of Science and Technology of China (USTC), School of Computer Science and Technology, Nature Inspired Computation and Applications Laboratory (NICAL), China
16. Zhan, Z.H., Zhang, J., Li, Y., Chung, H.H.: Adaptive particle swarm optimization. IEEE Trans. Syst. Man Cybern. Part B Cybern. 39(6), 1362–1381 (2009)
17. Zhang, Q.L., Li, X., Tran, Q.A.: A modified particle swarm optimization algorithm. In: Proceedings of 2005 International Conference on Machine Learning and Cybernetics, vol. 5, pp. 2993–2995, August 2005

Continuous Time Gathering of Agents with Limited Visibility and Bearing-only Sensing

Levi Itshak Bellaiche and Alfred Bruckstein

Technion, Israel Institute of Technology, Haifa, Israel
levi.itshak@gmail.com, freddy@cs.technion.ac.il

Abstract. A group of mobile agents, identical, anonymous, and oblivious (memoryless), having the capacity to sense only the relative direction (bearing) to neighboring agents within a finite visibility range, are shown to gather to a meeting point in finite time by applying a very simple rule of motion. The agents' rule of motion is: set your velocity vector to be the sum of the two unit vectors in $\mathbb{R}^2$ pointing to your "extremal" neighbours determining the smallest visibility disc sector in which all your visible neighbors reside, provided it spans an angle smaller than π, otherwise, since you are "surrounded" by visible neighbors, simply stay put. Of course, the initial constellation of agents must have a visibility graph that is connected, and provided this we prove that the agents gather to a common meeting point in finite time, while the distances between agents that initially see each other monotonically decreases.

Keywords: Gathering · Bearing-only · Convex polygon

1 Introduction

This paper studies the problem of mobile agent convergence, or robot gathering under severe limitations on the capabilities of the agent-robots. We assume that the agents move in the environment (the plane $\mathbb{R}^2$) according to what they currently "see", or sense in their neighborhood. All agents are identical and indistinguishable (i.e. they are anonymous having no i.d's) and, all of them are performing the same "reactive" rule of motion in response to what they see. Our assumption will be that the agents have a finite visibility range V, a distance beyond which they cannot sense the presence of other agents. The agents within the "visibility disk" of radius V around each agent are defined as its neighbors, and we further assume that the agent can only sense the direction to its neighbors, i.e. it performs a "bearing only" measurement yielding unit vectors pointing toward its neighbor. Therefore, in our setting, each agent senses its neighbors within the visibility disk and sets its motion only according to the distribution of unit vectors pointing to its current neighbors. Figure 1 shows a constellation of agents in the plane ($\mathbb{R}^2$), their "visibility graph" and the visibility disks of some of them, each agent moves based on the set of unit vectors pointing to its neighbors.

© Springer International Publishing Switzerland 2016
M. Dorigo et al. (Eds.): ANTS 2016, LNCS 9882, pp. 89–100, 2016.
DOI: 10.1007/978-3-319-44427-7_8

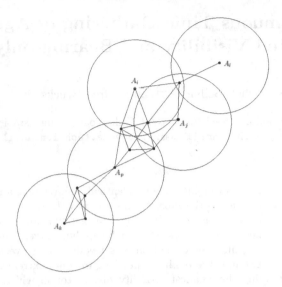

Fig. 1. A constellation of agents in the plane displaying the "visibility disks" of agents A_k, A_l, A_i, A_j, A_p and the visibility graph that they define, having edges connecting pairs of agents that can see each other.

In this paper we shall prove that continuous time limited visibility sensing of directions only and continuous adjustment of agents' velocities according to what they see is enough to ensure the gathering of the agents in finite time to a point of encounter. The literature of robotic gathering is vast and the problem was addressed under various assumptions on the sensing and motion capabilities of the agents. Here we shall only mention papers that deal with gathering assuming continuous time motion and limited visibility sensing, since these are most relevant to our work reported herein. The paper [6] by Olfati-Saber, Fox, and Murray, nicely surveys the work on the topic of gathering (also called consensus) for networked multi-agent systems, where the connections between agents are not necessarily determined by their relative position or distance. This approach to multi-agent systems was indeed the subject of much investigation and some of the results, involving "switching connection topologies" are useful in dealing with constellation-defined visibility-based interaction dynamics too. A lot of work was invested in the analysis of "potential functions" based multi-agent dynamics, where agents are sensing each other through a "distance-based" influence field, a prime example here being the very influential work of Gazi and Passino [7] which analyses beautifully the stability of a clustering process. Interactions involving hard limits on the "visibility distance" in sensing neighbors were analysed in not too many works. Ji and Eggerstedt in [2] analysed such problems using potential functions that are "visibility-distance based barrier functions" and proved connectedness-preservation properties at the expense of making some agents temporarily "identifiable" and "traceable" via a hysteresis process. Ando, Oasa, Suzuki and Yamashita in [8] were the first to deal with hard constraints of limited visibility and analysed the "point convergence" or gathering issue in a discrete-time synchronized setting, assuming agents can see and measure both distances and bearings to neighbors within the visibility range. Subsequently, in a series of papers, Gordon, Wagner, and Bruckstein, in [3–5], analysed gathering with limited visibility and bearing only sensing constraints imposed on the agents. Their work proved gathering or clustering results in discrete-time settings, and also proposed dynamics for the continuous-time settings. In the sequel we shall mention the continuous time motion model they analysed and compare it to our dynamic rule of motion. In our work, as well as most of the papers mentioned above one assumed that the agents can directly control their velocity with no acceleration constraints. We note that the literature of multi-agent systems is replete with papers assuming more complex and realistic dynamics for the agents, like unicycle motions, second order systems and double integration models relating the location to the controls, and seek sensor based local control-laws that ensure gathering or the achievement of some desired configuration. However we feel that it is still worthwhile exploring systems with agents directly controlling their velocity based on very primitive sensing, in order to test the limits on what can be achieved by agents with such simple, reactive behaviours.

2   The Gathering Problem

We consider N agents located in the plane ($\mathbb{R}^2$) whose positions are given by $\{P_k = (x_k, y_k)^T\}_{k=1,2,\ldots,N}$, in some absolute coordinate frame which is unknown to the agents. We define the vectors

$$u_{ij} = \begin{cases} \frac{P_j - P_i}{\|P_j - P_i\|} & 0 < \|P_j - P_i\| \le V \\ 0 & \|P_j - P_i\| = 0 \text{ or } \|P_j - P_i\| > V \end{cases}$$

hence u_{ij} are, if not zero, the unit vectors from P_i to all P_j's which are neighbors of P_i in the sense of being at a distance less than V from P_i, i.e. P_j's obeying:

$$\|P_j - P_i\| \triangleq [(P_j - P_i)^T (P_j - P_i)]^{1/2} \le V$$

Note that we have $u_{ij} = -u_{ji}, \forall (i,j)$. For each agent P_i, let us define the special vectors, u_i^+ and u_i^- (from among the vectors u_{ij} defined above). Consider the nonzero vectors from the set $\{u_{ij}\}_{j=1,2,\ldots,N}$. Anchor a moving unit vector $\bar{\eta}(\theta)$ at P_i pointing at some arbitrary neighbor, i.e. at $u_{ik} \ne 0$, $\bar{\eta}(0) = u_{ik}$ and rotate it clockwise, sweeping a full circle about P_i. As $\bar{\eta}(\theta)$ goes from $\eta(0)$ to $\eta(2\pi)$ it will encounter all the possible u_{ij}'s and these encounters define a sequence of angles $\alpha_1, \alpha_2, \ldots, \alpha_r$ that add to $2\pi = \alpha_1 + \ldots + \alpha_r$ (α_k = angle from k-th to (k+1)-th encounter with a u_{ij}, α_r = angle from last encounter to first one again, see Fig. 2). If none of the angles $\{\alpha_1, \ldots, \alpha_r\}$ is bigger than π, set $u_i^+ = u_i^- = 0$. Otherwise define $u_i^+ = u_{i(m)}$ and $u_i^- = u_{i(n)}$, the unit vectors encountered when entering and exiting the angle $\alpha_b > \pi$ bigger than π.

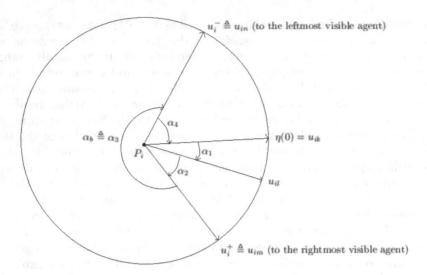

Fig. 2. Leftmost and rightmost visible agents of agent located at P_i.

One might call u_i^- the pointer to the "leftmost visible agent" from P_i and u_i^+ the pointer to the "rightmost visible agent" among the neighbors of P_i. If P_i has nonzero right and leftmost visible agents it means that all its visible neighbors belong to a disk sector defined by an angle less than π, and P_i will be movable. Otherwise we call it "surrounded" by neighbors and, in this case, it will stay in place while it remains surrounded. The dynamics of the multi-agent system will be defined as follows.

$$\frac{dP_i}{dt} = v_0(u_i^+ + u_i^-) \text{ for } i = 1, \dots, N \tag{1}$$

Note that the speed of each agent is in the span of $[0, 2v_0]$. With this we have defined a local, distributed, reactive law of motion based on the information gathered by each agent. Notice that the agents do not communicate directly, are all identical, and have limited sensing capabilities, yet we shall show that, under the defined reactive law of motion, in response to what they can "see" (which is the bearings to their neighboring agents), the agents will all come together while decreasing the distance between all pairs of visible agents. A simulated example of such a system is given in Fig. 3.

Assume that we are given an initial configuration of N agents placed in the plane in such a way that their visibility graph is connected. This just means that there is a path (or a chain) of mutually visible neighbors from each agent to any other agent. Our first result is that while agents move according to the above described rule of motion, the visibility graph will only be supplemented with new edges and old "visibility connections" will never be lost.

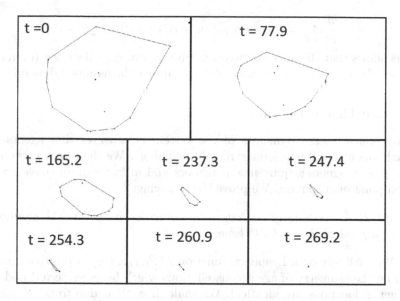

Fig. 3. Simulated evolution at different snapshots of a system composed of 15 agents obeying the laws of (1) with a random initial constellation. The convex hull of the set of agents is also represented.

2.1 Connectivity is Never Lost

We shall show that

Theorem 1. *A multi-agents system under the dynamics*

$$\{\dot{P}_i = v_0(u_i^+ + u_i^-)\}_{i=1,\ldots,N}$$

ensures that pairs of neighboring agents at $t = 0$ (i.e. agents at a distance less than V) will remain neighbors forever.

Proof. To prove this result we shall consider the dynamics of distances between pairs of agents. We have that the distance Δ_{ij} between P_i and P_j is

$$\Delta_{ij} = \|P_j - P_i\| = [(P_j - P_i)^T(P_j - P_i)]^{1/2}$$

hence

$$
\begin{aligned}
\frac{d}{dt}\Delta_{ij}^{(t)} &= \frac{1}{\|P_j - P_i\|}(P_j - P_i)^T(\dot{P}_j - \dot{P}_i) \\
&= u_{ij}^T(\dot{P}_j - \dot{P}_i) \\
&= -u_{ij}^T\dot{P}_i - u_{ji}^T\dot{P}_j \\
&= -v_0 u_{ij}^T(u_i^+ + u_i^-) - v_0 u_{ji}^T(u_j^+ + u_j^-)
\end{aligned}
$$

where we used the dynamics (1). However for every agent P_i we have either $u_i^+ + u_j^- \triangleq 0$ if agent is surrounded, or $u_i^+ + u_i^-$ is in the direction of the center of the disk sector in which all neighbors (including P_j) reside. Therefore the inner product $u_{ij}^T(u_i^+ + u_i^-) = < u_{ij}, (u_i^+ + u_i^-) >$ will necessary be positive, hence

$$\frac{d}{dt}\Delta_{ij}^{(t)} = -(v_0 * positive + v_0 * positive) \leq 0$$

This shows that distances between neighbors can only decrease (or remain the same). Hence agents never lose neighbors under the assumed dynamics.

2.2 Finite-Time Gathering

We have seen that the dynamics of the system (1) ensures that agents that are neighbors at $t = 0$ will forever remain neighbors. We shall next prove that, as time passes, agents acquire new neighbors and in fact will all converge to a common point of encounter. We prove the following:

Theorem 2. *A multi-agent system with dynamics given by (1) gathers all agents to a point in $\mathbb{R}^2$, in finite time.*

Proof. We shall rely on a Lyapunov function $L(P_1, \ldots, P_N)$, a positive function defined on the geometry of agent constellations which becomes zero if and only if all agents' locations are identical. We shall show that, due to the dynamics of the system, the function $L(P_1, \ldots, P_N)$ decreases to zero at a rate bounded away from zero, ensuring finite time convergence. The function L will be defined as the perimeter of the convex hull of all agents' locations, $CH\{P_i(t)\}_{i=1,\ldots,N}$. Indeed, consider the set of agents that are, at a given time t, the vertices of the convex hull of the set $\{P_i(t)\}_{i=1,\ldots,N}$. Let us call these agents $\{\tilde{P}_k(t)\}$ for $k = 1, \ldots, K \leq N$. For every agent $\tilde{P}_k$ on the convex hull (i.e. for every agent that is a corner of the convex polygon defining the convex hull), we have that all other agents, are in a region (wedge) determined by the half lines from $\tilde{P}_k$ in the directions $\tilde{P}_k \tilde{P}_{k-1}$ and $\tilde{P}_k \tilde{P}_{k+1}$, a wedge with an opening angle say θ_k. Since clearly $\theta_k \leq \pi$ for all k we must have that agent $\tilde{P}_k$ has all its visible neighbors in a wedge of its visibility disk with an angle $\alpha_k \leq \theta_k \leq \pi$ hence its u_k^+ and u_k^- vectors will not be zero, causing the motion of $\tilde{P}_k$ towards the interior of the convex hull. This will ensure the shrinking of the convex hull, while it exists, and the rate of this shrinking will be determined by the evolution of the constellation of agents' locations. Let us formally prove that indeed, the convex hull will shrink to a point in finite time. Consider the perimeter $L(t)$ of $CH\{P_i(t)\}_{i=1,\ldots,N}$

$$L(t) = \sum_{k=1}^{K(t)} \Delta_{k,k+1} = \sum_{k=1}^{K(t)} [(\tilde{P}_{k+1})(t) - \tilde{P}_k(t))^T (\tilde{P}_{k+1}(t) - \tilde{P}_k(t))]^{1/2}$$

where the indices are considered modulo $K(t)$.

We have, assuming that K remains the same for a while, that

$$\frac{d}{dt}L(t) = \sum_{k=1}^{K} \frac{d}{dt}\Delta_k = -\sum_{k=1}^{K} \left(v_0 \tilde{u}_{k,k+1}^T (u_k^+ + u_k^-) + v_0 \tilde{u}_{k,k+1}^T (u_{k+1}^+ + u_{k+1}^-)\right)$$

but note that $\tilde{u}_{k,k+1}$ does not necessarily lie between u_k^+ and u_k^- anymore, since, in fact, $\tilde{P}_k$ and $\tilde{P}_{k+1}$ might not even be neighbors.

Now let us consider $\frac{d}{dt}L(t)$ and rewrite it as follows

$$\frac{d}{dt}L(t) = -v_0 \sum_{k=1}^{K} \tilde{u}_{k,k+1}^T (u_k^+ + u_k^-) - v_0 \sum_{k=1}^{K} \tilde{u}_{k+1,k}^T (u_{k+1}^+ + u_{k+1}^-)$$

Rewriting the second term above, by moving the indices k by -1 we get

$$\frac{d}{dt}L(t) = -v_0 \sum_{k=1}^{K} \tilde{u}_{k,k+1}^T (u_k^+ + u_k^-) - v_0 \sum_{k=1}^{K} \tilde{u}_{k,k-1}^T (u_k^+ + u_k^-)$$

This yields

$$\frac{d}{dt}L(t) = -v_0 \sum_{k=1}^{K} < u_k^+, \tilde{u}_{k,k+1} + \tilde{u}_{k,k-1} > -v_0 \sum_{k=1}^{K} < u_k^-, \tilde{u}_{k,k+1} + \tilde{u}_{k,k-1} >$$

Note that we have here inner products between unit vectors, yielding the cosines of the angles between them. Therefore, defining $\theta_k =$ the angle between $\tilde{u}_{k,k-1}$ and $\tilde{u}_{k,k+1}$ (i.e. the interior angle of the convex hull at the vertex k, see Fig. 4), and the angles:

$$\begin{aligned}
\alpha_k^+ &\triangleq \gamma(u_k^+, \tilde{u}_{k,k+1}) \\
\beta_k^+ &\triangleq \gamma(\tilde{u}_{k,k-1}, u_k^+) \\
\alpha_k^- &\triangleq \gamma(\tilde{u}_{k,k-1}, u_k^-) \\
\beta_k^- &\triangleq \gamma(u_k^-, \tilde{u}_{k,k+1})
\end{aligned}$$

we have $\alpha_k^+ + \beta_k^+ = \alpha_k^- + \beta_k^- = \theta_k$ and all these angles are between 0 and π.

Using these angles we can rewrite

$$\frac{d}{dt}L(t) = -\sum_{k=1}^{K} v_0(\cos \alpha_k^+ + \cos \beta_k^+) - \sum_{k=1}^{K} v_0(\cos \alpha_k^- + \cos \beta_k^-)$$

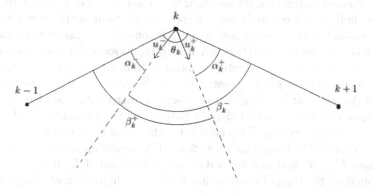

Fig. 4. Angles at a vertex of the convex hull.

Now, using the inequality (proved in Appendix 1)

$$\cos\alpha + \cos\beta \geq 1 + \cos(\alpha + \beta)$$
$$0 \leq \alpha, \beta, \alpha + \beta \leq \pi \tag{2}$$

we obtain that

$$-\frac{d}{dt}L(t) \geq 2v_0 \sum_{i=1}^{K}(1 + \cos\theta_i) \tag{3}$$

For any convex polygon we have the following result (see the detailed proof in Appendix 1):

Lemma 1. *For any convex polygon with K vertices and interior angles $\theta_1, \ldots, \theta_K$, with $(\theta_1 + \ldots + \theta_K) = (K - 2)\pi$ we have that*

$$\sum_{k=1}^{K}\cos(\theta_i) \geq \begin{cases} 1 + (K - 1)\cos\left(\frac{(K-2)\pi}{K-1}\right) & 2 \leq K \leq 6 \\ K\cos\left(\frac{(K-2)\pi}{K}\right) & K \geq 7 \end{cases} \tag{4}$$

Therefore, we obtain from (3) and (4) that

$$-\frac{d}{dt}L(t) \geq \mu(K) \tag{5}$$

where

$$\mu(K) = 2v_0\left(K + \begin{cases} 1 + (K-1)\cos\left(\frac{(K-2)\pi}{K-1}\right) & 2 \leq K \leq 6 \\ K\cos\left(\frac{(K-2)\pi}{K}\right) & K \geq 7 \end{cases}\right)$$
$$= 2v_0 K\left(1 - \max\left\{\cos\left(\frac{2\pi}{K}\right), \frac{K-1}{K}\cos\left(\frac{\pi}{K-1}\right) - \frac{1}{K}\right\}\right)$$

Note here that, since $(1 - max\{\ldots\}) > 0$ we have that the rate of decrease in the perimeter of the configuration is srictly positive while the convex hull of the agent location is not a single point.

The argument outlined so far assumed that the number of agents determining the convex hull of their constellation is a constant K. Suppose however that in the course of evolution some agents collide and/or some agents become "exposed" as vertices of the convex hull, and hence K may jump to some different integer value. At a collision between two agents we assume that they merge and thereafter continue to move as a single agent. Since irrespective of the value of K the perimeter decreases at a rate which is strictly positive and bounded away from zero we have effectively proved that in finite time the perimeter of the convex hull will necessarily reach 0. This concludes the proof of Theorem 2.

Figure 5 shows the bound as a function of K assuming $v_0 = 1$. Note that we always have $K \leq N$, and $\mu(K)$ is a decreasing function of K, hence we have an upper bound on the time of convergence for any configuration of N agents given by $\frac{L(0)}{\mu(N)}$.

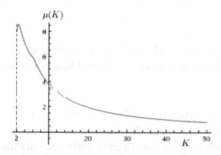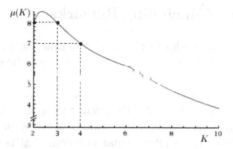

Fig. 5. Graph of the bound $\mu(K)$ of (5). The graph on the right is a zoom on small values of K. Note the change of curve between $K = 6$ and $K = 7$, due to the "interesting" discontinuity in the geometric result exhibited in Eq. (4).

The inequalities of (2) and of (4) become equalities for particular configurations of the agents (for example a regular polygon in which each pair of adjacent neighbors are visible to each other, if $K \geq 7$). In this case, the bound in (3) yields the exact rate of convergence of the convex-hull perimeter as long as K remains the same.

3   Generalizations

All the above analysis can be generalized for dynamics of the form

$$\frac{dP_i}{dt} = f(P^{(i)})(u_i^+ + u_i^-) \text{ for } i = 1, \ldots, N \tag{6}$$

$f(P^{(i)}) \geq 0$ is some positive function of the configuration of the neighbours seen by agent i. This generalization also guarantees that the rule of motion is locally defined and reactive, and defined in the same way for all agents. The dynamics (1) corresponds to a particular case of (6), with $f(P^{(i)}) = v_0 = constant$ for all agents.

It is easy to slightly change the proofs above in order to show that Theorem 1 (ensuring that connectivity is not lost) is still valid as long as $f(P^{(i)}) \geq 0$ for all i, and that Theorem 2 (ensuring finite time gathering) is also valid as long as $f(P^{(i)}) \geq \epsilon > 0$ for all i.

Note that in the work of Gordon et al. [3], a constant speed for the agents was considered, and this corresponds to setting $f(P^{(i)}) = \frac{1}{||u_i^+ + u_i^-||}$ for a mobile agent i, rather than v_0. Given that in this case $f(P^{(i)}) \geq \frac{1}{2}$, the conditions for Theorems 1 and 2 are verified, and hence the dynamics with constant speed also ensures convergence to a single point without pairs of initially visible agents losing connectivity. We therefore also have a proof for the convergence of the algorithm that was proposed in the above-mentioned paper.

4   Concluding Remarks

We have shown that a very simple local control on the velocity of agents in the plane, based on limited visibility and bearing only sensing of neighbors ensures their finite time gathering. We provided a very simple geometric proof that finite time gathering is achieved, and provided precise bounds on the rate of decrease of the perimeter of the agent configuration's convex hull. These bounds are based on a geometric lower bound on the sum of cosines of the interior angles of an arbitrary convex planar polygon, that is interesting on its own right (a curious breakpoint occurring in the bound at 7 vertices). Our result may be regarded as a convergence proof for a highly nonlinear autonomous dynamic system, naturally handling dynamic changes in its dimension (the events when two agents meet and merge). The reader is refered to [1] for a more complete analysis of these results including various simulations illustrating them.

Appendix 1: Proof of Lemma 1

We shall first prove the following facts:

Fact a. Let $0 \leq a \leq b \leq \pi$ and $0 \leq a + b \leq \pi$. Then we have

$$\sqrt{2(1 + \cos(a+b))} = 2\cos\left(\tfrac{a+b}{2}\right) \geq \cos(a) + \cos(b) \geq$$
$$2\cos^2\left(\tfrac{a+b}{2}\right) = 1 + \cos(a+b)$$

Proof. The function cosine is decreasing in $[0, \pi]$, and given that $\frac{a+b}{2} \geq \frac{b-a}{2}$:

$$1 \geq \cos\left(\frac{b-a}{2}\right) \geq \cos\left(\frac{a+b}{2}\right)$$

multiplying by $2\cos\left(\tfrac{a+b}{2}\right) \geq 0$:

$$2\cos\left(\tfrac{a+b}{2}\right) \geq 2\cos\left(\tfrac{a+b}{2}\right)\cos\left(\tfrac{b-a}{2}\right) \geq 2\cos^2\left(\tfrac{a+b}{2}\right)$$
$$2\cos\left(\tfrac{a+b}{2}\right) \geq \cos(a) + \cos(b) \qquad \geq 1 + \cos(a+b)$$

A direct consequence is the following fact.

Fact b. Let $0 \leq a, b \leq \pi$. Then

$$\cos(a) + \cos(b) \geq \begin{cases} 1 + \cos(a+b) : a + b \leq \pi \\ 2\cos\left(\tfrac{a+b}{2}\right) \quad : a + b \geq \pi \end{cases}$$

Proof. The first line is already part of Fact a. The second line can be proven by using the left inequality of Fact a with $\pi - a$ and $\pi - b$, noticing that $0 \leq \pi - a \leq \pi$, $0 \leq \pi - b \leq \pi$, and $\pi - a + \pi - b \leq \pi$ for $a + b \geq \pi$.

Now we can prove Lemma 1. Suppose any given initial configuration of the polygon with interior angles $0 \leq x_1, \ldots, x_n \leq \pi$. We then have $x_1 + \ldots + x_n = (n - 2)\pi$.

Now repeat the following step: Go through all the pairs of non-zero values (x_i, x_j). As long as there is still a pair verifying $x_i + x_j \leq \pi$, transform it from (x_i, x_j) to $(0, x_i + x_j)$. When there are no such pairs, then among all the non-zero values, take the minimum value and the maximum value, say x_i and x_j (they must verify $x_i + x_j \geq \pi$ ... the previously applied process), and transform the pair from (x_i, x_j) to $\left(\frac{x_i + x_j}{2}, \frac{x_i + x_j}{2}\right)$.

Repeat the above process until convergence. We prove that the process converges and that we can get as close as desired to a configuration where all non-zero values are equal. Note that after each step, the sum of the values equals $(n-2)\pi$, and that the values of all x_i's remain between 0 and π.

The number of values that the above process set to zero must be less or equal to 2 in order to have the sum of the n positive values equal to $(n-2)\pi$. Therefore it is guaranteed that after a finite number of iterations, there will be no pairs of nonzero values whose sum is less than π (otherwise this would allow us to add a zero value without changing the sum).

Once in this situation, all we do is replacing pairs of "farthest" non-zero values (x_i, x_j) with the pair $\left(\frac{x_i + x_j}{2}, \frac{x_i + x_j}{2}\right)$. Let us show that all the nonzero values converge to the same value, specifically to their average.

Let k be the number of remaining non-zero values after the iteration t_0 which sets the "last value" to zero. Denote these values at the i-th iteration by $(x_1^{(i)}, \ldots, x_k^{(i)})$. Define:

$$m = \frac{x_1^{(i)} + \ldots + x_k^{(i)}}{k} = \frac{(n-2)\pi}{k}$$

$$E_i = (x_1^{(i)} - m)^2 + \ldots + (x_k^{(i)} - m)^2$$

Without loss of generality, suppose that at the i-th iteration the extreme values were x_1 and x_2 and so we transformed $(x_1^{(i)}, x_2^{(i)})$ into $\left(x_1^{(i+1)} = \frac{x_1^{(i)} + x_2^{(i)}}{2},\right.$
$\left. x_2^{(i+1)} = \frac{x_1^{(i)} + x_2^{(i)}}{2}\right)$. So we have:

$$E_{i+1} - E_i = 2(\tfrac{x_1^{(i)} + x_2^{(i)}}{2} - m)^2 - (x_1^{(i)} - m)^2 - (x_2^{(i)} - m)^2)$$
$$= -\tfrac{1}{2}(x_1^{(i)} - x_2^{(i)})^2$$

But $x_1^{(i)}$ and $x_2^{(i)}$ being the extreme values, we have for any $1 \leq l \leq k$:

$$(x_1^{(i)} - x_2^{(i)})^2 \geq (x_l^{(i)} - m)^2$$

and by summing over l we get that:

$$k(x_1^{(i)} - x_2^{(i)})^2 \geq E_i$$

Hence

$$E_{i+1} - E_i = -\tfrac{1}{2}(x_1^{(i)} - x_2^{(i)})^2 \le -\tfrac{E_i}{2k}$$
$$E_{i+1} \quad \le \quad \left(1 - \tfrac{1}{2k}\right) E_i$$
$$0 \le \quad E_i \quad \le \quad \left(1 - \tfrac{1}{2k}\right)^{i-t_0} E_{t_0}$$

proving that E_i converges to zero, i.e. all the non-zero values converge to m.

At each step of the above described process, according to Fact b, the sum of cosines can only decrease. Therefore from any given configuration we can get as close as possible to a configuration in which all non-zero values are equal, without increasing the sum of the cosines. Hence, the minimum value must be reached in a configuration in which all non-zero values are equal.

Since there can be at most only two zero values, the minimum value of the sum of the cosines is the minimum of the following:

$$- 2 + (n - 2) \cos\left(\tfrac{(n-2)\pi}{n-2}\right) = -(n - 4) \text{ (case with 2 zeros)}$$

$$- 1 + (n - 1) \cos\left(\tfrac{(n-2)\pi}{n-1}\right) \text{ (case with 1 zero)}$$

$$- n \cos\left(\tfrac{(n-2)\pi}{n}\right) \text{ (case with no zero)}$$

An analytical comparison of these values depending on n leads to the result stated in Lemma 1.

References

1. Bellaiche, L.-I., Bruckstein, A.: Continuous time gathering of agents with limited visibility and bearing-only sensing (2015). arXiv:1510.09115
2. Ji, M., Egerstedt, M.: Distributed coordination control of multiagent systems while preserving connectedness. IEEE Trans. Robot. 23(4), 693–703 (2007)
3. Gordon, N., Wagner, I.A., Bruckstein, A.M.: Gathering multiple robotic a(ge)nts with limited sensing capabilities. In: Dorigo, M., Birattari, M., Blum, C., Gambardella, L.M., Mondada, F., Stützle, T. (eds.) ANTS 2004. LNCS, vol. 3172, pp. 142–153. Springer, Heidelberg (2004)
4. Gordon, N., Wagner, I.A., Bruckstein, A.M.: A randomized gathering algorithm for multipe robots with limited sensing capabilities. In: MARS 2005 Workshop Proceedings (ICINCO 2005), Barcelona, Spain (2005)
5. Gordon, N., Elor, Y., Bruckstein, A.M.: Gathering multiple robotic agents with crude distance sensing capabilities. In: Dorigo, M., Birattari, M., Blum, C., Clerc, M., Stützle, T., Winfield, A.F.T. (eds.) ANTS 2008. LNCS, vol. 5217, pp. 72–83. Springer, Heidelberg (2008)
6. Olfati-Saber, R., Fax, V., Murray, R.M.: Consensus and cooperation in networked multi-agent systems. Proc. IEEE 95(1), 215–233 (2007)
7. Gazi, V., Passino, K.M.: Stability analysis of swarms. IEEE Trans. Autom. Control 48(4), 692–697 (2003)
8. Ando, H., Oasa, Y., Suzuki, I., Yamashita, M.: Distributed memoryless point convergence algorithm for mobile robots with limited visibility. IEEE Trans. Robot. Autom. 15(5), 818–828 (1999)

Design and Analysis of Proximate Mechanisms for Cooperative Transport in Real Robots

Muhanad H. Mohammed Alkilabi[1,2](✉), Aparajit Narayan[1], and Elio Tuci[1]

[1] Computer Science Department, Aberystwyth University, Aberystwyth, UK
{mhm1,apn3,elt7}@aber.ac.uk
[2] Computer Science Department, Kerbala University, Kerbala, Iraq

Abstract. This paper describes a set of experiments in which a homogeneous group of real e-puck robots is required to coordinate their actions in order to transport cuboid objects that are too heavy to be moved by single robots. The agents controllers are dynamic neural networks synthesised through evolutionary computation techniques. To run these experiments, we designed, built, and mounted on the robots a new sensor that returns the agent displacement on the x/y plane. In this object transport scenario, this sensor generates useful feedback on the consequences of the robot actions, helping the robots to perceive whether their pushing forces are aligned with the object movement. The results of our experiments indicated that the best evolved controller can effectively operate on real robots. The group transport strategies turned out to be robust and scalable to effectively operate in a variety of conditions in which we vary physical characteristics of the object and group cardinality. From a biological perspective, the results of this study indicate that the perception of the object movement could explain how natural organisms manage to coordinate their actions to transport heavy items.

Keywords: Swarm robotics · Cooperative transport · Evolutionary robotics

1 Introduction

Collective object transport in a robot swarm is the ability of the robots to collect and transport objects that can not be transported by a single agent [5]. Cooperative transport is relatively ubiquitous in social insects, being known in at least 40 genera of ants [9]. It is primarily used to retrieve objects (e.g., food items) that are too heavy or too large to be moved by a single individual. For those ants species that live in environments in which the source of proteins are generally large carcass of insects, objects transport can be a solution to retrieve these precious food items reducing the time the food is exposed to competition [13]. It seems that a variety of parameters including the item's resistance to movement, the speed of transport, as well as the item size, shape, and mass play a significant role for the recruitment and for the active engagement of individuals into the

© Springer International Publishing Switzerland 2016
M. Dorigo et al. (Eds.): ANTS 2016, LNCS 9882, pp. 101–112, 2016.
DOI: 10.1007/978-3-319-44427-7_9

transport [8]. However, cooperative transport in ants remains a poorly understood process, with various hypothesis concerning the mechanisms for alignment and coordination of forces. There is not much empirical evidence to shed light on the proximate mechanisms underpinning this important cooperative process. In particular, it is still not clear what mechanisms are used to assess consensus or quorum information about directional movement [8]. Hypotheses vary from parsimonious explanations based on the perception of the object movement, to theories that require more complex structures for the perception of the forces exerted on the object, or for direct communication between the agents involved into the transport [11].

In recent years, the attempt of swarm roboticists to engineer groups of robots that generate interesting collective responses through self-organisation has provided biologists with an alternative method to investigate phenomena in social insects. The pioneering work of [7] on box-pushing by a multi-robot system has the merit of having formally represented in "hardware" the dynamics of collective object transport, pointing to issues of absolute relevance for a principled understanding of this form of cooperation. In the last 15 years, quite a few research works have tried to mimic the ants' cooperative behaviour with the double aim of engineering robust and scalable multi-robot systems and understanding nature. In [3], the authors carefully observed under experimental conditions the behaviour of a colony of ants (*Aphaenogaster cockerelli*) engaged in a cooperative transport task. They created a detailed model based on qualitative analysis of the role and contribution of single ants during transport of food items to the nest. The collected data has been used to create a model of the ants' behavioural rules during transport. The model has been validated by comparing the behaviour of simulated and real ants. In [12], the authors focus on the problem of alignment during transport showing that a robot leader that knows the direction of transport can induce the group to execute the desired cooperative manoeuvre by interacting with the group mates (i.e., followers) through forces exerted on the object. The swarm robotic model described in [6] demonstrated that communication between robots involved into the collective transport need not to be direct. Stigmergic forms of communication suffice to achieve coordination of forces and alignment in a group of robots retrieving heavy objects.

In this study, we describe a further swarm robotic model targeting cooperative transport. Real e-puck robots are required to push a cuboid object which, due to its mass/size, requires the cooperative effort of all the members of the group to be transported. The robots have to agree on a common direction of transport, to align their movements, and to push the object for an extended period of time. The distinctive feature of our model is the minimalist sensory apparatus provided to the robots. Contrary to the majority of previous similar studies, our robots have no means to feel forces. The objective of this study is to look at what the robots can collectively achieve with a sensory apparatus that allows them to indirectly perceive the movement of the object to transport. To run this study, we designed, built, and mounted a new sensor on the real e-pucks. This new sensor (hereafter, referred to as "optic-flow" sensor) is an optical camera positioned underneath the robot chassis, which returns the robot displacement on a x/y plane. In this collective transport scenario, the optic-flow sensor, in combination with the distance sensors, generates a sensory stimulation that effectively informs the robot on the direction of movement of the object. The results of our study show that this simple feedback suffices to allow the robots to agree on a common direction of transport and to maintain the transport for an extended period of time. A significant contribution of our study is in showing the robustness of the transport strategies evaluated in different scenarios (i.e., with objects of different mass and length, and with groups of different cardinality), and in the analysis of the behavioural mechanisms used by the robots to coordinate their actions. Our results point to a rather parsimonious explanation of the mechanisms required by real ants to transport object. In particular, our results suggest that feedback on the movement of the object modulates the frequency with which a robot changes the point of application of its pushing forces. This modulation is sufficient for a robot to sense a quorum with respect to the direction of travel, and to break "deadlocks" in which the robots cancel each others' forces. We also illustrate how the robots' shape influences the group performances. Interesting future lines of investigation dictated by our results are also discussed in Sect. 6.

2   The Task and the Simulation Model

In this study, neuro-controllers are synthesised using artificial evolution to allow a homogeneous group of four autonomous robots to push an elongated cuboid object (30 cm length, 6 cm width and height, 600 g mass) as far as possible from its initial position. Our study is run with groups of e-puck robots [10]. The parameters of the neuro-controllers are set in a simulation environment which model kinematic and dynamic features of the experimental conditions in which the simulated e-pucks are required to operate. The robot sensory apparatus includes infra-red sensors, the camera mounted on the robot chassis, and the optic-flow sensor appositely designed, built, and integrated into the e-puck structure for this task (see Fig. 1a). In simulation, the robots are initially positioned in a boundless arena with flat terrain, at 50 cm from the object. The objective of the robots is to move the object 2 m away from its initial position. The object mass is set so that the coordinated effort of all four robots is required to move the object. The best evolved controller is ported onto real e-puck robots, and extensively tested in various experimental conditions. This paper mainly focuses on the results of the evaluations on real robots[1].

In the remaining of this Section, we illustrate the characteristics of the new optic-flow sensor, which is an optical camera mounted underneath the robot chassis and located inside the slot originally hosting the robot battery (see Fig. 1a). This sensor captures a sequence of low resolution images (i.e., 18×18 pixels) of the ground at 1500 frames per second. The images are sent to the on board DSP which, by comparing them, calculates the magnitude and the direction of

---

[1] A detailed description of the simulation environment, of the robot model, including noise applied to sensors and motors, as well as results of all re-evaluation tests, and movies can be found at http://users.aber.ac.uk/elt7/ANTS2016/.

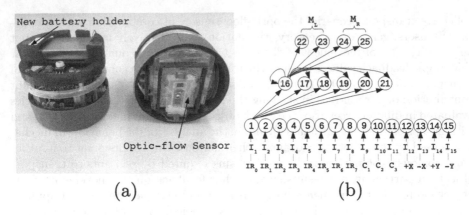

Fig. 1. (a) The e-puck robot with optic-flow sensor. (b) The robot's controller. The continuous line arrows indicate the efferent connections for only one neuron of each layer. Hidden neurons receive an afferent connection from each input neuron and from each hidden neuron, including a self-connection. Output neurons receive an afferent connection from each hidden neuron. Sensors to sensor neurons correspondence is indicated underneath the input layer.

movement of the robot. This information is subsequently communicated to the robot controller in the form of four normalized real values in $[0, 1]$: $+X$ and $-X$ representing the displacement on the positive and negative direction of the x axis, respectively; $+Y$ and $-Y$ representing the displacement on the positive and negative direction of the y axis, respectively. To improve portability of solutions to real hardware, in simulation, $+X$, $-X$, $+Y$, and $-Y$ are subjected to uniformly distributed random noise in $[-0.025, 0.025]$. The optic-flow sensor generates a sensory stimulus which is a direct feedback on the consequences of the signals sent to the motors. In a collective object transport scenario multiple contingencies can result in a robot failing to execute its desired action. For example, a forward movement command may not produce the desired action if the robot is pushing a stationary object, or an object that is moving in the opposite direction due to forces exerted by other robots. The optic-flow sensor generates readings that can be used by the agents to recognize these circumstances and to respond accordingly. The results of this study shows that this simple feedback, generated by the optic-flow sensor, is sufficient to allow a group of robots to coordinate their effort in order to collectively transport in an arbitrary direction an object that can not be moved by a single robot.

3   The Controller and the Evolutionary Algorithm

The robot controller is composed of a continuous time recurrent neural network (CTRNN) of 15 sensor neurons, 6 internal neurons, and 4 motor neurons (see [2] and also Fig. 1b which illustrates structure and connectivity of the network). The states of the motor neurons are used to control the speed of the left and right wheels. The values of sensory, internal, and motor neurons are updated using Eqs. 1, 2 and 3.

$$y_i = gI_i; \ i \in \{1, ..., N\}; \quad \text{with } N = 15; \tag{1}$$

$$\tau_i y_i = -y_i + \sum_{j=1}^{N} \omega_{ji} \sigma(y_i + \beta_j); \ i \in \{N+1, ..., N+6\}; \tag{2}$$

$$y_i = \sum_{j=N+1}^{j=N+6} \omega_{ji} \sigma(y_j + \beta_j); \ i \in \{N + 7, ..., N + 10\}; \tag{3}$$

with $\sigma(x) = (1+e^{-x})^{-1}$. In these equations, using terms derived from an analogy with real neurons, y_i represents the cell potential, τ_i the decay constant, g is a gain factor, I_i with $i = 1, .., N$ is the activation of the ith sensor neuron (see Fig. 1b for the correspondence between robot's sensors and sensor neurons), ω_{ij} the strength of the synaptic connection from neuron j to neuron i, β_j the bias term, $\sigma(y_j + \beta_j)$ the firing rate f_i. All sensory neurons share the same bias (β_I), and the same holds for all motor neurons (β_O). τ_i and β_i of the internal neurons, β_I, β_O, all the network connection weights ω_{ij}, and g are genetically specified networks' parameters. At each time step, the output of the left motor is $M_L = f_{N+7} - f_{N+8}$, and the right motor is $M_R = f_{N+9} - f_{N+10}$, with M_L, $M_R \in [-1, 1]$. Cell potentials are set to 0 when the network is initialised or reset, and Eq. 2 is integrated using the forward Euler method with an integration time step T = 0.13. A simple evolutionary algorithm using roulette wheel selection is employed to set the parameters of the networks [4]. The population contains 100 genotypes. Generations following the first one are produced by a combination of selection with elitism, recombination, and mutation. For each new generation, the eight highest scoring individuals ("the elite") from the previous generation are retained unchanged. The remainder of the new population is generated by fitness proportional selection from the 60 best individuals of the old population. A detailed description of the evolutionary algorithm can be found in [1].

4   The Fitness Function

During evolution each group undergoes a set of $E = 12$ evaluations or trials. A trial lasts 900 simulation steps (i.e., 117 s, with 1 stimulation step corresponding to 0.13 s). A trial is terminated earlier if the group manages to displace the object 2 m away from its initial position. At the beginning of each trial the controllers are reset, and the robots are positioned in the arena. Each trial differs from the others in the initialisation of the random number generator, which influences all the randomly defined features of the environment, such as the noise added to sensors and the robots initial position and orientation. The robots initial relative position with respect to the object is an important aspect which bears upon the complexity of this task. This is because the robots initial position contributes to determine the orientation with which they approach the object and consequently the nature of the manoeuvres required by the agents to coordinate and synchronise their actions. During evolution, the robots starting positions correspond to randomly chosen points on a circle's circumference of 50 cm radius that has the object in it's centre. This circle is divided in four equals parts. Each robot is randomly placed in one part of this circle with random orientation in a way that the object can be within an angular distance of $\pm 60°$ from its facing direction. These criteria should generate the required variability to develop solutions that are not sensitive to the robots initial positions.

In each trial (e), an evaluation function F_e rewards groups in which the robots remain close to the object, and transport the object as far as possible from its initial position. F_e is computed in the following:

$$F_e = f_1 + f_2 - f_3 \tag{4}$$

$$f_1 = \sum_{r=1}^{R}(1 - d_r); \quad f_2 = \Delta O^{pos}; \quad f_3 = t/T; \quad \text{with } T = 900; R = 4; \tag{5}$$

d_r is the Euclidean distance between the centroid of robot r and the centroid of the object. d_r is set to zero if the robot gets closer than 20 cm to the object. ΔO^{pos} is the Euclidean distance between the position of the object's centroid at the beginning and the end of the trial. t is the trial duration in simulation steps. f_1 rewards groups in which the robots approach the object. f_2 rewards groups that transport the object as far as possible. f_3 rewards groups that performs the task faster (i.e., required less number of simulation steps). The fitness of a genotype ($\bar{F}$) is the average team evaluation score after it has been assessed $E = 12$ times: $\bar{F} = \frac{1}{E}\sum_{e=1}^{E} F_e$.

5   Results

The primary aim of this study is to design control systems for homogeneous groups of real e-pucks required to transport objects in a cooperative way. Our objective is to generate solutions that are robust with respect to the object mass and length, and scalable with respect to the group cardinality. To design the controllers, we run 20 differently seeded evolutionary simulations, each simulation lasting 3000 generations. In order to choose the controller to be ported onto the real robots, we re-evaluated, in simulation, the best genotypes from generation 1000 to generation 3000 for every run. During re-evaluations, groups of simulated robots are tested with objects of different length and mass. Moreover, the group cardinality and the robots initial positions and orientations are systematically varied (see description and results of re-evaluation tests at http://users.aber.ac.uk/elt7/ANTS2016/).

The solution (i.e., the genotype coding for the controller) with the very best re-evaluation score has been selected to be ported onto the real e-pucks for further evaluations. In the next Section, we describe the results of the first test with real robots, and we compare these results with those of simulated robots controlled by the same controller, and evaluated in similar operational conditions.

5.1   First Evaluation Test with Real e-pucks

The first evaluation test with real e-pucks has been designed to investigate the scalability of the controllers with respect to the number of robots in the group, as well as the robustness with regard to objects of different length and mass, and with respect to varying initial conditions. Recall that during evolution, we used only groups of 4 robots, and only one type of elongated cuboid object (30 cm length, 6 cm width and height, 600 g mass). During the test with real robots, we evaluated homogeneous groups of 3, 4, 5 and 6 real e-pucks, for their capability to collectively transport cuboid objects of 30 cm and 40 cm lengths. Objects of each length were tried with two different masses. Object width and height are not changed with respect to evolutionary conditions. The total number of re-evaluation trials (160) with real e-pucks is given by all the possible combinations of the above mentioned parameters (i.e., 2 lengths, 2 masses, and 4 different values for group cardinality), each combination repeated 10 times, 5 trials with all the robots positioned in front of the long sides of the objects, and 5 trials with all the robots positioned in front of the short sides of the cuboid objects. In each trial, half of the group faces one side and the other half faces the other side of the object. In order to enforce the requirement of collective transport, the masses of the object vary with respect to the cardinality of the group in a way that in each of the 160 evaluation trials, the object is heavy enough to require the combined effort of all robots of the group to be successfully transported. The object masses are indicated in Fig. 2a. In each evaluation trial, the object is placed in the centre of 220 cm bounded square arena, and the robots are placed at about 50 cm from the object. Each evaluation trial can last 180 s (i.e. 1384 simulation steps), and it is terminated earlier if the group manages to transport the object at least 1 m away from its initial position. Only in this later case, the trial is considered successful.

The results of the first evaluation test are shown in Fig. 2a, where the bars indicate the success rate (%) of homogeneous groups controlled by the best evolved neural network in 16 different evaluation conditions. Black bars refer to the performance of groups of real e-pucks; white bars refer to the performances of groups of simulated e-pucks evaluated in similar experimental conditions (i.e., same object length, same mass, same group cardinality, and approximately same robots initial positions). The comparison between real and simulated robots is meant to capture differences in performance when moving from simulation to reality. We notice that the performance of both real and simulated robots is close to or largely above 80 % success rate in almost all evaluation conditions, demonstrating that the robots controller can successfully operate with larger groups than those used during the design phase, and with heavier and/or longer objects. At http://users.aber.ac.uk/elt7/ANTS2016/ the reader can find the results of further tests in simulations with groups of up to 16 robots. These tests could not be run on real e-pucks because in our Lab we only have 6 real e-pucks.

Results in Fig. 2a tell us that performances drop for the group of 6 e-pucks, transporting an object of 30 cm length, and of 980 g mass. This drop in performance can be explained with reference to two elements: the length of the longest

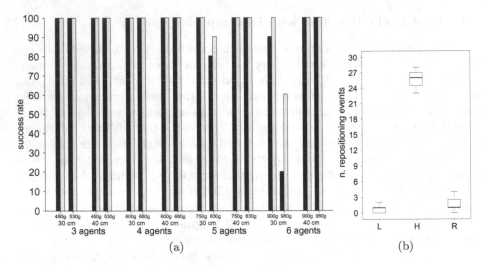

Fig. 2. (a) Graph showing the success rate (%) of homogeneous groups controlled by the best evolved neural network. Black bars refer to the performance of groups of real e-pucks; white bars refer to the performances of groups of simulated e-pucks. The x-axis shows mass and length of the object, and group cardinality. A trial is considered successful if the group manages to transport the object 1 m away from its initial position. Each bar refers to performances over 10 trials. (b) Graphs showing the results of evaluation tests with a single real robot. In test L, we use 30 cm length, and 150 g mass object. In test H, we use 30 cm length, and 600 g mass object. In test R, we use 400 g mass, and 40 cm length object.

size of the cuboid object (hereafter, referred to as $\bar{L}$), and the sum of the diameter of the robots in the group (hereafter, referred to as $\bar{D}$). The number of robots that are forced to indirectly push the object through physical contact with other robots progressively increases when $\bar{L}$ becomes smaller than $\bar{D}$. The higher the number of robots pushing other robots, the higher the frequency of "detachment events" during transport. A detachment event refers to the case in which a robot loses physical contact with the element that it is currently pushing. Thus, it needs to relocate itself in a new position in order to keep on actively contributing to the collective transport. Detachment events have a negative impact on the group performance, since during such an event the group loses the contribution of one robot. Detachment events are more frequent when robots are required to push other robots than when robots directly push the object. This is because the e-pucks have a cylindrical shape which makes it relatively difficult for a robot to push another non-stationary robot. Generally speaking, we could say that the smaller the $\bar{L}$ compared to $\bar{D}$, the higher the frequency of detachment events, the poorer the group performance. However, there are exceptions. As shown in Fig. 2a, the $\bar{L}$ smaller than $\bar{D}$ condition only minimally affects the performance of groups of 6 real e-pucks transporting a slightly lighter object (see Fig. 2a, 6 robots, 30 cm length, 900 g object, black bar). This is because, as long as the group manages to exert a sufficient force to move the object, the smaller linear momentum due to the object's lighter mass makes the detachment events less disruptive for the group performance. In other words, with a progressively lighter object, even if all the group members are required to initiate the transport, not all the robots are required to push a moving object to sustain the transport. Therefore, in this condition, detachment events are less disruptive with respect to the group performance.

Although, the results shown in Fig. 2a indicate that our simulation environment is a sufficiently accurate model of the "reality", modifications can be certainly made to improve the robustness of group strategies. For example, the performances of groups of 6 simulated robots transporting 30 cm length, and 980 g object drop with respect to the performances of simulated groups in the other experimental conditions (see Fig. 2a, white bars). However, this performance drop is less evident for other groups of real e-pucks. Moreover, this is the evaluation condition in which we observe the largest difference between the performances of real and simulated robots. This suggests that our simulation does not accurately capture the effect of the $\bar{L}$ smaller than $\bar{D}$ condition. If we could model the effects of this phenomenon, we could perhaps improve the performances and robustness of the transport strategies.

The result of the first set of evaluations tell us that we succeeded in designing a controller to allow a swarm of real e-pucks to effectively transport heavy objects in a cooperative way. Performances are scalable and robust to deal with varying operating conditions. The results also demonstrate that group coordination of actions and alignment of pushing forces can be reached with a simple sensory apparatus made of distance sensors and the optic-flow sensor to indirectly perceive the object movement. The cylindrical shape of the robots negatively impacts the group performance when the length of the object is shorter than the sum of the robots radius. This negative effect tends to disappear when the transport can be sustained by less robots than those required to initially move the object.

5.2 Behavioural Analysis

How do the robots manage to coordinate their actions to cooperatively transport the object? To answer this question, we describe the results of a further series of evaluation tests on a single real robot. In these tests, the robot undertakes multiple trials where it is required to push an object with varying characteristics (e.g., a light, a heavy, and a long object). During these tests, we record the number of repositioning events. That is the number of times the robot changes the point of exerting forces on the object. A repositioning event happens anytime the robot stops pushing the object and immediately after starts pushing the object again in a slightly different position. In the biological literature, repositioning events are considered to be direct evidence of "persistence": that is, the individual tendency to perseverate with a given behavioural strategy. As discussed in [8], persistence is an individual-level parameter that modulates transport efficiency.

Our objective is to use the concept of persistence as a tool to move a step forward in the understanding of the operational mechanisms underlying the alignment of forces required for group transport. In particular, we are looking for relationships between characteristics of the object (i.e., its mass, and its direction of movement with respect to the robot heading) and persistence.

In the first series of tests, a real robot is positioned in front of a cuboid object, facing the object at 20 cm from it. In each trial, the robot is given 60 s to push the object. All tests are repeated for 10 trials. In test L, the object length is set to 30 cm, and the object mass is 150 g. The robot can easily transport the object. In test H, the object length is set to 30 cm, and the object mass is 600 g. The object is too heavy to be moved by the robot. In test R, the object length is set to 40 cm, and the object mass is 400 g. The robot can rotate the object by exerting pushing forces on either end of the longest side, but it can not transport it. Figure 2b shows the number of repositioning events counted during each trial of each test. The results clearly show that the number of repositioning events change with respect to whether or not the object can be moved or simply rotated. When the object is so heavy that it can not be moved or rotated by the robot, we observe a very high number of repositioning events. This indicates that the agent persistence is low (see Fig. 2b, box H). When the object is light enough to be moved or to be rotated by the robot, we observe a very low number of repositioning events. This indicates that the agent persistence is very high (see Fig. 2b, box L, and box R). We conclude that, the agent perception of the object linear or rotational movement, through the optic-flow sensor, increases the agent persistence. In other words, the robot keeps on looking for new points on which to exert pushing forces if the object does not move. The robot does not change the point of contact with the object if the object moves while it is pushing it.

We also run a further test in which we looked at relationship between persistence and object movement. In this test, the object length is set to 30 cm, its mass to 600 g. This object is too heavy to be moved by the robot. We run 10 trials without interfering with the robot actions, and 10 trials in which we intentionally moved the object in the opposite direction of the robot heading while the robot is pushing the object. We refer to the trials with no experimenter interference as static object trials, and the trials with the intervention of the experimenter as non-static object trials. In each of the static and non-static trials, we counted the repositioning events with pushing forces exerted on the first touched long side of the object. We stopped counting as soon as the robot touches the other long side of the cuboid object. The aim of this test is to estimate how long it takes (in terms of repositioning events) the robot to invert the direction of its pushing forces when the object does not move (static), and when the object moves against its heading. The results of this test, shown in Table 1, clearly indicate that no repositioning events are observed when the robot perceives the object moving against its heading. In other words, the robot quickly changes direction of pushing forces if it perceives the object moving against its heading. The response of the robot is to move away from the object with a circular trajectory that rather quickly takes it to the opposite side of the object.

Table 1. Table showing the number of repositioning events during each trial of the evaluation test in which a single robot pushes either a static object, or a non-static object intentionally moved in the opposite direction of the robot heading.

Trial	1	2	3	4	5	6	7	8	9	10
static object	6	6	5	6	5	6	5	6	5	6
non-static object	0	0	0	0	0	0	0	0	0	0

As shown in Table 1 for the static object, when no object movement is perceived, the robot keeps on looking for new points on which to exert pushing forces on the same side of the object.

By visually inspecting the robots' strategies during group transport, keeping in mind the results of our single robot evaluation tests, we noticed that robots heavily rely on the perception of the object (rotational) movement as a mean to align their forces. Robots exerting forces on the direction of the object rotation tend to have high persistence, while the robots exerting forces on the opposite direction of the object rotational movement tend to swap sides. When all the robots are on a single side, the force exerted on the object causes the object to switch from rotational to translation movement, and the transport begins. In the absence of rotational movements (e.g., with very heavy objects), the alignment certainly becomes more difficult, and it definitely takes longer for the robots to coordinate their efforts. Nevertheless, the robots eventually manage to position themselves on the same side of the object and to exert the required forces to move it. In these circumstances, we think that alignment is favoured by correlation between robot-robot interactions and individual persistence. However, further investigations are required to better understand this process.

6   Conclusions

As shown in [8], cooperative transport in ants is a poorly understood process, with not much empirical evidence to shed light on the proximate mechanisms underpinning this important cooperative process. The results of this study suggest that a rather parsimonious explanation based on the perception of the object movement could account for the alignment and the coordination of forces observed in natural organisms. We showed that groups of robots capable of perceiving whether their pushing forces are aligned with the object movement can use this cue to arrange themselves on the same side of an elongated cuboid object to exert a sufficient force to transport objects that are too heavy to be moved by single robots. We also provided a basic description of how this sensory information influences individual strategies. In particular, we showed that the object movement correlates with the agent persistence. In other words, agents that perceive their pushing forces aligned with the object movement tend to keep on exerting forces on the same point on the object. Perception of no object movement induces the robot to change the point of contact with the object. Perception of object movement against the robot heading induces the robot to exert forces on the opposite side of the object. We also showed that the robot controllers synthesised using evolutionary computation techniques generate group strategies that are robust to deal with some variability in object length and mass, as well as scalable to successfully operate with groups of different cardinality. Future work will focus on the transport of objects with irregular shape and no symmetries, as well as on the analysis of the effects of robot-robot interactions on the development of successful group strategies.

Acknowledgements. M.H. Mohammed Alkilabi thanks Iraqi Ministry of Higher Education and Scientific Research for funding his PhD, P. Todd and D. Lewis for their help and support in modifying e-puck robot.

References

1. Alkilabi, M., Lu, C., Tuci, E.: Cooperative object transport using evolutionary swarm robotics methods. In: Proceedings of the European Conference on Artificial Life, vol. 1, pp. 464–471. MIT (2015)
2. Beer, R., Gallagher, J.: Evolving dynamic neural networks for adaptive behavior. Adapt. Behav. **1**(1), 91–122 (1992)
3. Berman, S., Lindsey, Q., Sakar, M., Kumar, V., Pratt, S.: Experimental study and modeling of group retrieval in ants as an approach to collective transport in swarm robotic systems. Proc. IEEE **99**(9), 1470–1481 (2011)
4. Goldberg, D.E.: Genetic Algorithms in Search, Optimization and Machine Learning. Addison-Wesley, Reading (1989)
5. Groß, R., Dorigo, M.: Cooperative transport of objects of different shapes and sizes. In: Dorigo, M., Birattari, M., Blum, C., Gambardella, L.M., Mondada, F., Stützle, T. (eds.) ANTS 2004. LNCS, vol. 3172, pp. 106–117. Springer, Heidelberg (2004)
6. Groß, R., Dorigo, M.: Evolution of solitary and group transport behaviors for autonomous robots capable of self-assembling. Adapt. Behav. **16**(5), 285–305 (2008)
7. Kube, C., Bonabeau, E.: Cooperative transport by ants and robots. Robot. Auton. Syst. **30**, 85–101 (2000)
8. McCreery, H., Breed, M.: Cooperative transport in ants: a review of proximate mechanisms. Insects Sociaux **61**, 99–110 (2014)
9. Moffett, M.: Ant foraging. Res. Explor. **8**, 220–231 (1992)
10. Mondada, F., et al.: The e-puck, a robot designed for education in engineering. In: Proceedings of the 9th International Conference on Autonomous Robot Systems and Competitions, vol. 1, pp. 59–65 (2009)
11. Robson, S., Traniello, J.: Resource assessment, recruitment behavior, and organization of cooperative prey retrieval in the ant Formica schaufussi (Hymenoptera: Formicidae). Insect Behav. **11**, 1–22 (1998)
12. Wang, Z., Takano, Y., Hirata, Y., Kosuge, K.: A pushing leader based decentralized control method for cooperative object transportation. In: Proceedings of IEEE/RSJ International Conference on Intelligent Robots and Systems, vol. 1, pp. 1035–1040. IEEE (2004)
13. Yamamoto, A., Ishihara, S., Fuminori, I.: Fragmentation or transportation: mode of large-prey retrieval in arboreal and ground nesting ants. Insect Behav. **22**, 1–11 (2009)

Dynamic Task Partitioning for Foraging Robot Swarms

Edgar Buchanan[⊠], Andrew Pomfret, and Jon Timmis

York Robotics Laboratory, Department of Electronics, University of York, York, UK
{edgar.buchanan,andrew.pomfret,jon.timmis}@york.ac.uk

Abstract. Dead reckoning error is a common problem in robotics that can be caused by multiple factors related to sensors or actuators. These errors potentially cause landmarks recorded by a robot to appear in a different location with respect to the actual position of the object. In a foraging scenario with a swarm of robots, this error will ultimately lead to the robots being unable to return successfully to the food source. In order to address this issue, we propose a computationally low-cost finite state machine strategy with which robots divide the total travelling distance into a variable number of segments, thus decreasing accumulated dead-reckoning error. The distance travelled by each robot changes according to the success and failure of exploration. Our approach is more flexible than using a previously used fixed size approach for the travel distance, thus allowing swarms greater flexibility and scaling to larger areas of operation.

Keywords: Swarm robotics · Task partitioning · Fault tolerance · Foraging

1 Introduction

Swarm robotics is defined by Şahin in [19] as:

> *"[...] the study of how large number of relatively simple physically embodied agents can be designed such that a desired collective behavior emerges from the local interactions among agents and between the agents and the environment."*

Swarm robotics is thought to overcome potential problems that are common in centralized systems, such as lack of scalability and flexibility [2]. In addition, such swarms are thought to be robust due to their being no single point of failure in the system [2]. Nevertheless, there are scenarios, such as swarm taxis and foraging, where total or partial failures on a collective group of robots might lead to performance and functionality degradation [18,23]. As a result, attempts have been made to increase robustness of the swarms in order to either detect [5,14,21] or, diagnose failures [12,15] or even to recover from failures [10,13,22].

© Springer International Publishing Switzerland 2016
M. Dorigo et al. (Eds.): ANTS 2016, LNCS 9882, pp. 113–124, 2016.
DOI: 10.1007/978-3-319-44427-7_10

Pini et al. [18] demonstrated that Static Partitioning Strategy(SPS), inspired by ponerine ants [20], leafcutter ants [9] and honey bees [11], and previously implemented to avoid bottlenecks in foraging [3,8,17] can provide fault tolerance against partial failures of robots foraging for items, thus allowing faulty robots to continue operation even in the presence of faults. The robots modelled a motion failure fault, a common real problem with multiple causes, including wear and tear of gears, wheel/track slippage and objects stuck in the gears [4]. The SPS approach is one to divide the main task of object collection into smaller subtasks performed by each individual robot. A robot will take an item to an exchange zone and wait for another robot to hand the item over and the second robot will then take the item to the nest. However, this strategy was only shown to work for the robot platform used in the authors experiments, in this case the foot-bot robot [6], and its respective travelling error. In addition, the number of subtasks (partitions) is fixed and provided by the user.

Ferrante et al. [7] showed that task partitioning improves performance in environments with slopes that slow the robots velocity. This was achieved by evolving controllers with basic actions until they achieve task partitioning similar to that observed in leafcutter ants [9]. However, the evolved controllers have the same limitations as for the previous partitioning method where controllers designed for specific scenarios.

In this paper a Dynamic Partitioning Strategy (DPS) is proposed which allows the number of partitions and the size of each partition to change according to the success, or failure, of item retrieval. Two different variants are shown. The first changes a robot's foraging distance in linear steps, and the second uses a exponential function to adapt the distance. Work in this paper shows that this strategy is able to find the optimal number of subtasks for different environments, swarm sizes and error magnitudes.

The structure of this paper is as follows. First, an overview the foraging case study task is given. DPS is then explained with reference to the SPS implementation. Experiments are described and results are explained in Sect. 3. Further work is discussed in Sect. 4.

2   Dynamic Task Partitioning

Pini et al. [18] propose SPS which consists of retrieving items in a foraging task, where robots hand over an item to each other until it reaches the home area. This foraging task is illustrated in Fig. 1a with the associated finite state machine shown in Fig. 1b. The objective of the strategy is to divide the total travelling distance D in to smaller segments in order to cope with the dead-reckoning navigation error inherent in the robots. The error is modelled as a bias in each robot to move slightly towards the left, causing a drift in the dead-reckoning position estimate.

The difference between a strategy with no partitions, a Non-partitioning Strategy (NPS), and SPS is that instead of going directly to nest, in a static partitioning approach robots make a stop at a specific distance to wait for another

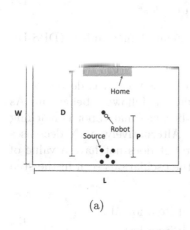

(a)   (b)

Fig. 1. Foraging scenario and finite state machine diagram. Foraging scenario (a) where robots take items from the source and takes them to the home area. D represents the distance between home area and source, P represents the partition distance and W and L represent environment dimensions. Finite state machine diagram (b) for task partitioning.

robot to hand the item over. This is done in the *wait for transfer* state. The distance that a robot moves before handing over an item is called the Partition Length (P) and is predefined by the authors with a value of 2 m.

In order to avoid any deadlocks, where robots will be waiting forever to hand an item over, a threshold time limit was implemented with a value of 2 min. If a robot waits over the limit it will go directly to home by entering the *go to nest* state.

However, as mentioned before, this approach presents a disadvantage which is that it is not flexible in terms or arena size or errors. For instance, if robots present different errors, or the arena size is changed, then performance provided by the strategy will not be optimal. On the other hand a DPS is able to select different number of subtasks for different error magnitudes and arena size.

The DPS is an approach proposed in this paper in which P changes according to the success, or failure, of last exploration. Every time an item is found by a robot, P will be increased as a reward. When the robot returns where the last object was found if it cannot find another item, then P will be decreased as a penalty. Each robot has its own P and changes it based on its own experience. In this paper, we present two different penalty/reward mechanisms.

The first mechanism, a step mechanism (DPS-S), changes P by a small fixed G as shown in Eq. 1. This means that if an object is not found then P will be decreased by G and if object is found then it will be increased by G. This approach has the advantage that there is only one parameter (G) to change and calibrate. However, as will be explained in more detail in the experiments section, robots can present oscillations in P.

$$P(t) = \begin{cases} P(t-1) + G & \text{if item found} \\ P(t-1) - G & \text{if item lost} \end{cases} \tag{1}$$

In our second proposed mechanism, an exponential mechanism (DPS-E), robots change P according to Eq. 2. N(t) is a measure of the success rate of finding an object for the robot itself at time t where $N(t)\epsilon[-10, 10]$. If the robot finds an item N will be incremented by one, and if not then N is decreased by one. G and α are constants. This equation provides the following behaviour. As N increases the smaller the changes to P will be because that robot is reaching a value of P that provides a good success rate. Alternatively, as N decreases the larger the change to P will be because the robot does not have a value of P that provides a good success rate. Therefore, the oscillations seen in the step mechanism are reduced with this approach.

$$P(t) = \begin{cases} P(t-1) + Ge^{-\alpha N(t)} & \text{if item found} \\ P(t-1) - Ge^{-\alpha N(t)} & \text{if item lost} \end{cases} \tag{2}$$

A disadvantage of the exponential mechanism is that if the value of N increases continuously for long periods of time, the robot becomes less able to change its behaviour and adapt to environmental changes. This means that the robot will take more time to recover from any change. The restriction of N to the interval [−10,10] is used to alleviate this, allowing robots to react faster to immediate possibles changes than with a wider interval.

3   Experiments and Results

In this section we present the experiments and results undertaken for the two DPS along with comparisons between the two approaches.

Experiments for DPS were implemented in ARGoS, a swarm robotics simulator [16]. ARGoS allows users to create controllers to test in different robot platforms such as e-puck and foot-bots in C++. The foot-bot [6] platform was chosen in order to be able to compare results with SPS previously implemented in [18] for the scenario shown in Fig. 1a and discussed in the previous section.

The number of repetitions for all the experiments shown in this paper is 130. We used Spartan [1] a statistical tool that has various statistical analysis techniques including a consistency analysis technique, known as the A-Test. An A-Test score was returned below 0.56 with 130 repeats of the simulation thus allowing us to conclude that 130 runs gave us statistically robust results with respect to the aleatory uncertainty in the simulation.

Experiments are divided into two sections, one for each mechanism implemented by DPS. In the first section, DPS uses a step mechanism to change P as shown in Eq. 1. Results for convergence to a single solution with fixed error and individual performance against different swarm and environment size are the experiments in the following section.

In the second section, DPS uses a exponential function to change P as shown in Eq. 2. This last section first describes the improvements with respect with the previous mechanism. Then, a comparison is shown to illustrate the robots getting lost rate for the different strategies. Finally, the last part describes how this last mechanism provides better and new solutions than with the step mechanism.

3.1 Step Mechanism

The step mechanism (DPS-S) consists of changing P by a fixed distance. The same dead reckoning error model as in [18], that provides an approximation to the real error in physical footbots, is used for these experiments. In this model every time a robot grips an object a value is sampled from a Rayleigh distribution with a scale parameter (σ) value of 0.0268. The previous distribution with the given value provides a similar error seen with physical foot-bots. This value multiplies actual wheel speed. However, the error term is only added to the right wheel when its speed is higher than zero, to the left wheel only if its speed is below zero. This is done to recreate the bias of real foot-bot robots moving towards the left.

Experiments are divided into two sets. The first set will show how this strategy makes P converge to the solution given in [18]. The second set compares the individual performance for each strategy.

Convergence to Solution. The objective of these experiments is to show that DPS-S is able to reach the solution proposed in [18]. The arena size is 4.5×6.7 m, with a distance between source and nest (D) of 4 m and 6 robots as swarm size. Two different initial partition length (P_0) values are tested the first P_0 has robots travelling a small P distance (0.5 m) and the second one is for a bigger P distance (3.5 m). This is done in order to illustrate convergence to the same solution from both sides. Finally, different values of G are used to illustrate the different behaviours that robots will have according to each value.

The swarm is considered to have reached the steady state when $|\tilde{P}(t) - \tilde{P}(t - 3600)| < 0.05$ m where $\tilde{P}(t)$ represents the median of P at time t. Finally, in order to measure stability an average of the confidence interval (CI) width is calculated from the samples once the swarm reached the steady state. Convergence times and the final average CI width are shown in Table 1.

Table 1. Convergence times and final average confidence intervals for different initial P_0 and G.

	$P_0 = 3.5$		$P_0 = 0.5$	
G (cm)	Time (h)	CI width (m)	Time (h)	CI width (m)
5	9.2	0.47	10.0	1.52
10	6.3	0.84	7.2	1.2
20	5.5	1.5	5.0	1.7

Table 2. Arena sizes and simulation parameters

Parameter	Normal	Large
Arena width W	4.5 m	6.7 m
Arena length L	6.7 m	9.9 m
Source-to-nest distance D	4.0 m	6.2 m
Experiments duration	15 h	20 h
Error intervals (σ)	.5σ, σ, 1.5σ	
Swarm size	2, 4, 6, 8, 10, 15, 20, 30	

As G increases, the convergence speed increases. However there is a trade-off with stability as shown in Fig. 2 and in Table 1. This is consistent with classical control theory where in the majority of systems, an increased loop gain will lead to a faster transient response but poorer damping and greater tendency towards oscillation. Figures 2a, c and e show this reduction in damping, where the whiskers become larger as G increases.

Additionally, Fig. 2b presents a different behaviour than Fig. 2a. In the first figure whiskers are shorter than the ones in the second figure. The main reason is that in some runs P and G are too small to allow robots to create a successful chain between the nest and the source. Robots get trapped with small values of P, and are never able to reach the ideal solution for this scenario.

For the values for G used in DPS-S, P was able to converge close to the distance given the author in [18] of 2 m and reach a steady state. This shows that distance provides the best performance for the actual environment and error used in robots. For the next experiments the value of G to be used will be 10 cm because it provides good balance between convergence speed and stability.

Individual Performance. This section is concerned with showing how DPS-S behaves and adapts under different arena sizes and error values. Arena sizes and simulation values are shown in Table 2. In the large environment robots take more time to find the food source, thus taking more time to converge to a solution. All robots start with a P_0 of 2 m.

Two individual performances from different strategies are considered different from one another whenever the Mann-Whitney U-test provides a p score lower than 0.05.

In Fig. 3 each graph represents the individual performance for different swarm sizes, environment sizes and errors. Individual performance is calculated as the total number of items collected at the end of the simulation, divided by the number of robots. When the error is high (1.5σ) and swarm size is larger than 8 robots for the normal environment and 15 robots for the large environment (Fig. 3e and f) DPS-S is better than SPS.

For the error σ individual performance is similar for SPS and DPS-S (Fig. 3c and d) especially in the large environment where there is no statistically

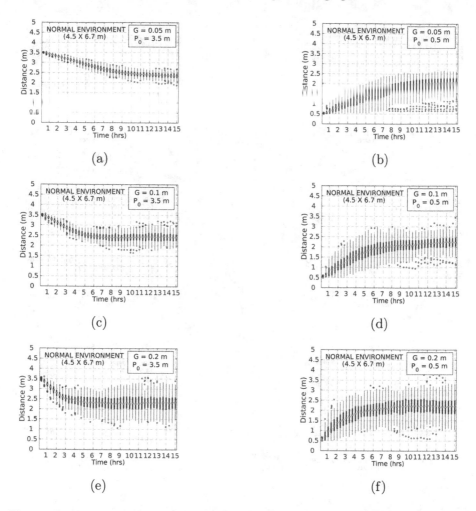

Fig. 2. Convergence graphs to optimal solution for two different values of P_0 and two different values of G. Left column graphs present robots starting with a P of 3.5 m (a, c, d) and on the right column robots start with a P of 0.5 m (b, d, f). Each row presents a different value of G used for DPS-S.

significant difference for any swarm size. This shows that the P distance of 2 m is the best solution provided by the author in [18] for the actual error. Also, as shown in the previous section, DPS-S converges to that solution.

In addition, DPS-S shares some of the same problems as SPS. When the swarm size is too small the robots have problems forming the chain that connects the source with the nest, causing an individual performance that is not significantly different from that of NPS. We find that the swarm must have at least 4 members for the normal environment and 6 members for the large environment to have an improvement with respect to NPS. On the other hand, when the swarm size is too large they spend more time avoiding each other than

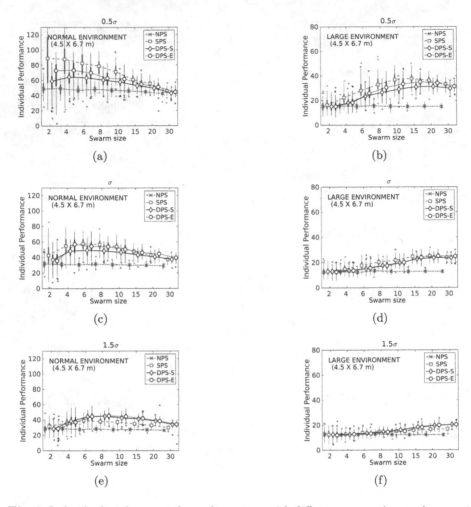

Fig. 3. Individual performance for each strategy with different swarm size, environment size and error. The left column represents a normal environment $(4.5 \times 6.7\,\text{m})$ and the right column represent a large environment $(6.7 \times 9.97\,\text{m})$. From top to bottom the errors are 0.5σ, σ and 1.5σ. For both environments, SPS performs better than the other strategies as the error decreases.

collecting items. For this reason individual performance decays as the swarm size increases.

3.2   Exponential Mechanism

Even though the previous approach was able to provide solutions for any environment, swarm size and error, the swarm performance is still affected by the continuous changes to P. A suitable approach to increase stability at steady state is to decrease G. However, this will affect convergence speed causing it to take more time to reach the steady state. Indeed, in some cases where the swarm size is small P might get trapped with small values that do not provide the best individual performance, as shown in the previous section. The exponential mechanism (DPS-E) can address this issue by dynamically adjusting the step size.

Experiments for this approach are divided into two parts. The first shows how the exponential function provides stability to the system by dynamically adjusting the size of the changes to P. The second provides the probability for the robots of not being able to return to the target for each strategy.

Stability. The behaviour that robots present using an exponential function is that as more items are successfully retrieved consecutively, their is less need to change P. This provides stability to the system. Conversely, if a robot becomes lost several times, the amount by which P will be changed increases. As a consequence, this provides a fast convergence to a steady state.

Figure 4 presents two different experiments with the same initial conditions, but each with a different approach. Each robot was given an inherent error of σ with a P_0 of 2 m that provides a reasonable performance for a normal environment. This means that robots are already in the steady state.

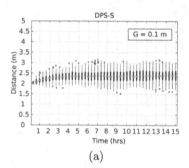
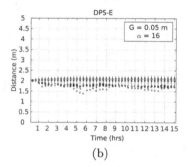

(a)   (b)

Fig. 4. Stability comparison between step and exponential functions for a normal environment with a 15 h simulation (4.5×6.7 m). Robots start at the steady state with an initial P of 2 m and they have an inherent error of σ.

Both graphs show that robots remain in the steady state, however, whiskers for step mechanism are larger for most of the simulation length (Fig. 4a) with a CI width of 1.03 m. The reason for this is that robots keep changing P continuously even though these robots have reached a solution that provides a continuous item collection.

On the other hand, the exponential function decreases the amount of change to P as the robots come closer to the solution. For this reason whiskers are smaller for Fig. 4b with a CI width of 0.4 m which is less than half than with step function.

In Fig. 2a, b, c and e, DPS-E performs better than DPS-S due to its fast convergence to steady state solutions. Furthermore, as mentioned before DPS-E provides better stability avoiding constant changes to P.

Probability of Robots Getting Lost. We now undertake a comparison to illustrate the different probabilities of getting lost for different strategies. The probability of a robot getting lost is given by $I_L/(I_F+I_L)$ where I_F is a counter that records the number of times an item is found since the beginning of the simulation and I_F is a counter that records the number of times an item is lost. An item is considered lost whenever a robot tries to retrieve it from the last place where it was found but the robot can no longer see any items and then it changes to *exploring* state. A comparison is shown in Fig. 5 between different strategies for two different scenarios and three different errors. The first scenario (Fig. 5a) is a normal environment ($4.5 \times 6.7\,\mathrm{m}$) with a swarm size of 6 members and a simulation length of 15 h. The second scenario (Fig. 5b) is a large environment ($6.7 \times 9.97\,\mathrm{m}$) with a swarm size 30 members and simulation length of 20 h. The probability was calculated after each simulation was over. This means that probability describes the last state of the robots.

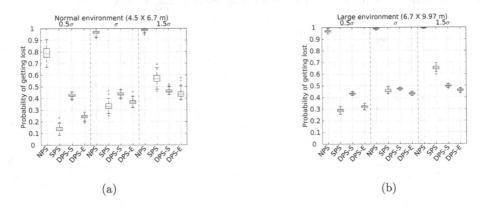

Fig. 5. Probability of getting lost comparison between different strategies for two given different scenarios against three errors.

For both scenarios SPS performs best when the odometric error is low, however, as the error increases this strategy becomes unsuitable as an optimal solution. The main reason is that the distance of 2 m is causing robots to get lost more frequently. On the other hand, DPS keeps a getting lost rate of 50 % independently of the error in the robots.

4   Conclusions and Future Work

In this paper a dynamic partitioning system (DPS) for foraging tasks was explained and results shown with simulated robots. For this strategy it is not necessary to provide a number of subtasks to be deployed. DPS is capable of evolving it by using penalties and rewards for each unsuccessful or successful search.

Two functions were presented that regulate changes to the search distance P. The first approach, DPS-S, changed P by small constants steps of value α. The second approach, DPS-E, used an exponential function to change P according to the success or failure of retrievals.

Experiments were divided into two parts one for each approach. In the first part it was shown that DPS is able to converge to the solution provided by the authors in [18] for specific parameters. Then DPS was compared with NPS and SPS and it was found that individual performance for item collection improves with respect with other strategies as the errors increase. This means that this strategy provides robustness, even when the error increases. Finally, an exponential function was discussed in detail and compared with the other strategies. It was shown that this approach provides a better stability in the steady state.

Further research will investigate the use of communication between robots to share information about successful strategies and increase convergence speed. In order to validate results, each strategy will also be implemented on real robots.

Acknowledgments. EB acknowledges financial support from CONACyT. JT is part sponsored by The Royal Society.

References

1. Alden, K., Read, M., Andrews, P.S., Timmis, J., Coles, M.: Applying spartan to understand parameter uncertainty in simulations. R J. **6**(2), 1–18 (2014)
2. Barca, J.C., Sekercioglu, Y.A.: Swarm robotics reviewed. Robot. **31**, 1–15 (2012)
3. Brutschy, A., Pini, G., Pinciroli, C., Birattari, M., Dorigo, M.: Self-organized task allocation to sequentially interdependent tasks in swarm robotics. Auton. Agents Multi-Agent Syst. **28**, 101–125 (2014)
4. Carlson, J., Murphy, R.R.: How UGVs physically fail in the field. IEEE Trans. Robot. **21**(3), 423–437 (2005)
5. Christensen, A.L., Grady, R.O., Dorigo, M.: From fireflies to fault-tolerant swarms of robots. IEEE Trans. Evol. Comput. **13**(4), 754–766 (2009)
6. Dorigo, M., Floreano, D., Gambardella, L.M., et al.: Swarmanoid: a novel concept for the study of heterogeneous robotic swarms. IRIDIA, Brussels, Belgium, Technical report 11–14 July (2011)
7. Ferrante, E., Turgut, A.E., Dué, E., Dorigo, M.: Evolution of self-organized task specialization in robot swarms. PLoS Comput. Biol. **11**, 1–21 (2015)
8. Goldberg, D., Matarie, M.J.: Design and evaluation of robust behavior-based controllers for distributed multi-robot collection tasks. In: Robot Teams: From Diversity to Polymorphism, pp. 1–24 (2001)
9. Hart, A.G., Ratnieks, F.L.W.: Task partitioning, division of labour and nest compartmentalisation collectively isolate hazardous waste in the leafcutting ant atta cephalotes. Behav. Ecol. Sociobiol. **49**(5), 387–392 (2001)

10. Humza, R., Scholz, O., Mokhtar, M., Timmis, J., Tyrrell, A.: Towards energy homeostasis in an autonomous self-reconfigurable modular robotic organism. In: Computation World: Future Computing, Service Computation, Adaptive, Content, Cognitive, Patterns, Computation World 2009, pp. 21–26 (2009)
11. Johnson, B.R.: Task partitioning in honey bees: the roles of signals and cues in group-level coordination of action. Behav. Ecol. **21**(6), 1373–1379 (2010)
12. Li, X., Parker, L.E.: Sensor analysis for fault detection in tightly-coupled multi-robot team tasks. In: Proceedings of the IEEE International Conference on Robotics and Automation, pp. 3269–3276, April 2007
13. Long, M., Murphy, R., Parker, L.: Distributed multi-agent diagnosis and recovery from sensor failures. In: Proceedings 2003 IEEE/RSJ International Conference on Intelligent Robots and Systems (IROS 2003), vol. 3, pp. 2506–2513, October 2003
14. Parker, L.E.: ALLIANCE: an architecture for fault tolerant multirobot cooperation. IEEE Trans. Robot. Autom. **14**(2), 220–240 (1998)
15. Parker, L.E., Kannan, B.: Adaptive causal models for fault diagnosis and recovery in multi-robot teams. In: IEEE International Conference on Intelligent Robots and Systems, pp. 2703–2710 (2006)
16. Pinciroli, C., Trianni, V., O'Grady et al.: ARGoS: a modular, multi-engine simulator for heterogeneous swarm robotics. In: IEEE International Conference on Intelligent Robots and Systems, pp. 5027–5034 (2011)
17. Pini, G., Brutschy, A., Birattari, M., Dorigo, M.: Task partitioning in swarms of robots: reducing performance losses due to interference at shared resources. In: Cetto, J.A., Filipe, J., Ferrier, J.-L. (eds.) Informatics in Control Automation and Robotics. LNEE, vol. 85, pp. 217–228. Springer, Heidelberg (2011)
18. Pini, G., Brutschy, A., Scheidler, A., et al.: Task partitioning in a robot swarm: object retrieval as sequence of subtasks with direct object transfer. Artif. Life **20**(3), 291–317 (2014)
19. Sahin, E.: Swarm robotics: from sources of inspiration. In: Swarm Robotics Workshop: State-of-the-Art Survey, pp. 10–20 (2005)
20. Schmickl, T., Karsai, I.: Sting, carry and stock: how corpse availability can regulate de-centralized task allocation in a ponerine ant colony. PloS one **9**(12), e114611 (2014)
21. Tarapore, D., Lima, P.U., Carneiro, J., Christensen, A.L.: To err is robotic, to tolerate immunological: fault detection in multirobot systems. Bioinspir. Biomim. **10**(1), 016014 (2015)
22. Timmis, J., Tyrrell, A., Mokhtar, M., Ismail, A., Owens, N., Bi, R.: An artificial immune system for robot organisms. In: Symbiotic Multi-Robot Organisms: Reliability, Adaptability, pp. 279–302 (2010)
23. Winfield, A.F.T., Harper, C.J., Nembrini, J.: Towards dependable swarms and a new discipline of swarm engineering. In: Şahin, E., Spears, W.M. (eds.) Swarm Robotics 2004. LNCS, vol. 3342, pp. 126–142. Springer, Heidelberg (2005)

Human-Robot Swarm Interaction with Limited Situational Awareness

Gabriel Kapellmann Tovar[⊠], Nicole Salomons, Andreas Kolling,
and Roderich Groß[⊠]

Natural Robotics Lab, Department of Automatic Control and Systems Engineering,
The University of Sheffield, Sheffield, UK
{gkapellmann,rgross}@sheffield.ac.uk

Abstract. This paper studies how an operator with limited situational
awareness can collaborate with a swarm of simulated robots. The robots
are distributed in an environment with wall obstructions. They aggregate
autonomously but are unable to form a single cluster due to the obstructions. The operator lacks the bird's-eye perspective, but can interact
with one robot at a time, and influence the behavior of other nearby
robots. We conducted a series of experiments. They show that untrained
participants had marginal influence on the performance of the swarm.
Expert participants succeeded in aggregating 85 % of the robots while
untrained participants, with bird's-eye view, succeeded in aggregating
90 %. This demonstrates that the controls are sufficient for operators to
aid the autonomous robots in the completion of the task and that lack
of situational awareness is the main difficulty. An analysis of behavioral
differences reveals that trained operators learned to gain superior situational awareness.

1 Introduction

As multi-robot systems continue to assist humans in an increasing variety of
roles, more and more humans will need to interact with them. Swarm robotic
systems are a subset of multi-robot systems with characteristics, also observed
in natural swarms, that seem to complicate such interactions. In particular,
they use local sensing and communication capabilities, have no access to global
information, and are governed by simple rules. Yet, complex behaviors may result
from interactions among the robots and of robots with their environment.

Krause et al. [9] proposes that swarm-intelligent systems could become a
useful tool for solving problems. Self-organization could lead to novel solutions
to problems, for example, path finding in dynamic environments, exploration,
or rescue and support. However, this does not mean that swarm intelligence
will necessarily be the best solution for a particular situation. Interaction with
humans can be beneficial, for example, to adapt and react to critical environment
changes or make decisions in which human experience is important.

A problem with swarm systems is that the attractive features of their social
structure also makes interactions with (external) users complex. There have been

M. Dorigo et al. (Eds.): ANTS 2016, LNCS 9882, pp. 125–136, 2016.
DOI: 10.1007/978-3-319-44427-7_11

several proposals suggested for the implementation of human interaction with robot swarms, surveyed in [8]. Some of these explored proposals are: controlling units as a leader [18], with haptic interactions [17] or with body gestures [1].

In this paper we consider further restrictions where operators can only receive local sensor information from a single robot and its local cluster and do not have access to global positions. This is more in line with the nature of distributed systems in which global state information can be difficult to obtain. In addition, it simulates better real-world scenarios such as search and rescue missions, where keeping visual contact with each member of the swarm would be infeasible.

The paper is organized as follows. In Sect. 2 related work is presented. Section 3 details the methodology used in this study. The results are presented in Sect. 4. Section 5 concludes the paper.

2   Related Work

Research on human-swarm interaction has produced a number of studies on the topic. A recent survey on human interaction with robotic swarms is available in [8]. One of the most frequently studied questions in human-swarm interaction is the design of appropriate control inputs for swarms. Four basic control approaches are distinguished in [8]: (1) algorithm switching; (2) parameter changing; (3) indirect control through environment influence; and (4) control through selected leaders. In our study we utilize algorithm switching and control through teleoperated leaders. These two approaches have been studied in a variety of scenarios.

In [3] a hybrid control approach allowed operators to teleoperate leaders and switch the swarm algorithm after teleoperation. In contrast to our work, the operator had access to global position information for all robots and algorithm switches did not propagate through the local swarm network. Teleoperation of leaders and their effect on the remaining swarm has been studied in [7] with an emphasis on determining what kind of flocking and motion behaviors can be generated from different human inputs.

The problem of obtaining and visualizing the information about the state of the swarm has been studied somewhat less than swarm controls. The studies that focused on controls usually assumed access to and present the position of all swarm robots in an interface. Work that considers limited access to state information due to bandwidth or latency restrictions has been presented in [14, 19]. An emphasis on how to display a limited amount of information while still allowing the human to detect patterns is found in [5]. In [11] a brief overview of potential display visualization for swarms is given.

We are not aware of any work in human-swarm interaction that studies the impact on and adaption of operators when removing access to global state information (such as position) and restricting the interaction to be strictly local and distributed. Such interaction schemes are pointed out as desirable in [2,4]. It is not clear, however, what the cost of such an interaction scheme is with regard to the operator's ability to observe and control the swarm effectively. Our study is aimed to contribute towards this area.

Neglect benevolence [13,19] is a concept that is concerned with the dynamic nature of emergent behaviors. Most swarm algorithms require time to converge to an emergent behavior and should their dynamics be disturbed, for example, by interacting with an operator, convergence may be delayed and the interaction may be detrimental. Hence, some swarms may benefit from a period of neglect. This stands in contrast to the concept of neglect tolerance studied in the context of multi-robot systems [15]. In these systems the performance deteriorates due to periods of neglect. In our study we observed positive effects and some learning of neglect benevolence dynamics by experienced operators, further supporting the evidence from [13] that human operators can learn to adapt the timing of their commands to the neglect benevolence of the swarm.

3 Methodology

3.1 Problem Formulation

We study a distributed interaction scheme between a human and a swarm of robots in the context of an aggregation task. The robots operate in a bounded environment with wall obstructions. They are equipped with motors, a communication device, a camera and proximity sensors. Initially, the robots are randomly distributed in the environment. Their goal is to aggregate into a single cluster in a given time period. By default, the robots execute the aggregation (clustering) behavior presented in [6]. Unlike [6], we consider environments with obstructions and robots which have limited range sensors, both of which can prevent aggregation.

The operator has access to a graphical interface that provides a connection to a single randomly selected robot. The robot, upon request, transmits either the readings from the proximity sensor or the camera. The operator can also issue motion commands to the selected robot and switch the behavior of it and all its neighbors to either clustering, following, or gossip, which can count the robots in the cluster. The operator does not have access to any other state information, but is shown a map of the environment prior to the experiment. Details on the robots, swarm behaviors and interface are provided in the following sections.

3.2 Robot and Simulation Platform

In our study, the operator interacts with a swarm of simulated robots. We use the open source physics simulator Enki [10], which treats the kinematics and dynamics of rigid objects in two dimensions.

We consider the e-puck miniature mobile robot [12]. Enki has a built-in model of the e-puck. The robot is represented as a disk with a diameter of 7.4 cm and a weight of 152 g. It is a differential wheeled robot. Each wheel can move backward and forward at different speeds with a maximum of 12.8 cm/s.

Each robot has a color camera, providing a horizontal field of view of 56 degree and a maximum range of 150 cm. We assume that the robot can use

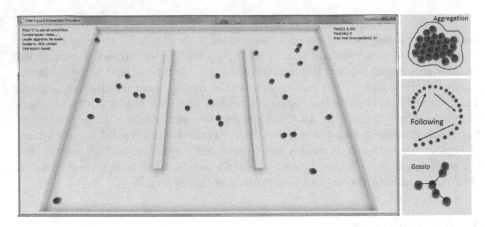

Fig. 1. Snapshot showing the simulation environment from a bird's-eye perspective. The operator is not provided with this global state information (except for the control experiments). The robots can perform three swarm behaviors: aggregation (top right), following (middle right), and gossip (bottom right).

the camera to detect other robots in the direct line of sight. In addition, the robot has eight infra-red sensors distributed around its body and a simulated Bluetooth communication device. These sensors help the operator interact with the robots.

Figure 1 provides an overview of the simulation environment. The robots operate in a rectangular arena of size 400×300 cm that contains two walls, which are symmetrically arranged. Their lengths are 2/3 of the corresponding side length of the arena and divide it in three equally sized areas joined only at the extremes. The walls are sufficiently tall to prevent robots at opposite sites from perceiving each other.

3.3   Swarm Behaviors

Each robot can execute three swarm algorithms (the corresponding behaviors are shown in Fig. 1):

- The *aggregation* algorithm is identical to the one reported in [6]. By default, this algorithm is executed. Each robot measures whether another robot is in its direct line of sight or not. It maps this binary sensor input onto a pair of constant wheel velocities. For simplicity we state the velocity values after scaling them from -1 to 1. If another robot is perceived, the velocity pair is $(1, -1)$; the robot thus turns clockwise on the spot. Otherwise, the scaled velocity pair is $(-0.7, -1)$; the robot thus moves backward, following a clockwise circular trajectory. As shown in [6], this simple algorithm leads to the overall aggregation of the swarm, provided the sensing range is sufficiently large and no obstacles are present in the environment.

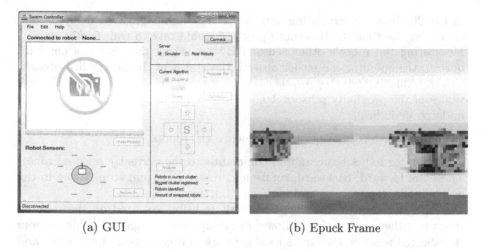

(a) GUI (b) Epuck Frame

Fig. 2. (a) Graphical user interface that the participants used in the human-robot swarm interaction study. (b) Image taken by a simulated robot and provided to the operator via the graphical user interface.

- The *follower* algorithm uses the same line-of-sight sensor and reactive control architecture as the aggregation algorithm. The wheel velocity constants are however different. If another robot is perceived, the robot moves straight forward $(1,1)$, attempting to approach the detected robot; otherwise, the robot rotates anti-clockwise on the spot $(-1,1)$.
- The *gossip* algorithm prevents the selected robot from changing its position (yet, the operator has control over its orientation). The robot requests all other robots in its neighborhood to stop. These requests get relayed, so that all 'connected' robots finally stop. Only in this mode the operator can obtain a count of the connected robots. The counting algorithm is explained in [16].

The robots do not use their IR sensors for obstacle avoidance. Nevertheless, the user can detect any obstacle by monitoring a robot's sensors (IR or camera).

3.4 User Interface

The interaction between the operator and the robot swarm occurs through the graphical user interface (GUI) shown in Fig. 2a. The operator can connect with one random robot at a time ("Request Bot" button). The operator is shown the robot's (unique) identification number and which of the three algorithms is currently being executed.

Once connected to a robot, the operator has two options to obtain information from its sensors. To simulate bandwidth limitations of the hardware, only one of these options can be selected at a time:

- Requesting an image of the camera: By clicking the "Image Request" button, the user is shown a 80×60 pixels snapshot of the robot's camera as shown in Fig. 2b. Between requesting and displaying the image, a 1 s delay occurs, emulating the time the Bluetooth protocol would take to transfer the data.

- Monitoring the robot's other sensors: By activating the "Sensors On/Off" button, the operator can either observe the status of the binary line-of-sight sensor, indicating whether another robot is perceived, or, they can see the raw values of the proximity sensors. Unlike the camera image, the sensor data is updated periodically.

The operator has two options to influence the robots:

- The operator issues basic motion commands to the currently selected robot. These are forward, backward, rotate left, rotate right and stop. When in the gossip mode, the forward and backward buttons are disabled.
- The operator changes the algorithm that is being executed on the selected robot to either aggregation, follower or gossip. The change is broadcast from the selected robot to the entire local network of robots connected via IR, and all robots in the network change their algorithm as well. When disconnecting from a robot, the algorithm which it is currently executing remains active. However, it is not possible to disconnect from a robot while in gossip mode. This is to avoid robots from being left in a static position.

3.5 Experimental Setup

A series of human-robot swarm interaction experiments were conducted. The study received ethical approval by The University of Sheffield. All participants were students of the university and their age ranged between 18 and 39.

Participants were given a 10 min presentation explaining the mission, the three swarm behaviors, and the user interface. They were also shown a snapshot of the simulation environment (see Fig. 1).

The default group of participants, referred to as *untrained participants*, were not provided with the opportunity to test the system in advance of the experiment. Overall, data for 38 untrained participants were collected. The data for three participants were excluded as they did not complete all three trials.

Six further participants received training on the system prior to conducting trials. Three of these received 60 min training (five to six trials), these are referred to as *trained participants*. Three further participants, chosen from the developer team, received several hours of training and are considered as *experts*.

All participants conducted three trials with 25 robots and lasting 10 min (600 s) each. The untrained participants were further assigned to one of two conditions at random:

- Blind-Blind-Blind (BBB): Participants of this group had no access to global state information (i.e., the bird's-eye perspective) during any of their trials. There were 19 participants in this group.
- Visual-Blind-Blind (VBB): Participants of this group had access to global state information for the entire duration of their first trial (referred to as VBB_V), but had no access to that information during the second and third trials (referred to as VBB_B). There were 16 participants in this group.

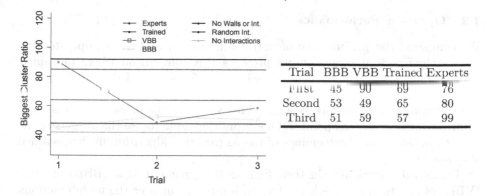

Trial	BBB	VBB	Trained	Experts
First	45	90	69	76
Second	53	49	65	80
Third	51	59	57	99

Fig. 3. The graph presents the percentage of robots in the biggest cluster at the end of the trial for each group of untrained participants (BBB and VBB). The performance of all baselines and the average performance in the last three trials of trained and expert participants are plotted as lines to provide a reference performance. The table presents the percentage of robots in the biggest cluster at the end of the trials with human participants.

Throughout all trials, the robots' positions and the participant's interactions through the interface were recorded.

4 Results

4.1 Performance Metrics and Baseline Performance

The main performance metric is the number of robots in the largest cluster. A pair of robots is considered in close proximity if the distance between their centers is less than 15 cm. We consider two robots that are in close proximity to belong to the same cluster. Moreover, if $\{a, b\}$ belong to the same cluster and $\{b, c\}$ belong to the same cluster, then the same holds true for $\{a, c\}$.

We establish the following baselines for comparison:

– *No Interaction*: This is the performance of the swarm in the absence of any interaction with an operator. In other words, each robot of the swarm executes the aggregation algorithm for the entire duration of the trial.
– *No Walls or Interactions*: This is the performance of the swarm when aggregating in the absence of wall obstructions and interactions with an operator. These represent the ideal conditions for the algorithm as presented in [6].
– *Random Interactions*: This is the performance of the swarm when interacting with a virtual operator agent choosing random commands drawn from a distribution that models the average participant across all trials.

For each of the baseline performance measures, 10 trials of 600 s were conducted. The table in Fig. 3 shows the average size of the biggest cluster at the end of the trial. Random commands resulted in slightly better performance than no interactions but with a larger standard deviation.

4.2 Operator Performance

We compared the performance of untrained, trained and expert operators to the baseline performance. Figure 3 presents this comparison where untrained operators with access to real-time global state information of the position of all robots (trial 1 for group VBB) aggregate 90 % of robots and perform as well as the 'no walls or interactions' baseline. This validates the efficacy of the swarm controls available to the operator. Operators were able to use the available controls to mitigate the shortcomings of the aggregation algorithm in the presence of obstacles.

Untrained participants in their final trial aggregated 51 % (BBB) or 59 % (VBB) of robots into a single cluster, an improvement over the no interactions baseline that aggregated 42 % (two-sided Mann–Whitney test, p-values = 0.049 and 0.029). The blind trials of both groups of untrained operators (trials 1, 2 and 3 for BBB and trials 2 and 3 for VBB) did not perform significantly better than the random interaction baseline (two-sided Mann–Whitney test, p-values = 0.985 and 0.481). Note that the proportion of the types of instructions is identical but the random interactions baseline does obviously not exploit any sensory information. This suggests that operators have similar difficulties in exploiting local sensory information.

A comparison between the blind trials of BBB and VBB shows no significant differences in performance (two-sided Mann–Whitney test, p-values = 0.215). This suggests a minimal learning effect of the initial trial with global state information. It further supports the conclusion that operator performance in blind trials was diminished due to a lack of situational awareness rather than lack of planning. If it were due to a lack of planning the trial with global state information would be expected to have facilitated the learning of plans.

Trained and expert operators were able to obtain significantly improved performance in their three trials over the random interactions baseline (two-sided Mann–Whitney test, p-values = 0.029 and 0.001). They aggregated 57–69 % and 76–99 % of robots respectively.

In summary, the results show a dramatic drop in performance of untrained operators when removing access to global state information, with performance on par with a random agent. The recovery of performance for trained and expert operators shows that learning does occur and warrants a closer look, in the following section, at the actions and strategies that are being learned.

4.3 Interaction Analysis

A detailed history of the operators' actions was recorded throughout all trials. The data is grouped into three categories: (i) the operator moves the robot, (ii) the operator uses the robot's sensors and (iii) the operator switches between algorithms. Figure 4a shows the distribution of time spent on these activities for the last three trials for untrained, trained and expert operators.

As expected, untrained operators with access to global state information (trial 1 in group VBB) rarely request local sensory information and instead

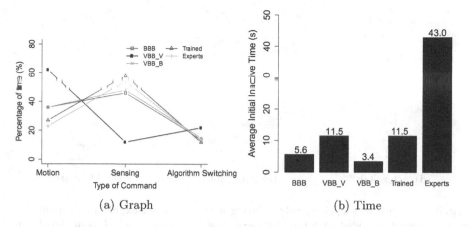

(a) Graph   (b) Time

Fig. 4. (a) Percentage of time spent with type of command. (b) Average initial inactive time.

move the robots and switch algorithms more frequently. Untrained operators in the blind trials, however, spend a larger proportion on obtaining sensor information to recover some situational awareness. The key observation is found by comparing trained and expert operators to untrained operators.

The improved performance of the later seems to rely on more requests for sensor observations while reducing the amount of time spent moving the robots. The time spent switching algorithms is identical between all groups. Given that the time spent on motion commands is significantly less for trained and expert operators than for untrained operators with global state information, the efficiency of the motion commands for the former group was higher. This is likely where the training effect materializes.

In addition to varying the time spent on certain activities we observed a difference in the initial interactions with the swarm, that is, the time the operators waited at the beginning of the trials before performing the first interaction. Figure 4b show the average time that operators waited at the beginning of the trials. This period of inactivity allows the swarm to exhibit local aggregation behavior and form small clusters within parts of the environment. These clusters may be controlled more effectively than dispersed robots. Operators that interact with the swarm too early may disturb this process and have hence less effective subsequent interactions. This suggests evidence for the concept of neglect benevolence in these experiments that is being learned and exploited by trained and expert operators. It is worth noting that untrained participants with access to global state information also increase their initial period of inactivity while observing the global dynamics, yet they do not repeat this in subsequent blind trials.

To illustrate the above more qualitatively, Fig. 5(a–f) shows a sequence of snapshots taken from an example trial. The initial positions of the robots are randomly distributed through the arena (a). Because of the aggregation

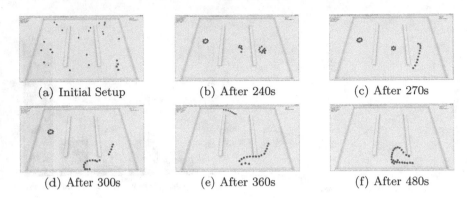

(a) Initial Setup   (b) After 240s   (c) After 270s

(d) After 300s   (e) After 360s   (f) After 480s

Fig. 5. Sequence of snapshots taken during a trial with an expert participant. The expert was not provided with the bird's-eye view of the scene, which is depicted here.

algorithm, the robots start grouping and form three clusters (b). The operator then starts moving the right cluster to the center area (c). The operator finds the third cluster and guides it to the center area (d). Again, when the robots are in visual range, they attempt to group together (e). Finally, the operator is monitoring the process until the swarm reports a complete aggregation of the swarm (f).

5   Conclusions and Future Work

This study investigated a distributed human-swarm interaction scheme in which operators have access to only local information when aiding a swarm in an aggregation task. Operators had access to swarm controls with which they were able to complete the aggregation task successfully when given global state information. When given only local information, however, untrained operators did not perform significantly better than random interactions. Nor did they exhibit a significant learning effect within three trials. Furthermore, operators that once were given global state information did not demonstrate improved performance on subsequent trials when being restricted to local information. This suggests no learning benefit from having observed the global dynamics once.

Trained and expert operators, with at least one hour of training, showed significantly improved performance suggesting the task is solvable. These operators compensated the lack in global situational awareness with increased requests for local sensory information while reducing the number of motion commands. Expert operators performed nearly as well as the baseline performance of the autonomous algorithm under ideal conditions, that is, without obstructions.

In addition, we observed evidence for neglect benevolence for trained and expert operators. These operators waited at the beginning of the trial for the swarm to converge to the emergent local clusters. From this configuration, interactions with the swarm were more beneficial as emerging clusters could be changed into leader-follower formations more easily. Untrained operators disturbed and interacted with the swarm prior to it settling into local clusters.

Overall, our findings suggest that exposure to global swarm dynamics does not necessarily accelerate learning, neither for improving situational awareness nor for understanding swarm dynamics to accommodate for neglect benevolence. In addition, learning to interact with a swarm through a distributed interaction scheme that relies on local information requires training times even for simple tasks and interfaces. This should inform future research on human-swarm interaction.

Simulation experiments, however, only offer a limited potential to validate human-swarm interaction schemes as they simulate simplified dynamics. Future work is planned to investigate the interaction scheme with physical robots and a wider range of tasks. This will answer whether the presented findings generalize to other scenarios and whether the dynamics of physical robots interfere with successful human-swarm interaction.

Acknowledgments. The first author acknowledges scholarship support by Consejo Nacional de Ciencia y Tecnologia (CONACYT). All authors thank the students of The University of Sheffield who volunteered to participate in the experiment.

References

1. Alonso-Mora, J., Haegeli Lohaus, S., Leemann, P., Siegwart, R., Beardsley, P.: Gesture based human-multi-robot swarm interaction and its application to an interactive display. In: Proceedings of 2015 IEEE International Conference on Robotics and Automation (ICRA 2015), pp. 5948–5953. IEEE (2015)
2. Barca, J.C., Sekercioglu, Y.A.: Swarm robotics reviewed. Robotica **31**(03), 345–359 (2013)
3. Bashyal, S., Venayagamoorthy, G.K.: Human swarm interaction for radiation source search and localization. In: Proceedings of 2008 IEEE Swarm Intelligence Symposium (SIS 2008), pp. 1–8. IEEE (2008)
4. Brambilla, M., Ferrante, E., Birattari, M., Dorigo, M.: Swarm robotics: a review from the swarm engineering perspective. Swarm Intell. **7**(1), 1–41 (2013)
5. Brown, D.S., Kerman, S.C., Goodrich, M.A.: Limited bandwidth recognition of collective behaviors in bio-inspired swarms. In: Proceedings of 13th International Conference on Autonomous Agents and Multiagent Systems (AAMAS 2014), pp. 405–412 (2014)
6. Gauci, M., Chen, J., Li, W., Dodd, T.J., Groß, R.: Self-organized aggregation without computation. Int. J. Robot. Res. **33**(8), 1145–1161 (2014)
7. Goodrich, M.A., Pendleton, B., Kerman, S., Sujit, P.: What types of interactions do bio-inspired robot swarms and flocks afford a human? In: Proceedings of 2013 Robotics: Science and Systems (RSS VIII), pp. 105–112. MIT Press (2013)
8. Kolling, A., Walker, P., Chakraborty, N., Sycara, K., Lewis, M.: Human interaction with robot swarms: a survey. IEEE Trans. Hum. Mach. Syst. **PP**(99), 1–18 (2015)
9. Krause, J., Ruxton, G.D., Krause, S.: Swarm intelligence in animals and humans. Trends Ecol. Evol. **25**(1), 28–34 (2010)
10. Magnenat, S.: Laboratory of Intelligent Systems, EPFL, Lausanne: Enki reference documentation (2005). http://lis2.epfl.ch/resources/download/doc1.0/libenki/. Accessed 25 Aug 2015

11. Manning, M.D., Harriott, C.E., Hayes, S.T., Adams, J.A., Seiffert, A.E.: Heuristic evaluation of swarm metrics' effectiveness. In: Proceedings of Tenth Annual ACM/IEEE International Conference on Human-Robot Interaction (HRI 2015), pp. 17–18. ACM (2015)
12. Mondada, F., Bonani, M., Raemy, X., Pugh, J., Cianci, C., Klaptocz, A., Magnenat, S., Zufferey, J.C., Floreano, D., Martinoli, A.: The e-puck, a robot designed for education in engineering. In: Proceedings of 9th Conference on Autonomous Robot Systems and Competitions, vol. 1, pp. 59–65 (2009)
13. Nagavalli, S., Chien, S.Y., Lewis, M., Chakraborty, N., Sycara, K.: Bounds of neglect benevolence in input timing for human interaction with robotic swarms. In: Proceedings of 10th Annual ACM/IEEE International Conference on Human-Robot Interaction (HRI 2015), pp. 197–204. ACM (2015)
14. Nunnally, S., Walker, P., Kolling, A., Chakraborty, N., Lewis, M., Sycara, K., Goodrich, M.: Human influence of robotic swarms with bandwidth and localization issues. In: Proceedings of 2012 IEEE International Conference on Systems, Man, and Cybernetics (SMC 2012), pp. 333–338. IEEE (2012)
15. Olsen, D.R., Goodrich, M.A.: Metrics for evaluating human-robot interactions. In: Proceedings of 2003 Workshop on Performance Metrics for Intelligent Systems (PerMIS 2013), vol. 2003, p. 5 (2003)
16. Salomons, N., Kapellmann-Zafra, G., Groß, R.: Human management of a robotic swarm. In: Alboul, L., Damian, D., Aitken, J.M. (eds.) TAROS 2016. LNCS, vol. 9716, pp. 282–287. Springer, Heidelberg (2016). doi:10.1007/978-3-319-40379-3_29
17. Setter, T., Fouraker, A., Kawashima, H., Egerstedt, M.: Haptic interactions with multi-robot swarms using manipulability. J. Hum. Robot Inter. 4(1), 60–74 (2015)
18. Walker, P., Amirpour Amraii, S., Chakraborty, N., Lewis, M., Sycara, K.: Human control of robot swarms with dynamic leaders. In: Proceedings of 2014 IEEE/RSJ International Conference on Intelligent Robots and Systems (IROS 2014), pp. 1108–1113. IEEE (2014)
19. Walker, P., Nunnally, S., Lewis, M., Kolling, A., Chakraborty, N., Sycara, K.: Neglect benevolence in human control of swarms in the presence of latency. In: Proceedings of 2012 IEEE International Conference on Systems, Man, and Cybernetics (SMC 2012), pp. 3009–3014. IEEE (2012)

Monotonicity in Ant Colony Classification Algorithms

James Brookhouse[✉] and Fernando E.B. Otero

School of Computing, University of Kent, Chatham Maritime, UK
{jb765,F.E.B.Otero}@kent.ac.uk

Abstract. Classification algorithms generally do not use existing domain knowledge during model construction. The creation of models that conflict with existing knowledge can reduce model acceptance, as users have to trust the models they use. Domain knowledge can be integrated into algorithms using semantic constraints to guide model construction. This paper proposes an extension to an existing ACO-based classification rule learner to create lists of monotonic classification rules. The proposed algorithm was compared to a majority classifier and the Ordinal Learning Model (OLM) monotonic learner. Our results show that the proposed algorithm successfully outperformed OLM's predictive accuracy while still producing monotonic models.

Keywords: Ant colony optimization · Semantic constraints · Monotonic · Data mining · Classification rules · Sequential covering

1 Introduction

Data mining is a research area focused on automating the search for useful patterns in data [6], where classification is one of the most studied tasks. A classification problem involves a set of examples, where each example is described by predictor attribute values and associated with a target class value. The goal of a classification algorithm is to find the best model that accurately represents the relationships between predictor and class attribute values, and therefore classification problems can be viewed as optimisation problems. Many algorithms concentrate on producing accurate models, however while accuracy is an important feature other properties of a model are also important, including a model's comprehensibility and its ability to preserve pre-existing domain knowledge. Both of these features can aid the acceptance of a model amongst its users who are normally experts in the domain being investigated.

Existing domain knowledge can be captured by semantic constraints, which can then be used to guide the construction of models. Algorithms that build models able to break these relationships can lead to increased model rejection by domain experts due to their counter intuitiveness [9]. One form of semantic constraints are monotonic constraints, which concern the sign of a relation between the predictor and target attributes. A problem that illustrates monotonic properties is house rental prices as it is expected that as the size of a house increases

© Springer International Publishing Switzerland 2016
M. Dorigo et al. (Eds.): ANTS 2016, LNCS 9882, pp. 137–148, 2016.
DOI: 10.1007/978-3-319-44427-7_12

so will its rental price—i.e., there is an increasing monotonic relation between size and rental price within the same location.

We investigate a strategy to add domain knowledge to the learning process of an Ant Colony Optimization (ACO) [4] classification rule learner to produce models that are both accurate and enforce monotonic constraints. We evaluate the impact of the proposed strategy on predictive accuracy and compare the results against an existing monotonic learner using publicly available data sets.

The rest of the paper is structured as follows. Firstly, Sect. 2 presents work from the literature that has been completed in related areas. Section 3 discusses the changes to cAnt-Miner$_{PB}$ allowing the enforcement of constraints. Next, Sect. 4 presents our computational results including a comparison with another monotonic learner, followed up by our conclusions and suggestions on possible future directions in Sect. 5.

2   Background

There are two main areas of related work, ACO-based classification rule learners and semantic constraints. First we will discuss existing sequential covering classification rule learners including the ACO-based Ant-Miner and its extensions. This will be followed by a summary of the literature surround semantic constraints, including monotonic constraints—the focus of this paper. Finally, we will discuss AntMiner+ in more detail, since it is an ACO-based classification rule learner that incorporates monotonic constraints.

2.1   Ant Colony Classification Algorithms

One of the most popular strategies for creating a list of classification rules from a given dataset is called *sequential covering* (or *separate-and-conquer*) [8]. It consists in transforming the problem of creating a list of rules into smaller problems of creating a single rule: (1) a single rule is created from the data (*conquer* step); (2) data instances that are covered by the rule are removed from the training data (*separate* step); these steps are repeated until the training data is empty or the number of uncovered data instances falls below a pre-defined threshold. Many rule induction algorithms follow the same separate-and-conquer strategy, their main difference is the way that individual rules are learn. In this context, ACO has been successfully applied to create classification rules.

The first ACO classification algorithm, called Ant-Miner, was proposed in [15]. Ant-Miner follows a sequential covering strategy, where individual rules are created by an ACO procedure. The main idea is to search for the best classification rule given the current training data at each iteration of the sequential covering. Ants traverse a construction graph selecting terms to create a rule in the form IF term$_1$ AND ... AND term$_n$ THEN class, where the IF-part represents the antecedent and the THEN-part is the class prediction. Each ant starts with an empty rule and iteratively selects terms to add to its partial rule based on their values of the amount of pheromone τ and a problem-dependent heuristic information η, similarly to Ant System (AS) [3]. Following on Ant-Miner's success, many extensions have been proposed in the literature [13]: they involve different rule pruning and pheromone update procedures, new rule quality measures and ~~l~~~~i~~~~m~~~~i~~~~t~~~~t~~~~i~~~~o~~~~n~~ ~~o~~~~f~~ ~~e~~~~x~~~~t~~~~e~~~~n~~~~s~~~~i~~~~o~~~~n~~~~s~~ ~~t~~~~h~~~~a~~~~t~~ ~~h~~~~a~~~~v~~~~e~~ ~~b~~~~e~~~~e~~~~n~~ ~~p~~~~r~~~~o~~~~p~~~~o~~~~s~~~~e~~~~d~~. Here are two Ant-Miner extensions relevant to this work, AntMiner+ [12] and cAnt-Miner$_{PB}$ [14].

AntMiner+ extends Ant-Miner in several aspects: (1) the complexity of the construction graph is reduced, in term of the number of edges connecting vertices, by defining it as a direct acyclic graph (DAG); (2) it makes a distinction between nominal attributes with categorical and ordered values, where ordinal attributes are used to create interval conditions; (3) the class value to be predicted and weight parameters used to control the influence of the pheromone and heuristic information are incorporated in the construction graph as vertices.

One potential drawback of using a sequential covering to create a list of rules is that there is no guarantee that the best list of rules is created. Ant-Miner (and the majority of its extensions) perform a greedy search for the list of best rules, using an ACO procedure to search for the best rule given a set of examples, and it is highly dependant on the order that rules are created. Therefore, they are limited to creating the *list of best rules*, which does not necessarily corresponds to the *best list of rules*. cAnt-Miner$_{PB}$ is an ACO classification algorithm that employs an improved sequential covering strategy to search for the best list of classification rules [14]. While Ant-Miner uses an ACO procedure to create individual rules in a one-at-a-time (sequential covering) fashion, cAnt-Miner$_{PB}$ employs an ACO procedure to create a complete list of rules. Therefore, it can search and optimise the quality of a complete list of rules instead of individual rules—i.e., it is not concerned by the quality of the individual rules as long as the quality of the entire list of rules is improving.

2.2 Semantic Constraints

When existing domain knowledge is available, semantic constraints can incorporate this knowledge into the construction of new models. For example, if you consider house rent the price can/will depend on the location and floor area. Table 1 shows a simple hypothetical rental dataset. One relationship in this data set is that houses in better locations (lower values of attribute *Location*) increases its rental price. This is the case for all possible pairs in the data set.

Model rejection by domain experts is a possibility if a model does not preserve existing patterns as it would seem counter intuitive. Hoover and Perez [9] state that the economic field scepticism towards data mining as a technique to search for models is due to the discovery of accidental correlations: *"Data mining is considered reprehensible largely because the world is full of accidental correlations, so that what a search turns up is thought to be more a reflection of what we want to find than what is true about the world."* [9, p. 197]. Semantic constraints allow model construction to be guided by providing information on real correlations present within the data. While there are a number of different semantic

Table 1. Simple house rental data set.

Target attribute	Predictor attributes	
Rental value	Floor area	Location
Medium	45	2
High	80	1
Low	33	3
Medium	65	2

constraint types, we explore the implementation of monotonic constraints in the discovery of classification rules.

2.3   Monotonicity

Monotonicity is found in many different fields including house/rental prices, medicine, finance and law. Looking at the first example of rental prices, it can be expected that as the location of a property becomes better (lower value of *Location*) its rental value will also increase—this can be seen in the example data shown in Table 1. The majority of data mining algorithm are not monotonically aware and do not enforce this relationship during model construction, yet still produce good models. However, if models violate these constraints they may not be accepted by experts as valid, and therefore, conforming to monotonicity constraints may help improve model acceptance [5,7].

Monotonicity can be defined formally in the following manner. Let $\mathcal{X} = \mathcal{X}_1 \times \mathcal{X}_2 \times \cdots \times \mathcal{X}_i$ be the instance space of i attributes, $\mathcal{Y}$ be the target space, and function $f : \mathcal{X} \to \mathcal{Y}$. It is also assumed that both the instance space and target space have an ordering. A function can then be considered monotone if:

$$\forall \mathbf{x}, \mathbf{x}' \in \mathcal{X} : \mathbf{x} \leq \mathbf{x}' \implies f(\mathbf{x}) \leq f(\mathbf{x}'), \tag{1}$$

where $\mathbf{x}$ and $\mathbf{x}'$ are two vectors in instance space, $\mathbf{x} = (x_1, x_2, \cdots, x_i)$ [16]. In other words, $f(\mathbf{x})$ is monotonic if and only if all the pairs of examples $\mathbf{x}, \mathbf{x}'$ are monotonic with respect to each other.

Monotonicity can be enforced in a number of different stages in the data mining process. The first is in the *pre-processing stage*, training data is manipulated so that the required attributes are monotonic with respect to the dependent attribute. Since this method is unable to enforce constraints in the model, it will be discussed no further. In the *model construction stage* the model construction algorithm creates monotonic models, possibly constraining the search. Finally, constraints can be enforced in a *post-processing stage* via the modification of constructed models to enforce monotonic constraints.

Constraints also appear in two different forms hard or soft. Hard constraints are enforced rigidly and will reject any new model or change to an existing model that would cause a violation. Good models can be rejected due to small violations in their monotonicity when this method is used. The second method, soft constraints, balances the monotonicity of a model against the models quality, allowing small violations to exist if they sufficiently increase the quality.

Model Construction. Soft constraints have been implemented in the model construction stage by Ben-David [1]. Ben-David assigns a non-monotonicity index to each tree produced. This index is the ratio between the number of non-monotonic leaf node pairs and the maximum number of pairs that could have been non-monotonic. First a non-monotonicity matrix m is constructed which has dimensions k (the number of branches in the tree). This matrix is used to find the number of violations in the current tree, given by:

$$W = \sum_{i=1}^{k} \sum_{j=1}^{k} m_{ij}, \text{ where } m_{ij} = \begin{cases} 1 & \text{, if } ij \text{ is non-monotonic} \\ 0 & \text{, otherwise} \end{cases}, \tag{2}$$

where i and j denote the current cell being referenced in the matrix. W can then be used to find a tree's non-monotonicity index, given by:

$$I_{a_1...a_v} = \frac{W_{a_1...a_v}}{k_{a_1...a_v}^2 - k_{a_1...a_v}}, \tag{3}$$

where $a_1...a_v$ are the constrained attributes with v being the total number of constrained attributes, the $I_{a_1...a_v}$ index can be converted to an ambiguity score A and then incorporated with a tree accuracy score T, given by:

$$A_{a_1...a_v} = \begin{cases} 0 & \text{, if } I_{a_1...a_v} = 0 \\ -(log_2(I_{a_1...a_v}))^{-1} & \text{, otherwise} \end{cases}, \tag{4}$$

$$T_{a_1...a_v} = E_{a_1...a_v} + R A_{a_1...a_v}, \tag{5}$$

where R is the importance given to the monotonicity of trees produced and E is an error based measure, usually the accuracy. The accuracy of the models produced were not significantly degraded compared to the original algorithm, however the combined metric did produce fewer models that breached the monotonicity constraints [1].

Ben-David has also investigated monotonic ordinal classifiers, proposing the hypothesis that adding monotonicity constraints to learning algorithms will impair their accuracy against those that do not. Ordinal classifiers are classifiers that allow discrete categories to have an order, for example credit rating has an obvious order if the categories are poor, acceptable and good. There were two unexpected results. It was found that ordinal classifiers did not significantly improve their accuracy over non-ordinal classifiers. Secondly, the monotonic algorithms were not able to significantly outperform a simple majority-based classifier. It is theorised that these results were due to noisy data sets: the monotonic classifiers enforced hard constraints, in the presence of noisy data a softer approach may lead to better results [2]. The algorithms also enforce constraints on all attributes, which may be unrealistic for real data sets as monotonically noisy attributes or those with no trend may masque the true monotonic attributes.

Qian et al. [17] have explored the possibility of fusing monotonic decision trees to improve the accuracy of the final model. This is achieved by reducing the original data set to create sets that maintain the monotonicity of the original. From these new reduced data sets, monotonic trees can be constructed. Each leaf node of a reduced tree then contain probabilities of the correctness of the prediction based on the training set. When a prediction is required, the probabilities at each tree's leaf nodes is averaged with the highest average being the class predicted by the model.

Post-processing. Feelders [7] has suggested that using non-monotonic criteria in tree construction is not beneficial as splits later in the construction process can transform a tree from a state of non-monotonicity to one that is. Therefore, Feelders has suggested several pruning methods to make the minimal number of changes to make a tree monotonic in a post-processing phase [7].

The first proposed pruner is the Most Non-monotone Parent (MNP) method, which aims to prune the node that gives the most number of monotone pairs. This method has the disadvantage of possibly creating more non-monotonic pairs than it removes leading to a net increase in non-monotonicity. The second method proposed is the best fix method, which prunes the node that gives the biggest reduction in non-monotonicity. While it solves the problem with the first pruner, it is more computationally expensive. The authors have also combined these pruning methods with existing complexity pruning methods and found that the monotonic trees produced no significant difference in performance compared to trees produced without monotonic pruning. However, it was observed that the trees produced were smaller, which aids the comprehensibility of the models produced further [7].

2.4   AntMiner+ with Monotonicity Constraints

As far as we are aware, the only implementation of an ACO that discovers monotonic classification rules was proposed by Martens et al. [11], who modified AntMiner+ to enforce hard and soft monotonic constraints. The basic idea is to limit the solution space by either removing nodes in the construction graph or manipulating the heuristic values of vertices. In the first approach, authors modified the construction graph by removing nodes, and subsequently closing off those areas of the search space, that could be used to create non-monotonic rules (hard constraints). This algorithm was applied to the binary classification problem of classifying customers as good or bad credit risks, where the algorithm could only create rules that predicted bad customers. For example, if there is a monotonic constraint on income, nodes corresponding to $income > x$ are removed leaving only those that express $income < x$, which will always produce monotonic rules when discovering the (negative) bad credit class. In the second approach, the heuristic value of a node that is monotonically related to the predicted class is adjusted to incorporate this preference, although they did not include experiments verifying how effective this would be.

It was found that AntMiner+ with hard constraints consistently produced rule lists that contained less rules and less terms per rule, when compared to the original algorithm without impacting the accuracy of the model produced. The comprehensibility of the models produced would be increased by the reduced model size [11]. While their results were positive overall, their approach seem to be limited to binary classification problems: the algorithm creates rules for the minority (bad credit) class, while a default rule predicts the majority (good credit) class; removal of conditions is based on a particular class value to be predicted and it is not clear how the removal of nodes can be used to enforce constraints in multi-class problems. Additionally, it has the side effect of limiting the search space of solutions, not taking into account that monotonicity is a global property [7] and a partial non-monotone rule might become monotone after additional conditions.

3   Discovering Monotonic Classification Rules

In this section we will provide an overview of cAnt-Miner$_{PB}$ and the modifications to the pruning strategies present in the proposed cAnt-Miner$_{PB+MC}$ (Pittsburgh-based cAnt-Miner with monotonicity constraints).

3.1 cAntMiner$_{PB}$ with Monotonicity Constraints

As we discussed in Sect. 2.1, cAnt-Miner$_{PB}$ is an ACO classification algorithm that employs an improved sequential covering strategy to search for the best list of classification rules. In summary, cAnt-Miner$_{PB}$ works as follows (Fig. 1). Each ant starts with an empty list of rules and iteratively adds a new rule to this list (*for loop*). In order to create a rule, an ant adds one term at a time to the rule antecedent by choosing terms to be added to the current partial rule based on the amount of pheromone (τ) and a problem-dependent heuristic information (η). Once a rule is created, it undergoes a pruning procedure. Pruning aims at removing irrelevant terms that might be added to a rule due to the stochastic nature of the construction process: it starts by removing the last term that was added to the rule and the removal process is repeated until the rule quality decreases when the last term is removed or the rule has only one term left. Finally, the rule it is added to current list of rules and the training examples covered by the rule are removed.[1] An ant creates rules until the number of uncovered examples is below a pre-defined threshold (inner *while loop*).

At the end of an iteration, when all ants have created a list of rules, the best list of rules (determined by an error-based list quality function) is used to update pheromone values, providing a positive feedback on the terms present

---

[1] An example is covered by a rule when it satisfies all terms (attribute-value conditions) in the antecedent of the rule.

Input: training instances
Output: best discovered list of rules
1. *InitialisePheromones();*
2. $list_{gb} \leftarrow \{\}$;
3. $t \leftarrow 0$;
4. **while** t < maximum iterations **and** not stagnation **do**
5. $list_{ib} \leftarrow \{\}$;
6.   **for** n $\leftarrow$ 1 **to** colony_size **do**
7.   *instances $\leftarrow$ all training instances;*
8. $list_n \leftarrow \{\}$;
9.   **while** $|instances|$ > maximum uncovered **do**
10.   *ComputeHeuristicInformation(instances);*
11. $rule \leftarrow CreateRule(instances)$;
12.   *SoftPruner(rule, $list_n$);*
13.   *examples $\leftarrow$ instances − Covered(rule, instances);*
14. $list_n \leftarrow list_n + rule$;
15.   **end while**
16.   **if** $Quality(list_n) > Quality(list_{ib})$ **then**
17. $list_{ib} \leftarrow list_n$;
18.   **end if**
19.   **end for**
20. $UpdatePheromones(list_{ib})$;
21.   **if** $Quality(list_{ib}) > Quality(list_{gb})$ **then**
22. $list_{gb} \leftarrow list_{ib}$;
23.   **end if**
24. $t \leftarrow t + 1$;
25. **end while**
26. *HardPruner($list_{gb}$);*
27. **return** $list_{gb}$;

Fig. 1. High-level pseudocode of the *c*Ant-Miner$_{PB+MC}$ algorithm. The main differences compared to *c*Ant-Miner$_{PB}$ [14] are found on lines 12, 16 and 26.

in the rules—the higher the pheromone value of a term, the more likely it will be chosen to create a rule. This iterative process is repeated until a maximum number of iterations is reached or until the search stagnates (outer *while loop*).

One of the main differences in *c*Ant-Miner$_{PB}$, when compared to other ACO classification algorithms, is that an ant creates a list of rules. Therefore, the ACO search is guided by and optimises the quality of a complete solution. Additionally, there is also the possibility of applying local search operators to the complete solution—e.g., a pruning procedure is an example of a local search operator. This is currently not explored in *c*Ant-Miner$_{PB}$, since pruning is applied to individual rules and not to the entire list of rules.

*c*Ant-Miner$_{PB+MC}$ is modified in three key places compared to the original *c*Ant-Miner$_{PB}$. The first change is a modification to the pruning method (line 12 of Fig. 1): this pruner is a soft pruner that balances monotonicity against accuracy. This modified quality is then used to update the pheromone levels ready for the next iteration. The second modification is the addition of a hard prune that rigidly enforces the monotonic constraints, this occurs immediately before the rule list is returned (line 26). Both pruners are explained in more detailing in the following section. The final modification is to the list quality function (line 16), this quality now uses both accuracy and NMI combined with a weighting term when assigning a quality measure to the list and comparing it to the best so far. This is the same function that is used in the soft pruner and shown by Eqs. 6 and 7.

3.2   Rule Pruning

There are two pruners used by $cAnt\text{-}Miner_{PB+MC}$: soft pruner that may allow constraint violations and a hard pruning that guarantees constraints are satisfied. In ACO terms, a pruner is a local search operator.

Soft Pruning. A soft monotonic prune allows violations in the monotonic constraint if the consequent improvement in accuracy is large enough. The pruner operates on an individual rule and iteratively removes the last term until no improvement in the rule quality is observed. Applying a soft pruner during model creation allows the search to be guided towards monotonic models while still allowing exploration of the search space.

As monotonicity is a global property of the model, the rule being pruned is temporarily added to the current list of rules, its non-monotonicity index (NMI) can then be used as a metric to assess the rules monotonicity and is given by:

$$NMI = \frac{\sum_{i=1}^{k} \sum_{j=1}^{k} m_{ij}}{k^2 - k}, \qquad (6)$$

where m_{ij} is 1 if the pair of rules $rule_i$ and $rule_j$ violate the constraint and 0 otherwise. k is the number of rules in the model. The NMI of a model is constrained between zero and one: it calculates the ratio of monotonic violating pairs over the total possible number of prediction pairs present in the model being tested, the lower a NMI is the better a model is considered. If this is the first rule in the partial model it will be automatically designated monotonic and be assigned a non-monotonicity Index of zero. The NMI is then incorporated into the quality metric by:

$$Q = (1 - \omega) \cdot Accuracy + \omega \cdot (1 - NMI), \qquad (7)$$

where Q is the quality of a model and ω is an adjustable weighting that sets the importance of monotonicity and accuracy to the overall rule quality. Note that Eq. 7 can be used to calculate the quality of either a single rule (used during the soft pruner) or a complete list of rules (line 16 of Fig. 1).

Hard Pruning. The hard monotonic pruner enforces the monotonic constraints rigidly. It operates on a list of rules as follows: (1) the NMI of a list is first calculated (Eq. 6); (2) if it is non zero, the last term of the final rule is removed or, if the rule contains no terms, the rule is removed; (3) the NMI is then recalculated for the modified list of rules. This is repeated until the NMI of the rule list is zero. Finally the default rule is added to the end of the list if it has been removed and the new monotonic rule list is returned.

4   Results

cAnt-Miner$_{PB+MC}$ has been compared to a majority classifier (ZeroR [18]), the original cAnt-Miner$_{PB}$ and a modified OLM [2]. The original OLM algorithm constrained all attributes, however our modified OLM constrains a single attribute to allow a fair comparison between the algorithms. The decision to only constrain a single attribute is more realistic to real world applications as it is unlikely that a monotonic relationship is present for every attribute. Forcing a relationship upon an algorithm is likely to negatively impact its performance.

In all experiments cAnt-Miner variations were configured with a colony size of 5 ants, 500 iterations, minimum cases covered by an individual rule of 10, uncovered instance ratio of 0.01, and constraint weighting (ω) of 0.5 (only used by cAnt-Miner$_{PB+MC}$). The four chosen algorithms were tested on five data sets taken from the UCI Machine Learning Repository [10]. Table 2 present the details of the chosen data sets, including a summary of the constraints used. All independent attributes had their NMI calculated to discover good monotonic relationships—the NMI results guided the choice of constrained attribute reported in the table.

Table 3 shows the predictive accuracy of all algorithms on the 5 data sets, with standard deviation shown in brackets. All results are the average of tenfold cross-validation, with the stochastic ACO-based algorithms running 5 times[2] on each fold to average out random differences.

The results show that cAnt-Miner$_{PB+MC}$ outperformed the majority classifier in every data set. OLM and the original cAnt-Miner$_{PB}$ implementation were beaten by cAnt-Miner$_{PB+MC}$ in four of the five data sets. The good performance of cAnt-Miner$_{PB+MC}$ compared to cAnt-Miner$_{PB}$ is very positive: it shows that using a pruning mechanism to enforce monotonic constraints does not affect the search process and the algorithm is able to create monotonic classification rules with good predictive accuracy

We further analysed the results of OLM and cAnt-Miner$_{PB+MC}$—both algorithms that enforce monotonic constraints—for statistical significance: cAnt-Miner$_{PB+MC}$ achieved statistically significantly better results than OLM in 3 out of 5 datasets, according to the Wilcoxon test with a significance level of 0.05. cAntMiner$_{PB+MC}$ enforces monotonic constraints on the entire list of rules, allowing global optimisation of monotonicity. OLM performs a local optimisation

---

[2] ACO-based algorithms therefore run a total of 50 times before the average is taken.

Table 2. The five UCI [10] data sets used in experiments including attribute and constraint information. The constraints information contain the attribute name, direction of constraint either ↑ (increasing) or ↓ (decreasing) and its corresponding NMI.

Name	Size	Attributes		Constraint		
		Nominal	Continuous	Constrained attribute	Direction	NMI
Cancer	698	0	10	Uniformity of Cell Size	↑	0.0059
Car	1727	6	0	Safety	↑	0.0460
Haberman	305	0	3	Positive Axillary Nodes	↑	0.0861
MPG	397	0	7	Horsepower	↓	0.0566
Pima	767	0	8	Plasma Glucose Conc.	↑	0.0947

Table 3. Accuracy results for the four algorithms being tested, the accuracy is based on the average of 10 cross-validation runs with the standard deviation shown in brackets. The datasets where cAnt-Miner$_{PB+MC}$'s performance is statistically significantly better than OLM (according to the Wilcoxon test with a significance level of 0.05) are marked with the symbol ▲; if no symbol is shown, no significant difference was observed. The best results are shown in boldface.

Data set	ZeroR	cAnt-Miner$_{PB}$	OLM	cAnt-Miner$_{PB+MC}$
Cancer	0.6552 [0.0156]	**0.9566 [0.0181]**	0.8355 [0.0149]	0.9554 [0.0178] ▲
Car	0.7002 [0.0201]	0.8929 [0.0151]	**0.9055 [0.0187]**	0.8954 [0.0154]
Haberman	0.7353 [0.0985]	0.7405 [0.0790]	0.6993 [0.0781]	**0.7552 [0.0664]** ▲
MPG	0.7286 [0.0542]	0.9200 [0.0293]	0.7663 [0.0367]	**0.9240 [0.0353]** ▲
Pima	0.6510 [0.0420]	0.7493 [0.0564]	0.7161 [0.0589]	**0.7599 [0.0640]**

as a rule cannot be added to the current list if it was to break the monotonicity of existing rules. This observation, together with the use of an ACO search strategy that aims at optimising both the accuracy and monotonicity of a model, are likely to account for the increased performance of cAnt-Miner$_{PB+MC}$ over OLM.

5   Conclusions

This paper presented an extension to cAnt-Miner$_{PB}$ that enforces monotonic constraints, called cAnt-Miner$_{PB+MC}$. This is achieved by modifying the pruning strategies used during solution construction: soft constraints are used to modify the quality of rules and this their pheromone levels; hard constraints were then enforced by a global pruner operating on the entire list of rules. Monotonicity is a global property of a data set, therefore the creation of complete list of rules rather than individual rules allows cAnt-Miner$_{PB+MC}$ to optimise the monotonicity of a model. cAnt-Miner$_{PB+MC}$ has been shown to outperform a majority classifier and an existing monotonic algorithm, while not losing predictive accuracy when compared to the original implementation.

Currently the global pruner is naïve in its approach, as it simply removes the last term in a rule list. Further work is required to optimise the pruning strategy, one approach is to remove the term that improves the monotonicity of the list by the greatest amount.

References

1. Ben-David, A.: Monotonicity maintenancs in information-theoretic machine learning algorithms. Mach. Learn. **19**, 29–43 (1995)
2. Ben-David, A., Sterling, L., Tran, T.: Adding monoticity to learning algorithms may impair their accuracy. Expert Syst. Appl. **36**, 6627–6634 (2009)
3. Dorigo, M., Maniezzo, V., Colorni, A.: Ant system: optimization by a colony of cooperating agents. IEEE Trans. Syst. Man Cybern. Part B **26**, 29–41 (1996)
4. Dorigo, M., Stutzle, T.: Ant Colony Optimization. A Bradford Book. The MIT Press, Cambridge (2004)
5. Duivesteijn, W., Feelders, A.: Nearest neighbour classification with monotonicity constraints. In: Daelemans, W., Goethals, B., Morik, K. (eds.) ECML PKDD 2008, Part I. LNCS (LNAI), vol. 5211, pp. 301–316. Springer, Heidelberg (2008)
6. Fayyad, U., Piatetsky-Shapiro, G., Smith, P.: From data mining to knowledge discovery: an overview. In: Advances in Knowledge Discovery & Data Mining, pp. 1–34. MIT Press (1996)
7. Feelders, A., Pardoel, M.: Pruning for monotone classification trees. In: Berthold, M., Lenz, H.-J., Bradley, E., Kruse, R., Borgelt, C. (eds.) IDA 2003. LNCS, vol. 2810, pp. 1–12. Springer, Heidelberg (2003)
8. Fürnkranz, J.: Separate-and-conquer rule learning. Artif. Intell. Rev. **13**(1), 3–54 (1999)
9. Hoover, K., Perez, S.: Three attitudes towards data mining. J. Econ. Methodol. **7**(2), 195–210 (2000)
10. Lichman, M.: UCI machine learning repository (2013). http://archive.ics.uci.edu/ml
11. Martens, D., De Backer, M., Haesen, R., Baesens, B., Mues, C., Vanthienen, J.: Ant-based approach to the knowledge fusion problem. In: Dorigo, M., Gambardella, L.M., Birattari, M., Martinoli, A., Poli, R., Stützle, T. (eds.) ANTS 2006. LNCS, vol. 4150, pp. 84–95. Springer, Heidelberg (2006)
12. Martens, D., Backer, M.D., Haesen, R., Vanthienen, J., Snoeck, M., Baesens, B.: Classification with ant colony optimization. IEEE Trans. Evol. Comput. **11**(5), 651–665 (2007)
13. Martens, D., Baesens, B., Fawcett, T.: Editorial survey: swarm intelligence for data mining. Mach. Learn. **82**(1), 1–42 (2011)
14. Otero, F., Freitas, A., Johnson, C.: A new sequential covering strategy for inducing classification rules with ant colony algorithms. IEEE Trans. Evol. Comput. **17**(1), 64–76 (2013)
15. Parpinelli, R., Lopes, H., Freitas, A.: Data mining with an ant colony optimization algorithm. IEEE Trans. Evol. Comput. **6**(4), 321–332 (2002)
16. Potharst, R., Ben-David, A., van Wezel, M.: Two algorithms for generating structured and unstructured monotone ordinal data sets. Eng. Appl. Artif. Intell. **22**(4), 491–496 (2009)
17. Qian, Y., Xu, H., Liang, J., Liu, B., Wang, J.: Fusing monotonic decision trees. IEEE Trans. Knowl. Data Eng. **27**(10), 2717–2728 (2015)
18. Witten, H., Frank, E.: Data Mining: Practical Machine Learning Tools and Techniques, 2nd edn. Morgan Kaufmann, San Francisco (2005)

Observing the Effects of Overdesign in the Automatic Design of Control Software for Robot Swarms

Mauro Birattari[1]([⊠]), Brian Delhaisse[1], Gianpiero Francesca[1],
and Yvon Kerdoncuff[1,2]

[1] IRIDIA, Université Libre de Bruxelles, Brussels, Belgium
mbiro@ulb.ac.be
[2] ENSTA ParisTech, Palaiseau, France

Abstract. We present the results of an experiment in the automatic design of control software for robot swarms. We conceived the experiment to corroborate a hypothesis that we proposed in a previous publication: the reality gap problem bears strong resemblance to the generalization problem faced in supervised learning. In particular, thanks to this experiment we observe for the first time a phenomenon that we shall call *overdesign*. Overdesign is the automatic design counterpart of the well known overfitting problem encountered in machine learning. Past an optimal level of the design effort, the longer the design process is protracted, the better the performance of the swarm becomes in simulation and the worst in reality. Our results show that some sort of early stopping mechanism could be beneficial.

Keywords: Swarm robotics · Automatic design · Evolutionary robotics · Reality gap · Generalization · Overdesign · Early stopping

1 Introduction

Designing the control software of the individual robots so that the swarm performs a given task is a difficult problem. A number of interesting approaches have been proposed to address specific cases—e.g., [3,7,28,32,34,45,56]. Nonetheless, there is no ultimate and generally applicable method on the horizon.

Automatic design is a viable alternative. To date, the automatic design of control software for robot swarms has been mostly studied in the framework of evolutionary swarm robotics [52], which is the application of evolutionary robotics [40] in the context of swarm robotics. In the classical evolutionary swarm

This research was conceived by MB and GF and was directed by MB. The experiment was performed by YK using automatic design software developed by BD on the basis of a previous version by GF. The article was drafted by MB and GF. All authors read the manuscript and provided feedback. BD is currently with the Department of Advanced Robotics, Istituto Italiano di Tecnologia (IIT), Genova, Italy.

M. Dorigo et al. (Eds.): ANTS 2016, LNCS 9882, pp. 149–160, 2016.
DOI: 10.1007/978-3-319-44427-7_13

robotics, the control software of each individual robot is a neural network that takes sensor readings as an input and returns actuation commands as an output. The parameters of the neural network are obtained via an evolutionary algorithm that optimizes a task-specific objective function. The optimization process relies on computer-based simulation. Once simulation shows that the swarm is able to perform the given task, the neural network is uploaded to the robots and the actual real-world performance of the swarm is assessed.

The *reality gap* [9,30] is one of the major issues to be faced in evolutionary swarm robotics—and in all automatic design methods that rely on simulation. The reality gap is the intrinsic difference between reality and simulation. As a consequence of the reality gap, differences should be expected between how an instance of control software behaves in simulation and in reality. Indeed, as pointed out by Floreano et al. [18], the control software is optimized "to match the specificities of the simulation, which differ from the real world."

A number of ideas have been proposed to reduce the impact of the reality gap, including methods to increase the realism of simulation [31,36] and design protocols that alternate simulation with runs in reality [5,33]. In a recent article, Francesca et al. [22] argued that the reality gap problem is reminiscent of the generalization problem faced in supervised learning. In particular, the authors conjectured that the inability to overcome the reality gap satisfactorily might result from an excessive representational power of the control software architecture adopted. Taking inspiration from a practice that is traditionally advocated in the supervised learning literature [13], the authors explored the idea of injecting bias in the process as a means to reduce the representational power.

In this article, we elaborate further on the relationship between the reality gap problem and the generalization problem faced in supervised learning. Understanding this relationship can enable the development of new approaches to handle the reality gap. We present an experiment whose goal is to highlight, in context of the automatic design of control software for robot swarms, a phenomenon similar to *overfitting*. Indeed, if the reality gap problem is similar to the generalization problem of machine learning, one should observe that, past an optimal level of the design effort, the further the control software is optimized in simulation, the worse the performance in reality gets. In the context of the automatic design of control software, we shall call this phenomenon *overdesign*.

2   Related Work

The automatic generation of control software is a promising approach to the design of robot swarms [8,19]. Most of the published research belongs in evolutionary swarm robotics [52], which is the application of the principles of evolutionary robotics [40] in the context of swarm robotics. Evolutionary robotics has been covered by several recent reviews [6,14,48,53]. In the following, we briefly sketch some of its notable applications in swarm robotics.

A number of authors adopted the classical evolutionary robotics approach: robots are controlled by neural networks optimized via an evolutionary algorithm. Quinn et al. [43] developed a coordinated motion behavior and tested it on three Kheperas. Christensen and Dorigo [11] developed a simultaneous hole-avoidance and phototaxis behavior and tested it on three s-bots. Baldassarre et al. [1] developed a coordinated motion behavior for physically connected robots and tested it on four s-bots. Trianni and Nolfi [51] developed a self-organizing synchronization behavior and tested it on two and three s-bots. Waibel et al. [54] developed an idealized foraging behavior and tested it on two Alices.

For completeness, we mention a number of studies in the automatic design of control software for robot swarms that departed from the classical evolutionary swarm robotics. Hecker et al. [29] developed a foraging behavior by optimizing the parameters of a finite state machine via artificial evolution. They tested the behavior on three custom-made robots. Gauci et al. [24,25] developed object clustering and self-organized aggregation by optimizing the six parameters of a simple control architecture using evolutionary strategy and exhaustive search, respectively. Experiments were performed with five and forty e-pucks, respectively. Duarte et al. [15,16] proposed an approach based on the hierarchical decomposition of complex behaviors into basic behaviors, which are then developed via artificial evolution or implemented manually. The authors obtained behaviors for object retrieval and patrolling. In a successive study [17], the authors used artificial evolution to produce control software for a swarm of ten aquatic robots and solve four different sub-tasks: homing, dispersion, clustering and area monitoring. The control software for the four sub-tasks was then combined in a sequential way to accomplish a complex mission. The authors performed experiments in a 330 m × 190 m waterbody next to the Tagus river in Lisbon, Portugal. The results show that the control software produced crosses the reality gap nicely. Francesca et al. [20–22] proposed AutoMoDe: an approach that automatically assembles and fine tunes robot control software starting from predefined modules. The authors developed behaviors for seven tasks: aggregation, foraging, shelter with constrained access, largest covering network, coverage with forbidden areas, surface and perimeter coverage, and aggregation with ambient cues. The developed behaviors were tested with swarms of twenty e-pucks.

3   Facts and Hypotheses

Neural networks have been studied for over seven decades, with alternating fortune—e.g., [12,35,37,46,55]. Around the year 2000, neural networks appeared to be superseded by other learning methods. They regained the general attention of researchers and practitioner in the last decade, thanks to the major success of deep learning—e.g., see [47]. In the context of our reasoning, we are interested in scientific facts about neural networks and their generalization capabilities that where established mostly in the 1990's. In particular, we are interested in the relationship between prediction error and two characteristics: (1) the complexity of the neural network; and (2) the amount of training effort.

A fundamental result for understanding the relationship between error and complexity is the so called *bias/variance decomposition* [26].[1] It has been proved that the prediction error can be decomposed into a bias and a variance component. Low-complexity neural networks—i.e., those with a small number of hidden neurons and therefore low representational power—present a high bias and a low variance. Conversely, high-complexity neural networks—i.e., those with a large number of hidden neurons and therefore a high representational power—present a low bias and a high variance.

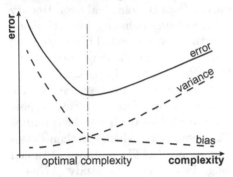

Fig. 1. Decomposition of the error into a bias and a variance component

As the bias and variance components combine additively, the error presents a U shape: for an increasingly large level of complexity, the error first decreases and then increases again. This implies that high complexity (i.e., high representational power and low bias) is not necessarily a positive characteristic: indeed an optimal value of the complexity exist. Beyond that value, prediction error increases. See Fig. 1 for a graphical illustration of the concept. In other terms, a complex network (i.e., high number of neurons and therefore high representational power) is able to learn complex functions but then generalizes poorly. Indeed, it is an established fact that the higher the complexity of a neural network (as of any functional approximator), the lower is the error on the training set and the higher is the error on a previously unseen test set—provided that we are beyond the optimal complexity. This fact is graphically represented in Fig. 2a: past the optimal level of complexity, the errors on training set and test set diverge.

Concerning the relationship between prediction error and training effort, a second important fact has been established, which goes under the name of *overfitting*—or alternatively overtraining. Overfitting is the tendency of a neural network (as of any functional approximator) to overspecialize to the examples used for training, which impairs its generalization capabilities. As a result of overfitting, one can observe that if the learning process is protracted beyond a given level, the error on the training and test sets diverge. Indeed, past an optimal level of the training effort, which is typically unknown a priori, the error on a previously unseen test set increases, while the one on the training set keeps decreasing. This fact is graphically represented in Fig. 2c.

It should be noted that the two facts illustrated in Figs. 2a and c are strictly related. The former considers the case in which the level of training effort is fixed and the complexity of the approximator is varied; the latter, considers the dual case in which the complexity of the approximator is fixed and the amount

---

[1] For a more advanced and general treatment of the issue, see also [57].

Supervised Learning

Automatic Design

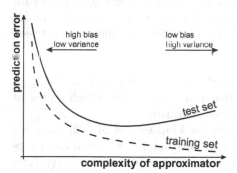

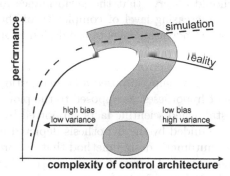

(a) Error on training and test sets vs complexity of approximator

(b) Performance in simulation and reality vs complexity of control architecture

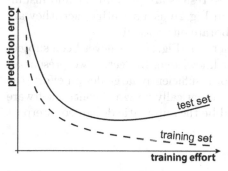

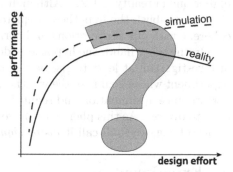

(c) Error on training and test sets vs training effort

(d) Performance in simulation and reality vs design effort

Fig. 2. Conceptual relationship between the bias-variance tradeoff in supervised learning and in automatic design (a/b) and between *overfitting* in supervised learning and *overdesign* in automatic design (c/d)

of training effort is varied. In both cases, past an a priori unknown level of the independent variable, the error on the training and test sets diverge.

Several ideas have been proposed to deal with these facts and produce so called *robust* learning methods. The most notable ones are cross-validation and regularization techniques—e.g., see [2,49]. In the context of this article, it is worth mentioning a technique known as *early stopping*, which consists in halting the learning process before the error on training and test set start to diverge— e.g., see [10,39,42,44].

In a previous article, Francesca et al. [22] argued that the reality gap problem faced in automatic design of robot control software is reminiscent of the generalization problem faced in supervised learning. If the two problems are indeed sufficiently similar, one should be able to observe in the automatic design the counterparts of the facts illustrated in Figs. 2a and c. In particular, one should observe that the performance in simulation and reality diverge (1) for an increasing level of complexity of the control architecture—Fig. 2b; and (2) for an increasing level of the design effort—Fig. 2d. The only difference between Figs. 2a and b (and between Figs. 2c and d) is that the former concerns the *minimization* of error, while the latter the *maximization* of performance. On Figs. 2b and d, we superimposed a large question mark to signify that these plots represent hypotheses, as opposed to the plots appearing on their left, which represent established scientific facts supported by a vast literature.

Guided by the hypothesis depicted in Fig. 2b, Francesca et al. [22] proposed an automatic design method that, according to their intentions, has a lower representational power (i.e., lower complexity) than the neural network typically adopted in evolutionary swarm robotics. Experimental results confirm that, with respect to a control architecture with a higher representational power, one with lower representational power yields a lower performance in simulation but a higher one in reality [20–22]. Although these results are preliminary and insufficient to establish the hypothesis depicted in Fig. 2b as a scientific fact, they are coherent with our expectations and corroborate our reasoning.

On the other hand, the hypothesis depicted in Fig. 2d has never been subject of investigation, at least to the best of our knowledge. In Sect. 4, we present an experiment whose goal is to see whether, for a sufficiently large design effort, the performance in simulation and reality of automatically designed control software tend to diverge. As this phenomenon would be the automatic design counterpart of overfitting, we shall call it *overdesign*.

4   Experiment

In this section, we present the material adopted in the experiment, the automatic design method, the task, the protocol, and the results.

Robots. We consider a particular version of the e-puck robot [38]. This version was formally defined in [22] via a reference model that describes the set of sensors and actuators exposed to the control software. In this section, we provide a brief sketch of the reference model. We refer the reader to [22] for the details. The e-puck moves thanks to a two-wheel differential steering system. The e-puck senses the obstacles (e.g., walls and other robots) via eight infrared proximity sensors. The e-puck measures the reflectance of the floor via three ground sensors placed under the front of the body. Thanks to a range-and-bearing extension board [27], the e-puck perceives the presence of other e-pucks in a 0.7 m range. For each perceived robot, the e-puck senses its relative distance and angle.

The control cycle has a period of 100 ms. At each time step, the control software receives the readings through the variables $prox_i$, $light_i$, gnd_i, r_m, and $\angle b_m$ that abstract respectively, proximity, light, ground sensors and the readings of the range-and-bearing board. Based on these variables, the control software decides the command values v_l and v_r to be applied to the wheel motors.

Design Method. We adopt `EvoStick`, an automatic design method presented in [22]. We briefly illustrate `EvoStick` here and we refer the reader to [22] for the details. `EvoStick` is an implementation of the classical evolutionary swarm robotics approach: an evolutionary algorithm optimizes the feed-forward neural network that controls each robot. Inputs and outputs of the neural networks are defined on the basis of the reference model. In particular, the neural network has 24 inputs: 8 readings from the proximity sensors, 8 from the light sensors, 3 from the ground sensors and 5 that are obtained by aggregating the range-and-bearing readings [22]. The outputs are the commands to the two wheel motors.

The neural network has 50 real-valued parameters that are optimized by an evolutionary algorithm that features mutation and elitism. The evolutionary algorithm operates on populations of 100 neural networks. At a given iteration, each neural network is tested 10 times in simulation. The population to be tested at the subsequent iteration is created as follows: the 20 best performing neural networks (the elite), are included unchanged; 80 further neural networks are generated from the elite via mutation. Simulations are performed using ARGoS [41].

Task. A swarm of $N = 20$ e-pucks must perform the aggregation task previously studied in [22]. The environment is a dodecagonal arena of 4.91 m² surrounded by walls—see Fig. 3. The floor is gray, except two circular black areas, a and b. These areas have the same radius of 0.35 m and are centered at 0.60 m from the center of the arena. The swarm must aggregate on either a or b. At the beginning of the run, each robot is randomly positioned in the arena. The run lasts for $T = 240$ s during which, the robots move in the arena according to their control software. At the end of a run, the performance of the swarm is computed using the objective function

$$F = max(N_a, N_b)/N, \tag{1}$$

where N_a and N_b are the number of e-pucks that, at the end of the run, are on a and b, respectively, and N is the total number of e-pucks. The objective function ranges from 0, when no e-puck is either on a or b, to 1, when all e-pucks are either on a or b.

Protocol. The experiment comprises two phases. In Phase 1, `EvoStick` is run 30 times for 256 iterations each. In order to evaluate the performance of the swarm at different levels of the design effort, for each run of `EvoStick` we collect the best neural network produced at four different stages: iteration 4, 16, 64, and 256. In Phase 2, we evaluate the neural networks collected in Phase 1. Each neural network is evaluated once in simulation and once in reality. The evaluation is performed under the same experimental conditions of Phase 1. Concerning the evaluation in reality, we tried to reduce human intervention as much as possible to avoid biasing the results: (1) the control software is automatically uploaded to each e-puck via the infrastructure described in [23]; (2) the performance of the swarm is formally evaluated using the objective function defined in Eq. 1

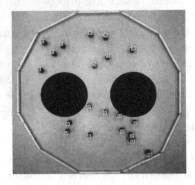

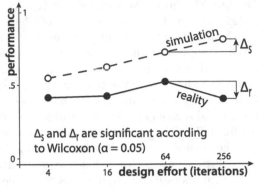

Fig. 3. Arena and twenty e-pucks   **Fig. 4.** Results of the experiment

and is computed automatically via the tracking system described in [50]; (3) the tracking system is also used to automatically drive the robots to random initial positions at the beginning of each evaluation.

Results. Figure 4 summarizes the results. Visually, the two curves representing the average performance in simulation and reality closely resemble the hypothetical ones that we sketched in Fig. 2d. In particular, between iteration 64 and 256 of the evolutionary algorithm, the performance in simulation increased while the one in reality decreased. To confirm that the observed trends are a genuine phenomenon rather than simply random fluctuations, we used the paired Wilcoxon signed rank test (with 95 % confidence level) to analyze the performance difference between iteration 64 and 256. We did this for both curves. In both cases, the null hypothesis we tested is that the performance at iteration 64 and 256 is the same and that the observed differences are the result of random fluctuations. As alternative hypotheses we used those suggested by Fig. 2d: from iteration 64 to 256, the performance in simulation increases while the one in reality decreases. In both cases, the observations reject the null hypothesis in favor of the alternative.

5   Conclusions

In the article, we presented results that corroborate a previously formulated hypothesis: the reality gap problem bears strong resemblance to the generalization problem faced in supervised learning. In particular, we presented an experiment that highlights a phenomenon that we shall call *overdesign*: as the training effort increases, past an optimal value, the performance that an automatically designed swarm obtains in reality diverges from the one it obtains in simulation.

The results presented in this article are preliminary, as they concern a single automatic design method and a single task. To establish overdesign as a scientific fact, further experimental work is needed and should involve a sufficiently large number of automatic design methods and tasks. Nonetheless, the results presented here are in line with our expectations and corroborate our hypothesis. Moreover, they are in line also with similar results previously obtained in the automatic fine-tuning of the parameters of metaheuristics. Within that context, Birattari [4] devised an experiment in which an iterated local search algorithm is fine tuned on an instance of the quadratic assignment problem. Is then tested on another instance of the same problem. The author recorded the cost of the best solution found by the algorithm on the two instances as a function of the tuning effort. The results show that, past an optimal value of the tuning effort, the costs diverge: on the tuning instance the cost keeps decreasing, while on the test instance it starts increasing. In the context of the automatic fine-tuning of metaheuristics, the phenomenon observed has been named *overtuning*.

In the article, we have developed our reasoning and conducted our experiment within the domain of the automatic design of control software for robot swarms. The choice was dictated simply by the fact that this is our research domain and it is within this domain that we wish to investigate the effects of the reality gap. Moreover, we have focused on a classical evolutionary swarm robotics setting because a relatively large number of studies have been developed under this setting. Indeed, there is an established research community that operates in the framework of evolutionary swarm robotics and that could be potentially affected by our contribution. Nonetheless, we do not have any reason to doubt that the phenomenon of overdesign could be observed in other approaches to the automatic design of control software for robot swarms and for single robots, as well. The experimental methodology we adopted in the study presented is sufficiently general and straightforward to be applicable in further studies. Yet, it should be noticed that an experiment to observe overdesign can be time consuming. The experiment presented in this article comprises 120 runs with 20 e-pucks and $30 \times 100 \times 10 \times 256 + 120 = 7,680,120$ runs in simulation.

Besides shedding new light on the reality gap problem, the concepts discussed in this article and the results presented could suggest improvements to the current practice in evolutionary (swarm) robotics and more generally in the automatic design of robot control software. In particular, the results suggest that one should check whether the control software obtained upon convergence of the design process is indeed the one that perform the best in reality. Moreover, these results suggest that a form of early stopping could be beneficial.

To summarize, future work should produce further evidence that the risk of overdesign is concrete in the automatic design of control software for robot swarms. Moreover, future research could be devoted to the development of early stopping mechanisms or similar overdesign-aware techniques that could contribute to mitigate the reality gap problem.

Acknowledgments. Mauro Birattari acknowledges support from the Belgian F.R.S.–FNRS, of which he is a Senior Research Associate.

References

1. Baldassarre, G., Trianni, V., Bonani, M., Mondada, F., Dorigo, M., Nolfi, S.: Self-organised coordinated motion in groups of physically connected robots. IEEE Trans. Syst. Man Cybern. Part B **37**(1), 224–239 (2007)
2. Bauer, F., Pereverzev, S., Rosasco, L.: On regularization algorithms in learning theory. J. Complex. **23**, 52–72 (2007)
3. Berman, S., Kumar, V., Nagpal, R.: Design of control policies for spatially inhomogeneous robot swarms with application to commercial pollination. In: International Conference on Robotics and Automation, ICRA 2011, pp. 378–385. IEEE Press, Piscataway (2011)
4. Birattari, M.: Tuning Metaheuristics: A Machine Learning Perspective. Springer, Germany (2009)
5. Bongard, J., Zykov, V., Lipson, H.: Resilient machines through continuous self-modeling. Science **314**(5802), 1118–1121 (2006)
6. Bongard, J.C.: Evolutionary robotics. Commun. ACM **56**(8), 74–83 (2013)
7. Brambilla, M., Brutschy, A., Dorigo, M., Birattari, M.: Property-driven design for swarm robotics: a design method based on prescriptive modeling and model checking. ACM Trans. Auton. Adapt. Syst. **9**(4), 17.1–17.28 (2015)
8. Brambilla, M., Ferrante, E., Birattari, M., Dorigo, M.: Swarm robotics: a review from the swarm engineering perspective. Swarm Intell. **7**(1), 1–41 (2013)
9. Brooks, R.A.: Artificial life and real robots. In: Varela, F.J., Bourgine, P. (eds.) Toward a Practice of Autonomous Systems. Proceedings of the First European Conference on Artificial Life, pp. 3–10. MIT Press, Cambridge (1992)
10. Caruana, R., Lawrence, S., Giles, L.: Overfitting in neural nets: backpropagation, conjugate gradient, and early stopping. In: Leen, T., Dietterich, T., Tresp, V. (eds.) Advances in Neural Information Processing Systems 13, NIPS 2000, pp. 402–408. MIT Press (2001)
11. Christensen, A.L., Dorigo, M.: Evolving an integrated phototaxis and hole-avoidance behavior for a swarm-bot. In: Artificial Life, ALIFE 2006, pp. 248–254. MIT Press, Cambridge (2006)
12. Cybenko, G.: Approximations by superpositions of a sigmoidal function. Math. Control Signals Syst. **2**(4), 303–314 (1989)
13. Dietterich, T., Kong, E.B.: Machine learning bias, statistical bias, and statistical variance of decision tree algorithms. Technical report, Department of Computer Science, Oregon State University (1995)
14. Doncieux, S., Mouret, J.B.: Beyond black-box optimization: a review of selective pressures for evolutionary robotics. Evol. Intell. **7**(2), 71–93 (2014)
15. Duarte, M., Oliveira, S.M., Christensen, A.L.: Evolution of hierarchical controllers for multirobot systems. In: Artificial Life, ALIFE 2014, pp. 657–664. MIT Press, Cambridge (2014)
16. Duarte, M., Oliveira, S.M., Christensen, A.L.: Hybrid control for large swarms of aquatic drones. In: Artificial Life, ALIFE 2014, pp. 785–792. MIT Press, Cambridge (2014)
17. Duarte, M., Costa, V., Gomes, J.C., Rodrigues, T., Silva, F., Oliveira, S.M., Christensen, A.L.: Evolution of collective behaviors for a real swarm of aquatic surface robots. arXiv-CoRR abs/1511.03154 (2015)
18. Floreano, D., Husbands, P., Nolfi, S.: Evolutionary robotics. In: Siciliano, B., Khatib, O. (eds.) Handbook of Robotics, pp. 1423–1451. Springer, Germany (2008)

19. Francesca, G., Birattari, M.: Automatic design of robot swarms: achievements and challenges. Front. Robot. AI **3**(29), 1–9 (2016)
20. Francesca, G., Brambilla, M., Brutschy, A., Garattoni, L., Miletitch, R., Podevijn, G., Reina, A., Soleymani, T., Salvaro, M., Pinciroli, C., Mascia, F., Trianni, V., Birattari, M.: AutoMoDe-Chocolate: automatic design of control software for robot swarms. Swarm Intell. **9**(2/3), 125–152 (2015)
21. Francesca, G., et al.: An experiment in automatic design of robot swarms. In: Dorigo, M., Birattari, M., Garnier, S., Hamann, H., Montes de Oca, M., Solnon, C., Stützle, T. (eds.) ANTS 2014. LNCS, vol. 8667, pp. 25–37. Springer, Heidelberg (2014)
22. Francesca, G., Brambilla, M., Brutschy, A., Trianni, V., Birattari, M.: AutoMoDe: a novel approach to the automatic design of control software for robot swarms. Swarm Intell. **8**(2), 89–112 (2014)
23. Garattoni, L., Francesca, G., Brutschy, A., Pinciroli, C., Birattari, M.: Software infrastructure for e-puck (and TAM). Technical report 2015–004, IRIDIA, Université Libre de Bruxelles, Brussels, Belgium (2015)
24. Gauci, M., Chen, J., Li, W., Dodd, T.J., Groß, R.: Self-organized aggregation without computation. Int. J. Robot. Res. **33**(8), 1145–1161 (2014)
25. Gauci, M., Chen, J., Li, W., Dodd, T.J., Groß, R.: Clustering objects with robots that do not compute. In: Lomuscio, A., et al. (eds.) Autonomous Agents and Multiagent Systems, AAMAS 2014, pp. 421–428. IFAAMAS, Richland (2014)
26. Geman, S., Bienenstock, E., Doursat, R.: Neural networks and the bias/variance dilemma. Neural Comput. **4**(1), 1–58 (1992)
27. Gutiérrez, Á., Campo, A., Dorigo, M., Donate, J., Monasterio-Huelin, F., Magdalena, L.: Open e-puck range & bearing miniaturized board for local communication in swarm robotics. In: International Conference on Robotics and Automation, ICRA 2009, pp. 3111–3116. IEEE Press, Piscataway (2009)
28. Hamann, H., Wörn, H.: A framework of space-time continuous models for algorithm design in swarm robotics. Swarm Intell. **2**(2), 209–239 (2008)
29. Hecker, J.P., Letendre, K., Stolleis, K., Washington, D., Moses, M.E.: Formica ex machina: ant swarm foraging from physical to virtual and back again. In: Dorigo, M., Birattari, M., Blum, C., Christensen, A.L., Engelbrecht, A.P., Groß, R., Stützle, T. (eds.) ANTS 2012. LNCS, vol. 7461, pp. 252–259. Springer, Heidelberg (2012)
30. Jacobi, N., Husbands, P., Harvey, I.: Noise and the reality gap: the use of simulation in evolutionary robotics. In: Morán, F., et al. (eds.) Advances in Artificial Life. LNCS (LNAI), vol. 929, pp. 704–720. Springer, London (1995)
31. Jakobi, N.: Evolutionary robotics and the radical envelope-of-noise hypothesis. Adapt. Behav. **6**(2), 325–368 (1997)
32. Kazadi, S., Lee, J.R., Lee, J.: Model independence in swarm robotics. Int. J. Intell. Comput. Cybern. **2**(4), 672–694 (2009)
33. Koos, S., Mouret, J., Doncieux, S.: The transferability approach: crossing the reality gap in evolutionary robotics. IEEE Trans. Evol. Comput. **17**(1), 122–145 (2013)
34. Lopes, Y.K., Trenkwalder, S.M., Leal, A.B., Dodd, T.J., Groß, R.: Supervisory control theory applied to swarm robotics. Swarm Intell. **10**(1), 65–97 (2016)
35. McCulloch, W., Pitts, W.: A logical calculus of ideas immanent in nervous activity. Bull. Math. Biophys. **5**(4), 115–133 (1943)
36. Miglino, O., Lund, H.H., Nolfi, S.: Evolving mobile robots in simulated and real environments. Artif. Life **2**(4), 417–434 (1995)
37. Minsky, M., Papert, S.: Perceptrons: An Introduction to Computational Geometry. MIT Press, Cambridge (1969)

38. Mondada, F., et al.: The e-puck, a robot designed for education in engineering. In: 9th Conference on Autonomous Robot Systems and Competitions, pp. 59–65. Instituto Politécnico de Castelo Branco, Portugal (2009)

39. Morgan, N., Bourlard, H.: Generalization and parameter estimation in feedforward nets: some experiments. In: Touretzky, D. (ed.) Advances in Neural Information Processing Systems 2, NIPS 1990, pp. 630–637. Morgan Kaufman, San Mateo (1990)

40. Nolfi, S., Floreano, D.: Evolutionary Robotics. MIT Press, Cambridge (2000)

41. Pinciroli, C., Trianni, V., O'Grady, R., Pini, G., Brutschy, A., Brambilla, M., Mathews, N., Ferrante, E., Di Caro, G., Ducatelle, F., Birattari, M., Gambardella, L.M., Dorigo, M.: ARGoS: a modular, parallel, multi-engine simulator for multi-robot systems. Swarm Intell. 6(4), 271–295 (2012)

42. Prechelt, L.: Early stopping-but when? In: Orr, G.B., Müller, K.-R. (eds.) NIPS-WS 1996. LNCS, vol. 1524, pp. 55–59. Springer, Heidelberg (1998)

43. Quinn, M., Smith, L., Mayley, G., Husbands, P.: Evolving controllers for a homogeneous system of physical robots: structured cooperation with minimal sensors. Philos. Trans. Royal Soc. London A Math. Phys. Eng. Sci. 361(1811), 2321–2343 (2003)

44. Raskutti, G., Wainwright, M.J., Yu, B.: Early stopping and non-parametric regression: an optimal data-dependent stopping rule. J. Mach. Learn. Res. 15, 335–366 (2014)

45. Reina, A., Valentini, G., Fernández-Oto, C., Dorigo, M., Trianni, V.: a design pattern for decentralised decision making. PLoS ONE 10(10), e0140950 (2015)

46. Rosenblatt, F.: The perceptron: a probabilistic model for information storage and organization in the brain. Psychol. Rev. 65(6), 386–408 (1958)

47. Schmidhuber, J.: Deep learning in neural networks: an overview. Neural Netw. 61, 85–117 (2015)

48. Silva, F., Duarte, M., Correia, L., Oliveira, S.M., Christensen, A.L.: Open issues in evolutionary robotics. Evol. Comput. (2016, in press)

49. Stone, M.: Cross-validatory choice and assessment of statistical predictions. J. Royal Stat. Soc. Ser. B (Methodol.) 36(2), 111–147 (1974)

50. Stranieri, A., Turgut, A., Salvaro, M., Garattoni, L., Francesca, G., Reina, A., Dorigo, M., Birattari, M.: IRIDIA's arena tracking system. Technical report 2013–013, IRIDIA, Université Libre de Bruxelles, Brussels, Belgium (2013)

51. Trianni, V., Nolfi, S.: Self-organising sync in a robotic swarm. A dynamical system view. IEEE Trans. Evol. Comput. 13(4), 722–741 (2009)

52. Trianni, V.: Evolutionary Swarm Robotics. Springer, Germany (2008)

53. Trianni, V.: Evolutionary robotics: model or design? Front. Robot. AI 1(13), 1–6 (2014)

54. Waibel, M., Keller, L., Floreano, D.: Genetic team composition and level of selection in the evolution of cooperation. IEEE Trans. Evol. Comput. 13(3), 648–660 (2009)

55. Werbos, P.: Beyond Regression: New Tools for Prediction and Analysis in the Behavioral Sciences. Ph.D. thesis, Harvard University, Cambridge (1974)

56. Werfel, J., Petersen, K., Nagpal, R.: Designing collective behavior in a termite-inspired robot construction team. Science 343(6172), 754–758 (2014)

57. Wolpert, D.: On bias plus variance. Neural Comput. 9(6), 1211–1243 (1997)

Parameter Selection in Particle Swarm Optimisation from Stochastic Stability Analysis

Adam Erskine, Thomas Joyce, and J. Michael Herrmann[(⊠)]

School of Informatics, Institute for Perception, Action and Behaviour,
The University of Edinburgh, Edinburgh, Scotland, UK
michael.herrmann@ed.ac.uk

Abstract. Particle swarm optimisation is a metaheuristic algorithm which finds reasonable solutions in a wide range of applied problems if suitable parameters are used. We study the properties of the algorithm in the framework of random dynamical systems (RDS) which, due to the quasi-linear swarm dynamics, yields exact analytical results for the stability properties in the single particle case. The calculated stability region in the parameter space extends beyond the region determined by earlier approximations. This is also evidenced by simulations which indicate that the algorithm performs best in the asymptotic case if parameterised near the margin of instability predicted by the RDS approach.

Keywords: Particle Swarm Optimisation · Criticality · Random dynamical systems · Random matrix products · Parameter selection

1 PSO Introduction

Particle Swarm Optimisation (PSO, [13]) is a metaheuristic algorithm which is widely used to solve search and optimisation tasks. It employs a number of particles as a swarm of potential solutions. Each particles shares knowledge about the current overall best solution and also retains a memory of the best solution it has encountered itself previously. Otherwise the particles, after random initialisation, obey a linear dynamics of the following form

$$
\begin{aligned}
\mathbf{v}_{i,t+1} &= \omega \mathbf{v}_{i,t} + \alpha_1 \mathbf{R}_1 (\mathbf{p}_i - \mathbf{x}_{i,t}) + \alpha_2 \mathbf{R}_2 (\mathbf{g} - \mathbf{x}_{i,t}) \\
\mathbf{x}_{i,t+1} &= \mathbf{x}_{i,t} + \mathbf{v}_{i,t+1}
\end{aligned}
\tag{1}
$$

Here $\mathbf{x}_{i,t}$ and $\mathbf{v}_{i,t}$, $i = 1, \ldots, N$, $t = 0, 1, 2, \ldots$, represent, respectively, the d-dimensional position in the search space and the velocity vector of the i-th particle in the swarm at time t. The velocity update contains an inertial term parameterised by ω and includes attractive forces towards the personal best location $\mathbf{p}_i$ and towards the globally best location $\mathbf{g}$, which are parameterised by α_1 and α_2, respectively. The symbols $\mathbf{R}_1$ and $\mathbf{R}_2$ denote diagonal matrices whose non-zero entries are uniformly distributed in the unit interval. The number of particles N is quite low in most applications, usually amounting to a few dozens.

© Springer International Publishing Switzerland 2016
M. Dorigo et al. (Eds.): ANTS 2016, LNCS 9882, pp. 161–172, 2016.
DOI: 10.1007/978-3-319-44427-7_14

In order to function as an optimiser, the algorithm uses a nonnegative cost function $F : \mathbb{R}^d \to \mathbb{R}$. In many problems, where PSO is applied, also states with near-optimal costs can be considered as good solutions. The cost function is evaluated for the state of each particle at each time step. If $F(\mathbf{x}_{i,t})$ is better than $F(\mathbf{p}_i)$, then the personal best $\mathbf{p}_i$ is replaced by $\mathbf{x}_{i,t}$. Similarly, if one of the particles arrives at a state with a cost less than $F(\mathbf{g})$, then $\mathbf{g}$ is replaced in all particles by the position of the particle that has discovered the new best solution. If its velocity is non-zero, a particle will depart even from the current best location, but can still return guided by the force terms in the dynamics (1).

In the next section we will consider an illustrative simulation of a particle swarm and move on to a standard matrix formulation of the swarm dynamics in order to describe some of the existing analytical work on PSO. In Sect. 3 we will argue for a formulation of PSO as a random dynamical system which will enable us to derive a novel exact characterisation of the dynamics of a one-particle system. In Sect. 4 we will compare the theoretical predictions with multi-particle simulations on a representative set of benchmark functions. Finally, in Sect. 5 we will discuss the assumption we have made in Sect. 3 based on the empirical evidence for our approach.

2   Swarm Dynamics

2.1   Empirical Properties

The success of the algorithm in locating good solutions depends on the dynamics of the particles in the state space of the problem. In contrast to many evolution strategies, it is not straight forward to interpret the particle swarm as following a landscape defined by the cost function. Unless the current best position $\mathbf{g}$ changes, the particles do not interact with each other and follow an intrinsic dynamics that does not even indirectly obtain any gradient information.

The particle dynamics depends on the parameterisation of the Eq. 1. To obtain the best result one needs to select parameter settings that achieve a balance between the particles exploiting the knowledge of good known locations and exploring regions of the problem space that have not been visited before. Although adaptive schemes are available [6,9,20], parameter values often need to be experimentally determined, and poor selection may result in premature convergence of the swarm to poor local minima or in a divergence of the particles.

Empirically we can execute PSO against a variety of problem functions with a range of ω and $\alpha_{1,2}$ values. Typically the algorithm shows performance of the form depicted in Fig. 1. The best solutions found show a curved relationship between ω and $\alpha = \alpha_1 + \alpha_2$, with $\omega \approx 1$ at small α, or $\alpha \gtrsim 4$ at small ω. Large values of both α and ω are found to cause the particles to diverge leading to results far from optimality, while at small values for both parameters the particles converge to a nearby solution which sometimes is acceptable. For other cost functions similar relationships are observed in numerical tests (see Sect. 4) unless no good solutions found due to problem complexity or runtime limits.

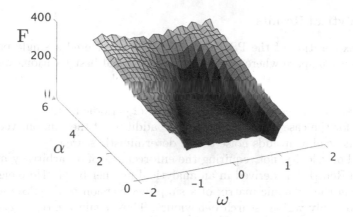

Fig. 1. Typical PSO performance as a function of its ω and α parameters. Here a 25 particle swarm was run for pairs of ω and α values ($\alpha_1 = \alpha_2 = \alpha/2$). Cost function here was the $d = 10$ non-continuous rotated Rastrigin function [15]. Each parameter pair was repeated 100 times and the minimal costs after 2000 iterations were averaged.

For simple cost functions, such as a single well potential, there are also parameter combinations with small ω and small α will usually lead to good results. The choice of α_1 and α_2 at constant α may have an effect for some cost functions, but does not seem to have a big effect in most cases.

2.2 Matrix Formulation

In order to analyse the behaviour of the algorithm it is convenient to use a matrix formulation by inserting the velocity explicitly in the second equation (1).

$$\mathbf{z}_{t+1} = M\mathbf{z}_t + \alpha_1 \mathbf{R}_1 (\mathbf{p}, \mathbf{p})^\top + \alpha_2 \mathbf{R}_2 (\mathbf{g}, \mathbf{g})^\top \tag{2}$$

with $\mathbf{z} = (\mathbf{v}, \mathbf{x})^\top$ and

$$M = \begin{pmatrix} \omega \mathbf{I}_d & -\alpha_1 \mathbf{R}_1 - \alpha_2 \mathbf{R}_2 \\ \omega \mathbf{I}_d & \mathbf{I}_d - \alpha_1 \mathbf{R}_1 - \alpha_2 \mathbf{R}_2 \end{pmatrix}, \tag{3}$$

where $\mathbf{I}_d$ is the unit matrix in d dimensions. Note that the two occurrence of $\mathbf{R}_1$ in Eq. 3 refer to the same realisation of the random variable. Similarly, the two $\mathbf{R}_2$'s are the same realisation, but different from $\mathbf{R}_1$. Since the second and third term on the right in Eq. 2 are constant most of the time, the analysis of the algorithm can focus on the properties of the matrix M. PSO's wide applicability has led to the analyses discussed in Sect. 2.3. These focused either on simplifying the algorithm to make it deterministic or on the expectation and variance values of the update matrix. Here we analyse the long term behaviour of the swarm considering both the stationary probability distribution of the particles within the z state space and the properties of the infinite product of the stochastic matrix.

2.3   Analytical Results

An early exploration of the PSO dynamics [12] considered a single particle in a one-dimension space where the personal and global best locations were taken to be the same. The random components were replaced by their averages such that apart from random initialisation the algorithm was deterministic. Varying the parameters was shown to result in a range of periodic motions and divergent behaviour for the case of $\alpha_1 + \alpha_2 \geq 4$. The addition of the random vectors was seen as beneficial as it adds noise to the deterministic search.

Control of velocity, not requiring the enforcement of an arbitrary maximum value as in Ref. [12], is derived in an analytical manner by [4]. Here eigenvalues derived from the dynamic matrix of a simplified version of the PSO algorithm are used to imply various search behaviours. Thus, again the $\alpha_1 + \alpha_2 \geq 4$ case is expected to diverge. For $\alpha_1 + \alpha_2 < 4$ various cyclic and quasi-cyclic motions are shown to exist for a non-random version of the algorithm.

In Ref. [19] again a single particle was considered in a one dimensional problem space, using a deterministic version of PSO, setting $\mathbf{R}_1 = \mathbf{R}_2 = 0.5$. The eigenvalues of the system were determined as functions of ω and a combined α, which leads to three conditions: The particle is shown to converge when $\omega < 1, \alpha > 0$ and $2\omega - \alpha + 2 > 0$. Harmonic oscillations occur for $\omega^2 + \alpha^2 - 2\omega\alpha - 2\omega - 2\alpha + 1 < 0$ and a zigzag motion is expected if $\omega < 0$ and $\omega - \alpha + 1 < 0$. As with the preceding papers the discussion of the random numbers in the algorithm views them purely as enhancing the search capabilities by adding a *drunken walk* to the particle motions. Their replacement by expectation values was thus believed to simplify the analysis with no loss of generality.

A weakness in these early papers stems from the treatment of the stochastic elements. Rather than replacing the R_1 and R_2 vectors by 0.5 the dynamic behaviour can be explored by considering their expectation values and variances. An early work doing this produced a predicted best performance region in parameter space similar to the curved valley of best values that is seen empirically [10]. The authors explicitly consider the convergence of means and variances of the stochastic update matrix. The curves they predict marks the locus of (ω, α)-pairs they believed guaranteed swarm convergence, i.e. parameter values within this line will result in convergence. Similar approaches yielded matching lines [17] and utilised a weaker stagnation assumption [16]. Ref. [1] provides an extensive recent review of such analyses. We will refer to this locus as the Jiang line [10]. It is included for comparison with the curves derived here, see Fig. 2 below.

We show in this contribution that the iterated use of these random factors $\mathbf{R}_1$ and $\mathbf{R}_2$ in fact adds a further level of complexity to the dynamics of the swarm which affects the behaviour of the algorithm in a non-trivial way. Essentially it is necessary to consider both the stationary distribution of particles in the system's state space and the properties of the infinite product of the stochastic update matrix. This leads to a loci of parameters leading to stable swarms that differs from previous solutions and depends upon the values of α_1 and α_2 used. All solutions lie outside the Jiang line [10]. We should note that they state that their solution is a guarantee of convergence but may not be its limit. Our analytical solution of the stability problem for the swarm dynamics explains why parameter settings derived from the deterministic approaches are not in line with experiences from practical tests. For this purpose we will now formulate the PSO algorithm as a random dynamical system and present an analytical solution for the swarm dynamics in a simplified but representative case.

3 Critical Swarm Conditions for a Single Particle

3.1 PSO as a Random Dynamical System

As in Refs. [12,19] the dynamics of the particle swarm will be studied here as well in the single-particle case. This can be justified because the particles interact only via the global best position such that, while $\mathbf{g}$ (1) is unchanged, single particles exhibit qualitatively the same dynamics as in the swarm. For the one-particle case we have necessarily $\mathbf{p} = \mathbf{g}$, such that shift invariance allows us to set both to zero, which leads us to the following is given by the stochastic-map formulation of the PSO dynamics (2).

$$\mathbf{z}_{t+1} = M\mathbf{z}_t \tag{4}$$

Extending earlier approaches we will explicitly consider the randomness of the dynamics, i.e. instead of averages over $\mathbf{R}_1$ and $\mathbf{R}_2$ we consider a random dynamical system with dynamical matrices M chosen from the set

$$\mathcal{M}_{\alpha,\omega} = \left\{ \begin{pmatrix} \omega\mathbf{I}_d & -\alpha\mathbf{R} \\ \omega\mathbf{I}_d & \mathbf{I}_d - \alpha\mathbf{R} \end{pmatrix}, \ \mathbf{R}_{ij} = 0 \text{ for } i \neq j \text{ and } \mathbf{R}_{ii} \in [0,1], \right\} \tag{5}$$

with $\mathbf{R}$ being in both rows the same realisation of a random diagonal matrix that combines the effects of $\mathbf{R}_1$ and $\mathbf{R}_2$ (1). The parameter α is the sum $\alpha_1 + \alpha_2$ with $\alpha_1, \alpha_2 \geq 0$. As the diagonal elements of $\mathbf{R}_1$ and $\mathbf{R}_2$ are uniformly distributed in $[0,1]$, the distribution of the random variable $\mathbf{R}_{ii} = \frac{\alpha_1}{\alpha}\mathbf{R}_{1,ii} + \frac{\alpha_2}{\alpha}\mathbf{R}_{2,ii}$ in Eq. 4 is given by a convolution of two uniform random variables, namely

$$P_{\alpha_1,\alpha_2}(s) = \begin{cases} \frac{\alpha^2 s}{\alpha_1 \alpha_2} & \text{if } 0 \leq s \leq \min\{\frac{\alpha_1}{\alpha}, \frac{\alpha_2}{\alpha}\} \\ \frac{\alpha}{\max\{\alpha_1,\alpha_2\}} & \text{if } \min\{\frac{\alpha_1}{\alpha}, \frac{\alpha_2}{\alpha}\} < s \leq \max\{\frac{\alpha_1}{\alpha}, \frac{\alpha_2}{\alpha}\} \\ \frac{\alpha^2(1-s)}{\alpha_1 \alpha_2} & \text{if } \max\{\frac{\alpha_1}{\alpha}, \frac{\alpha_2}{\alpha}\} < s \leq 1 \end{cases} \tag{6}$$

if the variable $s \in [0,1]$ and $P_{\alpha_1,\alpha_2}(s) = 0$ otherwise. $P_{\alpha_1,\alpha_2}(s)$ has a tent shape for $\alpha_1 = \alpha_2$ and a box shape in the limits of either $\alpha_1 \to 0$ or $\alpha_2 \to 0$. Thus, the selection of particular α_1 and α_2 parameters will determine the distribution for the random multiplier $\mathbf{R}_{ii}$ in Eq. 5.

We expect that the multi-particle PSO is well represented by the simplified version for $\alpha_2 \gg \alpha_1$ or $\alpha_1 \gg \alpha_2$, the latter case being irrelevant in practice. For $\alpha_1 \approx \alpha_2$ deviations from the theory may occur because in the multi-particle case $\mathbf{p}$ and $\mathbf{g}$ will be different for most particles. We will discuss this as well as the effects of the switching of the dynamics at discovery of better solutions in Sect. 5.

3.2   Marginal Stability

As the PSO algorithm runs, the particles locate new and better solutions. These result in updates to the personal best locations of the particles, and sometimes to the swarm's global best location. Typically, these updates become rarer over time. When the swarm is not discovering new and better solutions, the dynamics of the system is determined by an infinite product of matrices from the set $\mathcal{M}_{\alpha,\omega}$ (5). Such products have been studied for several decades [7] and have found applications in physics, biology and economics. Here they provide a convenient way to explicitly model the stochasticity of the swarm dynamics such that we can claim that the performance of PSO is determined by the stability properties of the random dynamical system (4).

Since the equation (4) is linear, the analysis can be restricted to vectors on the unit sphere in the $(\mathbf{v}, \mathbf{x})$ space, i.e. to unit vectors $\mathbf{a} = (\mathbf{x}, \mathbf{v})^{\top} / \| (\mathbf{x}, \mathbf{v})^{\top} \|$, where $\|\cdot\|$ denotes the Euclidean norm. Unless the set of matrices shares the same eigenvectors (which is not the case here) standard stability analysis in terms of eigenvalues is not applicable. Instead we will use tools from the theory of random matrix products in order to decide whether the set of matrices is stochastically contractive. The properties of the asymptotic dynamics can be described based on a double Lebesgue integral over the unit sphere S^{2d-1} and the set $\mathcal{M}_{\alpha,\omega}$ [14]. As in Lyapunov exponents, the effect of the dynamics is measured in logarithmic units in order to account for multiplicative action.

$$\lambda(\alpha, \omega) = \int d\nu_{\alpha,\omega}(\mathbf{a}) \int dP_{\alpha,\omega}(M) \log \|M\mathbf{a}\| \tag{7}$$

If $\lambda(\alpha, \omega)$ is negative the algorithm will converge to $\mathbf{p}$ with probability 1, while for positive λ arbitrarily large fluctuations are possible. While the measure for the inner integral (7) is given by Eq. 6, we have to determine the stationary distribution $\nu_{\alpha,\omega}$ (called invariant measure in [14]) on the unit sphere for the outer integral. It tells us where (or rather in which sector) the particles are likely to be in the system's state space. It is given as the solution of the integral equation

$$\nu_{\alpha,\omega}(\mathbf{a}) = \int d\nu_{\alpha,\omega}(\mathbf{b}) \int dP_{\alpha,\omega}(M) \delta(\mathbf{a}, M\mathbf{b}/\|M\mathbf{b}\|), \quad \mathbf{a}, \mathbf{b} \in S^{2d-1}, \tag{8}$$

which represents the stationarity of $\nu_{\alpha,\omega}$, i.e. the fact that under the action of the matrices from $\mathcal{M}_{\alpha,\omega}$ the distribution of particles over sectors remains unchanged. Obviously, if the particles are more likely to reside in some part then this part should have a stronger influence on the stability, see Eq. 7.

The existence of the invariant measure requires the dynamics to be ergodic which is ensured if at least some of elements of $\mathcal{M}_{\alpha,\omega}$ have complex eigenvalues, such as being the case for $\omega^2 + \alpha^2/4 - \omega\alpha - 2\omega - \alpha + 1 < 0$ (see above, [19]). This condition excludes a small region in the parameters space at small values of ω, such that there we have to take all ergodic components into account. There are not more than two components which due to symmetry have the same stability properties. It depends on the parameters α and ω and differs strongly from a homogenous distribution. Critical parameters are obtained from Eq. 7 by the relation

$$\lambda(\alpha, \omega) = 0. \tag{9}$$

A similar goal was followed in Ref. [6], where, however, an adaptive scheme rather than an analytical approach was invoked in order to identify critical parameters. Solving Eq. 9 is difficult in higher dimensions, so we rely on the linearity of the system when considering the $(d = 1)$-case as representative. In Fig. 2 critical loci of parameter values are plotted. Two lines are plotted in black: one (outer) derived for the case of $\alpha = \alpha_1 + \alpha_2$, and $\alpha_1 = \alpha_2$, the other (inner) for the case of $\alpha = \alpha_2$, and $\alpha_1 = 0$. We also plot a line (in dark green) showing the earlier solution of swarm stability [10]. Inside the contour $\lambda(\alpha, \omega)$ is negative, meaning that the state will approach the origin with probability 1. Along the contour and in the outside region large state fluctuations are possible. Interesting parameter values are expected near the curve where due to a coexistence of stable and unstable dynamics (induced by different sequences of random matrices) a theoretically optimal combination of exploration and exploitation is possible. For specific problems, however, deviations from the critical curve can be expected to be beneficial.

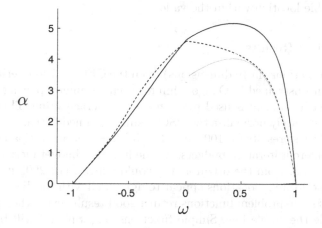

Fig. 2. Solution of Eq. 9 representing a single particle in one dimension with a fixed best value at $\mathbf{g} = \mathbf{p} = 0$. The curve that has higher α-values on the right (solid) is for $\alpha_1 = \alpha_2$, the other curve (dashed) is for $\alpha = \alpha_2$, $\alpha_1 = 0$. Except for the regions near $\omega = \pm 1$, where numerical instabilities can occur, a simulation produces an indistinguishable curve. In the simulation we tracked the probability of a particle to either reach a small region (10^{-12}) near the origin or to escape beyond a radius of 10^{12} after starting from a random location on the unit circle. Along the curve both probabilities are equal. For comparison the line of stability predicted by [10] is shown in green (the innermost line). (Color figure online)

4   Optimisation of Benchmark Functions

4.1   Experimental Setup

Metaheuristic algorithms are often tested in competition against benchmark functions designed to present different problem space characteristics. The 28 functions [15] contain a mix of unimodal, basic multimodal and composite functions. The domain of the functions in this test set are all defined to be $[-100, 100]^d$ where d is the dimensionality of the problem. Particles were initialised uniformly randomly within the same domain. We use 10-dimensional problems throughout. It may be interesting to consider higher dimensionalities, but $d = 10$ seems sufficient in the sense that random hits at initialisation are already very unlikely. Our implementation of PSO performed no spatial or velocity clamping. In all trials a swarm of 25 particles was used. For the competition 50000 fitness evaluation were allowed which corresponds to 2000 iterations with 25 particles. Other iteration numbers (20, 200, 20000) were included here for comparison. Results are averaged over 100 trials. This protocol was carried out for pairs of $\omega \in [-1.1, 1.1]$ and $\alpha \in [0, 6]$. This was repeated for all 28 functions. The averaged solution costs as a function of the two parameters showed curved valleys similar to that in Fig. 1 for all problems. For each function we obtain different best values along (or near) the theoretical curve (9). There appears to be no preferable location within the valley.

4.2   Empirical Results

Using the 28 functions (in 10 dimensions) from the CEC2013 competition [15] we can run our unconstrained PSO algorithm for each parameter pairing. Randomly sampling of each problem is used to estimate its average value. This average is used to approximately normalise the PSO results obtained for each the function. We combined these results for 100 runs. The 5 % best parameter pairs are shown in Fig. 3 for different iteration budgets. As the iteration budget increases the best locations move out from the origin as we would expect. For 2000 iterations per run the best performing locations appear to agree well with the Jiang line [10]. It is known that some problem functions return good results even when parameters are well inside the stable line. Simple functions (e.g. Sphere) will benefit from early swarm convergence. Thus, our average performance may mask the full effects. Figure 3 also shows an example of a single function's best performing parameter for 2000 iterations. This function now shows many locations beyond the Jiang line for which good results are obtained.

In Fig. 4 detailed explorations of two functions are shown. For these, we set $\omega = 0.55$, while α is varied with a much finer granularity between 2 and 6. 2000 repetitions of the algorithm are performed for each parameter pairing. The curves shown are for increasing iteration budgets (20, 200, 2000, 20000). Vertical lines mark where the two predicted stable loci sit on these parameter space slices.

The best results lie outside the Jiang line for these functions. Our predicted stable limit appears to be consistent with these results. In other words, if the

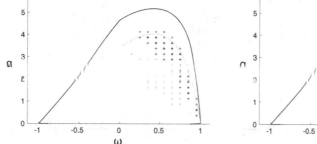 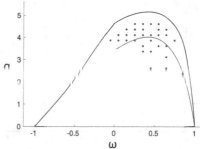

Fig. 3. Empirical cost function value results. (left) 5 % best parameter pair locations across all 28 functions plotted against our curve (black) and Jiang curve [10] (green). Iteration budgets are 20 (green circles), 200 (blue crosses), 2000 (red ×'s). (right) 5 % best parameter pair locations for function 21 plotted against our curve (black) and Jiang curve (green). Red dot is best location. (Color figure online)

solution is to be found in a short time a more stable dynamics is preferable, because the particles can settle in a nearby optimum at smaller fluctuations. If more time is available, then parameter pairs more close to the critical curve lead to an increased search range which obviously allows the swarm to explore better solutions. Similarly, we expect that in larger search spaces (e.g. relative to the width of the initial distribution of the particles) parameters near the critical line will lead to better results.

5 Discussion

Our analytical approach predicts a locus of α and ω pairings that maintain the critical behaviour of the PSO swarm. Outside this line the swarm will diverge unless steps are taken to constrain it. Inside, the swarm will eventually converge to a single solution. In order to locate a solution precisely in the search space, the swarm needs to converge at some point, so the line represents an upper bound on the exploration-exploitation mix that a swarm manifests. For parameters on the critical line, fluctuations are still arbitrary large. Therefore, subcritical parameter values can be preferable if the settling time is of the same order as the scheduled runtime of the algorithm. If, in addition, a typical length scale of the problem is known, then the finite standard deviation of the particles in the stable parameter region can be used to decide about the distance of the parameter values from the critical curve. These dynamical quantities can be approximately set, based on the theory presented here, such that a precise control of the behaviour of the algorithm is in principle possible.

The observation of the distribution of empirically optimal parameter values along the critical curve, confirms the expectation that critical or near-critical behaviour is the main reason for success of the algorithm. Critical fluctuations are a plausible tool in search problem if apart from certain smoothness assumptions

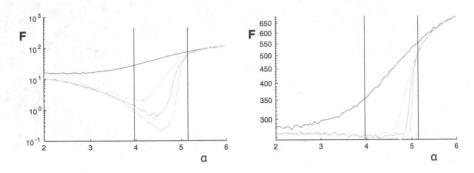

Fig. 4. Detailed empirical cost function value results. Detailed PSO performance along the ($\omega = 0.55$)-slice of parameter space for functions 7 (left) and 21 (right) [15]. Different iteration budgets are shown: 20 (red), 200 (yellow), 2000 (green) and 20000 (cyan) fitness evaluations. Vertical lines show our limit (black) and Jiang limit [10] (dark green). (Color figure online)

nothing is known about the cost landscape: The majority of excursions will exploit the smoothness of the cost function by local search, whereas the fat tails of the jump distribution allow the particles to escape from local minima.

The critical line in the PSO parameter space has been previously investigated and approximated by various authors [2,8,11,17,18]. Many of these approximations are compared alongside empirical simulation in [16]. As the authors of Ref. [3] note, the most accurate calculation of the critical line so far is provided by Poli in Refs. [17,18], however, not without pointing out that the effects of the higher-order terms were actually ignored. In contrast, the method we present here uses an approach which does not exclude the effects of higher order terms. Thus, where our results differ from those previously published, we can conclude that the difference is a result of incorporating the effects of these higher order terms. Further, a second result is that these higher order terms do not have noticeable effect for ω values close to ± 1, and thus in these regions of the parameter space both methods coincide.

The critical line (9) defines the best parameters for a PSO allowed to run for infinite steps. As the number of steps (and the size of the problem space) decrease, the best parameters move inwards, such that for e.g. 2000 steps the line proposed by Poli in Refs. [17,18] provides a good estimate for good parameters.

The work presented here can be seen as a Lyapunov condition based approach to uncovering the phase boundary. Previous work considering the Lyapunov condition has produced rather conservative estimates for the stability region [8, 11] which is a result of the particular approximation used, while we avoid this by directly calculating the integral (7) for the one-particle case.

Equation 2 shows that the discovery of a better solution affects only the constant terms of the linear dynamics of a particle, whereas its dynamical properties are governed by the (linear) parameter matrices. However, in the time step after a particle has found a new solution the corresponding force term in the dynamics is zero (see Eq. 1) such that the particle dynamics slows down compared to the theoretical solution which assumes a finite distance from the best position at all (finite) times. As this affects usually only one particle at a time and because new discoveries tend to become rarer over time, this effect will be small in the asymptotic dynamics, although it could justify the empirical optimality of parameters in the unstable region for some test cases.

The question is nevertheless, how often these changes occur. A weakly converging swarm can still produce good results if it often discovers better solutions by means of the fluctuations it performs before settling into the current best position. For cost functions that are not 'deceptive', i.e. where local optima tend to be near better optima, parameter values far inside the critical contour (see Fig. 2) may give good results, while in other cases more exploration is needed.

A numerical scan of the (α_1, α_2)-plane shows a valley of good fitness values, which, at small fixed positive ω, is roughly linear and described by the relation $\alpha_1 + \alpha_2 = $ const, i.e. only the joint parameter $\alpha = \alpha_1 + \alpha_2$ matters. For large ω, and accordingly small predicted optimal α values, the valley is less straight. This may be because the effect of the known solutions is relatively weak, so the interaction of the two components becomes more important. In other words, if the movement of the particles is mainly due to inertia, then the relation between the global and local best is non-trivial, while at low inertia the particles can adjust their **p** vectors quickly towards the **g** vector such that both terms become interchangeable.

6   Conclusion

In previous approaches, inherent stochasticity of PSO was handled via various simplifications such as the consideration of expectation values, thus excluding higher order terms that were, however, included in the present approach. It was shown here that the system is more correctly understood by casting PSO as a random dynamical system. Our analysis shows that there exists a locus of (ω, α)-pairings that result in the swarm behaving in a critical manner. This plays a role also in other applications of swarm dynamices, e.g., the behaviour reported in Ref. [5] occurred as well in the vicinity of critical parameter settings.

A weakness of the current approach is that it focuses on the standard PSO [13] which is outperformed on benchmark sets as well as in practical applications by many of the existing PSO variants. Similar analyses are certainly possible and can be expected to be carried out for some of these variants.

Acknowledgments. This work was supported by the Engineering and Physical Sciences Research Council (EPSRC), grant number EP/K503034/1.

References

1. Bonyadi, M.R., Michalewicz, Z.: Particle swarm optimization for single objective continuous space problems: a review. Evol. Comput (2016). doi:10.1162/EVCO_r_00180

2. Cleghorn, C.W., Engelbrecht, A.P.: A generalized theoretical deterministic particle swarm model. Swarm Intell. **8**(1), 35–59 (2014)
3. Cleghorn, C.W., Engelbrecht, A.P.: Particle swarm convergence: an empirical investigation. In: IEEE Congress on Evolutionary Computation, pp. 2524–2530 (2014)
4. Clerc, M., Kennedy, J.: The particle swarm-explosion, stability, and convergence in a multidimensional complex space. IEEE Trans. Evol. Comput. **6**(1), 58–73 (2002)
5. Erskine, A., Herrmann, J.M.: Cell-division behavior in a heterogeneous swarm environment. Artif. Life **21**(4), 481–500 (2015)
6. Erskine, A., Herrmann, J.M.: CriPS: Critical particle swarm optimisation. In: Andrews, P., Caves, L., Doursat, R., Hickinbotham, S., Polack, F., Stepney, S., Taylor, T., Timmis, J. (eds.) Proceedings of European Conference Artificial Life, pp. 207–214 (2015)
7. Furstenberg, H., Kesten, H.: Products of random matrices. Ann. Math. Stat. **31**(2), 457–469 (1960)
8. Gazi, V.: Stochastic stability analysis of the particle dynamics in the PSO algorithm. In: IEEE International Symposium on Intelligent Control (2012)
9. Hu, M., Wu, T.F., Weir, J.D.: An adaptive particle swarm optimization with multiple adaptive methods. IEEE Trans. Evol. Comput. **17**(5), 705–720 (2013)
10. Jiang, M., Luo, Y., Yang, S.: Stagnation analysis in particle swarm optimization. In: IEEE Swarm Intelligence Symposium, pp. 92–99 (2007)
11. Kadirkamanathan, V., Selvarajah, K., Fleming, P.J.: Stability analysis of the particle dynamics in particle swarm optimizer. IEEE Trans. Evol. Comput. **10**(3), 245–255 (2006)
12. Kennedy, J.: The behavior of particles. In: Porto, V.W., Saravanan, N., Waagen, D., Eiben, A.E. (eds.) Evolutionary Programming VII. LNCS, vol. 1447, pp. 579–589. Springer, Heidelberg (1998)
13. Kennedy, J., Eberhart, R.: Particle swarm optimization. In: Proceedings of IEEE International Conference on Neural Networks, vol. 4, pp. 1942–1948 (1995)
14. Khas'minskii, R.Z.: Necessary and sufficient conditions for the asymptotic stability of linear stochastic systems. Theory Prob. Appl. **12**(1), 144–147 (1967)
15. Liang, J.J., Qu, B.Y., Suganthan, P.N., Hernández-Díaz, A.G.: Problem definitions and evaluation criteria for the CEC 2013 special session on real-parameter optimization. Technical report, 201212, Comput. Intelligence Lab., Zhengzhou Univ. (2013)
16. Liu, Q.: Order-2 stability analysis of particle swarm optimization. Evol. Comput. **23**(2), 187–216 (2014)
17. Poli, R.: Mean and variance of the sampling distribution of particle swarm optimizers during stagnation. IEEE Trans. Evol. Comput. **13**(4), 712–721 (2009)
18. Poli, R., Broomhead, D.: Exact analysis of the sampling distribution for the canonical particle swarm optimiser and its convergence during stagnation. In: Proceedings of the 9th Annual Conference Genetic and Evolutionary Computation, pp. 134–141. ACM (2007)
19. Trelea, I.C.: The particle swarm optimization algorithm: convergence analysis and parameter selection. Inf. Process. Lett. **85**(6), 317–325 (2003)
20. Zhan, Z.H., Zhang, J., Li, Y., Chung, H.S.H.: Adaptive particle swarm optimization. IEEE Trans. Syst. Man Cybern. B **39**(6), 1362–1381 (2009)

Population Coding: A New Design Paradigm for Embodied Distributed Systems

Heiko Hamann[1]([✉]), Gabriele Valentini[2], and Marco Dorigo[2]([✉])

[1] Department of Computer Science, Heinz Nixdorf Institute,
University of Paderborn, Paderborn, Germany
`heiko.hamann@uni-paderborn.de`
[2] IRIDIA, Université Libre de Bruxelles, Brussels, Belgium
`{gvalenti,mdorigo}@ulb.ac.be`

Abstract. Designing embodied distributed systems, such as multi-robot systems, is challenging especially if the individual components have limited capabilities due to hardware restrictions. In self-organizing systems each component has only limited information and a global, organized system behavior (macro-level) has to emerge from local interactions only (micro-level). A general, structured design approach to self-organizing distributed systems is still lacking. We develop a general approach based on behaviorally heterogeneous systems. Inspired by the concept of population coding from neuroscience, we show in two case studies how designing an embodied distributed system is reduced to picking the right components from a predefined set of controller types. In this way, the design challenge is reduced to an optimization problem that can be solved by a variety of optimization techniques. Our approach is applicable to scenarios that allow for representing the component behavior as (probabilistic) finite state machine. We anticipate the paradigm of population coding to be applicable to a wide range of distributed systems.

1 Introduction

The complexity of engineered systems is getting more and more difficult to govern. We require novel methodologies to enable us to reliably engineer systems also in the future. Combining distributed systems with self-organization has high potential to solve this curse of complexity and is a promising pathway. However, distributed computing systems are more difficult to program than a single-CPU computer due to parallelism, asynchronism, and uncertain interactions between components. This problem is even more pronounced for self-organizing systems whose high standards of scalability and robustness are usually achieved through methods restricted to local interactions and local information. In embodied distributed systems we additionally face hardware limitations concerning computational power, communication range, and energy autonomy. Examples of embodied self-organizing systems are self-organizing networks [8], multi-robot systems [11], and robot swarms [6]. The main challenge is due to the strict locality of individual components which requires the program code to be written from the local component perspective (micro-level) while tasks are defined

M. Dorigo et al. (Eds.): ANTS 2016, LNCS 9882, pp. 173–184, 2016.
DOI: 10.1007/978-3-319-44427-7_15

at the system level (macro-level) [1, 2]. An exhaustive design strategy needs to establish a so-called micro-macro link [3, 14] that connects the micro-level information processing with its effect on the macro-level. An additional challenge of distributed systems that have mobile components (e.g., robot swarms) is their dynamic interaction network (time-variant neighborhoods) which complicates the derivation of a micro-macro link.

In some applications of embodied distributed systems, as nanorobotics [15], the hardware requirements are extremely strict [17] and limit the core functions of such robots. While robots are usually built as reprogrammable devices, it might prove difficult to build nanorobots with that property. In certain scenarios the only feasible approach might be to hardwire the control logics. This potential lack of flexibility in programming individual robots motivates us to implement flexibility at the macro-level. We do so by composing heterogeneous swarms of robots with different hardwired controllers to obtain a desired macro-level behavior. In other words, our swarm is behaviorally heterogeneous, that is, individual components or subpopulations are allowed to differ in their controller. Examples of heterogeneous robot swarms include the Swarmanoid project [7] and an approach inspired by honeybees [16].

Related to our approach are the methods proposed by Berman et al. [4] and Prorok et al. [19]. These methods have the advantage of high scalability because they operate on continuous, macroscopic models. Their disadvantage is that they either rely on non-communicating agents or they require a centralized authority that gathers information. Hence, there is either no cooperation or a single point of failure which is not coherent with swarm intelligence.

2   Population Coding and Hardwired Controllers

Our main idea is inspired by the concept of population coding which is a method from neuroscience to relate a stimulus to the activity of a neuron population [10, 18]. For example, the direction of movement can be encoded within a population of neurons with each of them representing a preferred direction. Population coding, according to Georgopoulos et al. [10, p. 1416], can be understood in the following way: "When individual cells were represented as vectors that make weighted contributions along the axis of their preferred direction [. . .] the resulting vector sum of all cell vectors (population vector) was in a direction congruent with the direction of movement". Population coding can be mathematically interpreted as a function approximation with basis functions [18]. Each neuron's preference for a certain direction is represented by a Gaussian function as basis function and each neuron's activity gives the weight of the respective basis function to approximate a 'stimulus function'. We define an approach to compose heterogeneous distributed systems by combining subpopulations of components of different predetermined, possibly hardwired behavioral types (see Fig. 1). In analogy to population coding, we select quantities of different controller types of the micro-level (weighted contributions of neurons) that sum up to a system behavior of the macro-level (population vector). The choice of controller type compositions is implemented

input: macro-behavior requirements

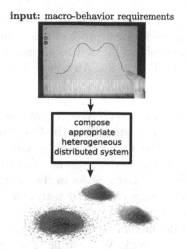

output: number of required controllers of each type

Fig. 1. Schematic representation of our approach. A user specifies the desired system behavior, for example, in the form of a potential field. Our algorithm derives an appropriate heterogeneous composition of controller types (microscopic behavior), and outputs the respective type numbers to compose the macroscopic behavior.

as an optimization process that minimizes deviations from the user-specified system behavior.

We allow to specify the desired system behavior in two different ways. The preferable approach is to define the macroscopic behavior, that is, working at the same level at which the actual task is defined. However, this approach requires to first define the control states and possible transitions and then, in a second step, to analytically derive a micro-macro link [14] to guide the optimization process. The alternative approach is to skip the second step. Then control states and a performance measure of the macroscopic behavior are required but not the micro-macro link. For example, one specifies the states of a finite state machine (FSM) where the conditions of state transitions are undetermined but parameterized. In this way we define a simple, user-friendly methodology to design the behavior of a distributed system. In the following, we give an example for both options: the definition of the desired system via a macroscopic behavior together with a micro-macro link or via a microscopic behavior using a FSM.

3 Scenario A: Task Allocation

As first example we investigate a task allocation problem in the form of a special collective decision-making scenario [20]. Instead of having a single optimal assignment of agents to tasks, we assume that our task allocation problem allows two or more different assignments of equal utility. This is therefore a collective decision-making problem because the group of agents is free to choose one of the different assignments but has to collectively agree on which option to choose.

We allow the agent group to switch between the desired task assignments at stochastic time intervals to allow for a probabilistic control approach. We focus on a binary task allocation problem [5] that requires a group of robots to obtain a desired allocation to tasks T_1 and T_2. All robots in the swarm are capable of performing both tasks and the overall goal is to reach an appropriate distribution of workforce that maximizes the swarm performance. For example, the user could specify a swarm fraction $s = N_1/(N_1 + N_2)$ of how many robots N_1 should be assigned to task T_1 which in turn defines the fraction $1 - s = N_2/(N_1 + N_2)$ to be assigned to task T_2. The user can also specify several swarm fractions s_1, s_2, etc., which requires a multistable system. We take a bistable distribution as an example (e.g., see Fig. 3b). Both peaks in the distribution define a particular allocation of robots (the variance around each peak influences the switching time between allocations).

Similarly to [13, 20] we define the controller types (i.e., the microscopic behavior) as a chemical reaction network. We assume that a robot perceives the current task allocations of its neighbors and decides to switch between tasks or to recruit a neighbor based on this information. For simplicity, we define reaction rules depending on a fixed neighborhood size of seven (i.e., the considered robot and its six neighbors). We define a rule for each neighborhood configuration (except for neighborhoods where all robots are assigned to the same task):

$$(7 - x)T_1 + xT_2 \xrightarrow{r} (7 - x + \delta_i)T_1 + (x - \delta_i)T_2, \tag{1}$$

where $x \in \{1, 2, \ldots, 6\}$ is the number of neighbors assigned to task T_2, $\delta_i \in \{+1, -1\}$ define the behavior of the focal robot, $i \in \{1, \ldots, 6\}$ is the rule index, and r is the reaction rate coefficient. The parameter δ_i defines the effect of a rule, that is, whether the current number of robots assigned to task T_1 is increased or decreasd by 1 unit. Depending on its current task, the considered robot either switches its own task assignment or recruits a neighbor to do so. The combinatorics of all assignments δ_i, $i \in \{1, 2, \ldots, 6\}$ gives $2^6 = 64$ different controller types that we enumerate and their index gives the δ_i as binary encoding. For example, controller type $R^{56} = (+ + + - - -)$ implements a majority rule because an observed majority of T_1 (respectively T_2) has the effect of increasing the majority by one robot. Type $R^7 = (- - - + + +)$ implements a minority rule because an observed minority of T_2 (respectively T_1) has the effect of increasing the minority by one robot. Finally, we define two more reactions to model a spontaneous switching behavior: $T_1 \xrightarrow{e} T_2$ and $T_2 \xrightarrow{e} T_1$ with a reaction rate coefficient e. Spontaneous switching is required to avoid absorption in the macroscopic states where all robots of the swarm are assigned to one of the two tasks.

We defined 64 different robot controller types that we can use to compose heterogeneous swarms. The idea of producing 64 different hardwired controllers might seem to come with considerable overhead, however, in the following we show that only a few types are used in a controller composition and minimizing the number of controller types can be an additional optimization objective (sparsity).

3.1   Micro-macro Model

In the second step of our approach we need to establish a micro-macro link to model mathematically the contribution of each controller type to the macroscopic behavior of the swarm. Based on this micro-macro link we can derive a proper composition C of controller types that forms a heterogeneous swarm satisfying the input of the user. A composition is defined as $C = (n_1, \ldots, n_{64})$ based on the above defined 64 controller types, where each n_i gives the number of required robots of the corresponding type and $\sum_i n_i = N$ for swarm size N. Similarly to [13], we define a micro-macro link based on the expected contribution of each controller type to the change of the swarm state (macro-level). The swarm state is the current fraction $s \in [0, 1]$ of robots that are assigned to task T_1 (respectively, $1 - s$ for task T_2). The swarm state s varies because robots interact with each other. The dynamics of the swarm state is modeled by the expected change Δs of s which, in turn, is the sum over the contributions of each controller type.

In the following we assume for simplicity that the robots are spatially well-mixed with respect to their current task allocation. That allows us to calculate the probability of a certain configuration of a robot's neighborhood using the hypergeometric distribution

$$P(k, m) = \frac{\binom{N-m}{G-k}\binom{m}{k}}{\binom{N}{G}}, \tag{2}$$

whereas k is the number of robots allocated to task T_1 in the neighborhood and m is the number of robots allocated to task T_1 in the whole swarm. With probability $P(k, m)$ a controller of type j contributes to the swarm behavior with a change $\Delta R_k^j \in \{+1, -1\}$. As a consequence, its contribution to the expected change is $\Delta R_k^j P(k, m)$. A robot also contributes by spontaneously switching its task allocation. With probability $P = s$ a robot allocated to task T_1 switches to task T_2 contributing a change of -1 robots allocated to T_1 and vice versa. The contribution to the expected change is $-1s + 1(1 - s) = (1 - 2s)$.

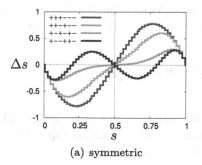

(a) symmetric

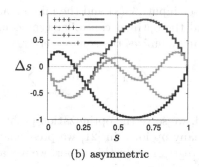

(b) asymmetric

Fig. 2. Examples of individual contributions to the expected change Δs of the swarm behaviors according to Eq. 3 with $e = 0$. Symbols '+' and '−' corresponds to values of $\delta_i \in \{+1, -1\}$.

In Fig. 2 we give examples of the expected change Δs for a few controller types. The main effect of Δs on the system can be interpreted visually. For $s > 0.5$ in Fig. 2, $\Delta s > 0$ represents positive feedback that drives the system towards the extreme of $s = 1$, while $\Delta s < 0$ represents negative feedback that drives the system towards the balanced state of $s = 0.5$. In Fig. 2a we show the symmetric expected change Δs of 'symmetric' controller types. In Fig. 2b we give expected changes of 'asymmetric' controller types.

The micro-macro link is established by calculating the expected swarm change Δs which is a sum over all controller types in a chosen composition C and for each of them all possible neighborhood configurations are considered. We obtain

$$\Delta s(s, C) = \sum_{j=1}^{64} \frac{n_j}{N} \left[\frac{r}{r+e} \sum_{k=1}^{G-1} \Delta R_k^j P(k, m = sN) + \frac{e}{r+e}(1 - 2s) \right], \quad (3)$$

where n_j is the number of robots of controller type j in the swarm and hence n_j/N weights the contribution of each controller type.

3.2   Evolutionary Approach

For a given user input, we formulate the derivation of the appropriate heterogeneous swarm as an optimization problem using the micro-macro link. A user provides as input a potential field $p(x)$ that characterizes the desired allocation of robots. For swarm size N the potential field p is defined by $N + 1$ data points $p(i) = y$, $i \in \{0, 1, \ldots, N\}$. Each maximum defines a desired allocation. For example, a maximum $p(j) = c_{\max}$ defines that the user requires the allocation of j robots to T_1 and $N - j$ robots to T_2. First, we translate the desired potential field to its corresponding expected change $\widehat{\Delta s}$ via the discrete derivative

$$\widehat{\Delta s}(s) = \frac{d}{ds}p(sN). \quad (4)$$

Second, we formulate an optimization problem. We consider the error between the user input $\widehat{\Delta s}(s)$ and the micro-macro link Δs as defined in Eq. 3. We want to find the optimal controller type composition C_{opt} (and optimal rates r and e) that minimizes the squared error

$$C_{\mathrm{opt}} = \arg \min_{C} \sum_{x \in \{0,1,\ldots,N\}} (\widehat{\Delta s}(xN) - \Delta s(xN, C))^2. \quad (5)$$

Third, we solve the optimization problem with an appropriate technique. There are many options, in [21] we present an efficient, model-driven approach using lasso regression. In this paper, we use a genetic algorithm[1].

---

[1] We use an implementation for the R project "NMOF: Numerical Methods and Optimization in Finance" ('NMOF') by Enrico Schumann, see http://cran.r-project.org/web/packages/NMOF/.

We evolve controller type compositions with a population size of 50 compositions for 50 generations. Mutation is implemented as bit flip with probability 0.02 and mutated compositions are corrected to guarantee $\sum_i n_i = N$. The fitness function is defined by the sum in the right side of Eq. 5. We have tested this approach for the two different user inputs shown in Fig. 3. Figures 3a and b show the user input as potential fields (2 maxima, hence 2 optimal task assignments, which requires collective decision-making at runtime). The desired macroscopic behavior can be understood as a hill climber that is greedily walking uphill towards the peaks but is also subject to fluctuations. In Figs. 3c and d we give the expected change $\widehat{\Delta s}$ as defined by the user input (Eq. 4) and the resulting expected change of the evolved (fitted) controller type composition. In the first

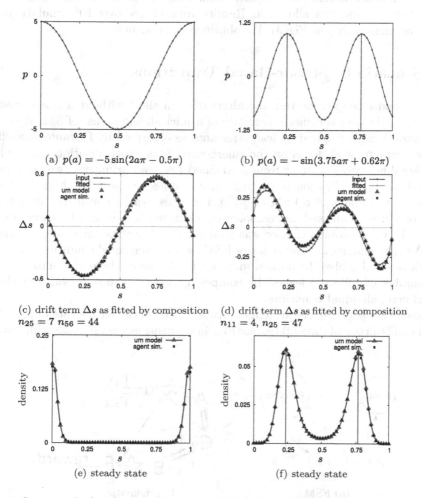

(a) $p(a) = -5\sin(2a\pi - 0.5\pi)$

(b) $p(a) = -\sin(3.75a\pi + 0.62\pi)$

(c) drift term Δs as fitted by composition $n_{25} = 7$ $n_{56} = 44$

(d) drift term Δs as fitted by composition $n_{11} = 4$, $n_{25} = 47$

(e) steady state

(f) steady state

Fig. 3. Scenario A, (a, b) examples of potential fields $p(x)$ defined using sine waves as user input, (c, d) expected change $\widehat{\Delta s}$, resulting expected change using the evolved controller type compositions, and the validation (urn model and agent-based simulations), (e, f) steady states for the evolved controller type compositions.

example, we obtain an almost perfect fit (Fig. 3c) by a composition of $n_{25} = 7$ and $n_{56} = 44$ (all other $n_j = 0$). Controller type 56 corresponds to decision rule $(+ + + - - -)$ that implements a majority decision. Controller type 25 corresponds to rule $(- + + - - +)$ which shifts the maxima towards the boundaries $(s = 0, s = 1)$ and lowers the amplitude of the expected change Δs to match the user input. In the second example we obtain a controller type composition consisting of types $n_{11} = 4$ $(- - + - + +)$ and $n_{25} = 47$ $(- + + - - +)$, see Fig. 3d. Despite some errors, the zeros of the user input (i.e., desired task allocations) are well approximated. We validate our approach using a simple urn model following [12] and determine the expected change and the steady state numerically (see Fig. 3c–f). We also use a simple, agent-based simulator. Agents are massless points randomly walking in a square area. Each agent is characterized by its controller type and task allocation. Results are averaged over 10^4 simulations of 10^4 time units each (see Fig. 3). We obtain very good fits.

4   Scenario B: Sensor-Based Transitions

As a second example, we test the alternative method without a micro-macro link where the user specifies a template of a micro-behavior as a FSM. We take a scenario loosely inspired by leafcutter ants as described by Ferrante et al. [9]. While Ferrante et al. focus on the emergence of task specialization and evolve individual behaviors starting from predefined low-level primitives, we get a predefined task specialization (e.g., cutting, collecting) as user input in the form of the control states of a FSM (see Fig. 4a). This can be considered as a template of a class of allowed microscopic behaviors and is in contrast to scenario A where the macroscopic behavior was predefined but not the microscopic behavior. We then enumerate a finite set of FSMs with determined conditions of state transitions and evolve the desired macroscopic behavior (here, maximization of the number of collected leaves) by composing a heterogeneous swarm of these predefined individual behaviors.

Leaves are added to the system at a rate r_{in} and decay with a rate of r_{out}. An agent can be in one of three states (see Fig. 4a): cutting leaves (A), collecting leaves

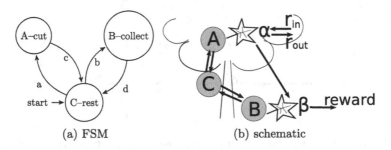

(a) FSM   (b) schematic

Fig. 4. Scenario B, finite state machine (FSM) and schematic representation of FSM showing a tree, leaves on tree α, leaves at ground β.

(B), or resting (C). The area is divided into two spaces: leaf cutting agents A are on the tree and collecting agents B are at the ground. Once an agent has cut a leaf α on the tree, the leaf falls down to the floor and becomes β ($\alpha \rightarrow \beta$, see Fig. 4b). We only allow transitions between states A and C and between B and C but not directly between A and B. Additionally, the number of Leaf cutting agents A can only perceive 20 % of other leaf cutting agents and 20 % of the leaves on the tree. Collecting agents B can only perceive 20 % of other collecting agents and 20 % of leaves on the floor. The desired global behavior is an efficient system that maximizes the number of collected leaves. We say that agents in state resting (C) save energy and give a reward for each agent spending a time step in C.

Next, we define the controller types used to compose a heterogeneous system. Each agent locally perceives the number of neighboring agents that are in the same state and also the number of nearby leaves. For each transition as labeled in Fig. 4a, we define a rule using the notation of reaction equations:

$$a : x_1\alpha + C \rightarrow x_1\alpha + A, \tag{6}$$
$$b : x_2\beta + C \rightarrow x_2\beta + B, \tag{7}$$
$$c : x_3\alpha + y_1A \rightarrow x_3\alpha + (y_1 - 1)A + C, \tag{8}$$
$$d : x_4\beta + y_2B \rightarrow x_4\beta + (y_2 - 1)B + C, \tag{9}$$

and for two transitions that model the leaves we have $\alpha + A \rightarrow \beta + A$ and $\beta + B \rightarrow B$ (associated with a reward for collecting a leaf). We limit the six parameters $x_i, y_j \in \{0, 1, 2, 3\}$ for simplicity giving us a total of $6^4 = 1296$ rules to choose from. We can represent a controller type by a 6-tuple: $(x_1, x_2, x_3, x_4, y_1, y_2)$. A particular controller type can have any choice of x_i and y_j for each individual rule (Eqs. 6–9). An example controller is

$$a : \alpha + C \rightarrow \alpha + A, \tag{10}$$
$$b : 2\beta + C \rightarrow 2\beta + B, \tag{11}$$
$$c : 3\alpha + 2A \rightarrow 3\alpha + A + C, \tag{12}$$
$$d : 2\beta + B \rightarrow 2\beta + C. \tag{13}$$

We test a setup with $N = 50$ agents. The experiment is done in four phases by changing the leaf adding rate r_{in} every 50 time steps for a total of 200 time steps. We evaluate each controller type composition in six tests (the fitness is the average over these six tests) with different sequences of r_{in}: (0, 50, 0, 20), (50, 0, 20, 0), (20, 20, 20, 20), (10, 10, 10, 10), (1, 5, 10, 15), (15, 10, 5, 1). Such a task allocation problem could be solved with adaptive response thresholds in each agent, but we restrict the agents to be non-adaptive. Hence, the adaptivity has to emerge at the macro-level. We use a genetic algorithm to find good controller type compositions. We reward (each with equal weight) for each collected leaf, for agents staying in state C (rest) per time step, and for sparsity (i.e., use of few different controller types). In Fig. 5 we give results for the best evolved controller type composition. It receives a fitness of 0.64 averaged over all six tested leaf inflow sequences. The best homogeneous swarm (i.e., using the same controller type for all agents) received a fitness of 0.56. The best heterogeneous composition assigns 17 different controller types to the 50 agents, most agents (eight) are assigned the controller type with values ($x_1 = 3, x_2 = 3, x_3 = 0, y_1 = 2, x_4 = 2, y_2 = 0$) (cf. Eqs. 6–9). Figures 5a and b give the cumulative number of agents with transitions for 0, 1 or less, 2 or less, and any number of seen leaves as sum over all controller types used by the evolved composition for reaction rules 6 and 7 that depend on leaves only. We observe that fewer leaves suffice for transition a while transition b requires more leaves, hence a switch from C to state A is done more easily. Figures 5c and d give the cumulative number of agents with transitions as weighted sum over all controller types used by the evolved composition for reaction rules 8 and 9 that depend on two variables each (agents and leaves). We notice that few leaves suffice for transition c while transition d requires more. Hence, a switch back from A to C is done more easily which corresponds to our finding for transition a. Figures 5e and f give the number of agents per state, their transitions, and the number of leaves in the system over time for the fitness evaluation with leaf adding rate sequence (0, 50, 0, 20). For $t < 50$ we observe only up to 12 agents that are not in state C which is efficient although suboptimal. For $50 < t < 100$ there are 32 agents cutting leaves (A), 18 agents collecting leaves (B), and none resting. Having no resting agents in this period is important because otherwise more α leaves would be lost due to $r_{out} > 0$ (see Fig. 5f). For $t < 100$ the number of collecting agents B is increased at the cost of cutting agents A which is reasonable to process the pile of β leaves. Note that an optimal solution for this particular leaf inflow sequence may limit the success for other sequences, hence, the controller type composition needs to be a compromise.

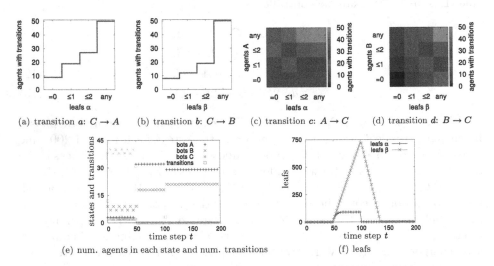

(a) transition a: $C \rightarrow A$ (b) transition b: $C \rightarrow B$ (c) transition c: $A \rightarrow C$ (d) transition d: $B \rightarrow C$

(e) num. agents in each state and num. transitions   (f) leafs

Fig. 5. Scenario B, (a–d) resulting number of state transitions (transition labels as in Fig. 4a) for evolved controller type composition based on 17 different controller types, (e) number of agents per state, their transitions, and (f) the number of leaves in the system over time for the evaluation with leaf inflow r_{in} sequence (0, 50, 0, 20).

5   Discussion and Conclusion

We have described our new design paradigm for embodied distributed systems which is inspired by population coding. Our approach relies on predetermined ⅰⅰⅰⅼⅰⅰⅰⅼⅼ ⅰ ⅼⅼⅼⅼ ⅰⅼⅰⅰ ⅰ ⅰⅰ ⅼⅰ ⅰⅰⅰⅰⅼⅰⅼⅰⅰⅰⅼ ⅼⅰ ⅰⅼⅼⅰⅼⅼⅼⅼ ⅰⅰ ⅰⅰ ⅰⅰⅰⅰⅼⅼⅰⅼ ⅰ heterogeneous swarm. In scenario A, we have shown how we can evolve a heterogeneous swarm with the desired behavior for a user-specified macroscopic behavior by leveraging on a micro-macro link. In scenario B, we have shown how a heterogeneous swarm can be evolved for a user-specified microscopic behavior template in the form of a FSM using agent-based simulations. Scalability and robustness might impose a challenge to our approach.

Scaling the number of states and state transitions in the FSM is potentially problematic due to the combinatorial explosion of the search space. This issue can be addressed by limiting a priori the number of possible state transitions as done in scenario B where the FSM is not a complete graph. An alternative approach is to leverage on optimization methods specifically conceived to achieve sparsity and that are computationally efficient also in high-dimensional search spaces (e.g., lasso for regularized regression as done in [21]).

Robustness might be problematic due to the heterogeneity of the system. In a homogeneous system any loss of an agent is compensated by all other agents. In a heterogeneous system, however, agents are different and cannot be replaced by every other agent. In our approach we tackle this problem by pushing towards sparse solutions, that is, controller type compositions that make use of only a few different controllers. With this approach, the probability that a single controller type is represented by few agents is lowered. Still, sparsity is not sufficient because only few robots may be assigned to a certain controller type. A solution could be to maximize this quantity in addition to minimizing the number of controller types. Furthermore, a radical approach could be to provide each agent with all controller types (i.e., back to homogeneous swarms) and to allow the agents to switch between controller types probabilistically. Then each agent would execute each controller from the composition with an appropriate probability that depends on how many agents are assigned to that controller type in the composition. However, we would loose the property that we can prefabricate the different controller types. Hence, it seems that there is an unavoidable tradeoff between robustness and design flexibility at the macro-level.

In future work, we plan to experiment with many different case studies both in simulation and in hardware to show the generality of our approach and also to show how it scales to more complex tasks.

References

1. Abelson, H., Allen, D., Coore, D., Hanson, C., Homsy, G., Knight, T., Nagpal, R., Rauch, E., Sussman, G., Weiss, R.: Amorphous computing. Commun. ACM **43**(5), 74–82 (2000)

2. Beal, J., Dulman, S., Usbeck, K., Viroli, M., Correll, N.: Organizing the aggregate: languages for spatial computing. In: Formal and Practical Aspects of Domain-Specific Languages, pp. 436–501. Information Science Reference (2012)
3. Beckers, R., Holland, O.E., Deneubourg, J.L.: From local actions to global tasks: stigmergy and collective robotics. Artif. Life **4**, 181–189 (1994)
4. Berman, S., Halasz, A., Hsieh, M., Kumar, V.: Optimized stochastic policies for task allocation in swarms of robots. IEEE Trans. Robot. **25**(4), 927–937 (2009)
5. Brutschy, A., Pini, G., Pinciroli, C., Birattari, M., Dorigo, M.: Self-organized task allocation to sequentially interdependent tasks in swarm robotics. Auton. Agents Multi-Agent Syst. **28**(1), 101–125 (2014)
6. Dorigo, M., Birattari, M., Brambilla, M.: Swarm robotics. Scholarpedia **9**(1), 1463 (2014)
7. Dorigo, M., et al.: Swarmanoid: a novel concept for the study of heterogeneous robotic swarms. IEEE Robot. Autom. Mag. **20**, 60–71 (2013)
8. Dressler, F.: Self-organization in Sensor and Actor Networks. Wiley, New York (2008)
9. Ferrante, E., Turgut, A.E., Duez-Guzmn, E., Dorigo, M., Wenseleers, T.: Evolution of self-organized task specialization in robot swarms. PLoS Comput. Biol. **11**(8), 1–21 (2015)
10. Georgopoulos, A.P., Schwartz, A.B., Kettner, R.E.: Neuronal population coding of movement direction. Science **233**(4771), 1416–1419 (1986)
11. Gerkey, B.P., Matarić, M.J.: A formal analysis and taxonomy of task allocation in multi-robot systems. Int. J. Robot. Res. **23**(9), 939–954 (2004)
12. Hamann, H.: Towards swarm calculus: Urn models of collective decisions and universal properties of swarm performance. Swarm Intell. **7**(2–3), 145–172 (2013)
13. Hamann, H., Valentini, G., Khaluf, Y., Dorigo, M.: Derivation of a micro-macro link for collective decision-making systems. In: Bartz-Beielstein, T., Branke, J., Filipič, B., Smith, J. (eds.) PPSN 2014. LNCS, vol. 8672, pp. 181–190. Springer, Heidelberg (2014)
14. Hamann, H., Wörn, H.: A framework of space-time continuous models for algorithm design in swarm robotics. Swarm Intell. **2**(2–4), 209–239 (2008)
15. Hogg, T.: Coordinating microscopic robots in viscous fluids. Auton. Agents Multi-Agent Syst. **14**(3), 271–305 (2006)
16. Kengyel, D., Hamann, H., Zahadat, P., Radspieler, G., Wotawa, F., Schmickl, T.: Potential of heterogeneity in collective behaviors: a case study on heterogeneous swarms. In: Chen, Q., Torroni, P., Villata, S., Hsu, J. (eds.) PRIMA 2015. LNCS, vol. 9387, pp. 201–217. Springer, Heidelberg (2015)
17. Lenaghan, S., Wang, Y., Xi, N., Fukuda, T., Tarn, T., Hamel, W., Zhang, M.: Grand challenges in bioengineered nanorobotics for cancer therapy. IEEE Trans. Biomed. Eng. **60**(3), 667–673 (2013)
18. Pouget, A., Dayan, P., Zemel, R.: Information processing with population codes. Nat. Rev. Neurosci. **1**, 125–132 (2000)
19. Prorok, A., Hsieh, M.A., Kumar, V.: Fast redistribution of a swarm of heterogeneous robots. In: International Conference on Bio-inspired Information and Communications Technologies (BICT) (2015)
20. Valentini, G., Ferrante, E., Hamann, H., Dorigo, M.: Collective decision with 100 Kilobots: speed versus accuracy in binary discrimination problems. Auton. Agents Multi-Agent Syst. **30**(3), 553–580 (2015)
21. Valentini, G., Hamann, H., Dorigo, M.: Global-to-local design for self-organized task allocation in swarms. Technical report TR/IRIDIA/2016-002, IRIDIA, Université Libre de Bruxelles, Brussels, Belgium, March 2016

Random Walks in Swarm Robotics: An Experiment with Kilobots

Cristina Dimidov[1], Giuseppe Oriolo[1], and Vito Trianni[2](✉)

[1] DIAG, Sapienza University of Rome, Rome, Italy
dimidovc@yahoo.com, oriolo@diag.uniroma1.it
[2] ISTC, National Research Council, Rome, Italy
vito.trianni@istc.cnr.it

Abstract. Random walks represent fundamental search strategies for both animal and robots, especially when there are no environmental cues that can drive motion, or when the cognitive abilities of the searching agent do not support complex localisation and mapping behaviours. In swarm robotics, random walks are basic building blocks for the individual behaviour and support the emergent collective pattern. However, there has been limited account for the correct parameterisation to be used in different search scenarios, and the relationship between search efficiency and information transfer within the swarm has been often overlooked. In this study, we analyse the efficiency of random walk patterns for a swarm of Kilobots searching a static target in two different environmental conditions entailing a bounded or an open space. We study the search efficiency and the ability to spread information within the swarm through numerical simulations and real robot experiments, and we determine what kind of random walk best fits each experimental scenario.

1 Introduction

Animal search patterns are often described as random walks to represent situations in which the location of the target is not a priori known and the individual cognitive limitations and ecological conditions do not support more complex search strategies [2,4,6]. Since the early studies of the botanist Robert Brown about the motion of pollen particles—usually referred to as Brownian motion—the theory about random walks has been thoroughly developed and applied in disparate contexts, from animal behaviour to human cognition [1,10]. Among the several possible random walk variants, two classes have emerged as the most useful models for describing animal search patterns: correlated random walks (CRWs) and Lévy walks (LWs) [6,22]. The former are characterised by some correlation between the orientation of consecutive movements, while the latter are characterised by several small displacements interleaved by long relocations. LWs, in particular, provide an optimal search behaviour in case of sparse targets, thanks to the long motion steps that allow to search in different areas without frequently passing over sites that have been already visited [20,21]. For this reason, several experimental studies have been conducted to demonstrate Lévy

© Springer International Publishing Switzerland 2016
M. Dorigo et al. (Eds.): ANTS 2016, LNCS 9882, pp. 185–196, 2016.
DOI: 10.1007/978-3-319-44427-7_16

behaviour in Nature, sometimes generating strong controversies [7,11]. Recently, even theoretical results about the superiority of Lévy strategies have been questioned, showing that the optimal strategy is highly influenced by the specific contingencies of the search problem, such as the existence of a direction bias [13].

In swarm robotics too, it is important to deliver efficient search strategies for a number of relevant tasks, from search & rescue to demining, from surveillance to space exploration. The basic assumptions of swarm robotics entail limited individual abilities (i.e., local sensing, low processing power) which do not support complex localisation and mapping. As a consequence, random walks represent fundamental building blocks for the individual behaviour, and are often used when no environmental/social cue can be exploited [17]. For instance, a biased random walk was exploited for the basic motion of robots in the context of a commercial pollination task [3]. In a resource exploitation task, robots were programmed to search for resources within a bounded space exploiting a simple random walk with obstacle avoidance [5]. In collective decision-making problems, robots used a CRW to move in the different parts of a bounded space to find available options and share information with other robots [14,19]. In a collective foraging task, the parameter of a biased CRW have been tuned to maximise search efficiency [9]. In the context of consensus decisions, the effects of the diffusion coefficient on the collective dynamics and the robot interaction network have been investigated [18]. These are just a few recent studies that demonstrate the pervasiveness and relevance of random walks in swarm robotics research.

Despite the importance of random walks for the design of swarm robotics systems, there is no systematic study that can help in the choice of the correct type and parameterisation, to the best of our knowledge. In some cases, a LW is chosen on the basis of the theoretical results only [8,16]. More often, the type and parameterisation of the random walk behaviour are chosen heuristically without an analysis of their effect. This may lead to lower performance as soon as the working conditions change (e.g., when the size of the working space is increased [5]). In other cases, parameters are tuned with some optimisation algorithm [9]. Additionally, the type and parameterisation of the random walk are often chosen in relation to the efficiency of the individual behaviour, and the effects they have on information sharing within the robot swarm are often overlooked [18]. Given that the way in which robots move determines also the probability of their encounters, there may be a trade-off between the ability to widely search the environment and the ability to share information with other robots, which sometime requires special reverse behaviours (i.e., homing to a central place [14]) to allow information sharing. Overall, we believe that there is a compelling need for a systematic study of random walks in swarm robotics, taking into account possible trade-offs between search efficiency and information sharing, and investigating scenarios relevant for a wide range of applications.

In this paper, we move a step in this direction by studying different types of random walk for two specific search problems involving a single static target in either a bounded or an open space. We develop our study with respect to a specific robotic platform—the Kilobot robot [15]—and consider its properties and limitations in the performance analysis. We devise a random walk behaviour determined by the distribution of step lengths and of turning angles. The former is a Lévy distribution controlled by the parameter α, which allows one to obtain step-length distributions varying from Gaussian—resulting in a (correlated) random walk—to a power law resulting in a LW. The distribution of turning angles corresponds to a wrapped Cauchy distribution controlled by the parameter ρ, which allows to obtain a distribution varying from uniform—resulting in a isotropic random walk—to a delta (i.e., ballistic motion, see Sect. 2). We implement the target search scenarios in both multiagent simulations and physical robots (see Sect. 3), and we measure the efficiency in searching the target and in sharing information about its discovery for a wide range of parameterisations and swarm sizes (see Sect. 4). We find that the search efficiency and the information transfer highly depend on the scenario and on the local robot density. These results can be exploited in future swarm robotics research to support a principled choice of the random walk behaviour to be used as building block for more complex problems (see Sect. 5).

2 Random Walk Models

In its simplest form, a random walk can be thought of as a sequence of straight movements and direction changes. For instance, the simplest isotropic random walk in one dimension has a fixed step-length δ and equal probability of moving left or right $p_l = p_r = 1/2$ at each time step τ. In these conditions, the resulting motion is diffusive with a diffusion constant $D = \delta^2/2\tau$ [6].

In two or more dimensions, changes of directions are not limited to left-right motion, but any possible orientation must be taken into account, leading to the need of introducing a probability distribution for the turning angles. An isotropic random walk in multiple dimensions is obtained with a uniform distribution, while a biased or correlated random walk is obtained if such distribution is not uniform. A biased random walk has a preferential (absolute) direction of motion that does not depend on the current orientation of the random walker, but may depend on its location in space (e.g., a drift from wind or currents). A CRW, instead, is characterised by a positive correlation between consecutive movements, that is, the walker with higher probability moves in a similar direction to the previous one. In this study, we focus on random walks in two dimensions, and the turning angle θ is chosen from a wrapped Cauchy distribution, characterised by the following PDF [2,12]:

$$f_w(\theta; \mu, \rho) = \frac{1}{2\pi} \frac{1 - \rho^2}{1 + \rho^2 - 2\rho\cos(\theta - \mu)}, \qquad 0 < \rho < 1, \tag{1}$$

where μ represents the average value of the distribution ($\mu = 0$ in this study), while ρ determines the distribution skewness: for $\rho = 0$ the distribution becomes uniform and provides no correlation between consecutive movements, while for $\rho = 1$ a Dirac distribution is obtained, corresponding to straight-line motion.

For what concerns the straight motion steps, these may be of fixed length or can vary according to a certain step-length distribution. A Brownian motion is characterised by a step-length distribution with finite second moment, so that the distribution tends to a normal distribution according to the central limit theorem. On the other hand, a LW is characterised by a step-length distribution that follows a power law:

$$P_\alpha(\delta) \sim \delta^{-(\alpha+1)}, \quad 0 < \alpha \leq 2 \tag{2}$$

so that long movements are performed with non-null probability, as the distribution is heavy-tailed [22]. The Lévy distribution can be defined in terms of its Fourier transformation:

$$F(k) = e^{-\beta|k|^\alpha}, \quad 0 < \alpha \leq 2, \tag{3}$$

where β is a scale parameter, and α is the parameter defining the power law scaling. In particular, for $\alpha = 2$ the distribution becomes Gaussian, while for $\alpha \to 0$ the random walk reduces to straight-line paths.

To summarise, a pure CRW can be obtained by controlling the distribution of turning angles through the parameter ρ, while having a Gaussian step-length distribution—corresponding to $\alpha = 2$ in (3). On the other hand, a pure LW can be obtained by controlling the step-length distribution through the parameter α, while having a uniform turning-angle distribution—corresponding to $\rho = 0$ in (1). As a special case, a Brownian motion is obtained when $\alpha = 2$ and $\rho = 0$. In this work, we study pure CRWs and LWs, and we also address a hybrid form that joins together the non-uniform distribution of turning angles and the heavy-tail distribution of step lengths [2]. In this way, both the properties of correlated movements and long relocations can be obtained at the same time, which may lead to improved search efficiency.

3   Experimental Setup

As already mentioned, the type and parameterisation of a random walk must be chosen on the basis of the search problem to be faced. In this study, we focus on the search of a single static target by a swarm of N robots, and we also allow robots to exchange information about the target discovery. The target is represented by a circle of radius $r_t = 10\,\mathrm{cm}$, and robots recognise the target when they pass over it. Robots can communicate with all neighbours within a radius $r_c = 10\,\mathrm{cm}$, and can exchange short messages to communicate whether the target was discovered (by themselves or by some teammate). Robots always move following the random walk behaviour, even after discovering the target: in this way, they can interact with other robots upon encounters.

We look for the effects of different parameterisation and swarm sizes on the search performance. We measure the efficiency of the individual search as the average *first passage time* t_f, measured as the average time taken by robots to pass over the target for the first time. The *fraction* of robots that individually discover the target is referred to as ϕ_t. We also measure the efficiency of information sharing as the *convergence time* t_c, which is the time in which all robots have information about the target (e.g., an identification code). Robots can obtain such information directly from the target when passing over it, or indirectly from other robots that already have such information. An experiment is terminated after a fixed amount of time T or when a sufficient number of robots have discovered the target.

We consider two simple scenarios that represent two common situations in swarm robotics. The first scenario consists in a *bounded space* surrounded by walls (square area with side L) in which robots and target are uniformly distributed. Given that Kilobots are not able to perceive obstacles, they are let free to collide with walls and with each other, and eventually disentangle owing to the random turns determined by their random walk behaviour. As we will discuss, collisions with walls have a bearing on the efficiency of the random search. The second scenario consists in a *open space* with a central place (e.g., a "home" location) from which all robots start searching. The central place is globally known to the robots, thanks to some form of dead reckoning or by some globally visible cue (e.g., a light source for the Kilobots [15]). In this scenario, the target is placed at a fixed distance d_t from the central place, but robots can travel very long distances away from the central place because of the absence of boundaries. To avoid that robots overly depart from the central place, we implement a biased random walk, so that a motion step is performed towards the central place with probability $p_b = 0.2$, otherwise following the direction given by the wrapped Cauchy distribution. In this way, we provide an elegant mechanism to maintain the swarm bounded in the vicinity of the central place, with the possibility of tuning the probability p_b to vary the diffusion properties. As a final remark, note that the motion step is interrupted and a new random direction is chosen every time a robot passes over the target or the central place.

Multi-agent Simulations. In order to analyse the properties of several parameterisations for the random walk as well as several swarm sizes, we devised a simple multi-agent simulation that abstracts the physical details of the Kilobots and focuses on the collective motion pattern. This computational model has been devised to provide a link between abstract analytical models and the robotic implementation [18], and is particularly useful to test a wide range of parameters for the random walk and the swarm size (see Sect. 4). Our simulation treats agents as dimensionless particles that can move at constant speed $v = 1\,\mathrm{cm/s}$ and can communicate with all neighbours within the radius r_c, much as the Kilobots can do. Differently from Kilobots, however, agents do not collide with each other and they can change direction instantaneously. Finally, agents can collide with walls—if present—so that the motion vector orthogonal to the wall is cancelled, and only the parallel component is executed. For the bounded space scenario, we use a square arena with side $L = 1\,\mathrm{m}$. For the open space scenario, we vary the target distance $d_t \in \{0.25, 0.5, 0.75, 1.0\}$ m. Each simulation is run for $T = 10^5\,steps$ with an integration time step $\Delta t = 0.5\,\mathrm{s}$, to grant enough time for the agents to individually find the target, hence having a sufficiently large sample to compute the statistics of the first passage time t_f. Given the discrete-time simulation and the finite velocity of the agents, the random walk is implemented by letting agents move straight for a number of simulation steps drawn from the Lévy distribution of Eq. (3), with $\beta = 5$. Turning is instantaneous and the turning angle is directly sampled from the wrapped Cauchy distribution of Eq. (1), with $\mu = 0$.

Experiments with Kilobots. The experiments performed with the Kilobots were made only in the bounded space scenario.[1] We built a square arena with $L = 90$ cm and distributed the robots and the target uniformly. The target here is represented by an immobile Kilobot programmed to continuously and frequently broadcast a target identification code id_t. As soon as a robot enters the communication range of the target Kilobot and receives the id_t code for the first time, it stores a time stamp to be used for the average first passage time statistics. Additionally, robots communicate with each other and share information about the target discovery by broadcasting a discovery identification code id_d, either when a robot has discovered the target on its own or when a robot has received the information from another robot. In the latter case, robots just act as relay. Upon reception of id_d for the first time, a robot stores a time stamp to be used to compute the convergence time t_c. The experimental run is terminated when a sufficient number of robots has discovered the target (i.e., $\phi_t > 0.7$) or after one hour of experimentation (i.e., $T = 3600$ s).

The implementation of the random walk behaviour for the Kilobot is rather straightforward, with the main differences with respect to simulation given by collisions and finite angular velocity. The distribution function for CRW and LW have been implemented as custom library functions in C++ and then ported to AVR C—the Kilobot programming language. Given the discrete control step of the Kilobots, both straight motion and turning are obtained through counters drawn from the Lévy and wrapped Cauchy distribution, respectively.

4   Results

Simulations of the Bounded Space Scenario. We have performed a wide simulation study to analyse different random walk behaviours by varying the parameteres $\rho \in [0, 0.9]$ and $\alpha \in [1.0, 2.0]$, and by testing the search efficiency for varying swarm size $N \in [10, 100]$. The parameter ρ spans the whole range of possible values for the wrapped Cauchy distribution, excluding only very high values $\rho > 0.9$. The parameter α varies in the range in which the Lévy distribution has a finite mean. For each experimental condition, we performed 100 independent runs. The statistics for the individual search efficiency are shown in Fig. 1A, D. Here, the heat map shows average statistics over different runs and

---

[1] Given the size of the robots and characteristics of the random walks, we have found particularly impractical to run experiments in the unbounded arena scenario due to the small robot arena available for experimentation with Kilobots.

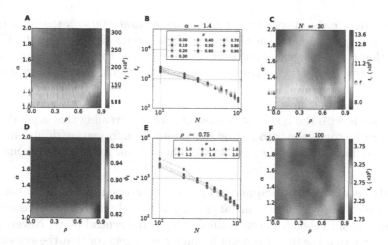

Fig. 1. Bounded space scenario. The search efficiency is represented by the averge first passage time t_f (A) and the fraction of agents that discovered the target ϕ_t (D). The efficiency of information diffusion is represented by the convergence time t_c. The scaling for some fixed parameterisation is shown in panel B for $\alpha = 1.4$ and panel E for $\rho = 0.75$. The joint dependency on α and ρ is shown in panel C and F respectively for $N = 30$ and $N = 100$.

different swarm sizes. Indeed, the search efficiency is an individual measure that does not depend on the swarm size and robot density. By looking at the average first passage time t_f in Fig. 1A, it is possible to note that the search efficiency is higher when $\alpha \geq 1.8$ and $\rho = 0.7$, which corresponds to the areas in which t_f is minimised. This means that a pure CRW is sufficient to maximise individual search efficiency, and that the correlation coefficient ρ needs to be adequately tuned because an excessive persistence in maintaining a certain direction of motion is deleterious. Indeed, due to the absence of a collision avoidance strategy, agents that persist in moving in the same direction remain blocked against walls or corners for long time. For the same reason, the LW does not provide any advantage here, as the long relocations lead the agents to collide with walls for long time without any possibility to escape until a new direction away from the wall is chosen. The fraction of agents visiting the target ϕ_t is near 1 for much of the parameter space (see Fig. 1D). In particular we can see a slight influence on the results when $\alpha = 1$ confirming that for small Lévy exponents the agents collide with walls too often due to excessively long relocation steps.

The above measures are mainly related to the individual search behaviour, and do not depend on the swarm size. The situation is different for the diffusion of information, which instead can be influenced by the number of agents in the swarm. Within a bounded space, the swarm size determines also the agent density, so that higher densities correspond to more chances of agents to interact with each other. This is reflected in the convergence time, which decreases with increasing swarm size, as shown in Fig. 1B, E where we plot the convergence time for some specific values of α and ρ. Both parameters have a minor impact on the convergence time, which is mainly dependent on the swarm size N.

To appreciate the effect of the random walk parameters on the convergence time, we have plotted t_c for specific values of the swarm size (see Fig. 1C, F). It is evident that the convergence time is higher either when the agents perform a very localised random walk (i.e., a Brownian motion), especially for small swarm size, as shown in the top left corner of Fig. 1C or when the agents perform almost a ballistic motion (bottom-right corner of Fig. 1C, F). Instead, the smallest values for t_f coincide with the region of highest efficiency, revealing that a good search behaviour also corresponds to a good behaviour for information diffusion, as the agents meet more often if they efficiently move within the bounded arena.

Simulations of the Open Space Scenario. In an open space, agents can move large distances away from the central place. The biased random walk ensures that the search remains somehow constrained around the central place. Nevertheless, it can happen that the target is never found by any agent, or that the system does not converge. To evaluate the performance of the system, we perform 100 runs for each experimental condition obtained by varying the parameters as for the bounded space scenario, and we report the statistics for those parameterisation in which at least 75 % of the runs were successful. We report here a thorough analysis for a fixed target at distance $d_t = 0.5\,\mathrm{m}$, while other distances are discussed in less detail later on. Looking at Fig. 2A, we note that the parameter α controlling the Lévy distribution has the most influence on the search efficiency, while ρ as a smaller effect. The mean first passage time t_f is minimised for $\alpha \approx 1.4$ and $\rho \geq 0.75$. This parameterisation corresponds to a random walk characterised by both highly correlated movements and long relocations, which proves useful to explore widely the space around the central place. The fraction of agents visiting the target is highest for similar parameterisation (see Fig. 2D).

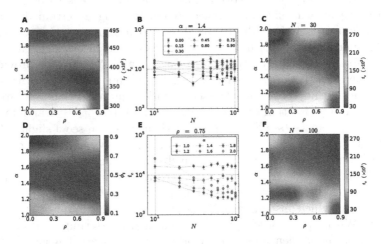

Fig. 2. Open space scenario. Results for a target at distance $d_t = 0.5\,\mathrm{m}$. See the caption of Fig. 1 for a description of the different panels.

We have also analysed the effects of the different parameterisations on the convergence time t_c. By varying the Lévy exponent α and fixing the correlation to the best-efficiency value ($\rho = 0.75$), we can appreciate how the long relocations of the LW affect the convergence time (see Fig. 2B). When the behaviour is close to a CRW ($\alpha \geq 1.6$), the convergence time decreases with the swarm size N. Indeed, without long relocations the agents remain close to the central place, hence the convergence time is mainly determined by the local density of agents, which in turn depends on N. On the other hand, when the random walk has the typical characteristics of a LW ($\alpha < 1.6$), the influence of the swarm size N on the convergence time vanishes. In this case, the long relocations coupled with the biased random walk allow agents to search widely the arena and to interact with each other in a way that is not dependent on the local density, leading to a very scalable behaviour. This is confirmed by the analysis of t_c for a fixed Lévy parameter $\alpha = 1.4$ (see Fig. 2E), which highlights that this scalability of the convergence time is determined by the feature of the step-length distribution, and not by the correlated movements, because for any value of ρ the convergence time appears to be independent from the swarm size N. If we look at the combined effects of α and ρ on t_c for a fixed swarm size (Fig. 2C, F), we can see a faster convergence for high values of both α and ρ. This means that the scalable behaviour offered by the LW does not minimise convergence time, but a good trade-off can be found to obtain at the same time scalability and fast convergence (e.g., $\alpha = 1.4$ and $\rho = 0.9$).

The other cases analysed in the open space scenario validate the analysis exposed above. When the distance of the target from the central place is small ($d_t = 0.25$ m, Fig. 3A), the search efficiency is maximised by a random walk with few long relocations (high values for α) and high persistence of movements

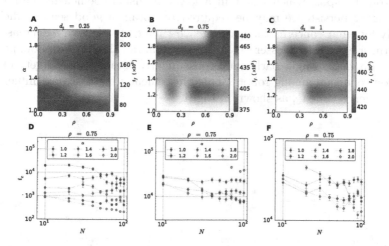

Fig. 3. Average first passage time t_f (top) and convergence time t_c (bottom) in the open space scenario for varying target distance (A, D: $d_t = 0.25$ m; B, E: $d_t = 0.75$ m; C, F: $d_t = 1.0$ m).

(high values for ρ). With a very close target, a localised random walk is more efficient because long relocations are not necessary, similarly to the bounded space scenario. With increasing distance (see Fig. 3B, C), ρ loses its influence and the search efficiency is mainly determined by the extent to which agents are able to perform long relocations.

The convergence time presents similar dynamics to the case with target distance $d_t = 0.5\,\mathrm{m}$ (see Fig. 3D, F). When the target is very close, there is a generalised tendency to have slightly lower values when N increases. This is because the target is quickly found and hence the information spreads faster for larger swarms as the agents return to the central place. We note also that the parameter α has a clear influence on the convergence time, with higher values corresponding to faster convergence. When $d_t \geq 0.75$ instead, high values of α lead to a low success rate (hence data are not plotted). Here, too, smaller values of α lead to a scalable behaviour with respect to the swarm size N.

Results with Kilobots. The experiments with Kilobots have been performed with groups of 10 and 30 robots. Following the simulation results, the highest search efficiency in the bounded space scenario was obtained with a pure CRW. Consequently, we have decided to examine the cases in which $\alpha = 2$ and $\rho \in \{0.1, 0.5, 0.9\}$ to evaluate the effects of different CRWs on the search efficiency.

We perform 20 runs for each experimental condition, and we evaluate the performance of the system in case at least 75 % of the experiments were successful. The results obtained are in line with those obtained in simulation, with smaller t_f for larger ρ values (see Fig. 4). Differently from what observed in simulation, the high persistence provided by $\rho = 0.9$ does not lead to a lower efficiency. We argue that this is due to the effects of collisions and the time taken by Kilobots to turn on the spot, which result in a lower diffusion coefficient. This means that a higher persistence may be required to obtain a good search efficiency. Similarly for what concerns the convergence time t_c we observe a decrease with the swarm size N, with a lesser extent for $\rho = 0.9$. In this case, Kilobots perform a CRW with long straight paths, and consequently it takes time to get out from a collision condition among robots. This phenomenon has a strong influence on the convergence time t_c, as shown in Fig. 4.

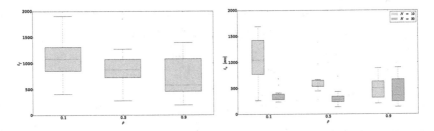

Fig. 4. Average first passage time t_f (left) and convergence time t_c (right) in the bounded space scenario in the experiments with kilobots. Boxes represent the inter-quartile range from the median. Whiskers extend 1.5 times beyond the inter-quartile range. Empty circles mark the outliers.

5 Conclusions

The analysis of different random walks in a bounded space shows that a CRW with a relatively high persistence is the best strategy to adopt. The LW has worse performance due to the effect of collisions with walls (or other robots) that result in a poor overall performance. In the unbounded space scenario, instead, the best strategy is the LW, although some correlation in the movement provide some advantage as well. The distance between the target and the central place can have a high influence on the performance of the system. Additionally, the LW provides scalability to the system in terms of information diffusion, as the convergence time becomes independent of the swarm size, especially for the values of the Lévy exponent α that maximise efficiency. Hence, the Lévy strategies are advantageous because they provide a very scalable behaviour, even if at the cost of some performance. Notwithstanding the specificities of the Kilobot platform, these results can help in selecting the type of random walk to use in a swarm robotics context, on the basis of the particular experimental scenario to be tackled.

In future work, we plan to analyse other free parameters that have not been tested in this study (e.g., the amount of bias). Additionally, we plan to perform a systematic study with varying density of targets in order to analyse the system efficiency and the diffusion of information when there are more than one possible outcomes, in particular for what concerns the unbounded arena scenario. Finally, robots could exploit their communication abilities to provide locally some bias to the random walk performed by the neighbours. In this way, the transmission of information between robots could alter the random walk pattern and improve the search efficiency beyond the individual capabilities.

Acknowledgments. Vito Trianni acknowledges support from the project DICE (FP7 Marie Curie Career Integration Grant, ID: 631297).

References

1. Baronchelli, A., Radicchi, F.: Lévy flights in human behaviour and cognition. Chaos Solitons Fractals **56**(C), 101–105 (2013)
2. Bartumeus, F., da Luz, M., Viswanathan, G., Catalan, J.: Animal search strategies: a quantitative random-walk analysis. Ecology **86**(11), 3078–3087 (2005)
3. Berman, S., Kumar, V., Nagpal, R.: Design of control policies for spatially inhomogeneous robot swarms with application to commercial pollination. In: Proceedings of the 2011 IEEE International Conference on Robotics and Automation (ICRA 2011), pp. 378–385. IEEE (2011)
4. Blackwell, P.: Random diffusion models for animal movement. Ecol. Model. **100**(1–3), 87–102 (1997)
5. Campo, A., Garnier, S., Dédriche, O., Zekkri, M., Dorigo, M.: Self-organized discrimination of resources. PLoS ONE **6**(5), e19888 (2011)
6. Codling, E., Plank, M., Benhamou, S.: Random walk models in biology. J. Roy. Soc. Interface **5**(25), 813–834 (2008)
7. Edwards, A., Phillips, R., Watkins, N., Freeman, M., Murphy, E., et al.: Revisiting Lévy flight search patterns of wandering albatrosses, bumblebees and deer. Nature **449**(7165), 1044–1048 (2007)

8. Fujisawa, R., Dobata, S.: Lévy walk enhances efficiency of group foraging in pheromone-communicating swarm robots. In: 2013 IEEE/SICE International Symposium on System Integration (SII), pp. 808–813. IEEE (2013)

9. Hecker, J., Moses, M.: Beyond pheromones: evolving error-tolerant, flexible, and scalable ant-inspired robot swarms. Swarm Intell. 9(1), 1–28 (2015)

10. Hills, T., Todd, P., Lazer, D., Redish, A., Couzin, I.: The cognitive search research group: exploration versus exploitation in space, mind, and society. Trends Cogn. Sci. 19(1), 46–54 (2015)

11. Humphries, N., Queiroz, N., Dyer, J., Pade, N., Musyl, M., et al.: Environmental context explains Lévy and brownian movement patterns of marine predators. Nature 465(7301), 1066–1069 (2010)

12. Kato, S., Jones, M.: An extended family of circular distributions related to wrapped Cauchy distributions via Brownian motion. Bernoulli 19(1), 154–171 (2013)

13. Palyulin, V., Chechkin, A., Metzler, R.: Lévy flights do not always optimize random blind search for sparse targets. Proc. Natl. Acad. Sci. U S A 111(8), 2931–2936 (2014)

14. Reina, A., Miletitch, R., Dorigo, M., Trianni, V.: A quantitative micro–macro link for collective decisions: the shortest path discovery/selection example. Swarm Intell. 9(2–3), 75–102 (2015)

15. Rubenstein, M., Ahler, C., Hoff, N., Cabrera, A., Nagpal, R.: Kilobot: a low cost robot with scalable operations designed for collective behaviors. Robot. Auton. Syst. 62(7), 966–975 (2014)

16. Sutantyo, D., Kernbach, S., Levi, P., Nepomnyashchikh, V.: Multi-robot searching algorithm using Lévy flight and artificial potential field. In: IEEE International Workshop on Safety Security and Rescue Robotics (SSRR), pp. 1–6. IEEE (2010)

17. Trianni, V., Campo, A.: Fundamental collective behaviors in swarm robotics. In: Kacprzyk, J., Pedrycz, W. (eds.) Springer Handbook of Computational Intelligence, pp. 1377–1394. Springer, Berlin, Germany (2015)

18. Trianni, V., De Simone, D., Reina, A., Baronchelli, A.: Emergence of consensus in a multi-robot network: from abstract models to empirical validation. IEEE Robot. Autom. Lett. 1(1), 348–353 (2016)

19. Valentini, G., Ferrante, E., Hamann, H., Dorigo, M.: Collective decision with 100 kilobots: speed versus accuracy in binary discrimination problems. Auton. Agents Multi-Agent Syst. 30, 1–28 (2015)

20. Viswanathan, G., Afanasyev, V., Buldyrev, S., Havlin, S., da Luz, M., et al.: Lévy flights in random searches. Phys. A: Stat. Mech. Appl. 282(1–2), 1–12 (2000)

21. Viswanathan, G., Raposo, E., da Luz, M.: Lévy flights and superdiffusion in the context of biological encounters and random searches. Phys. Life Rev. 5(3), 133–150 (2008)

22. Zaburdaev, V., Denisov, S., Klafter, J.: Lévy walks. Rev. Mod. Phys. 87(2), 483–530 (2015)

Synthesizing Rulesets for Programmable Robotic Self-assembly: A Case Study Using Floating Miniaturized Robots

Bahar Haghighat$^{(\boxtimes)}$, Brice Platerrier, Loic Waegeli, and Alcherio Martinoli

Distributed Intelligent Systems and Algorithms Laboratory,
School of Architecture, Civil and Environmental Engineering,
École Polytechnique Fédérale de Lausanne, Lausanne, Switzerland
`bahar.haghighat@epfl.ch`

Abstract. Programmable stochastic self-assembly of modular robots provides promising means to formation of structures at different scales. Formalisms based on graph grammars and rule-based approaches have been previously published for controlling the self-assembly process. While several rule-synthesis algorithms have been proposed, formal synthesis of rulesets has only been shown for self-assembly of abstract graphs. Rules deployed on robotic modules are typically tuned starting from their abstract graph counterparts or designed manually. In this work, we extend the graph grammar formalism and propose a new encoding of the internal states of the robots. This allows formulating formal methods capable of automatically deriving the rules based on the morphology of the robots, in particular the number of connectors. The derived rules are directly applicable to robotic modules with no further tuning. In addition, our method allows for a reduced complexity in the rulesets. In order to illustrate the application of our method, we extend two synthesis algorithms from the literature, namely Singleton and Linchpin, to synthesize rules applicable to our floating robots. A microscopic simulation framework is developed to study the performance and transient behavior of the two algorithms. Finally, employing the generated rulesets, we conduct experiments with our robotic platform to demonstrate several assemblies.

1 Introduction

Self-assembly (SA) plays a key role in many of the natural structuring phenomena at all scales. SA is defined as the reversible and spontaneous phenomenon of an ordered spatial structure emerging from the aggregate behavior of simpler preexisting entities, through inherently local and random interactions in the system. In recent years, SA has been extensively studied both as an enabling technique for micro/nano-fabrication, and as a coordination mechanism for distributed robotic systems of miniaturized modules with limited capabilities, where highly stochastic sensing, actuation, and interactions are inevitable.

© Springer International Publishing Switzerland 2016
M. Dorigo et al. (Eds.): ANTS 2016, LNCS 9882, pp. 197–209, 2016.
DOI: 10.1007/978-3-319-44427-7_17

SA has been used as a means for coordination in several robotic systems [2,8,11,12]. Programmable SA has been demonstrated in [8,11]. In [11], a deterministic and quasiserial approach to shape formation is implemented in a large swarm of miniaturized Kilobot robots. Stochastic SA can be realized by taking advantage of the stochastic ambient dynamics for module transportation. In [8], the robots stochastically self-assemble on an air table based on their internal rule-based behavior. Using a synthesis algorithm, a ruleset is first derived for SA of a similar abstract target graph. The rules are then tuned to suit the specific morphology of the robots.

The problem of ruleset synthesis for programmable SA of graphs was first addressed in [9]. In [10], the formalism of graph grammars is applied to the SA of graphs and two rule synthesis algorithms are presented. A deadlock situation is discussed, where the number of copies of the target being built in parallel is higher than the maximum feasible number, considering the total number of available agents. In the same work, in order to avoid deadlocks the authors propose a disassociation rule which requires implementation of a consensus algorithm among the agents. In [3], the formalism of graph grammars is employed and it is shown that SA of graphs can be achieved while avoiding deadlocks by introducing probabilistic dissociating rules. Two formal rule-synthesis algorithms, Singleton and Linchpin, are introduced in the same work. In [4], weighted graphs are considered in a case study to encode the geometric orientations of the edges. Stochastic SA of simulated underwater robots in 3D using a rule-based approach has been studied in [5]. A rule-based approach incorporating a state machine is manually designed for the specific simulated platform and targets under study.

While several formal rule-synthesis algorithms have been proposed for programmable SA of graphs, the derived rules are not directly applicable to robotic SA where orientation of the bonding links determines the structure and is part of the internal state of the modules. In this work, we extend the graph grammars formalism for the problem of ruleset synthesis for programmable SA of robots. In particular, we extend the concept of abstract graphs by introducing vertices with link-slots and propose a new way to encode a robot's internal state. This allows formulating general methods for synthesizing rules directly applicable to robotic modules. Each module is associated with one vertex in the graph and its internal state is encoded by a control state label and an orientation index. For a module with N connectors, we achieve a ruleset complexity of $O(N)$ compared with $O(N^2)$ obtained in [8]. Using our method, we extend the Singleton and Linchpin algorithms from [3] to synthesize rules for our miniature floating robots. These two algorithms incorporate reversible rules, a feature offering two key advantages. First, reversibility is necessary for scenarios in highly stochastic environments, where permanent bonds are not always feasible. Second, by exploiting reversible rules the system can recover from deadlock situations.

We begin in Sect. 2 by describing the SA process in our robotic system. In Sect. 3, the graph grammars formalism for SA of graphs is summarized. Section 4 discusses our proposed extension for the case of SA of robots. Section 5 describes synthesis of rules for SA of our robots using two algorithms. In Sect. 6, we detail the simulation framework. Simulated and experimental results are presented in Sect. 7, with the conclusions offered in Sect. 8.

2   Fluidic Self-assembly of Lily Robots

Our system consists of two main components: (1) the Lily robots, originally presented in [7], which serve as the building blocks of the SA process, and (2) the experimental setup built around them. Lilies are endowed with four custom-designed Electro-Permanent Magnets (EPM) to latch and also to communicate locally with their neighbors. They can also communicate over a radio link to a base station to receive commands, new firmware, or to report specific information. Being power-autonomous, the robots can actively take part in the assembly process at all times. Given a target structure, an appropriate ruleset is derived as explained in Sect. 5, and deployed on all robots through wireless bootloading. The robots' EPM latches are by default enabled, resulting in a default latching upon meeting another robot. Once latched, the EPM-to-EPM inductive communication channel is physically established. The robots then exchange their internal states and look for an applicable rule in their ruleset. If no applicable rule is found, they unlatch by turning off their EPM latches; otherwise they remain latched and update their internal states accordingly. Each robot then updates the base station with its new internal state over the radio. Lilies are not self-locomoted, they are instead stirred by the flow field produced within a tank by several peripheral pumps. To monitor the evolution of the system, we use an overhead camera to visually track a passive marker on the top of each robot (Fig. 1).

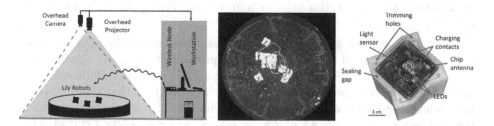

Fig. 1. An overview of the system: The experimental setup (left). Visual tracking of ten Lily robots during an experiment (middle). The Lily robot (right).

3   Graph Grammars for Self-assembly of Graphs

In this section we summarize the graph grammars formalism for formulating SA of graphs as presented in [3,8]. A labeled graph is a triple $G = (V, E, \ell)$ where $V = \{1, ..., N\}$ is the set of vertices, $E \subset V \times V$ is the set of edges, and $\ell : V \to \Sigma$ is a labeling function, with Σ being a set of labels. A pair of vertices $\{x, y\} \in E$ is represented by xy. The $n_E(k)$ represents the neighbors of vertex k relative to the edge set E. Two graphs are considered to be isomorphic when there exists a bijection $h : V_{G1} \to V_{G2}$ such that $ij \in E_{G1} \Leftrightarrow h(i)h(j) \in E_{G2}$. The function h is called a witness. A label-preserving isomorphism has the additional property that $\ell_{G1}(x) = \ell_{G2}(h(x)), \forall x \in V_{G1}$. A graph G is said to contain a graph H if a subgraph of G is isomorphic to H.

Definition: A rule is an ordered pair of graphs $r = (L, R)$ such that $V_L = V_R$. The graphs L and R are the left hand side (LHS) and right hand side (RHS) of the rule r. A binary rule can be depicted as $a \quad b \to c - d$, with the characters denoting the labels of the two engaged vertices.

Definition: A rule $r = (L, R)$ is applicable to a graph G if there exists $I \subset V_G$ such that the subgraph $G \subset I$ has a label-preserving isomorphism $h : I \to V_L$.

Definition: The triple (r, I, h) is called an action. Application of an action with $r = (L, R)$ to G gives a new graph $G' = (V_G, E_{G'}, l_{G'})$ defined by

$$E_{G'} = (E_G - xy : xy \in E_G \cap I \times I) \cup (xy : h(x)h(y) \in E_R)$$

$$\ell_{G'}(x) = \begin{cases} \ell_G(x), & \text{if } x \in V_G - I \\ \ell_R(h(x)), & \text{otherwise} \end{cases}$$

Definition: The complement or reverse of a rule $r = (L, R)$, is $\bar{r} = (R, L)$, such that $G \xrightarrow{r,I,h} G' \xrightarrow{\bar{r},I,h} G'' = G$.

Definition: A trajectory of a system (G_0, ϕ), where G_0 is the initial graph of the system and ϕ is a ruleset, is a finite or infinite sequence of $G_0 \xrightarrow{r_1,I,h} G_1 \xrightarrow{r_2,I,h} G_2 \xrightarrow{r_3,I,h} ...$

Given a set of rules ϕ, we can study the sequences of graphs obtained from successive application of the rules in ϕ. For a probabilistic ruleset, a probability may be associated with each rule by the mapping $P : \phi \to (0, 1]$, indicating the tendency for the corresponding event to take place provided that the conditions under which the rule is applicable are met. The formal rule-synthesis methods proposed for programmable SA of graphs automatically generate a ruleset ϕ for assembling a desired target by iteratively browsing and parsing the target graph [3,8,10]. Section 5 provides details on the functionality of such methods and how they can be extended to generate rules for SA of robots.

4   Graph Grammars for Self-assembly of Robots

In this section we explain how we extend the graph grammars formalism to formulate the synthesis problem for programmable SA of robots. While the SA process in a system of atomic agents can be directly modeled by abstract graphs evolving over time, for the case of robotic modules the morphology of the robots, in particular the orientation of the links they may form, strictly determines the shape of the resulting structure. This information can not be directly encoded in the abstract graphs. Figure 2 (left) gives a simple illustration of this issue.

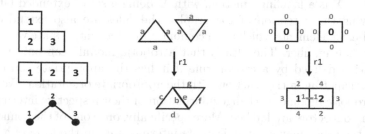

Fig. 2. Different structures with similar graph representation (left). Association of one label with one latch [8] (middle). Relative CCW hop numbering (right).

The method in [8] associates each latching connector on the robot with one vertex in the graph and connects them using permanent links, as depicted in Fig. 2 (middle). This method of encoding the internal state of the robots within a graph grammar formalism has several drawbacks. First, the graph modeling the system is augmented with vertices and edges which encode redundant information, resulting in an increased complexity of model analysis and simulation. Second, manual tuning of the rules is necessary to obtain a ruleset applicable on the robots. A synthesis algorithm is first run on an abstract description of the desired target, the resulting rules are then manually adapted to account for the correct orientation of the forming links. Third, for a robot with N connectors each acquiring a dedicated state label, the ruleset complexity grows in $O(N^2)$.

Our goal is to be able to formulate general methods for automatic synthesis of rules for programmable SA of robots. To this end, we extend the notion of labeled graphs by extending the definition of vertices and labels. While we are particularly interested in scenarios involving our Lily robots in 2D, the assumptions we make are general enough to be directly applied to similar platforms. The method is also easily applicable to 3D SA with similar assumptions.

Definition: An extended vertex has ordered link-slots which correspond to the latching connectors of a robotic module. The numbering on the slots is assumed to match the one of the robot, following a counter-clockwise (CCW) rotation convention. We assume that the robotic modules have a rotational symmetry. As a result, for an isolated module the connectors are anonymous.

Definition: An extended label is a pair $l = (l_a, l_n)$ encoding the internal state of a module. l_a represents the control state of the robotic module and l_n represents the index of the most recently engaged connector.

Definition: An extended labeled graph is a quadruple $G = (V, E, S, \ell)$ where $V = \{1, ..., N\}$ is the set of extended vertices, $E \subset V \times V$ is the set of edges, $S : E \to K \times K$ defines which slots are involved in a link between two vertices, and $\ell : V \to \Sigma$ is a labeling function, with Σ being a set of extended labels.

Following the extension of the graphs, the rules are also extended to be described using elements which are a combination of a control state variable and a relative hop number. The idea is that a robotic module can only take part in a reaction defined by a certain rule if it has the appropriate control state and is participating in the reaction with the appropriate orientation. We assume that the robotic modules exchange information of their respective internal states once their connectors are latched. More specifically, once one of the connectors is engaged, the robot may communicate its internal state in the form of a relative extended label of $l = (l_a, l_h)$ with l_a being the robot's control state and l_h being a relative hop number which represents the relative orientation of the currently engaged connector with respect to its predecessor, assuming a CCW hop convention (see Fig. 2, right). For a vertex with an extended label of (l_a, l_n) on a robot with N connectors $l_h = [(l_n - l_c)modN] + 1$, where l_n and l_c are the indexes of the most recently and the currently engaged connectors, respectively.

Definition: An extended rule is an ordered pair of extended graphs $r = (L, R)$. An extended binary rule can be depicted as $l_1 \quad l_2 \rightharpoonup l_3 - l_4$, with the $l_i = (l_{ia}, l_{ih})$ values being the relative extended label of the engaged vertex.

5   Synthesizing Rules for Robots

In the previous section, we explained the extension of the graph grammars formalism to the case of SA of robots. Our goal is to employ the extended formalism to (1) automatically synthesize rules to control programmable SA of robotic modules, and (2) model and simulate the evolution of the SA process in a system of robotic modules. Here we explain how our extended formalism may be used to formulate formal methods for deriving rules for SA of robots of arbitrary shapes, for a given target. In particular, we pick two synthesis algorithms from the literature, namely Singleton and Linchpin, presented in [3], which are capable of deriving rules for SA of graphs for any given acyclic target. Using our formalism, we extend these algorithms such that they generate rules for programmable SA of robots, for a given target represented as an extended graph. We then use the extended Singleton and Linchpin to synthesize rulesets for SA of our Lily robots for two specific targets, a chain and a cross structure, consisting of 6 robots.

For a given target graph G, *Singleton* generates a serial ruleset where each rule progresses the SA of the target graph by appending an isolated vertex to the structure. In contrast, *Linchpin* synthesizes a parallel ruleset, where the target graph is assembled from each leaf towards a final vertex, with the process culminating in two subgraphs joining together [3]. As an example consider $G = (V = \{1, 2, 3, 4, 5, 6\}, E = \{12, 23, 34, 45, 56\})$, assuming vertex 2 as the root vertex fed to the algorithms in [3], the resulting rulesets are as below:

$$\phi_{Singleton} = \begin{cases} 0 & 0 \leftrightharpoons 1 - 2 & (r1, \bar{r}1) \\ 1 & 0 \leftrightharpoons 3 - 4 & (r2, \bar{r}2) \\ 4 & 0 \leftrightharpoons 5 - 6 & (r3, \bar{r}3) \\ 6 & 0 \leftrightharpoons 7 - 8 & (r4, \bar{r}4) \\ 8 & 0 \leftrightharpoons 9 - 10 & (r5, \bar{r}5) \end{cases} \quad \phi_{Linchpin} = \begin{cases} 0 & 0 \leftrightharpoons 1 - 2 & (r1, \bar{r}1) \\ 0 & 0 \leftrightharpoons 7 - 8 & (r2, \bar{r}2) \\ 2 & 0 \leftrightharpoons 3 - 4 & (r3, \bar{r}3) \\ 4 & 0 \leftrightharpoons 5 - 6 & (r4, \bar{r}4) \\ 8 & 6 \leftrightharpoons 9 - 10 & (r5, \bar{r}5) \end{cases}$$

5.1   Singleton and Linchpin for Robots

Algorithm 1 depicts the pseudo codes for the extended Singleton algorithm for robots with N connectors, denoted as SingletonR, and the original one for abstract graphs, denoted as SingletonG. l, k, and $N_E(k)$ denote the largest label, the root vertex, and the neighbors of node k with respect to edge set E, respectively. For a given target graph $\hat{G}$, running $SingletonG((V_{\hat{G}}, E_{\hat{G}}, k, 0))$ for any $k \in V_{\hat{G}}$ generates a ruleset. The ruleset allows the SA process to grow the target graph outwards from the starting vertex k. Similarly, SingletonR generates a ruleset for robots based on a given target structure, represented by an extended graph $G = (V_G, E_G, S_G)$, where $S(v_i, v_j)$ returns the ordered pair of (s_i, s_j), the involved link-slots on the two linked vertices. $L(v)$ returns the current extended label of a vertex, (l_a, l_n). The GVL (short for Get Vertex Label) procedure returns the ordered pair of (l_a, l_h) by updating the value of l_h such that it indicates the relative position of the currently engaged slot, s, with respect to the previously engaged one. The SVL (short for Set Vertex Label) procedure updates the extended label (l_a, l_n) by updating the value of l_n considering the value of the applied label. Compared to the SingletonG algorithm where only the state labels are synthesized, SingletonR produces the relative hop number l_h indicating the proper linking orientation as well. The combination of these two values provides a general description of the full internal state of a robot. Alternatively for a robot with N connectors, the internal state may be fully described using an ordered N-tuple by associating one state label to each connector. Considering interactions between any two connectors, this would result in a ruleset complexity of $O(N^2)$. Utilizing our extended label convention, we obtain a ruleset complexity of $O(N)$. LinchpinR is similarly obtained by extending the standard Linchpin algorithm with the notion of link-slots. We skip its pseudo code is for brevity here.

```
1:  C : (V, E, S, L, k, l)
2:  procedure SINGLETONR(C)
3:      φ ← ∅
4:      if |n_E(k)| = 0 then
5:          return (l, φ)
6:      else
7:          {v_j : j - 1, 2, ..., |n_E(k)|} ← n_E(k)
8:          for j = 1 to |n_E(k)| do
9:              (s_k, s_j) ← S(v_k, v_j)
10:             l_k ← GVL(L, s_k, v_k)
11:             l_j ← GVL(L, s_j, v_j)
12:             l̄ ← INCREMENTSTATE(l, 1)
13:             l ← INCREMENTSTATE(l, 2)
14:             φ ← φ ∪ {l_k  l_j ⇌ l̄ - l}
15:             SVL(L, v_k, s_k, l̄)
16:             SVL(L, v_j, s_j, l)
17:             Let (V^j, E^j, S^j) be the
        component of (V, E - {kv_j}) containing v_j
18:             C_j : (V^j, E^j, S, L, v_j, l)
19:             (l, φ_j) ← SINGLETONR(C_j)
20:             φ ← φ ∪ φ_j
21:         end for
22:     end if
23:     return (l, φ)
24: end procedure

25: procedure GVL(L, s, v)
26:     (l_a, l_n) ← L(v)
27:     l_h ← (l_n - s + 1) (mod N)
28:     return (l_a, l_h)
29: end procedure

30: procedure SVL(L, v, s, l)
31:     (l_a, l_h) ← l(1 : 2)
32:     l_n ← s
33:     L(v) ← (l_a, l_n)
34: end procedure

35: procedure INCREMENTSTATE(l, k)
36:     return (l_a + k, l_n)
37: end procedure
```

```
1:  C : (V, E, k, l)
2:  procedure SINGLETONG(C)
3:      φ ← ∅
4:      if |n_E(k)| = 0 then
5:          return (l, φ)
6:      else
7:          {v_j : j = 1, 2, ..., |n_E(k)|} ← n_E(k)
8:          l̄ ← l
9:          for j = 1 to |n_E(k)| do
10:             φ ← φ ∪ {l̄ 0 ⇌ (l + 1) - (l + 2)}
11:             l̄ ← l + 1
12:             l ← l + 2
13:             Let (V^j, E^j) be the
        component of (V, E - {kv_j}) containing v_j
14:
        C_j : (V^j, E^j, v_j, l)
15:             (l_j, φ_j) ← SINGLETONG(C_j)
16:             φ ← φ ∪ φ_j
17:             l ← l_j
18:         end for
19:     end if
20:     return (l, φ)
21: end procedure
```

Alg. 1: SingletonR for robotic SA and SingletonG for SA of graphs [3].

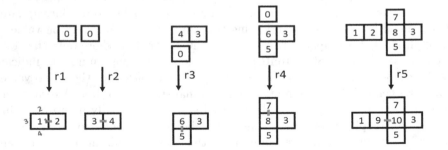

Fig. 3. Progress of the SA process for cross shape employing ϕ_L.

5.2 Rulesets for Self-assembly of Lily Robots

The rulesets returned by SingletonR for a chain, ϕ_S, and the one returned by LinchpinR for a cross, ϕ_L, using 6 Lilies are reported below. The (l_a, l_h) notation is used for the relative extended labels and the reverse rules are separated.

$$
\phi_S = \begin{cases}
(0,0) \;\; (0,0) \;\; \xrightarrow{r1} \;\; (1,1)-(2,1) \\
(1,3) \;\; (0,0) \;\; \xrightarrow{r2} \;\; (3,1)-(4,1) \\
(4,3) \;\; (0,0) \;\; \xrightarrow{r3} \;\; (5,1)-(6,1) \\
(6,3) \;\; (0,0) \;\; \xrightarrow{r4} \;\; (7,1)-(8,1) \\
(8,3) \;\; (0,0) \;\; \xrightarrow{r5} \;\; (9,1)-(10,1) \\
(1,1)-(2,1) \;\; \xrightarrow{\bar{r}1} \;\; (0,0) \;\; (0,0) \\
(3,1)-(4,1) \;\; \xrightarrow{\bar{r}2} \;\; (1,3) \;\; (0,0) \\
(5,1)-(6,1) \;\; \xrightarrow{\bar{r}3} \;\; (4,3) \;\; (0,0) \\
(7,1)-(8,1) \;\; \xrightarrow{\bar{r}4} \;\; (6,3) \;\; (0,0) \\
(9,1)-(10,1) \;\; \xrightarrow{\bar{r}5} \;\; (8,3) \;\; (0,0)
\end{cases}
\qquad
\phi_L = \begin{cases}
(0,0) \;\; (0,0) \;\; \xrightarrow{r1} \;\; (1,1)-(2,1) \\
(0,0) \;\; (0,0) \;\; \xrightarrow{r2} \;\; (3,1)-(4,1) \\
(0,0) \;\; (4,4) \;\; \xrightarrow{r3} \;\; (5,1)-(6,1) \\
(0,0) \;\; (6,3) \;\; \xrightarrow{r4} \;\; (7,1)-(8,1) \\
(2,3) \;\; (8,2) \;\; \xrightarrow{r5} \;\; (9,1)-(10,1) \\
(1,1)-(2,1) \;\; \xrightarrow{\bar{r}1} \;\; (0,0) \;\; (0,0) \\
(3,1)-(4,1) \;\; \xrightarrow{\bar{r}2} \;\; (0,0) \;\; (0,0) \\
(5,1)-(6,1) \;\; \xrightarrow{\bar{r}3} \;\; (0,0) \;\; (4,2) \\
(7,1)-(8,1) \;\; \xrightarrow{\bar{r}4} \;\; (0,0) \;\; (6,3) \\
(9,1)-(10,1) \;\; \xrightarrow{\bar{r}5} \;\; (2,3) \;\; (8,4)
\end{cases}
$$

Consider ϕ_S. While the state labels returned by SingletonR for Lilies are similar to the ones for a chain shape in abstract graphs, it can be seen that the values of $l_h = 3$ on the LHS of the rules dictate 2 hops between the successive latching events, resulting in a linear structure considering the square shaped modules. The reverse rules all have $l_h = 1$ at the LHS, indicating that the rule happens at the slot engaged the latest. Figure 3 depicts the SA process employing ϕ_L on 6 Lilies. Each square represents a Lily, labeled with the l_a value. The most recent engaged link-slot is indicated with a blue mark, while the relative hop numbers of l_h are marked in red for one Lily. For each Lily, numbering the slots always starts with $l_h = 1$ at the most recently engaged slot and follows a CCW convention. Note that the synthesis algorithms only generate the rules; appropriate probabilities should be associated with forward and reverse rules to allow the system to recover from deadlocks, while reliably forming the target.

6 Simulation Framework

In order to compare the performance of our rulesets for SA of robots and to study the transient behavior, we develop a microscopic simulation framework. Our approach is based upon the abstract model for randomized interactions among atomic agents introduced in [3]. We build on this method in two ways. First, in order to model interactions between robots the notion of extended graphs along with appropriate geometrical constraints is utilized. Second, we introduce a new shape recognition method which is an extension over a graph isomorphism check to track the progress of the SA process in the system.

6.1 Random Pairwise Interactions

In our extended formalism, a random pairwise interaction dynamics is defined as a quadruple (G, F, ϕ, P). Rule probabilities are assigned by $P : \phi \to (0, 1]$.

The set of pairs of disjoint vertices is defined as $PW(G) = \{(x,y) : \nexists I \subset G | (x,y) \in V_I, x \neq y\}$, where I is a connected subgraph of G. The set $PW(G)$ defines modules among which an interaction is feasible as they are not on the same sub-assembly. $F(G)$ maps an extended graph G to probabilities of pairwise vertex selections from V_G. A random trajectory of the system, is generated by sampling $F(G_t)$ at each time instant to obtain a pair (x,y) and then executing an appropriate action on the selected pair. For two selected vertices to interact, the link-slots are chosen randomly from the available slots. Sampling from $F(G_t)$ introduces an inherent stochasticity to the trajectories even if the ruleset contains only deterministic rules. The interaction probabilities, defined by $F(G_t)$, depend on the current graph G_t and can be calibrated.

6.2   Shape Recognition

Tracking the progress of the SA process of the simulated system requires a mapping between the connected components of the graph of the system and the shape of the corresponding sub-assemblies. For the case of SA of graphs where the system is represented by an abstract graph at each time instant, this describes a problem of graph isomorphism. However, for the case of our extended graphs, the relative position of the engaged slots need to be taken into account to recognize the shapes. We propose a simple method for recognizing the shapes based on traversing the connected components of the extended graph and constructing a series of locations of the Center Of Mass (COM) of the robotic modules. The relative ordering of the slots of neighboring modules determines the orientation of each traverse. The series of locations are then rotated and translated such that all coordinates are positive. The resulting ordered set is used as the identifier of the structure. This method can be applied to modules with a variety of shapes. Our method is sufficient for the case of structures confined in 2D and is substantially less computationally expensive than general approaches [1,6].

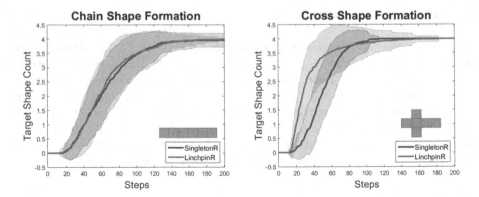

Fig. 4. Comparison of rulesets derived by the two extended synthesis algorithms for the two target structures of chain and cross shape. The solid lines and shaded regions summarize the mean and standard deviation of 100 runs, respectively.

7   Experiments and Results

SingletonR and LinchpinR algorithms are utilized to derive rules for (1) a target assembly of a chain shape, and (2) a target assembly of a cross shape, both of size 6. The resulting rulesets are deployed in microscopic simulations with 24 modules, and on 6 real robots. Within a ruleset, all the rules with identical LHS are set to be equi-probable. For forward rules $P(.) = 1$ and for reverse rules $P(.) = 0.1$ is chosen. The finishing rule is chosen to be irreversible in all the rulesets, giving rise to stable target assemblies once they are formed. Care should be taken in comparing simulated and experimental results. First, a higher number of available modules compared to the target size in simulation allows for inherently larger opportunities for interaction, particularly in the early stages of the process. Second, the simulation framework assumes all interactions to be equiprobable, this can be a good assumption when the number of available modules is much higher than the target size. Third, the simulation results are reported as a function of steps, representing formation events in the system, a progress unit suitable for measuring the concurrency of the rulesets.

Table 1. Formation time statistics

Algorithm	Target	Mean (s)	Std. (s)
SingletonR	Chain shape	844.3	165.8
LinchpinR	Chain shape	941.1	138.9
SingletonR	Cross shape	181.1	25.8
LinchpinR	Cross shape	190.3	77.6

Figure 4 shows the performance of the rulesets derived by the two extended synthesis algorithms for the two target assemblies in simulation. The vertical axis shows the number of copies of the target assembly in the system at each step. For the cross shape target, the naturally serial ruleset of SingletonR is outperformed by the more concurrent one of LinchpinR. For the chain shape target, the rulesets of the two algorithms perform similarly. Looking into the generated rules, LinchpinR builds dimers with two possible labeling assigned probabilistically, while SingletonR adds modules one by one, labeled deterministically.

For the experimental studies, 6 Lily robots were programmed with the derived rulesets to build the two target structures. Each experiment was repeated five times. Table 1 details the formation time statistics. Considering the chain shape, while the average formation time for SingletonR is less than that of LinchpinR, SingletonR exhibits a higher standard deviation. This can be ascribed to the assembly strategy of the rulesets. LinchpinR builds the target out of dimers and requires two dimers labeled differently. Since the labeling is done at random, when the available modules are scarce this can easily result in longer formation times. More generally, LinchpinR does not necessarily make the best use of the available resources. For the cross shape, both the smallest and the largest

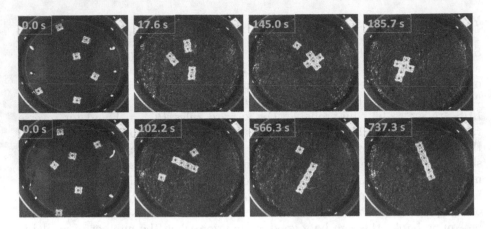

Fig. 5. SingletonR rulesets for chain and cross shapes on six Lily robots.

formation times were obtained by LinchpinR. This can be explained by considering the interaction between the intermediate sub-assemblies. While LinchpinR builds the target through four concurrent steps as opposed to SingletonR's five, the relative orientation of the connecting sub-assemblies is more easily achieved for SingletonR where one component, i.e. the isolated Lily, is always symmetric (Fig. 5).

8   Conclusion

In this paper, we addressed the problem of rule synthesis for programmable SA of robots. We extended the graph grammar formalism to account for the morphology of the robots and proposed a formal method to automatically synthesize rules for robots. We introduced the notion of extended graphs comprising vertices with ordered link-slots representing the robotic modules' connectors. The state of each module is represented by an extended label. We showed that our formalism achieves a ruleset complexity of $O(N)$ compared to the conventional methods' $O(N^2)$. Using our method, two synthesis algorithms originally introduced for SA of graphs were then extended to synthesize rules for our robots. Studies on the synthesized rulesets in simulation and real experiments demonstrated the functionality of our method. In the future, we will investigate novel rule-synthesis algorithms allowing for higher concurrency in the process by considering geometrical features of the target. Finally, we plan to fully utilize our setup to conduct systematic real experiments involving up to 100 Lily robots.

Acknowledgments. This work has been sponsored by the Swiss National Science Foundation under the grant numbers 200021_137838/1 and 200020_157191/1.

References

1. Asadpour, M., Ashtiani, M.H.Z., Sproewitz, A., Ijspeert, A.: Graph signature for self-reconfiguration planning of modules with symmetry. In: IEEE/RSJ International Conference on Intelligent Robots and Systems, pp. 5295 5290 (2009)
2. Avallaii, N., White, P.J., Halasz, A., Yim, M., Kumar, V.. Stochastic control for self-assembly of xbots. In: International Design Engineering Technical Conferences and Computers and Information in Engineering Conference, pp. 1169–1176 (2008)
3. Fox, M., Shamma, J.: Probabilistic performance guarantees for distributed self-assembly. IEEE Trans. Autom. Control **60**(12), 3180–3194 (2015)
4. Fox, M.J., Shamma, J.S.: Communication, convergence, and stochastic stability in self-assembly. In: IEEE International Conference on Decision and Control, pp. 7245–7250 (2010)
5. Ganesan, V., Chitre, M.: On stochastic self-assembly of underwater robots. IEEE Robot. Autom. Lett. **1**(1), 251–258 (2016)
6. Golestan, K., Asadpour, M., Moradi, H.: A new graph signature calculation method based on power centrality for modular robots. In: Martinoli, A., Mondada, F., Correll, N., Mermoud, G., Egerstedt, M., Hsieh, M.A., Parker, L.E., Støy, K. (eds.) Distributed Autonomous Robotic Systems. STAR, vol. 83, pp. 505–516. Springer, Heidelberg (2013)
7. Haghighat, B., Droz, E., Martinoli, A.: Lily: a miniature floating robotic platform for programmable stochastic self-assembly. In: IEEE International Conference on Robotics and Automation, pp. 1941–1948 (2015)
8. Klavins, E.: Programmable self-assembly. IEEE Control Syst. **27**(4), 43–56 (2007)
9. Klavins, E.: Automatic synthesis of controllers for distributed assembly and formation forming. In: IEEE International Conference on Robotics and Automation, pp. 3296–3302 (2002)
10. Klavins, E., Ghrist, R., Lipsky, D.: A grammatical approach to self-organizing robotic systems. IEEE Trans. Autom. Control **51**(6), 949–962 (2006)
11. Rubenstein, M., Cornejo, A., Nagpal, R.: Programmable self-assembly in a thousand-robot swarm. Science **345**(6198), 795–799 (2014)
12. Salemi, B., Moll, M., Shen, W.M.: Superbot: a deployable, multi-functional, and modular self-reconfigurable robotic system. In: IEEE/RSJ International Conference on Intelligent Robots and Systems, pp. 3636–3641 (2006)

Using Ant Colony Optimization to Build Cluster-Based Classification Systems

Khalid M. Salama[1] and Ashraf M. Abdelbar[2(✉)]

[1] School of Computing, University of Kent, Canterbury, UK
kms39@kent.ac.uk
[2] Department of Mathematics & Computer Science,
Brandon University, Manitoba, Canada
abdelbara@brandonu.ca

Abstract. Learning cluster-based classification systems is the process of partitioning a training set into data subsets (clusters), and then building a local classifier for each data cluster. The class of a new instance is predicted by first assigning the instance to its nearest cluster, and then using that cluster's local classification model to predict the instance's class. In this paper, we use the Ant Colony Optimization (ACO) meta-heuristic to optimize the data clusters based on a given classification algorithm in an integrated cluster-with-learn manner. The proposed ACO algorithms use two different clustering solution representation approaches: instance-based and medoid-based, where in the latter the number of clusters is optimized as part of the ACO algorithm's execution. In our experiments, we employ three widely-used classification algorithms, k-nearest neighbours, Ripper, and C4.5, and evaluate performance on 30 UCI benchmark datasets. We compare the ACO results to the traditional c-means clustering algorithm, where the data clusters are built prior to learning the local classifiers.

Keywords: Ant Colony Optimization (ACO) · Data mining · Classification · Clustering · Cluster-based classification system

1 Introduction

Classification is an important supervised learning task, concerned with predicting the class of a given instance based on its input attributes, using a well-constructed classification model [28]. The classification process consists of two stages. The training stage utilizes a *training set* of labelled instances, that is a set of instances along with their correct class labels, that should be sufficiently representative of the domain of interest. A classification algorithm uses the training set to construct an internal model of the relationships between the attributes of the input instances and their corresponding class labels. Then, during the subsequent operating stage, the classifier uses its internal model to predict the class of new unlabelled instances, which have not been presented to the algorithm during the training stage.

© Springer International Publishing Switzerland 2016
M. Dorigo et al. (Eds.): ANTS 2016, LNCS 9882, pp. 210–222, 2016.
DOI: 10.1007/978-3-319-44427-7_18

A cluster-based classification system consists of several local classifiers, one for each subset of the dataset, to model an asymmetric set of relationships between the predictor attributes and the predictable class for each data subset. Clustering techniques [3] are utilized to discover data partitions in which similar instances tend to occur together in the same partition and dissimilar subset in the partition. Consequently, more effective local classifiers are built for each data subset.

Ant Colony Optimization (ACO) [2] is a meta-heuristic for solving combinatorial optimization problems, inspired by observations of the behaviour of ant colonies in nature. While ACO has been used for data clustering in general [1,4,6,23], the focus of this paper is on using ACO to build classification systems, based on data partitions of the original training set. In other words, the performance of the proposed methods is evaluated mainly in terms of the predictive accuracy of the constructed classification system, rather than the cohesion/separation quality of the clusters *per se*.

In this paper we introduce AntClust-Miner, an algorithm which employs the ACO meta-heuristic to learn the data clusters and build the local classification models in a "cluster-with-learn" fashion. Such an integrated approach aims to find the best data partitions that improve the overall predictive accuracy of the cluster-based classification system. We use the AntClust-Miner algorithm with two ACO clustering methods: (1) instance-based, where a solution is a set of instance-class assignments, and (2) medoid-based, where a solution is a set of instances to be used as the mediods of clusters. In this paper, we extend the medoid-based ACO clustering method to automatically optimize the number of clusters as part of the ACO algorithm execution. For building the local classifiers, we use three widely used classification algorithms from three different classification families, namely, k-nearest neighbours from instance-based classification, Ripper from classification rule induction, and C4.5 from decision tree construction. We evaluate the performance of our proposed ACO algorithms on 30 UCI benchmark datasets, using 3, 5 and 8 clusters. We compare the ACO results to a cluster-based classification system based on the traditional c-means clustering algorithm, where the data clusters are built before learning the local classifiers.

The rest of the paper is structured as follows. We begin in Sect. 2 with a brief overview on ACO related work in the field of classification and clustering data mining problems. We then present our ACO approach for learning cluster-based classification systems in Sect. 3. Experimental methodology and results are presented in Sect. 4, and final remarks are offered in Sect. 5.

2   ACO Related Work

Inspired by the "intelligent" behaviour of natural ant colonies foraging to find the shortest path between a food source and the nest, Dorigo et al. have introduced Ant Colony Optimization (ACO) [2] as a population-based, global search meta-heuristic to solve a wide range of (mainly combinatorial) optimization problems.

A number of ACO-based classification algorithms have been introduced in the literature with different classification learning approaches [8]. Ant-Miner [12] is the first ant-based classification algorithm, which discovers a list of classification rules. The algorithm has been followed by several extensions in [7,9,10,12,15]. Two different ACO-based algorithms were proposed in [11,22] for inducing decision trees. ACO was also employed by Salama and Freitas in [18,19,21] to learn various types of Bayesian network classifiers. Blum and Socha applied an ACO variation for continuous optimization [5,25] to train feed-forward neural networks [24]. ANN-Miner [13] was introduced by Salama and Abdelbar as an ACO-based algorithm for learning neural network topologies. ACO has recently been utilized in data reduction for classification [14]. Furthermore, ACO has recently been applied to feature weighting in the context of instance-based learning [16].

The authors have introduced the idea of using ACO in building cluster-based classification systems in [17,20], but only using Bayesian network classifiers. In other words, in [17,20], ACO was employed to produce cluster-based Bayesian multi-nets models, which consist of only Naïve-Bayes or Tree-Augmented Naïve-Bayes local classifiers. However, in the present work we explore using ACO for building cluster-based classification models by employing three different algorithms to build the local classifiers: the k-nearest neighbour algorithm, the Ripper rule induction algorithm, and the C4.5 decision tree construction algorithm. Also, while the Medoid-based method for clustering solution representation was introduced in previous work [17,20], it had the limitation of needing the number of clusters to be supplied by the user. In this work, we extend the Medoid-based ACO method for building cluster-based classification systems by automatically optimizing the number of clusters to be used in the system.

A useful general review of (unsupervised) clustering is [29]. ACO algorithms for clustering are reviewed in [4].

3   Ant Colony for Building Cluster-Based Classifiers

3.1   The AntClust-Miner Overall Algorithm

The AntClust-Miner algorithm for building cluster-based classification systems carries out the data clustering process as well as the local classifiers construction process in a synergistic fashion via the ACO meta-heuristic. In such a "cluster-with-learn" approach, each ant in the colony creates a complete cluster-based classification system, rather than just a clustering solution. This is in contrast to having a—conventional or evolutionary-based—clustering algorithm complete the creation and optimization of the data clusters *before* the local models are constructed. The advantage of the integrated "cluster-with-learn" approach is that the clusters are optimized to maximize the predictive accuracy of the classification system, rather than just optimizing the cohesion/separation of the clusters. The overall procedure of AntClust-Miner is shown in Algorithm 1.

Before the ACO procedure begins, the *trainingSet* data is split into a *learningSet* and a *validationSet* (lines 6–7). The *learningSet* is 75 % of the

---

Algorithm 1. Pseudo-code of AntClust-Miner.

1: **begin**
2:   K $\Leftarrow$ *input*; /* number of clusters */
3:   algorithm $\Leftarrow$ *input*; /* classification algorithm */
4:   *trainingSet* $\Leftarrow$ *input*;
5:   *system_gbest* = ϕ; /* final cluster-based classification system */
6:   *datasets* = *Split(training_set)*;
7:   *learningSet* = *datasets*[0]; *validationSet* = *datasets*[1];
8:   *InitializeConstructionGraph(learningSet, K)*;
9:   *quality_gbest* = 0; t = 1;
10: **repeat**
11:     *system_tbest* = ϕ;
12:     *quality_tbest* = 0;
13:     **for** $i = 1 \rightarrow$ colonySize **do**
14:         *clustSolution_i* = *ant_i.CreateClusteringSolution()*;
15:         **for** $k = 1 \rightarrow$ K **do**
16:             *dataSubset* = *clustSolution_i.GetDataCluster(k)*
17:             *classifier_k* = *LearnClassifier(dataSubset, algorithm)*;
18:             **append** *classifier_k* to *system_i*;
19:         *quality_i* = *ComputeQuality(system_i, validationSet)*;
20:         **if** *quality_i* > *quality_tbest* **then**
21:             *system_tbest* = *system_i*;
22:             *quality_tbest* = *quality_i*;
23:     *PerformLocalSearch(system_tbest)*;
24:     *UpdatePheromone()*;
25:     **if** *quality_tbest* > *quality_gbest* **then**
26:         *system_gbest* = *system_tbest*;
27:         *quality_gbest* = *quality_tbest*;
28:     $t = t + 1$;
29: **until** t = maxIterations **or** *Convergence()*;
30: **return** *system_gbest*;
31: **end**

---

trainingSet and is used to construct the data clusters and build the local classifiers, while the *validationSet*, consisting of the remaining 25 % of the training set, is used for evaluating the constructed classification system. Note that the class distribution in *learningSet* and *validationSet* is kept roughly the same as in *trainingSet*. The construction graph (discussed in the following subsections) is initialized in line 8 prior to the commencement of the ACO procedure.

In essence, the AntClust-Miner algorithm works as follows. In the inner **for**-loop (lines 13 to 22), each *ant_i* in the colony constructs a complete cluster-based classification *system_i*. A candidate *system_i* is produced by first constructing a clustering solution *clustSolution_i* in line 14 (this is based on the ACO clustering method used, which will be discussed in the following two subsections), then for each data cluster k, a local *classifier_k* is created using the input **algorithm**, and appended to the classification *system_i* (lines 15 to 18). Then, the *quality_i* of the candidate *system_i* produced by *ant_i* is evaluated using the *validationSet* in line 19 (this will be discussed in Subsect. 3.4). The iteration-best $system_{tbest}$ produced in the colony at iteration t is maintained (lines 20 to 22).

At the end of iteration t, a local search procedure is performed on the iteration-best cluster-based classification $system_{tbest}$ (line 23). Basically, the clustering solution of $system_{tbest}$ undergoes c-means clustering, initialized by the centroids of the clustering solution. Then the pheromone amounts are updated (line 24) and the global-best cluster-based classification $system_{gbest}$ produced throughout the execution of the ACO algorithm is maintained (lines 25 to 27). This concludes one iteration of the outer **repeat**-loop, which continues until either the maxIteration is reached, or the ACO algorithm converges on a solution. The ACO algorithm converges when it produces the same solution in convIteration consecutive iterations. In our experiments, we set colonySize to 10, maxIteration to 10000, and convIteration to 10. Finally, $system_{gbest}$ is returned as the output of the algorithm.

3.2 Instance-Based ACO Clustering Method

As discussed in [17,20], the instance-based method for ACO clustering assigns each of the N instances in the *learningSet* to one out of K clusters. The construction graph contains $N \times K$ solution components: each instance with each possible cluster assignment. Each ant in the colony starts with a list of N elements with unassigned clusters (an empty solution). Then, the ant selects a cluster assignment from the construction graph for each element. The selection is performed probabilistically, based on the pheromone amount associated with each instance-cluster decision component. When every instance has been assigned to a cluster, the ant has a complete candidate clustering solution.

A candidate clustering solution in the instance-based method consists of N elements, the index of an element represents the instance, and the element represents the cluster assignment of this instance. For example, a candidate clustering solution for a dataset with 10 instances and 4 clusters is represented in the following form:

3	1	3	4	1	2	1	3	4	2

This representation means that in this candidate clustering solution, for example, the first instance belongs to cluster number 3, along with the third and the eighth instances. However, such a clustering solution representation method has two drawbacks. First, the mapping between a clustering solution and this representation is one-to-many [20]. That is, the same clustering solution can be obtained by several instance-based representations. This is an example of the classical *competing conventions* problem studied for example by Whitley et al. [27]. The redundancy of this kind of encoding enlarges the size of the search space, which affects the search's efficiency, and may have a noticeable impact on the effectiveness of the ACO algorithm in terms of the quality of the solution found. Second, the number of the clusters has to be supplied to the algorithm, rather than being optimized within the algorithm.

3.3   Medoid-Based ACO Clustering Extended Method

The medoid-based ACO clustering method avoids the competing conventions problem of the instance-based method. In the medoid-based method, a clustering solution is represented by the choice of V instances to act as the cluster medoids, where V is the number of clusters. More precisely, the construction graph is a complete (fully connected) graph containing only N solution components (recall that N denotes the number of instances), each representing an instance that is a candidate cluster medoid.

When constructing a solution, an ant chooses V instances based on the pheromone information associated with each solution component. The chosen instances represent a medoid-based clustering solution, where the k-th element (instance) represents the medoid of the k-th cluster. The medoid selection is performed under the constraint that a node can be visited at most once by an ant during a single solution construction.

Once a medoid-based candidate solution has been constructed by an ant, each instance i in the *learningSet* is assigned to the k-th cluster for which the similarity between instance i and the k-th medoid is the highest (compared to the other medoids). The similarity measure is discussed in the following subsection.

In this paper, we extend the medoid-based method to allow the ACO procedure to optimize the number of clusters. The algorithm receives K as the maximum number of clusters that can be produced. Every integer within the inclusive range 2 to K has an associated decision component in the construction graph, and an associated pheromone amount. Each training instance also has an associated decision component and associated pheromone amount. Thus, the construction graph consists of $(N + K)$ decision components.

When constructing a candidate solution, an ant first probabilistically selects the number of clusters V (between 2 and K) by selecting one of these decision components based on their pheromone amounts. It then selects V instances to act as cluster medoids. The V instances are selected one by one; each selection is made probabilistically based on pheromone amounts and under the constraint that an instance cannot be selected more than once.

3.4   Quality Evaluation and Pheromone Update

The AntClust-Miner algorithm evaluates the quality of a candidate solution as a classifier, rather than a clustering solution. That is, we use predictive accuracy, a widely-used measure in the context of classification, as an evaluation measure for the quality of the produced cluster-based classification system as a whole, rather than the cohesion/separation measure of the clusters per se. The *validationSet* is used to calculate the predictive accuracy of a candidate classification system as follows. First, each instance is assigned to its nearest cluster. Then, the local classifier of that cluster is used to predict the class of the validation instance. The predictive accuracy is computed as the ratio of the number of correctly classified instances to the total number of instances in the validation set.

The nearest cluster for instance i is the one that has the maximum total similarity between instance i and each instance j in the cluster. The similarity between any two instances i and j is computed according to:

$$\mathbf{Similarity}(i,j) = 1 - \sum_{v=1}^{a} \sum_{l=1}^{|C|} |P(C_l|i_v) - P(C_l|j_v)|, \qquad (1)$$

where a is the number of attributes and $P(C_l|i_v)$ is the conditional probability of the class value C_l given the attribute value i_v. This conditional probability is measured empirically as the ratio of the number of instances with attribute value i_v and the class value C_l to the number of instances with attribute value i_v in the *learningSet*. Accordingly, if a class value occurs frequently with two attribute values, then these two values are considered similar; the same applies if the class value does not occur frequently with both of the attribute values. On the other hand, if a class value occurs frequently with one attribute value, but does not occur frequently with the other attribute value, then these two attribute values are considered dissimilar. Note that the continuous attributes in the *learningSet* are discretized using the supervised C4.5-disc algorithm [28].

As for pheromone update, pheromone level τ_x is increased on each solution component x of the construction graph included in the clustering solution, based on the quality of the iteration-based cluster-based classification solution ($system_{tbest}$), using the following formula:

$$\tau_x(t+1) = \tau_x(t) + \tau_x(t) \cdot quality_{tbest}(t) \qquad (2)$$

To simulate pheromone evaporation, normalization is then applied; each τ_x is divided by the total pheromone amounts in the construction graph.

4   Experimental Methodology and Results

In our experiments, we used three classification algorithms to learn the local classifiers of the cluster-based classification systems constructed by our AntClust-Miner algorithm, namely the k-nearest neighbour lazy learning algorithm, the Ripper classification rule induction algorithm, and the C4.5 decision tree construction algorithm [26,28]. We used the WEKA implementation for these algorithms: k-NN, JRip, and J48, and used WEKA's default parameter settings in each case. We evaluated the performance of the two versions of the AntClust-Miner algorithm (IB-AntClust-Miner and MB-AntClust-Miner), using each algorithm g to build the local classifiers, against several methods. Specifically, for each classification algorithm g, we evaluated IB-AntClust-Miner (with 3, 5, and 8 clusters) and MB-AntClust-Miner, using g as the underlying local classification algorithm. We compared these to the base algorithm g (using the whole training set to build the classifier without any data clustering). We further compared performance to a cluster-based classification system with the c-means algorithm as the clustering algorithm and g as the underlying local classifier (without any

ACO)—this was evaluated with 3, 5, and 8 clusters. All of these evaluations used 30 benchmark datasets from the University of California at Irvine (UCI) Machine Learning repository. In all, 24 algorithms were evaluated and compared in this study.

Table 1. Predictive accuracy (%) results using k-NN as the local classifier.

Dataset	k-NN	c-means-3	c-means-5	c-means-8	IB-Ant-3	IB-Ant-5	IB-Ant-8	MB-Ant
audiology	50.00	78.00	36.42	54.43	65.00	62.50	58.07	**79.17**
automobile	48.36	71.64	68.85	**74.62**	56.02	56.69	60.03	65.05
breast-1	61.09	63.99	64.20	63.93	67.04	63.18	64.69	**74.89**
breast-p	65.24	65.18	64.88	63.68	**70.21**	67.55	65.48	68.58
breast-w	93.85	93.61	94.26	95.39	95.09	94.31	**95.88**	95.22
car	66.67	59.81	65.78	66.31	72.75	74.62	63.85	**74.77**
chess	78.18	82.53	76.49	72.33	**86.07**	79.25	79.39	85.60
credit-a	77.68	79.02	79.32	78.92	80.29	**81.01**	79.77	79.57
credit-g	65.40	69.50	68.30	68.91	68.00	68.80	66.98	**69.98**
cylinder	55.92	66.75	72.41	72.29	60.38	50.37	72.60	**72.91**
dermat	82.21	92.53	87.55	91.53	**92.62**	88.77	86.12	89.92
ecoli	71.82	79.31	77.67	77.41	**81.88**	77.72	79.34	80.11
heart-c	53.18	50.52	53.36	53.16	52.44	51.23	**53.77**	53.16
heart-h	59.30	44.55	60.81	50.81	56.57	58.16	62.61	**62.76**
horse	71.07	77.05	75.24	78.01	77.87	78.89	**79.15**	77.30
ionospere	73.66	85.38	79.42	78.09	69.68	79.97	80.67	**85.81**
liver	53.34	58.87	63.21	61.22	62.05	**65.20**	62.01	64.58
lymphography	75.00	77.10	81.09	**81.21**	77.00	76.48	78.95	79.10
monks	58.18	54.73	58.93	60.48	60.91	59.27	**69.58**	61.64
pima	65.63	68.31	67.58	67.31	65.24	68.98	67.66	**71.11**
s-heart	78.52	71.33	80.79	79.10	77.78	74.07	82.19	**82.52**
segmentation	78.48	**93.60**	81.42	84.87	88.74	82.46	85.82	93.17
soybean	32.07	**86.62**	84.50	56.81	86.55	84.97	58.99	86.55
thyroid	85.89	94.23	**96.42**	95.43	93.48	89.31	95.84	96.41
transfusion	62.85	59.55	63.42	62.55	62.84	64.33	**65.20**	64.74
ttt	70.53	65.37	65.23	70.17	72.11	**73.79**	70.40	72.32
vertebral-2c	80.00	78.97	80.22	82.50	77.10	**84.65**	83.61	82.35
vertebral-3c	73.87	76.71	71.59	79.47	75.81	79.29	**79.93**	79.35
voting	86.85	86.73	87.29	**88.35**	88.28	86.84	86.91	88.17
wine	88.17	92.94	95.48	96.55	96.63	**97.52**	97.21	97.49
Rank (avg.)	6.7	5.2	5.0	4.7	4.3	4.3	3.5	**2.3**

The experiments were carried out using the *stratified* 10-fold cross validation procedure. The results (accuracy rate on the test set) are averaged and reported as the accuracy rate of the classifier. Because ACO is a stochastic method, we ran our AntClust-Miner algorithms ten times—using a different random seed to initialize the search each time—in each iteration of the cross-validation procedure, and took the average accuracy as the iteration result. The c-means algorithm was also run ten times in each cross validation iteration with different cluster initializations, and the average accuracy was taken as the iteration result.

Tables 1, 2 and 3 report the predictive accuracy results of our experiments, one for each base algorithm: k-NN, Ripper, and C4.5, respectively. In each table, the first column shows the results for the base algorithm (i.e., using the whole training set to build the classifier without any data clustering). The second, third and fourth columns show the results for the c-means algorithm, where the number of clusters are 3, 5 and 8 respectively. The fifth, sixth and seventh column show the results for the IB-AntClust-Miner algorithm, with 3, 5 and 8 clusters, respectively. The last column shows the results for the MB-AntClust-Miner algorithm—note that the latter optimizes the number of clusters, and the maximum number of clusters was set to 8. The last row of each table shows the average rank of each algorithm over the 30 datasets in terms of the predictive accuracy results. Note that in the

Table 2. Predictive accuracy (%) results using Ripper as the local classifier.

Dataset	Ripper	c-means-3	c-means-5	c-means-8	IB-Ant-3	IB-Ant-5	IB-Ant-8	MB-Ant
audiology	**77.17**	49.17	43.33	43.92	51.67	44.48	49.17	56.83
automobile	66.69	62.14	66.07	60.12	72.12	68.96	68.43	**80.91**
breast-1	67.44	69.13	67.54	69.42	69.92	69.85	68.24	**70.87**
breast-p	73.79	**78.82**	64.71	66.85	74.58	66.96	72.63	70.06
breast-w	92.20	90.82	87.89	**94.89**	92.39	93.94	85.23	93.79
car	**85.66**	78.30	69.82	65.54	78.60	70.56	66.50	74.77
chess	**97.00**	93.18	87.39	85.61	92.61	87.70	86.10	91.58
credit-a	83.51	82.93	81.59	75.23	84.03	85.98	**86.96**	86.17
credit-g	70.20	69.20	69.00	66.80	**70.50**	69.39	68.45	70.36
cylinder	62.29	56.72	52.56	65.55	72.97	**75.80**	72.68	73.38
dermat	86.01	86.91	31.66	88.17	86.51	91.75	79.21	**93.80**
ecoli	79.86	65.50	64.00	80.58	81.18	81.82	81.44	**82.67**
heart-c	52.15	47.49	49.78	52.48	52.47	54.56	54.74	**54.81**
heart-h	61.72	61.60	57.83	63.77	64.70	65.13	62.68	**65.34**
horse	81.54	74.92	79.59	75.97	82.19	81.00	80.19	**82.32**
ionospere	**87.66**	66.95	69.99	73.46	70.05	72.93	76.46	73.96
liver	64.34	56.81	60.02	60.34	**64.71**	63.31	64.70	63.22
lymphography	**77.95**	57.24	64.86	68.86	74.57	76.44	73.89	74.78
monks	58.36	61.64	61.09	61.51	62.36	61.88	60.18	**62.94**
pima	71.55	68.88	69.78	62.63	71.61	**73.07**	72.28	72.41
s-heart	76.52	62.22	78.52	83.29	77.30	83.65	81.11	**83.81**
segmentation	**92.10**	76.54	84.81	74.22	88.88	83.84	79.98	90.05
soybean	**81.10**	42.41	42.07	49.47	50.34	40.00	48.62	50.35
thyroid	90.53	75.80	79.83	73.23	91.70	93.45	91.92	**93.80**
transfusion	71.71	67.94	71.00	69.41	**72.48**	71.89	70.06	72.06
ttt	**96.00**	72.11	61.05	52.41	69.05	60.40	51.16	69.83
vertebral-2c	80.58	81.29	80.00	78.55	**83.87**	79.04	76.13	82.52
vertebral-3c	78.32	74.19	79.35	78.71	79.68	81.08	80.03	**82.34**
voting	91.66	92.95	90.53	89.29	92.93	92.37	90.48	**93.14**
wine	90.19	79.38	83.63	82.55	92.65	95.07	92.91	**96.05**
Rank (avg.)	4.1	5.8	6.4	6.0	3.2	3.5	4.9	**2.0**

following tables, IB-Ant refers to AntClust-Miner with the instance-based clustering method, while MB-Ant refers to AntClust-Miner with the medoid-based clustering method.

As shown in Table 1, MB-AntClust-Miner with k-NN obtained the best overall average rank of 2.3, and achieved the best results in 9 datasets. IB-AntClust-Miner using 8 clusters came in second place with an overall rank of 3.4, achieving the best results in 6 datasets, followed by IB-AntClust-Miner using 3 clusters, which obtained 4.2 as an overall rank and achieved the best results in 5 datasets. With k-NN, the Friedman test with the Holm *post hoc* test, at the conventional 0.05 significance level, indicates that MB-AntClust-Miner is significantly better than the other algorithms, except for IB-AntClust-Miner with 8 clusters.

Table 3. Predictive accuracy (%) results using C4.5 as the local classifier.

Dataset	C4.5	c-means-3	c-means-5	c-means-8	IB-Ant-3	IB-Ant-5	IB-Ant-8	MB-Ant
audiology	**80.50**	46.67	55.75	52.50	64.42	50.00	55.93	65.83
automobile	**79.36**	56.07	69.25	61.50	76.92	67.43	60.08	78.79
breast-1	**70.86**	69.49	68.17	65.74	69.42	69.48	67.20	67.12
breast-p	69.08	71.29	72.04	67.13	**74.44**	70.24	72.01	72.68
breast-w	92.91	90.49	94.59	86.48	94.46	91.18	**95.03**	94.04
car	**90.98**	72.28	67.67	63.63	72.10	68.07	64.05	73.74
chess	**97.47**	91.38	87.68	84.97	91.00	88.71	84.88	89.75
credit-a	83.80	78.84	82.44	77.10	**85.59**	84.10	83.90	82.03
credit-g	67.60	69.20	68.70	68.50	**70.08**	65.80	67.21	68.90
cylinder	72.50	53.95	67.29	56.74	70.15	58.51	68.19	**72.74**
dermat	**92.00**	43.39	86.62	84.02	86.94	82.80	86.71	91.01
ecoli	81.66	50.26	80.34	64.05	80.21	**81.82**	79.24	81.66
heart-c	49.21	50.80	53.96	49.92	54.93	51.82	53.71	**55.88**
heart-h	64.73	31.12	63.35	63.58	**65.54**	64.97	61.85	64.42
horse	**80.75**	78.94	80.03	76.25	80.43	79.34	78.83	80.36
ionospere	**86.26**	70.69	70.21	61.91	71.94	72.14	71.28	75.37
liver	62.56	61.42	58.25	58.05	**63.71**	62.82	63.22	63.39
lymphography	74.38	68.24	**76.98**	62.24	74.68	72.86	76.38	74.95
monks	59.46	60.55	60.67	58.55	61.25	61.64	60.11	**63.09**
pima	70.51	72.01	71.08	67.43	73.48	**74.52**	73.67	64.99
s-heart	73.56	75.56	75.19	77.41	**84.65**	83.78	83.07	75.93
segmentation	**93.59**	87.04	80.49	74.95	88.07	81.62	70.72	84.64
soybean	**81.11**	45.17	37.61	39.66	49.99	38.97	37.88	53.45
thyroid	89.15	79.03	94.09	93.31	**94.47**	93.01	92.92	93.48
transfusion	**71.78**	71.37	70.44	66.33	71.25	69.78	68.62	71.57
ttt	**83.58**	79.26	67.59	54.95	80.92	68.95	55.49	81.89
vertebral-2c	79.29	80.32	77.10	69.68	**80.63**	78.06	78.63	79.55
vertebral-3c	76.71	80.32	75.81	80.32	**81.22**	79.72	79.75	72.90
voting	92.48	**93.92**	92.01	90.53	93.50	92.80	90.63	92.68
wine	91.30	87.12	83.66	93.04	**96.15**	94.22	93.13	91.60
Rank (avg.)	3.6	5.2	5.1	6.7	**2.4**	4.5	5.1	3.3

The results shown in Table 2 indicate that MB-AntClust-Miner with Ripper obtained the best overall rank of 2.0, and achieved the best results in 13 datasets. In second place came IB-AntClust-Miner using 3 clusters with an overall rank of 3.1, achieving the best results in 4 datasets. IB-AntClust-Miner using 5 clusters came in third place by obtaining 3.5 as an overall rank and achieving the best results in 2 datasets. With Ripper, the Friedman test with the Holm *post hoc* test, at the conventional 0.05 significance level, indicates that MB-AntClust-Miner is significantly better than the other algorithms except for IB-AntClust-Miner with 3 and 5 clusters.

The results for C4.5 shown in Table 3 indicate that IB-AntClust-Miner using 3 clusters obtained the best overall rank of 2.4, and achieved the best results in 10 datasets. MB-AntClust-Miner came in the second place with an overall rank of 3.3, achieving the best results in 3 datasets. In third place came the baseline C4.5 algorithm, which obtained 3.6 as an overall rank and achieved the best results in 12 datasets. With C4.5, the Friedman test with the Holm *post hoc* test, at the conventional 0.05 significance level, indicates that IB-AntClust-Miner with 3 clusters is significantly better than c-means with 3, 5, and 8 clusters, and also significantly better than IB-AntClust-Miner with 5 and 8 clusters.

5   Conclusions and Future Work

In this paper, we have employed Ant Colony Optimization to create cluster-based classification systems. The AntClust-Miner algorithm produces the data clusters and learns the local models in an integrated fashion so that the clusters are optimized to maximize the predictive accuracy of the overall classification system. We used two ACO clustering methods, instance-based and medoid-based, and we extended the medoid-based method to automatically optimize the number of clusters. In our experiments, we used three widely-used classification algorithms, namely k-nearest neighbours, Ripper, and C4.5. We compared our ACO algorithm to the baseline classifiers and to the cluster-based classifiers using the c-means algorithm to produce the clusters (instead of the ACO algorithms), using 30 datasets. The results indicate that the ACO algorithms perform statistically significantly better than c-means in terms of the predictive accuracy of the produced classification models with k-NN, Ripper, and C4.5, and also significantly better than the base k-NN and Ripper algorithms (however, in the case of the C4.5 base algorithm, the difference was not statistically significant). It is not clear why the C4.5 algorithm benefited the least from the cluster-based classification approach, and we would like to explore this further in future work.

We would also like to consider allowing different classification algorithms to be used to learn the local models, based on the characteristics of each cluster, with the choice of the algorithm to use per data cluster being automatically optimized by the ACO procedures. Furthermore, we would like to investigate using all the constructed local models to decide on the class of an instance using a weighted voting ensemble method, where the weight would be computed based on the fuzzy membership of the instance in each cluster.

Acknowledgments. Partial support of a grant from the Brandon University Research Council is gratefully acknowledged.

References

1. Abdelbar, A.M., Salama, K.M.: Clustering with the ACOR algorithm. In: Swarm Intelligence, LNCS, vol. 9882, pp. 210–222 (2016)
2. Dorigo, M., Stützle, T.: Ant Colony Optimization. MIT Press, Cambridge (2004)
3. Gan, G., Ma, C., Wu, J.: Data Clustering: Theory, Algorithms, and Applications. SIAM Press, Philadelphia (2007)
4. Jafar, M., Sivakumar, R.: Ant-based clustering algorithms: a brief survey. Int. J. Comput. Theor. Eng. **2**, 787–796 (2010)
5. Liao, T., Socha, K., de Montes Oca, M., Stützle, T., Dorigo, M.: Ant colony optimization for mixed-variable optimization problems. IEEE Trans. Evol. Comput. **18**(4), 503–518 (2014)
6. Liu, X.Y., Fu, H.: An effective clustering algorithm with ant colony. J. Comput. **5**, 598–605 (2010)
7. Martens, D., De Backer, M., Haesen, R., Vanthienen, J., Snoeck, M., Baesens, B.: Classification with ant colony optimization. IEEE Trans. Evol. Comput. **11**(5), 651–665 (2007)
8. Martens, D., Baesens, B., Fawcett, T.: Editorial survey: swarm intelligence for data mining. Mach. Learn. **82**(1), 1–42 (2011)
9. Otero, F.E., Freitas, A.A., Johnson, C.: A new sequential covering strategy for inducing classification rules with ant colony algorithms. IEEE Trans. Evol. Comput. **17**(1), 64–74 (2013)
10. Otero, F.E., Freitas, A.A., Johnson, C.G.: Handling continuous attributes in ant colony classification algorithms. In: IEEE Symposium on Computational Intelligence in Data Mining (CIDM 2009), pp. 225–231 (2009)
11. Otero, F.E., Freitas, A.A., Johnson, C.G.: Inducing decision trees with an ant colony optimization algorithm. Appl. Soft Comput. **12**(11), 3615–3626 (2012)
12. Parpinelli, R.S., Lopes, H.S., Freitas, A.A.: Data mining with an ant colony optimization algorithm. IEEE Trans. Evol. Comput. **6**(4), 321–332 (2002)
13. Salama, K.M., Abdelbar, A.M.: Learning neural network structures with ant colony algorithms. Swarm Intell. **9**(4), 229–265 (2015)
14. Salama, K.M., Abdelbar, A.M., Anwar, I.M.: Data reduction for classification with ant colony optimization. Intelligent Data Analysis (2016, to appear)
15. Salama, K.M., Abdelbar, A.M., Freitas, A.A.: Multiple pheromone types and other extensions to the ant-miner classification rule discovery algorithm. Swarm Intell. **5**(3–4), 149–182 (2011)
16. Salama, K.M., Abdelbar, A.M., Helal, A.Z., Freitas, A.A.: Instance-based classification with ant colony optimization. Intelligent Data Analysis (accepted, 2016)
17. Salama, K.M., Freitas, A.A.: Clustering-based Bayesian multi-net classifier construction with ant colony optimization. In: IEEE Congress on Evolutionary Computation (IEEE CEC), pp. 3079–3086 (2013)
18. Salama, K.M., Freitas, A.A.: Learning Bayesian network classifiers using ant colony optimization. Swarm Intell. **7**(2–3), 229–254 (2013)
19. Salama, K.M., Freitas, A.A.: ABC-Miner+: constructing Markov blanket classifiers with ant colony algorithms. Memetic Comput. **6**(3), 183–206 (2014)
20. Salama, K.M., Freitas, A.A.: Classification with cluster-based Bayesian multi-nets using ant colony optimization. Swarm Evol. Comput. **18**, 54–70 (2014)

21. Salama, K.M., Freitas, A.A.: Ant colony algorithms for constructing Bayesian multi-net classifiers. Intell. Data Anal. **19**(2), 233–257 (2015)
22. Salama, K.M., Otero, F.E.: Learning multi-tree classification models with ant colony optimization. In: 6th International Conference on Evolutionary Computation Theory and Applications (ECTA 2014), pp. 38–48 (2014)
23. Shelokar, P.S., Jayaraman, V.K., Kulkarni, B.D.: An ant colony approach for clustering. Anal. Chim. Acta **509**(2), 187–195 (2004)
24. Socha, K., Blum, C.: An ant colony optimization algorithm for continuous optimization: application to feed-forward neural network training. Neural Comput. Appl. **16**, 235–247 (2007)
25. Socha, K., Dorigo, M.: Ant colony optimization for continuous domains. Eur. J. Oper. Res. **185**, 1155–1173 (2008)
26. Tan, P.N., Steinbach, M., Kumar, V.: Introduction to Data Mining, 2nd edn. Addison Wesley, Reading (2005)
27. Whitley, D., Dominic, S., Das, R., Anderson, C.: Genetic reinforcement learning for neurocontrol problems. Mach. Learn. **13**(2–3), 259–284 (1993)
28. Witten, I.H., Frank, E.: Data Mining: Practical Machine Learning Tools and Techniques, 3rd edn. Morgan Kaufmann, San Francisco (2010)
29. Xu, R., Wunsch, D.: Clustering. Wiley-IEEE Press, Hoboken (2009)

Short Papers

A Swarm Intelligence Approach in Undersampling Majority Class

Haya Almutlaq Alhakbani[(✉)] and Mohammad Majid al-Rifaie[(✉)]

Department of Computing, Goldsmiths, University of London, London, UK
{h.alhakbani,m.majid}@gold.ac.uk

Abstract. Over the years, machine learning has been facing the issue of imbalance dataset. It occurs when the number of instances in one class significantly outnumbers the instances in the other class. This study investigates a new approach for balancing the dataset using a swarm intelligence technique, Stochastic Diffusion Search (SDS), to undersample the majority class on a direct marketing dataset. The outcome of the novel application of this swarm intelligence algorithm demonstrates promising results which encourage the possibility of undersampling a majority class by removing redundant data whist protecting the useful data in the dataset. This paper details the behaviour of the proposed algorithm in dealing with this problem and investigates the results which are contrasted against other techniques.

Keywords: Swarm intelligence · Class imbalance · Stochastic diffusion search · SVM

One of the major issues in machine learning is the presence of imbalanced datasets. It occurs in most real world applications, including customers related dataset. When mining a customer data, potential buyers and churners are usually classified as minority class and data mining algorithms tend to be influenced by the majority class and misclassifying the minority class. In order for the classifiers to be accurately trained and not be influenced by the majority class, the datasets need to be balanced. In this work, a swarm intelligence algorithm (SDS) is used in order to undersample the majority class. The outcome is then analysed and the results are compared against other techniques. The research questions raised in this work are the following:

1. How does SDS help dealing with imbalanced datasets?
2. What are the other comparable techniques applicable to the problem of imbalanced datasets?
3. Does the application of SDS maintains the spread of the original data?
4. How does SDS deal with the computational cost of undersampling?

1 Related Work

In class imbalance [8], the difference in the numbers of the instances causes a skewed data distribution which affects the classifiers' capabilities in modelling

© Springer International Publishing Switzerland 2016
M. Dorigo et al. (Eds.): ANTS 2016, LNCS 9882, pp. 225–232, 2016.
DOI: 10.1007/978-3-319-44427-7_19

some cases leading to low accuracy and bad classification model. Other factors affecting the classifier performance on imbalanced dataset are the sample size and difficulty of separating the minority class instances from the majority class instances [24]. Therefore, class imbalance issue has received attention in the literature [9,12] and various types of solutions were proposed which include data level and algorithmic level solutions. This paper focuses on data level solutions where several solutions are proposed to overcome the class imbalance problem [7,14,18]. These include: random oversampling, random undersampling and a combination of both to balance the data [3,7,16,18]. However, it has been argued that these techniques can result in removing useful information in the case of random undersampling, and over-fit in the case of random oversampling [7]. In spite of the above mentioned disadvantage, re-sampling are still popular to deal with class imbalance issue. Moreover, various researches have suggested better ways to both oversample and undersample such as Synthetic Minority Oversampling Technique (SMOTE) [7].

2   Stochastic Diffusion Search

SDS was first described by Bishop [5] as a population based matching algorithm that uses direct communication patterns such as cooperative transport found among social insects to perform evaluation of search hypothesis. Unlike other nature inspired search methods, SDS has a strong mathematical framework which describes the behaviour of the algorithm by investigating convergence to global continuum, linear time complexity and resource allocation [5,22]. The SDS algorithm is applicable to changing the objective function, thus enabling a more robust response in dynamically changing environments. This feature of SDS makes the algorithm more attractive for various applications including but not limited to: eye tracking in facial images by using a combination of a Stochastic Search network and an n-tuple network [6], site decision for transmission equipment for wireless networks [15]; mouth locating in human faces images [13]; and more recently global optimisation and medical imaging applications [1]. A recent and comprehensive review of SDS details the key phases (test and diffusion phases) and use of this algorithm in the last two decades [23]. In the test phase each agent is labelled as active or inactive and in the diffusion phases agents communicate with each other (more details are provided in Sect. 3.1).

3   Experiments and Results

In this study, a set of experiments at the data level have been conducted to compare a few undersampling approaches which are applied to the direct marketing campaigns of Portuguese bank dataset which can be accessed at the UCI Machine Learning Repository[1]. From the metadata, it has been found that there

---

[1] Link to the dataset: http://mlr.cs.umass.edu/ml/datasets/Bank+Marketing.

is a class imbalance which is caused by the dramatic difference between the number of subscribers that is equal to 451 and that of the non-subscribers which is equal to 3668. The proposed model uses support vector machine (SVM), which is one of the common and widely used classification algorithm. The model makes prediction using the radial kernel with Gamma set to 1.00 and the cost to 1.00. To prepare the dataset for SVM, the following pre-processing steps have been taken: all nominal values are converted to numerical; and all values are normalised to avoid the value scale difference among all attributes. As mentioned before, in order to oversample the minority class to 2000, SMOTE algorithm will be used. The aim is to oversample the minority class in order to reach a comparable size with the undersampled majority class.

3.1 Balancing the Dataset

There are several methods to deal with the class imbalance problem in the dataset; the proposed model will investigate balancing the dataset by applying two different approaches: undersampling the majority class, and oversampling the minority class, which will be conducted using SMOTE. The undersampling process is performed by SDS whose performance is then contrasted against random undersampling as well as undersampling with Euclidean Distance (ED).

Applying SDS: The initial work is to use SDS to undersample the majority class from 3668 to 2000 non-subscribers. In this experiment, the empirical value of 100 agents are used. Initially the model is selected from the search space (the entire non-subscribers) and the agents are set to find the closest match from the remaining items of the search space. Once a match or the most similar item is found, it is removed from the majority class with the aim of removing redundant data. Given this process aims at reducing the size of the search space without removing useful data, removing the closest item to a randomly selected model discourages the deletion of useful data. This hypothesis is later validated (in Sect. 4.3) when the spread and the central tendency of the data are investigated before and after the undersampling process [19].

Following the initialisation phase where each agent is allocated to a hypothesis from the search space (a random non-subscriber), in the *test phase*, a randomly selected micro-feature (attribute) from the hypothesis is compared against the corresponding micro-feature of the model; if the randomly selected micro-feature of the hypothesis is within a specific threshold (which will be discussed later) from the model's micro-feature, the agent is set to active, otherwise inactive. This process is repeated for all the agents.

In the next phase, the *diffusion phase*, a passive recruitment mode is applied where each inactive agent chooses another agent and adopts the same hypothesis if the randomly selected agent is active. If the randomly selected agent is inactive, the selecting agent picks a random hypothesis (i.e. a random non-subscriber from the search space). This process is repeated for all the inactive agents.

The cycle of test-diffusion is repeated 10 times, which is an empirically chosen value, at the end of which a non-subscriber with the maximum number of active agent is removed from the search space and the model is moved to another list (e.g. model list). This guarantees that while the most similar item is removed from the search space, the model, which represents the deleted item is kept and used later during the classification process. This process is repeated until the dataset is undersampled.

In the experiments reported in the paper, three different thresholds, including 1.00, 0.50 and 0.00 have been used and thus three different datasets of non-subscribers have been generated all sized 2000. As the input dataset is normalised, SDS algorithm with threshold 1.00 *randomly* undersamples the data; threshold 0.00 looks for exact micro-feature match from the model; and threshold 0.50 is a state between random and exact-match undersampling.

Applying ED: ED is a metric used to measure distances between n points in the space. Over the past years, this measure has been widely used for database dimensionality reductions [4,17]. Although a comprehensive metric, acknowledging the high computational expense of applying ED to undersampling problem, it will be used in this work as the mean to contrast with the proposed cheaper computationally expensive swarm intelligence technique. ED will be used to undersample the majority class; in each iteration, a model is picked randomly, then the ED of the model with each element in the search space is calculated; once all the distances are calculated, the closest element to the model is removed. This process process is repeated until the size of the search space is reduced to the number required (i.e. 2000 entries).

3.2   Results

In this work, various performance measures are used. Predictive accuracy is a widely used evaluation metric, however in the case of imbalanced data it is not in itself, a comprehensive evaluation tool as it does not show how the model correctly classifies the minority class, which is the class of interest [7]. To complement predictive accuracy rate, other performance metrics are also used: sensitivity, specificity, Area Under the Curve (AUC), f-measure and precision. The experimental results show that the new approach (i.e. a combination of SDS at threshold 0.00 to undersample the majority class, and SMOTE to oversample the minority class) achieves the best performance in terms of accuracy, specificity, F-measure and precision, as shown in Table 1. The proposed model achieves higher accuracy because of the higher specificity. On the other hand, obtaining higher F-measure is attributable to the higher precision rate as opposed to the ED undersampling. However when using ED for undersampling, the results exhibit higher sensitivity and AUC which can be justified given the much higher computational expense; this claim will be explored further in the next section along with a more in-depth discussion about SDS and the impact of the varying thresholds on the results. For all the experiments, 10-fold cross-validation is applied. Moreover, The results reported in this paper has shown that the proposed method can offer a promising results when compared against previous work on the same dataset, as shown in Table 2.

Table 1. Performance measurements comparison

Threshold	0.00	0.50	1.00	Euclidean distance
Accuracy	**90.46%**	88.56 %	88.56 %	89.47 %
Sensitivity	05.16 %	06.06 %	90.00 %	90.70 %
Specificity	**85.45%**	81.04 %	81.04 %	82.15 %
AUC	0.959	0.96	0.96	**0.965**
F-measure	**90.93%**	89.41 %	89.41 %	90.91 %
Precision	**86.82 %**	83.67 %	83.67 %	84.48 %

Table 2. Results for previous models on the direct marketing dataset

Models	AUC	Accuracy	Sensitivity	Specificity
Moro et al. [21]	0.938	NA	NA	NA
Moro et al. [20]	0.8	NA	NA	NA
G. Feng et al. [11]	NA	83 %	NA	NA
Elsalamony [10]	NA	90.09 %	59.06 %	**93.23%**
Bahnsen et al. [2]	NA	88.28 %	NA	NA
Proposed model	**0.959**	**90.46 %**	**95.46 %**	85.45 %

4 Discussion

In this section, the research questions raised in this work are discussed in the context of the experiments conducted and the results reported in the Sect. 3.

4.1 Applying SDS to Imbalance Data

SDS presents itself as an effective tool to persisting problems encountered in search and optimisation. This is due to SDS's strong partial function evaluation feature which assists the agents to explore the existing large search space and gather a global knowledge without having to evaluate all the existing dimensions; the in-depth analysis of the dimensions occurs only once a viable solution is found, at which stage, agents explore further dimensions of the plausible solutions.

In other words, the partial evaluation enables an agent to form a quick "opinion" about the quality of the investigated solution without exhaustive testing which potentially leads to increased computational complexity. However, using ED, the search for a close match to the model is more computationally expensive because of the complete (vs. partial) function evaluation that accompanies each evaluation.

In the experiments report earlier, three SDS threshold values are used. The activity of the agents in each of the three presented threshold are illustrated in

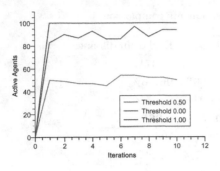 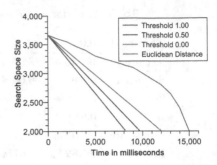

Fig. 1. SDS agent's activity   **Fig. 2.** SDS & EUC time comparison

Fig. 1. As expected, when the threshold is set to 1.00, all agents become active at the end of the first iteration, thus stopping communicating with other agents in the diffusion phase; when the threshold is set to 0.00, the algorithm only "settles" on an exact match, thus as shown in the figure, while around half of the agents are active, the other half searches for the closer match. The middle ground status of SDS when the threshold is set to 0.50, is also illustrated in the figure.

4.2   SDS and Analysing the Spread of Data

Several metrics have already being used in the paper to evaluate the quality of the undersampled data during the classification phase. However another important metric to verify that useful data have not been removed during undersampling, is the spread of data and the central tendency. Using these measures, the mean and the standard deviation of all data points are calculated. The difference of each undersampled dataset from the original dataset (before undersampling) is 0.01095 ± 0.00925 and 0.00945 ± 0.00775 for SDS with threshold 0.0 and when using ED respectively. The results highlight the lack of any significant change in the spread of data with threshold set to 0.00 and when ED is used. This shows not only the success of the algorithm in keeping the useful data, but also the presence of redundant data in the dataset.

4.3   SDS and Computational Complexity

As stated before, due to the partial function evaluation feature of SDS, the computational cost of running SDS on a huge dataset is only dependant on the number of agents and the number of iterations. In the presented work, where the initial size of the majority class is 3668, having 100 agents performing 10 iterations, means that the agents population partially evaluate more than quarter of the search space (i.e. 100 agents × 10 iterations = 1000 micro-features evaluated). Overtime, with the shrinkage of the search space – thanks to the removal of the redundant data – the algorithm's coverage increases to half. One possible approach, which is the subject of an ongoing research, is to reduce the computational expense further by keeping the coverage of the swarm at a constant rate throughout the undersampling process. Figure 2 shows the time taken for SDS in all three thresholds to undersample the data as well as when ED is used. As can be seen in the figure, the undersampling process with SDS demonstrate a linear time complexity throughout the undersampling process (where the search space is shrinking but the number of agents and the iterations allowed are constant), thus exhibiting the time complexity of $O(n)$.

5 Conclusion and Future Work

Various researches proposed advanced undersampling strategies to reduce the majority class samples without removing useful information. This work proposes a swarm intelligence based undersampling approach that reduces the sizes of the majority class in a reliable yet cheap computational way, using the agents and partial evaluation of the majority instance, in which the individuals of the swarm move through the solution space in search of solution that is close to the model. In the proposed method, the capability of SDS to perform majority class undersampling has been investigated on the real-world Portuguese bank dataset. The obtained results imply that SDS can be used as a good undersampling tool for class imbalance. Future work include the investigation of the SDS on other imbalanced dataset, as well as comparison with other swarm intelligence techniques that have been applied to overcome the class imbalance issue. Another topic of ongoing research is the relationship between (and the impact of) the population size of the SDS and the coverage percentage of the dynamically shrinking search space of the dataset being undersampled.

References

1. al-Rifaie, M.M., Aber, A., Sayers, R., Choke, E., Bown, M.: Deploying swarm intelligence in medical imaging. In: 2014 IEEE International Conference on Bioinformatics and Biomedicine (BIBM), pp. 14–21. IEEE (2014)
2. Bahnsen, A.C., Aouada, D., Ottersten, B.: Ensemble of example-dependent cost-sensitive decision trees. arXiv preprint (2015). arXiv:1505.04637
3. Batista, G.E., Prati, R.C., Monard, M.C.: A study of the behavior of several methods for balancing machine learning training data. ACM Sigkdd Explor. Newslett. **6**(1), 20–29 (2004)
4. Beckmann, M., Ebecken, N.F., de Lima, B.S.P.: A KNN undersampling approach for data balancing. J. Intell. Learn. Syst. Appl. **7**(04), 104 (2015)
5. Bishop, J.: Stochastic searching networks. In: Procedings of the 1st IEE Conference on Artifical Neural Networks, pp. 329–331 (1989)
6. Bishop, J., Torr, P.: The stochastic search network. In: Linggard, R., Myers, D.J., Nightingale, C. (eds.) Neural Networks for Vision, Speech and Natural Language. BT Telecommunications Series, vol. 1, pp. 370–387. Springer, Cambridge (1992)
7. Chawla, N.V., Bowyer, K.W., Hall, L.O., Kegelmeyer, W.P.: Smote: synthetic minority over-sampling technique. J. Artif. Intell. Res. **16**, 321–357 (2002)

8. Chawla, N.V., Japkowicz, N., Kotcz, A.: Editorial: special issue on learning from imbalanced data sets. ACM Sigkdd Explor. Newslett. **6**(1), 1–6 (2004)
9. Drown, D.J., Khoshgoftaar, T.M., Narayanan, R.: Using evolutionary sampling to mine imbalanced data. In: Sixth International Conference on Machine Learning and Applications, ICMLA 2007, pp. 363–368. IEEE (2007)
10. Elsalamony, H.A.: Bank direct marketing analysis of data mining techniques. Int. J. Comput. Appl. **85**(7), 12–22 (2014)
11. Feng, G., Zhang, J.D., Liao, S.S.: A novel method for combining bayesian networks, theoretical analysis, and its applications. Pattern Recogn. **47**(5), 2057–2069 (2014)
12. García, V., Sánchez, J.S., Mollineda, R.A.: On the effectiveness of preprocessing methods when dealing with different levels of class imbalance. Knowl. Based Syst. **25**(1), 13–21 (2012)
13. Grech-Cini, H., McKee, G.T.: Locating the mouth region in images of human faces. In: Optical Tools for Manufacturing and Advanced Automation, pp. 458–465. International Society for Optics and Photonics (1993)
14. Han, H., Wang, W.-Y., Mao, B.-H.: Borderline-SMOTE: a new over-sampling method in imbalanced data sets learning. In: Huang, D.-S., Zhang, X.-P., Huang, G.-B. (eds.) ICIC 2005. LNCS, vol. 3644, pp. 878–887. Springer, Heidelberg (2005)
15. Hurley, S., Whitaker, R.M.: An agent based approach to site selection for wireless networks. In: Proceedings of the 2002 ACM Symposium on Applied Computing, pp. 574–577. ACM (2002)
16. Japkowicz, N., et al.: Learning from imbalanced data sets: a comparison of various strategies. In: AAAI Workshop on Learning from Imbalanced Data Sets, vol. 68, pp. 10–15, Menlo Park, CA (2000)
17. Keogh, E., Chakrabarti, K., Pazzani, M., Mehrotra, S.: Dimensionality reduction for fast similarity search in large time series databases. Knowl. Inf. Syst. **3**(3), 263–286 (2001)
18. Kubat, M., Matwin, S., et al.: Addressing the curse of imbalanced training sets: one-sided selection. In: ICML, vol. 97, pp. 179–186, Nashville, USA (1997)
19. McCluskey, A., Lalkhen, A.G.: Statistics II: central tendency and spread of data. Conti. Educ. Anaesth. Crit. Care Pain **7**(4), 127–130 (2007)
20. Moro, S., Cortez, P., Rita, P.: A data-driven approach to predict the success of bank telemarketing. Decis. Support Syst. **62**, 22–31 (2014)
21. Moro, S., Laureano, R., Cortez, P.: Using data mining for bank direct marketing: an application of the crisp-dm methodology. In: Proceedings of the European Simulation and Modelling Conference, Eurosis (2011)
22. Nasuto, S.: Resource allocation analysis of the stochastic diffusion search. Ph.D. thesis, University of Reading (1999)
23. al Rifaie, M.M., Bishop, J.M.: Stochastic diffusion search review. J. Behav. Robot. **3**, 155–173 (2013)
24. Sun, Y., Wong, A.K., Kamel, M.S.: Classification of imbalanced data: a review. Int. J. Pattern Recogn. Artif. Intell. **23**(04), 687–719 (2009)

Optimizing PolyACO Training with GPU-Based Parallelization

Torry Tufteland[⊠], Guro Ødesneltvedt[⊠], and Morten Goodwin[⊠]

Department of ICT, Institute for Technology and Sciences,
University of Agder, Agder, Norway
torry.tufteland@gmail.com, guro.odesneltvedt@gmail.com,
morten.goodwin@uia.no

Abstract. A central part of Ant Colony Optimisation (ACO) is the function calculating the quality and cost of solutions, such as the distance of a potential ant route. This cost function is used to deposit an opportune amount of pheromones to achieve an apt convergence, and in an active ACO implementation a significant part of the runtime is spent in this part of the code. In some cases, the cost function accumulates up towards 94 % in its run time making it a performance bottle neck.

In this paper we parallelize and move the central parts of the cost function to Graphics Processing Unit (GPU). We further test and measure the performance using the ACO classification approach PolyACO. This GPU based parallelization has a tremendous impact on the performance. The duration of the cost function is reduced to 0.5 % of its original runtime. The over all performance of PolyACO implementation is reduced down towards a remarkable 7 % of its original running time — an improvement factor of 14.

Keywords: ACO · Cost function · GPU

1 Introduction

An essential part of Swarm Intelligence, including Ant Colony Optimization (ACO), is an environment informing the algorithms of the quality of proposed or establish solutions — often referred to as the cost function. The cost function is problem dependent and could be the distance of a path for a Travelling Salesman Problem (TSP) [10], the edge quality for image edge detection [16], or the fitness when dealing with classification [9].

Even though the meta-heuristic Swarm Intelligence algorithms are mostly problem independent, the cost function is typically what connects the high-level approaches with the actual problem area. In its base form, the ACO cost function informs of the route distance from a source to a goal via the selected nodes [7]. To do so, it measures the distance, Euclidean or otherwise, whenever the length of a path needs to be known. In this scenario, the cost function is calculated either after each ant or, with caching implemented, when an ant finds a new previously

© Springer International Publishing Switzerland 2016
M. Dorigo et al. (Eds.): ANTS 2016, LNCS 9882, pp. 233–240, 2016.
DOI: 10.1007/978-3-319-44427-7_20

unknown solution. There is no doubt that the cost function is a critical part of any ACO implementation, and improving the performance has the potential to reduce the over-all run time.

Recent advances in supervised learning has proposed using ACO in a Euclidean space to encompass nodes to create a polygon and in turn use the polygon as a classifier [9]. The approach, called PolyACO, classifies items depending on whether they are inside or outside of the training polygon and relies upon defining polygons that efficiently separate two classes. This is different from mathematically based classifiers, such as SVM which defines mathematical functions for similar separations. SVM relies upon the right choice of kernel functions and corresponding parameters, which PolyACO does not. However, a significant disadvantage with PolyACO is its speed during the training — making it impractical when the data set or the granularity grows large. It is slow because much time needs to be spent optimising with the Euclidean training data, which means that the cost of the path is calculated frequently.

This paper makes a powerful update to ACO by parallelizing and adapting the most costly part of the algorithm, the cost function, to Graphics Processing Unit (GPU) using CUDA [1,3]. As a case for testing the improvement, we use PolyACO. The improvement significantly reduces the training speed of Poly-ACO, and can be generalized to any ACO that relies upon a cost function.

The paper is organized as follows. Section 2 gives, for completeness of the paper, a brief introduction of ACO classifiers with most focus on the algorithm used for optimisation PolyACO. Section 3 introduces programming for GPUs and continues with with an approach parallelization PolyACO on GPUs. Section 4 presents results on the parallelization compared to out-of-the-box PolyACO and with optimisation. Finally, Sect. 5 presents the conclusion and future work.

2   PolyACO Classification

Supervised Learning is one of the most central tasks in pattern recognition. The task is challenging whenever the data to be classified cannot easily be separated in a feature space. Many classification algorithms have been proposed in the literature with various limitations.

Much work on ACO classification has been reported in the literature as well. The existing approaches fall into three main categories: (1) Rule based extractors [12], (2) Hybrid approaches involving ACO that attempt to improve and enhance the quality of existing classifiers [14], and lastly (3) PolyACO [9]. This paper focuses on the latter.

2.1   PolyACO

For reasons of completeness, this section presents a brief overview of PolyACO [9], an algorithm for solving classification problems with ACO based on polygons and ray casting. We refer the reader to [9] for details on the algorithm.

In PolyACO, the ants explore solutions in a grid-like graph environment that is generated around some training data. Training data is a set of labeled items where the target class is known. Ants are released sequentially with random initial positions, thus making it an iterative process. The ants explore and find ~~paths around an area in search for path finding. The instant of finding a path~~ from a source to a goal, they end up at the same position they started and their travelled path will have formed a polygon. PolyACO uses a combination of the polygon length and a score of how well the training data is positioned relative to the polygon. This quality measurement is called the cost function, and is the objective to minimize for the algorithm.

After each ant walk, part of the pheromone trail is evaporated to avoid stagnation. Evaporation on an edge sets the edge to the minimum pheromone value, and is applied to each edge with the probability ρ, called the evaporation rate. For example with an evaporation rate of 0.01, a random sample of 1 % of the edges will have their pheromone value reset to the initial value on each ant walk.

Ants only deposit pheromones on the ground if their solution is better than the global best solution. Additionally, the global best solution is reinforced after each iteration to save it from gradually evaporating. This is in line with the approach used in $\mathcal{MAX}$ - $\mathcal{MIN}$ Ant System ($\mathcal{MMAS}$) [15].

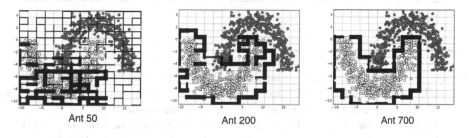

Ant 50   Ant 200   Ant 700

Fig. 1. Pheromone trail development over multiple ant walks. The pheromone amount is indicated by the thickness of the lines.

Environment. The environment where the ants explore solutions is constructed based on the training data. It is a squared graph (see Fig. 1) where all edges along a given axis have equal length forming a grid-like environment. The resolution of the graph environment can be manually set through a granularity factor μ provided to the grid on initialization. μ is an integer argument where $\mu > 2$ and μ is length of the grid for all axes.

Pheromone Update. After every completed ant walk, the pheromones in the graph environment are updated. The amount of pheromone laid in an area of the graph depends on the score of the ant solution. The score is measured by the cost function $f(s)$. The cost function calculates a score based on the length of the polygon, and the number of elements that are correctly placed within it.

$$f(s) = \frac{\sum_{t_i \in T} h(t_i, s)}{|T|} \tag{1}$$

$h(t_i, s)$ is a function that determines whether an element t is on the inside of the solution s, and T is the training data. Ray casting is used to determine if an element is on the inside or outside of a solution. Algorithm 1 presents the most pertinent part of the algorithm, the cost function.

Algorithm 1. PolyACO Cost function

Require: *training_data*
1: **function** Cost(*polygon_solution*)
2:      *num_correctly_inside* ← 0
3:      **for all** $t \in training\_data$ **do**
4:          *inside* ← H($t, polygon\_solution$)
5:          **if** (*inside* **and** $t \in class1$) **or** (**not** *inside* **and** $t \in class2$) **then**
6:              *num_correctly_inside* ← *num_correclty_inside* + 1
7:          **end if**
8:      **end for**
9:      **return** $1 - \frac{num\_correctly\_inside}{|training\_data|}$
10: **end function**

2.2 CUDA

CUDA is a parallel computing platform and an API model created by NVIDIA. The CUDA platform is a software layer that gives direct access to the GPU's virtual instruction set and parallel computational elements [1,3].

CUDA has a two-level architecture consisting of threads and blocks. A thread is a single execution unit that can perform independent tasks. A block is a group of threads that share memory and is executed simultaneously. The number of threads running per block is defined by the programmer when invoking CUDA, and is dependent on both the problem at hand and the GPU hardware.

2.3 GPU-Based ACO Solutions

GPU-based ACO solutions with parallelization are available in the literature [13]. Perhaps most notably is a general GPU-based ACO for TSP [4] which were able to run almost all parts of the code on GPU and reached a speed improvement of a factor of 2. A similar implementation, by however only parallelizing the roulette wheel selection, has resulted in a more than 8 times speed improvement [6]. ACO has also recently been applied for the protein folding problem [11], and reached a 7-fold speed improvement by parallelizing part of the code to GPU.

To the best of our knowledge, no reported work uses GPU based programming for ACO classification, and certainly not for PolyACO.

3   Parallelizing the Cost-Function to GPU

A GPU is a piece of hardware optimized to run many parallel computations. Programming on a GPU is a lot more challenging than programming on a Central Processing Unit (CPU) since parallel programs have a completely different flow than normal sequential programs.

PolyACO is very computationally demanding and takes a long time to train. The cost function takes up a large and disproportionate amount of the total runtime. Profiling results show that this function uses up to 94.9 % of the total run time of the algorithm which obviously makes it a huge bottleneck. Ray casting is part of the cost function and works by computing the intersection of all data points with all the edges in the polygon (see Algorithm 1), where $h(t_i, s)$ computes the intersection for a single data point and edge. On one single ant walk $h(t_i, s)$ is called for every sample in the training set multiplied with the number of edges in the polygon created by the ant. For example, if an ant creates a polygon with 50 segments and the training set contains 10 000 samples, then the $h(t_i, s)$ is called $50 \times 10000 = 500000$ times for this ant only. Each function call to $h(t_i, s)$ average to only about $2\,\mu s$, however with 500 000 calls per ant walk this quickly sums up to a lot of time.

Implementation. The $h(t_i, s)$ function is an independent operation and is computed for the combination of all data points and edges in a given training set and polygon. This makes it ideal as a kernel function as it can perform a lot of parallel computations on the GPU without much expensive communication between the GPU and CPU. The GPU is invoked once per ant, and returns a two-dimensional array where the length of the x-axis corresponds to the number of points in the training set, and the length of the y-axis corresponds to the number of edges in the polygon produced by the ant.

The specifications of the GPU has to be taken into consideration when designing the thread and block layout. This implementation is designed to run on the Nvidida Tesla K40 GPU. The K40 is limited to running 16 blocks per multiprocessor simultaneously and a maximum of 2048 threads in total per multiprocessor. In order the maximize thread occupancy, the block size (number of threads per block) should be sufficiently large so that the running blocks occupy all available threads in the multiprocessor.

Since the block size is set to 128, the kernel will in most cases launches more threads than needed. Therefore, in order to avoid that the threads tries to access data with indexes that are out of bounds, a simple check is performed before the data access. If the thread is out of bounds, the thread is simply terminated.

The performance of the GPU implementation is evaluated by comparing it to the regular implementation that runs on CPython, and for a fair comparison, an optimized the cost function using a library called Numba [2].

4   Experiments and Results

This section presents performance results for PolyACO applied to CUDA. Figure 2a presents results for 3 variants of PolyACO: (1) CPython-version of PolyACO, (2) PolyACO using Jit for optimization, (3) PolyACO where the cost function is moved to GPU through CUDA.[1]

The figure shows that the GPU implementation performs significantly better than both the CPython implementation and the implementation that is optimized using a Just-in-time (JIT) compiler. The results are similar regardless of the size of the dataset. Note that the values on the y-axis follows a logarithmic scale, so the performance gain is much more dramatic than it may look at the first look: — Up to a 6.6X increase from the JIT implementation to the GPU implementation, — Up to a 29.3X increase from CPython to JIT, — Up to a 193.8X increase from CPython to the GPU implementation.

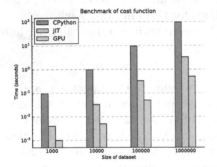
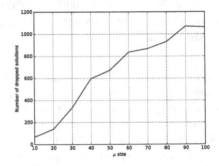

(a) Performance comparison of cost function in (1) CPython, with (2) Numba's JIT compiler, and the (3) GPU implementation

(b) The number of dropped solutions as μ increases. Ants: 1500, iterations: 20

Fig. 2. Performance benchmarkings

The results in Fig. 2a shows the performance of the cost function itself isolated from the rest of the algorithm. To measure the impact of parallelization on the entire algorithm we measure the time it takes to run 1500 ants on both the normal CPython implementation and on the GPU implementation. Correspondingly, the results in Fig. 3a shows that with the cost function running on the GPU this speeds with a factor of 12.98X.

4.1   Declined Performance Gain

Figure 3b shows that the performance gain of the GPU over CPython declines as the grid granularity increase. Profiling results show that the cost function only

---

[1] All GPU results presented in Sect. 4 are run on a Nvidia Tesla K40 GPU and the algorithm implementation is optimized for this device in particular.

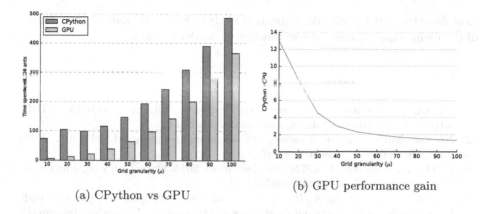

(a) CPython vs GPU

(b) GPU performance gain

Fig. 3. Performance gain of GPU compared to normal CPython implementation

uses about 1.5 % of the total runtime when the granularity factor is set to a high value as opposed to the 94.9 % with a low granularity factor.

This is explained by a higher granularity factors mean more edges in the environment and more paths for the ants to choose, and more paths to choose means that it is easier for the ants to get stuck and create unsuitable solutions. The PolyACOs cost function is optimized for GPU usage to increase performance, but when an ant gets stuck the ant is dropped and the cost function is never run. This means that if the algorithm spends more time on construction solutions than running the cost function, the GPU based parallelization is less used. We therefore tested to see how the drop rate of unsuitable solutions changes with the μ. Figure 2b shows that the drop rate increases with grid granularity μ. A conclusion to be drawn from this is that another factor that influences time spent is the construction of the grid it self.

5   Conclusion and Future Work

In this paper we have improved practical implementations of Ant Colony Optimization by a GPU based parallelizing of the cost function with CUDA. The performance was tested with a reference implementation of the ACO classification algorithm PolyACO — and it had a tremendous effect. The duration of the cost function was reduced to 0.5 % of its original runtime, and the speed of training PolyACO was improved by factors up towards 14. The same approach is applicable to other ACO variants, but the effects will be less apparent for algorithms that spend less time in the cost function.

The future work includes examining the impact of parallelizing and moving cost functions to GPU for other variants of ACO. Even though our improvement had a major impact on the PolyACO performance, and is likely to have a significant impact on other ACO variants as well, this remains to be tested. The future work also includes examining the effect with fuzzy cost functions [8] and constraints [5].

Cost functions with stochastic elements is likely to have a similar or better impact of parallelization because the cost function is harder to cache.

References

1. Parallel Programming and Computing Platform | CUDA | NVIDIA|NVIDIA. http://www.nvidia.com/object/cuda_home_new.html
2. Numba: NumPy aware dynamic Python compiler using LLVM (2012–2016). https://github.com/numba/numba/
3. CUDA, page Version ID: 697481561, December 2015. https://en.wikipedia.org/w/index.php?title=CUDA&oldid=697481561
4. Bai, H., OuYang, D., Li, X., He, L., Yu, H.: Max-min ant system on gpu with cuda. In: 2009 Fourth International Conference on Innovative Computing, Information and Control (ICICIC), pp. 801–804. IEEE (2009)
5. Brito, J., Martínez, F.J., Moreno, J.A., Verdegay, J.L.: An aco hybrid metaheuristic for close-open vehicle routing problems with time windows and fuzzy constraints. Appl. Soft Comput. **32**, 154–163 (2015)
6. Dawson, L., Stewart, I.: Improving ant colony optimization performance on the gpu using cuda. In: 2013 IEEE Congress on Evolutionary Computation (CEC), pp. 1901–1908. IEEE (2013)
7. Dorigo, M., Birattari, M., Stützle, T.: Ant colony optimization. IEEE Comput. Intell. Mag. **1**(4), 28–39 (2006)
8. Garcia, M.P., Montiel, O., Castillo, O., Sepúlveda, R., Melin, P.: Path planning for autonomous mobile robot navigation with ant colony optimization and fuzzy cost function evaluation. Appl. Soft Comput. **9**(3), 1102–1110 (2009)
9. Goodwin, M., Yazidi, A.: Ant Colony Optimisation Based Classification using Two-Dimensional Polygons, September 2016
10. Lian, T.A., Llave, M.R., Goodwin, M., Bouhmala, N.: Towards multilevel ant colony optimisation for the euclidean symmetric traveling salesman problem. In: Ali, M., Kwon, Y.S., Lee, C.-H., Kim, J., Kim, Y. (eds.) IEA/AIE 2015. LNCS, vol. 9101, pp. 222–231. Springer, Heidelberg (2015)
11. Llanes, A., Vélez, C., Sánchez, A.M., Pérez-Sánchez, H., Cecilia, J.M.: Parallel ant colony optimization for the hp protein folding problem. In: Ortuño, F., Rojas, I. (eds.) IWBBIO 2016. LNCS, vol. 9656, pp. 615–626. Springer, Heidelberg (2016). doi:10.1007/978-3-319-31744-1_54
12. Martens, D., De Backer, M., Haesen, R., Vanthienen, J., Snoeck, M., Baesens, B.: Classification with ant colony optimization. IEEE Trans. Evol. Comput. **11**(5), 651–665 (2007)
13. Pedemonte, M., Nesmachnow, S., Cancela, H.: A survey on parallel ant colony optimization. Appl. Soft Comput. **11**(8), 5181–5197 (2011)
14. Salama, K.M., Freitas, A.A.: Ant colony algorithms for constructing bayesian multi-net classifiers. Intell. Data Anal. **19**(2), 233–257 (2015)
15. Sttzle, T., Hoos, H.H.: MAXMIN ant system. Future Gener. Comput. Syst. **16**(8), 889–914 (2000). http://www.sciencedirect.com/science/article/pii/S0167739X00000431
16. Tao, C., Xiankun, S., Hua, H., Xiaoming, Y.: Image edge detection based on aco-pso algorithm. Image **6**(7), 47–54 (2015)

Motion Reconstruction of Swarm-Like Self-organized Motor Bike Traffic from Public Videos

Benjamin Reh[✉] and Katja Mombaur[✉]

Optimization in Robotics and Biomechanics, Interdisciplinary Center for Scientific Computing, Heidelberg University, Heidelberg, Germany
orb@uni-hd.de

Abstract. The process of modeling swarm behaviour based on natural phenomena usually involves the comparison to real world motion data. Our research focuses on analyzing and reproducing realistic behavior of self-organized traffic of motorbikes as it can be observed in some Asian metropoles such as Hanoi or Ho Chi Minh City. We introduce a semiautomatic method to extract motion trajectories of motorbikes in dense traffic situations from public video material. This technique can also be applied to other scenarios with a high density of entities that are only partialally visible on the video frame. To reconstruct these motions as trajectories on the ground plane, the camera pose is estimated using hints found in the videos. In addition we introduce a geometrical model for the locomotion of bikes which enables us to reconstruct the steering angle from the trajectories which gives more insight to the decision making process of the driver. A controlled experiment presented in this paper verifies the validity of our methods.

Keywords: Motion reconstruction · Image recognition · Self-organizing traffic · Crowd simulation

1 Introduction

For the simulation of swarm behaviour, models need to be validated against real-world motion data. An approach often used in crowd simulation is to obtain this data by using motion capture systems in controlled environments. While being very precise this method has the drawback that the number of participants in an experiment is very limited and that they need to be priorly instructed which can lead to an unnatural behavior. Our research focuses on self-organizing behavior of scooter traffic in Vietnamese cities like Hanoi or Ho Chi Minh City where for obvious reasons motion capture cannot be applied. Examples of such traffic situations can be seen in Fig. 1. We therefore pursue the approach of reconstructing motion trajectories directly by processing videos found on internet platforms. This gives us access to a large number of different scenarios with a high traffic density. The methods we present in this paper are not only applicable to traffic

© Springer International Publishing Switzerland 2016
M. Dorigo et al. (Eds.): ANTS 2016, LNCS 9882, pp. 241–248, 2016.
DOI: 10.1007/978-3-319-44427-7_21

Fig. 1. Typical traffic situation ([10]+[1])

situations but can also be used for other scenarios with a high density of entities in a swarm or crowd. Software to track entities in a swarm is freely available to the community. However, none of these tools can be adapted in such a way that their methods can be applied our video material. SwisTrack [4] for example is a very modular software suite to automatically track objects by methods of image recognition. Like most tools it requires a camera position perpendicular to the plane the entities move in. Ctrax [3] is specialized on tracking large numbers Drosophila flies automatically. This is a very specific area of application which is different to tracking bikes that can shadow each other. We decided to develop our own method specific to the requirements imposed by our video source material. In Sect. 2 we present our semi-automatic method to extract trajectories by tracking features on the 2D video frame and projecting them back onto the ground surface. As a second part we introduce a model for the locomotion of a (motor) bike in Sect. 3 to show the difference to other existing models usually found in crowd simulation. This model enables us to reconstruct the steering of the driver from the trace of a single reference point. To verify the accuracy of both methods we conducted a real-world experiment described in Sect. 4. We reconstructed the motion trajectory and steering of a cyclist with our method and compared it to reference data obtained in a controlled environment. In part Sect. 5 we conclude and summarize our findings.

2   Data Acquisition

Internet platforms like youtube provide a variety of videos covering typical scooter traffic filmed from elevated positions. These clips provide sufficient information to extract trajectories semi-automatically. However, unknown properties of the setup and the camera lead to uncertainties which will be evaluated in an experiment in Sect. 4. The three video clips from two sources are chosen for their high resolution (1280×720) as well as for using a tripod to keep the camera stable relative to the scene. They also provide features on the ground helping to estimate the camera pose as described in Sect. 2.

Tracking the Trace of a Motorbike. A reference point $P_{ref}(x, y)$ for a given scooter is placed manually on the ground plane (street) in such a way that it

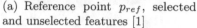

(a) Reference point p_{ref}, selected
and unselected features [1]

(b) Ground plane calibrated using a sewer cover [10]

Fig. 2. Screenshots from our software used for the reconstruction

is in the center between the contact points of the two wheels with the ground
(see Fig. 2(a)). This is performed manually in one frame of the video clip making
it a keyframe. Tracking the reference point itself during the motion is virtually
impossible since especially the lower parts of the motorbike are obscured by
other traffic participants. A feature detector therefore marks distinctive features
on the frame that are visible and easy to track. This detector is based on the
work of Shi and Tomasi [9] which is available in openCV. Adequate features
F_i on the scooter are manually selected and then tracked automatically from
this keyframe forwards and backwards in time. The algorithm used for tracking
is a sparse iterative version of the Lucas-Kanade optical flow in pyramids [2]
that is also provided by openCV. The displacement of the reference point P_{ref}
from frame $(t-1) \rightarrow t$ is computed as the average of the displacements of the
features F_i: $P_{ref}(t) = P_{ref,t-1} + \frac{1}{n} \sum_{i=0}^{n}(F_i(t) - F_i(t-1))$. Manual intervention
is only needed if features get obscured by other traffic participants. Defining the
motion of P_{ref} in such a way is an assumption that needs to be validated. The
experiment described in Sect. 4 takes a closer look at this method's accuracy and
validity.

Pose Estimation and Back Projection. In general, the projection from a two
dimensional pixel P' on the video frame back to a 3D point P in space requires an
estimation of the camera pose relative to the three dimensional space it captures.
For the reconstruction of trajectories only points on the ground plane ($P_z = 0$)
are of interest. This reduces the complexity of the problem allowing for a unique
transformation between pixel P' and point P. A quadratic sewer cover which
can be found in both videos is used to correlate pixels with their counterparts
on the street (see Fig. 2(b)). It provides limited but sufficient information to
estimate the pose. OpenCV offers a function to do this estimation by numerically
optimizing the pose parameters. It uses Levenberg-Marquardt [5] optimization to
minimize the projection error that occurs when projecting a 3D point P onto the
2D frame as P'. Once the camera pose is determined, projecting a point P in 3D
space forward to a pixel P' on the screen is unique $P' = F(P), P' \in \mathbb{R}^2, P \in \mathbb{R}^3$.

Generally, the back projection $P = F^{-1}(P')$ is ambiguous. Several P in space can be projected on the same pixel P' on the screen. Since only points on the ground plane (street surface) with $P(x, y, 0)$ are of interest, a unique solution of the back projection can be computed. We achieve this by numerically inverting the forward projection available from the openCV library using a Nelder Mead simplex algorithm [6] to minimize the error of the forward projection as $\min_P(|F(P) - P'|)$. The reference points of each scooter and each time frame are back-projected thereby obtaining a complete trajectory on the ground plane in the real world 3D space.

3   Geometric Model of a Bike

In the field of swarm and crowd simulation agents are typically described by a point $P(x, y)$ on a ground plane and a velocity vector $\boldsymbol{v}$ or a heading angle α in combination with a scalar velocity $v = |\boldsymbol{v}|$. In a time discrete case with a fixed time step of dt the equations of locomotion are $P_t = P_{t-1} + \boldsymbol{v}_t \cdot dt$.

The form of locomotion of a realistic, two-dimensional bike model can be described as follows and is illustrated in Fig. 3(a). A bike can only move in a given direction. The steering angle β describes the angle of the front wheel (F) in respect to the back wheel (B). Assuming the non-trivial case $\beta \neq 0$, the front and the back wheel describe circular trajectories with different radii $|\overline{CF}|$ and $|\overline{CB}|$. These radii are defined by the intersection point C of two lines, each perpendicular to one of the wheel's orientation. C becomes the pivot point for a rotation of F and B with angle ϕ. Rotations are affine transformations hence applying to each point on the vehicle. We conveniently define a reference point P in the center between both wheels. P travels with velocity v for the next time step dt on a circle section with a length of $s = v \cdot dt$. Looking at this problem from a geometrical point of view one can deduce Eqs. (1) and (2).

$$|\overline{CP}| = \sqrt{|\overline{CB}|^2 + b^2/4} = b \cdot \sqrt{(\tan \beta)^{-2} + 1/4} \tag{1}$$

$$\phi = \text{sign}\,(\beta) \cdot \frac{s}{|\overline{CP}|} = \text{sign}\,(\beta) \cdot \frac{v \cdot dt}{|\overline{CP}|} \tag{2}$$

The displacement of the reference point ΔP with the update of the orientation $\Delta \theta = \phi$ is then given by

$$\Delta P = |\overline{CP}| \cdot \text{sign}\,(\beta) \cdot \begin{pmatrix} \sin(\theta + \phi) - \sin(\theta) \\ \cos(\theta) - \cos(\theta + \phi) \end{pmatrix} \tag{3}$$

It becomes obvious that the direction of motion described by ΔP and the orientation angle θ are not pointing in the same direction. This is a simplified model of a bike as it is limited to two dimensions. The bike is always assumed to stand upright perpendicular to the ground plane. Another simplification is that in this model the pivot axis of the front wheel coincides with its center which is not the case for most (motor) bikes.

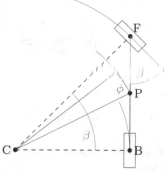

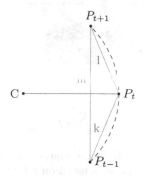

(a) Geometric model of locomotion

(b) k, l, m form a triangle with a circumscribed circle with radius $|\overline{CP}|$

Fig. 3. Geometric models for a bike

Reconstruction of Motions. In this section we reconstruct the orientation angle θ which is not identical to the direction of locomotion and the steering angle β based on trajectories obtained as described before. Pedestrian trajectories obtained with motion capture systems are usually filtered with a low pass filter of 0.5 Hz to remove the swaying motion that is produced during walking [7,8]. In the case of scooter traffic the motions are much faster and more fluent. Nevertheless a Butterworth low-pass filter (second order) with a cut-off frequency of 2 Hz is used to smoothen out noise. Only a subset of the data is selected for further analysis. Data outside a certain range around the image center is neglected to reduce the effect of lens distortions. Figure 4 shows the selected trajectories for all 3 clips. To reconstruct the orientation θ and steering β for time t a total of three points is needed. P_{t-1}, P_t and P_{t+1} define a triangle with a unique circumscribed circle. The radius of this circle is $|\overline{CP}|$ in Fig. 3(a) and is expressed in Eq. (4) using Heron's formula. For simplification we identify the triangle's sides with $k = |\overline{P_{t-1}P_t}|$, $l = |\overline{P_tP_{t+1}}|$ and $m = |\overline{P_{t-1}P_{t+1}}|$ (see Fig. 3(b)):

$$|\overline{CP}| = klm \cdot \left(4k^2l^2 - (k^2 + l^2 - m^2)^2\right)^{-1/2} \qquad (4)$$

Equations (1) and (2) now allow us to compute ϕ and β with a given wheelbase b analytically. Due to the complexity of Eq. (3) the value of θ is computed numerically by solving the problem defined in (5).

$$\min_{\theta} \left| \Delta P - |\overline{CP}| \left(\frac{\sin(\theta + \phi) - \sin(\theta)}{\cos(\theta) - \cos(\theta + \phi)} \right) \right| \qquad (5)$$

The ability to reconstruct to steering β in each time frame is a major benefit when developing a swarm model to describe scooter traffic. The steering directly reflects the intention of the driver which allows a deeper insight into the decision making process compared to looking at the trajectory itself.

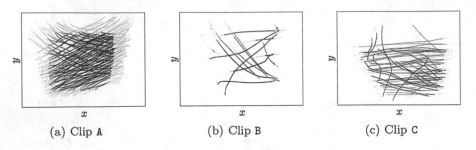

(a) Clip A   (b) Clip B   (c) Clip C

Fig. 4. Points marked for analysis in paths (black) vs. neglected points (gray). The selection is based on a filter in the position (x, y) and time.

4   Experiment for Evaluation

The convenience of using already existing video material contrasts with inaccuracies imposed by unknown parameters and factors of the scene and camera. It is therefore very advisable to evaluate and estimate the accuracy of the data obtained by this method. In the controlled experiment we conducted a cyclist was filmed from an elevated position the same way as it has been done in the public videos from the internet. This material was then analyzed and compared to reference data obtained by aerial photography. The bicycle was modified to leave a trace of sand from the center between both wheels. Furthermore a small camera was mounted on the bicycle's handlebar to record a video for the purpose of reconstructing the steering angles. To resemble a motorcycle behaviour as observed in the public videos, the person on the bicycle was given the instructions to ride in an upright position using a low to medium speed and not to lean to the side while cornering. Three paths are specified by marking its start and end points with arrows on the ground. Figure 5(a) shows these paths marked as a, b, c. Path c is a slalom course with two additional markers to avoid. To reconstruct the camera pose a square of $1.5\,\mathrm{m} \times 1.5\,\mathrm{m}$ was drawn on the ground to serve as a hint similar to the sewer covers as described in Sect. 2. The main camera placed in a height of $4.5\,\mathrm{m}$ records a video with 1920×1080 pixels and $25\,\mathrm{fps}$.

4.1   Results and Discussion

Back Projection. The path is reconstructed in a similar way as described in Sect. 2. Figure 5(a) shows the reprojected trace as crosses overlayed on an areal photograph. It can be observed that the general form and position of the path is followed. Two main causes for deviations can be stated. Coming from the nature of a reconstruction with only one camera an error due to perspective distortion of the bike has to be expected. Features marked in one view do not have to transform necessarily in such a way that their average displacement equals the translation of the reference point P_{ref} as it was assumed. The other important factor that has not been taken into account are lens distortions. Since videos

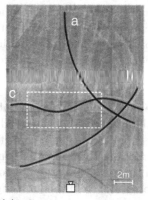

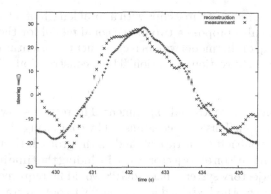

(a) Comparison between reconstructed and actual path.

(b) Reconstructed vs. measured steering.

Fig. 5. Results of the reconstruction

from the internet have insufficient information available to compensate for this effect we also did not apply any corrections to our video as well. Overall it can be stated that the reconstructed path lies within a margin of 60 cm − 80 cm of the original trace left on the ground. This result can be regarded as more than sufficient especially when taking into account that the videos from the internet are recorded form a steeper angle thus making perspective distortions less of an issue.

Reconstruction of the Steering. The objective in this part is to compare the steering reconstructed from the trajectory to the actual steering recorded by the on-board camera capturing the handlebar. For that purpose a section of a trajectory has to be chosen in which reconstructed and actual path coincide well. This section of path c is marked with a dashed rectangle in Fig. 5(a). Figure 5(b) shows the reconstructed steering compared to the actual steering recorded by the on-board camera for the above mentioned section. Data from the camera was filtered by a low pass filter with a cut-off frequency of 5 Hz to reduce the noise introduced by the image recognition. One can clearly observe that the amplitude of the reconstructed steering matches the recorded one. Even though the exact values cannot be reproduced the overall shape is preserved. This is regarded as sufficient as in further analyses the reconstructed steering will be compared to the reconstructed path only.

5   Conclusions and Outlook

We successfully demonstrated our method of extracting trajectories of scooters using image recognition techniques applied on videos found on internet platforms.

We analyzed three clips with a total length of 32.2 s and obtained 176 trajectories. We also propose a two-dimensional model for the locomotion of a bike. With the help of this model we can reconstruct the orientation of a bike which is not identical to the direction of motion. The reconstruction of the driver's steering angle from the recorded trajectories gives a deeper insight into the intentions and the decision making process of each entity. To evaluate the accuracy of our methods we conducted a controlled experiment. The results show the validity within a reasonable margin. This was accomplished by comparing the path obtained by our method to the one left by a trace of sand on the ground. Further experiments can include the comparison of trajectories e.g. including the time information. To obtain a reference trajectory systems like a dGPS would be required. In this paper we presented our new method, applied it successfully to obtain trajectories and confirmed it using a controlled experiment.

References

1. Allround vision: Crazy Hanoi Traffic. https://www.youtube.com/watch?v=Gf8_lzCWvq4. Accessed 10 Nov 2014
2. Bouguet, J.Y.: Pyramidal implementation of the affine lucas kanade feature tracker description of the algorithm. Intel Corporation 5 (2001)
3. Branson, K., Robie, A.A., Bender, J., Perona, P., Dickinson, M.H.: High-throughput ethomics in large groups of drosophila. Nat. Methods **6**(6), 451–457 (2009)
4. Lochmatter, T., Roduit, P., Cianci, C., Correll, N., Jacot, J., Martinoli, A.: Swistrack - a flexible open source tracking software for multi-agent systems. In: 2008 IEEE/RSJ International Conference on Intelligent Robots and Systems, pp. 4004–4010, September 2008
5. Mor, J.: The levenberg-marquardt algorithm: implementation and theory. In: Watson, G. (ed.) Numerical Analysis. LNCS, vol. 630, pp. 105–116. Springer, Heidelberg (1978)
6. Nelder, J.A., Mead, R.: A simplex method for function minimization. Comput. J. **7**, 308–313 (1965)
7. Olivier, A.H., Marin, A., Crétual, A., Berthoz, A., Pettré, J.: Collision avoidance between two walkers: role-dependent strategies. Gait Posture **38**(4), 751–756 (2013)
8. Pettré, J., Ondřej, J., Olivier, A.H., Cretual, A., Donikian, S.: Experiment-based modeling, simulation and validation of interactions between virtual walkers. In: Proceedings of the 2009 ACM SIGGRAPH/Eurographics Symposium on Computer Animation, SCA 2009, New York, NY, USA, pp. 189–198 ACM (2009)
9. Shi, J., Tomasi, C.: Good features to track. In: 1994 IEEE Computer Society Conference on Computer Vision and Pattern Recognition, Proceedings CVPR 1994, pp. 593–600. IEEE, June 1994
10. Whitworth, R.: Ho Chi Minh City (Saigon), Vietnam Rush Hour Traffic in Real Time. https://www.youtube.com/watch?v=Op1hdgzmhXM. Accessed 10 Nov 2014

On Heterogeneity in Foraging by Ant-Like Colony: How Local Affects Global and Vice Versa

Yuichiro Sueoka[⊠], Kazuki Nakayama, Masato Ishikawa, Yasuhiro Sugimoto, and Koichi Osuka

Department of Mechanical Engineering, Osaka University, Osaka, Japan
sueoka@mech.eng.osaka-u.ac.jp

Abstract. In this paper, we discuss influence of heterogeneity in ant-like colony, i.e., how the ratio of individuals (ants) obeying two different action rules affects the behavior of whole colony. For this purpose, we focus on the foraging task – searching the field for food sources, transporting the food packets to the nest. The two types of ants include what we call hard-working and lazy ants, and we perform statistical analyses to show that moderate existence of the lazy ants would boost efficient food transportation; in particular, we point out that the lazy ants play as explorer of newly emerged food sources, but also as global sensor to capture global information through their local experience, thanks to their moving-around behavior. Based on these observations, we propose a distributed estimation method of global information, i.e., to estimate the global mixture ratio by local encounter frequency with other lazy ants. Finally, we expand the estimation method to distributed control strategy of the global mixture ratio, called on-line switching strategy, where every ant dynamically alternates its obeying rules from the hard-working to the lazy and vice versa, based on its local encounter experience.

1 Introduction

In discussing swarm systems, it has a great meaning for an individual to know states of a whole group, e.g., how many agents engage in the same work or attend to different works. This paper is motivated by natural insect phenomena: ants or termites exhibit us wonderful performance, such as: role division, environment adaptability, nevertheless they have physically tiny brains with limited deduction capacity [1]. These phenomena have been strongly attracted control engineers as well as biologists to motivate them to make a great deal of effort [3].

This paper also challenges to grasp outstanding ideas of swarm intelligence by exploiting the food transporting task by ant-like colonies, which was inspired by real ants' foraging behavior. The point we wish to emphasis here is that our research is not aimed at perfect models of real ants, but focuses attention on influence of heterogeneity in ant-like colony. Our previous research [5] have attempted to demonstrate the foraging behavior by heterogeneous ants obeying

© Springer International Publishing Switzerland 2016
M. Dorigo et al. (Eds.): ANTS 2016, LNCS 9882, pp. 249–256, 2016.
DOI: 10.1007/978-3-319-44427-7_22

two different action rules. In the process of examining the foraging task, heterogeneity would boost efficient transporting task, whose results are the same as the previous report on insect societies [2], but lead us to a fundamental question, such as: How an individual knows global without global point of view? Is it possible to control the ratio of working ants to resting ants from local experience?

In this paper, we dare to exploit an issue by exploring an estimation strategy of global from local. First, we prepare the simulation setups with reference to cellular automata approach [7]. Then, we introduce not only pheromone pursuing ants, called hard-working ants, but also lazy ants which move randomly and take a rest with moderate frequency. Throughout statistical examination of the foraging task by these heterogeneous agents, we noticed that lazy ants have two important roles:

1. Field explorer: they search new food source efficiently by exploring in the field.
2. Global sensor: they experience a wide range of the field (global information).

From this viewpoint, we examine distributed estimation method: local encounter frequency with other lazy ants reflects the global mixture ratio, i.e., true mixture ratio of lazy ants to total ants. The authors try to expand the estimation method to distributed control of global mixture ratio based on on-line switching strategy: every ant dynamically alternates its obeying rules from a hard-working to a lazy state and vice versa, based on its local encounter experience.

2   Preliminaries

This section is dedicated to the modeling of food transportation by ants-like colony, inspired by real ants' foraging behavior. First, we try to build the model by extracting ideas in food transportation by real ants' colony; real ants obey different pheromones in food exploration and transportation cases. Then, we introduce the two types of ants obeying different action procedure, what we call hard-working and lazy ants.

2.1   Discrete Model of Food Transportation by Ants-Like Colony

Let us begin with building a model of foraging task by ant-like colony. Each ant is supposed to possess two modes: exploration and transportation, and switches these two modes dynamically as shown in Fig. 1. The duration from leaving their nests to reaching food sources is called as exploration mode. On contrast, the duration returning from the food source to their nest is called as transportation mode. Ants deposit and perceive two types of pheromones (recruitment/homing pheromones). Each unit of food is allowed to be transported only by single ant.

Mode 1 (Exploration mode) Ants pursue homing pheromone and deposit recruitment pheromone. Each ant switches to transportation mode after picking up a food packet at a food source.

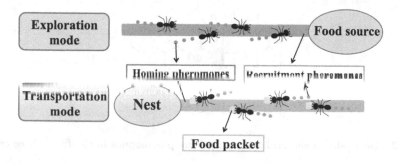

Fig. 1. Exploration and transportation modes in the foraging behavior of ants.

Mode 2 (Transportation mode) Ants pursue recruitment pheromone and deposit homing pheromone. Each ant switches to exploration mode after transporting a food packet to their nest.

This paper introduces a discrete version of a pheromone model inspired by the natural ones deposited by real ants. As mentioned above, each ant deposits two types of pheromones: homing/recruitment pheromones. Both pheromones are volatile, which means they evaporate from the field and diffuse into space as a time function, with reference to [4]. We call the deposited pheromone to the ground as ground pheromone, and also call the diffused pheromone in the air as air pheromone. The detailed explanation about the equations of evaporation and diffusion are written in our previous work [5].

2.2 Setting of Action Types

Let us turn to discuss the action of ants. Suppose that every ant is positioned at the center of a hexagonal cell as shown in Fig. 2. Also, there is no limit on the number of ants in a single cell in this paper - namely, we do not adopt excluded volume. We suppose that ants perceive both ground and air pheromones on the three blue cells in Fig. 2; i.e. their front, front right and front left cells. Moreover, we assume that ants perceive whether their nest is in the direction of movement based on the navigational abilities of real ones such as a solar compass [6].

Each ant tries to choose one action rule from the following five rules and execute the action in the cellular world.

Turn In transportation mode, if the direction of their nest is toward the rear direction, they turn to a cell selected randomly from the rear three cells.

Ground pheromone pursuing When ants perceive ground pheromones in their front, front right or front left cells, they follow this rule. Ants decide their moving cell based on the concentrations of ground pheromone in three cells. The following integers $k = -1, 0, 1$ coincide with front-left/front/front-right cells, respectively.

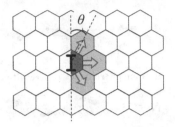

Fig. 2. Ant model in the grid space to pursue pheromones in the front three cells.

$$k = \begin{cases} -1 & (0 \le \theta < \frac{\pi}{3}) \\ 0 & (\frac{\pi}{3} \le \theta \le \frac{2\pi}{3}) \,, \\ 1 & (\frac{2\pi}{3} < \theta \le \pi) \end{cases} \qquad \theta = \tan^{-1} \frac{\mathbf{g}^T \mathbf{s}}{\mathbf{g}^T \mathbf{c}} \qquad (1)$$

Each component of vectors is written as

$$\mathbf{g} = \begin{bmatrix} G^{-1}(n_x, n_y, \tau) \\ G^0(n_x, n_y, \tau) \\ G^1(n_x, n_y, \tau) \end{bmatrix}, \quad \mathbf{s} = \begin{bmatrix} \frac{1}{2} \\ 1 \\ \frac{1}{2} \end{bmatrix}, \quad \mathbf{c} = \begin{bmatrix} \frac{\sqrt{3}}{2} \\ 0 \\ -\frac{\sqrt{3}}{2} \end{bmatrix} \qquad (2)$$

This action rule determines the ants movement based on the collection of three vectors whose gain is the concentration of pheromone in each cell.

Air pheromone pursuing When ants do not perceive ground pheromones on their front, front right or front left cell, but perceive air pheromones, they follow this rule. Their movement is determined based on the concentration of air pheromone, whose equation is the same in the case of ground pheromone pursuing.

Random walk If ants cannot perceive neither grounding nor air pheromones on their front, front right or front left cell, they obey this rule. They try to move to their front cell with probability ε ($0 \le \varepsilon \le 1$) and their front right or front left cells with probability $\frac{1-\varepsilon}{2}$, respectively. In this paper, we set ε to 0.5.

Rest Take a rest at the cell

2.3   Heterogeneous Ants Obeying Different Action Procedure

Let us turn to introduce two types of ants, called hard-working and lazy ants. We would like to special emphasis on these heterogeneous ants, because this work gives weight to influence of heterogeneity.

Hard-working ants This type of ants tries to pursue ground/air pheromones.

- Exploration mode: Ground pheromone pursuing → Air pheromone pursuing → Random walk

– Transportation mode: Turn → Ground pheromone pursuing → Air pheromone pursuing → Random walk

Lazy ants This type of ants move randomly. An ant tries to take a rest at a constant probability

– Exploration mode: Rest or Random walk
– Transportation mode: Rest or Turn → Random walk

3 Analysis of Food Transportation by Heterogeneous Ants

This section examines the foraging task by heterogeneous ants based on an evaluation index, called energy efficiency. After preparing simulation environment, we carry out statistical analyses by changing two parameters: the rest probability of lazy ants, the global mixture ratio of lazy ants.

3.1 Fundamental Simulation Settings

Suppose the field is occupied by 107×107 cells; there exist one nest with ants at the center and food sources in the radial direction. The number of food packets is fixed at 600 per food source, and if one food source is exhausted, a new food source is emerged. The new food source is on the extended line from their nest in the radial directions, and the distance from their nest to food sources is fixed. The maximum number of food sources is set to three at the same time.

3.2 Statistical Analysis in Foraging Behavior by the Heterogeneous Ants

It is helpful to introduce an evaluation index, called energy efficiency before moving on to the further analysis of foraging behavior.

Energy efficiency Suppose that each ant costs 1 energy to execute actions except for rest. Energy efficiency is calculated as the equation:

$$\text{Energy efficiency} = \frac{\text{Sum of transported food packets}}{\text{Total energy consumption}}. \tag{3}$$

We demonstrate the foraging behavior by changing two parameters: the rest probability of lazy ants and the global mixture ratio of lazy ants. The values of rest probability is set within $[0,1]$, for example, if the rest probability is 1, the lazy ants always take a rest; in contrast, if the rest probability is 0, the lazy ants always move randomly. We conducted 20 times repeated simulations for each parameter value, where the ratio of lazy ants changes from 0 % to 90 % in every 10 % and the rest probability of lazy ants changes at $0, 1/2, 3/4, 7/8, 15/16$. Figure 3 shows the averages of energy efficiency for each parameter value.

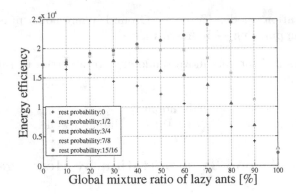

Fig. 3. Energy efficiency in food transporting task by the heterogeneous ants

A whole tendency in Fig. 3 indicates that the foraging task gets to more efficient as the density of lazy ants increase, except for no rest cases. By focusing on the role of lazy ants, lazy ants help to guide hard-working ants to newly emerged food sources quickly after one food source is exhausted. In addition, the results also say that lazy ants need not to move frequently. On these grounds we have come to the conclusion that the foraging task gets to efficient with the aid of lazy ants.

4   Distributed Control of Global Mixture Ratio Based on Local Encounter Experience

This section discusses another role of lazy ants – estimating the global mixture ratio through their local experience, thanks to moving-around behavior. This section also proposes a distributed control method of global mixture ratio.

4.1   Estimation of Global Mixture Ratio from Local Encounter Experience

Before it is possible to enter into a detailed discussion of estimation, we must clarify some terms. The term "global mixture ratio" can be defined as the true ratio of lazy ants to total ants. The term "empirical mixture ratio" is also defined as a calculated ratio from the local encounter frequency with lazy ant from lazy or hard-working ants' experience. First, we examine the relation between the empirical mixture ratio and the global mixture ratio. Figure 4 shows the empirical mixture ratio: the averages with error bars by changing the global mixture ratio of lazy ants from 0 % to 90 % in every 10 %. In the case of hard-working ants, empirical mixture ratio does not reflect the global mixture ratio, because hard-working ants mainly engage in food transporting work on the pheromone trail, in other words, their experience reflects only on the pheromone trail. On the other hand, in the case of lazy ants, empirical mixture ratio has proportional

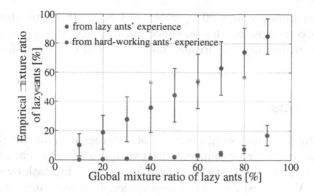

Fig. 4. Global mixture ratio of lazy ants vs. Empirical mixture ratio of lazy ants

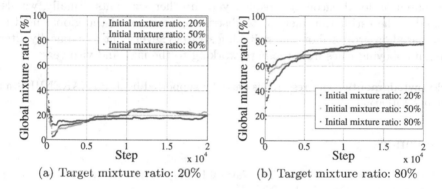

(a) Target mixture ratio: 20%   (b) Target mixture ratio: 80%

Fig. 5. Distributed control of the global mixture ratio based on the estimated mixture ratio calculated from ant's local encounter experience.

relation to the global mixture ratio. In summery, empirical mixture ratio from lazy ants' experience reflects the global mixture ratio.

4.2 Distributed Control of Global Mixture Ratio

Suppose that ants record a memory in previous n step of local encounter frequency with lazy ants. We propose on-line switching strategy, where every ant alternates its obeying rule from the hard-working to the lazy and vice versa, based on its local encounter experience. If the encountered ratio with lazy ant passes under a pre-determined threshold C_1, the ant switches its obeying rule from the hard-working to the lazy. And if the encounter rate with lay ant passes over a pre-determined threshold C_2, the ant switches its obeying rule from the lazy to the hard-working. When we set the targeting value of the global mixture ratio as 20% or 80%, the thresholds C_1 and C_2 is set as $C_1 = 5.02 \times 10^{-3}, C_2 = 1.79 \times 10^{-1}$, and $C_1 = 4.82 \times 10^{-2}, C_2 = 7.81 \times 10^{-1}$, respectively. These values are determined based on local encounter frequency in heterogeneous simulations. Time series of the global mixture ratio is shown in

Fig. 5 with the initial values 20 %, 50 %, and 80 %. It seems that the global mixture ratio converges to the reference values. Therefore, we can say that global mixture ratio can be controlled based on local encounter frequency with lazy ants.

5 Conclusions

This paper aimed at discussing influence of heterogeneity in foraging behavior by ant-like colony. After introducing the two types of ants: hard-working and lazy ants, we performed statistical analyses of the foraging task by these hetero-geneous ants. We noticed from the investigation that lazy ants play important roles as global sensor to capture global information thanks to moving-around behavior. Then, we proposed distributed estimation method of global informa-tion based on local encounter frequency with other lazy ants. Finally, we also expanded the estimation method to distributed control of the global mixture ratio based on proposed on-line switching strategy: every ant dynamically alter-nates its obeying rules from the hard-working to the lazy and vice versa.

Acknowledgments. This research is partially supported by JSPS KAKENHI Grant Number 15H06360.

References

1. Hansell, M.: Built by Animals: The Natural History of Animal Architecture. Oxford University Press, New York (2009)
2. Hasegawa, E., Ishii, Y., Tada, K., Kobayashi, K., Yoshimura, J.: Lazy workers are necessary for long-term sustainability in insect societies. Sci. Rep. 6, Article No. 20846 (2016). doi:10.1038/srep20846
3. Hölldobler, B., Wilson, E.: The Ants. Belknap Press of Harvard University Press, Cambridge (1990)
4. Nakamura, M., Kurumatani, K.: A method for designing ant colony models and two examples of its application. In: Capcarrère, M.S., Freitas, A.A., Bentley, P.J., Johnson, C.G., Timmis, J. (eds.) ECAL 2005. LNCS (LNAI), vol. 3630, pp. 530–539. Springer, Heidelberg (2005)
5. Nakayama, K., Sueoka, Y., Ishikawa, M., Sugimoto, Y., Osuka, K.: Control of trans-portation trails by distributed autonomous agents inspired by the foraging behavior of ants. Nonlinear Theory Appl. 5(4), 487–498 (2014)
6. Wehner, R., Müller, M.: The significance of direct sunlight and polarized skylight in the ant's celestial system of navigation. PNAS **103**(33), 12575–12579 (2006)
7. Wolfram, S.: Cellular Automata and Complexity: Collected Papers. Westview Press, Boulder (1994)

On Stochastic Broadcast Control of Swarms

Ilana Segall$^{(\boxtimes)}$ and Alfred Bruckstein

Technion, Israel Institute of Technology, Haifa, Israel
segall.ilana@gmail.com

Abstract. We present a model for controlling swarms of mobile agents via a broadcast control, detected by a random number of agents in the swarm. The agents that detect the control signal become the ad-hoc leaders of the swarm, while they detect the exogenous control. The agents are assumed to be velocity controlled, identical, anonymous, oblivious units with unlimited visibility. Assuming unlimited visibility decouples the problem of emergent behavior in a swarm from that of keeping the visibility graph complete, which has been thoroughly discussed in [10]. Each agent applies a linear local gathering control, based on the relative position of its neighbors. The detected exogenous control is superimposed by the leaders on the local gathering control. We show that in each time interval of a piecewise constant system, where the system evolves as a time-independent dynamic linear system, the swarm asymptotically aligns on a line in the direction of the exogenous control and all the agents move with identical speed. The speed of the swarm is set by the ratio between the numbers of agents receiving the control signal and the total number of agents in the swarm. A new time interval is triggered by a change in the broadcast control signal or in the agents detecting it, i.e. the "leadership team".

1 Introduction

We present a system composed of agents and a controller. All the agents apply a distributed gathering control, providing cohesion to the swarm, and the controller sets the desired velocity to the cloud. The signal sent by the controller is received by a random set of agents. We show that if all agents receive the signal then the cloud will move with the desired velocity. If only part of the agents receive the signal then the cloud will move in the desired direction but with a speed that is proportional to the ratio of the number of agents receiving the signal (the leaders) to the total number of agents in the swarm. Thus, this ratio can be viewed as representing the inertia or the reluctance of the cloud to move.

1.1 Statement of Problem

We consider a system composed of n homogeneous agents, modeled by single integrators, evolving in $\mathbb{R}^2$. Moreover, the agents are assumed to be memoryless and to have unlimited visibility, i.e. each agent senses all other agents at all times.

© Springer International Publishing Switzerland 2016
M. Dorigo et al. (Eds.): ANTS 2016, LNCS 9882, pp. 257–264, 2016.
DOI: 10.1007/978-3-319-44427-7_23

Each agent can measure only the *relative position* of other agents in its own local coordinate system. The orientation of all local coordinate systems is aligned to that of a global coordinate system.

We assume that the agents do not to have data transmission capabilities, but all the agents are capable of detecting the exogenous, broadcast control. At any time, a random set of agents detect the broadcast control. These agents will be referred to as ad-hoc *leaders*, while the remaining agents will be the *followers*. The exogenous control, a velocity vector u, is common to all leaders. The agents are unaware of which of their neighbors are leaders. The sets of the leaders and of the followers are denoted by N^l, N^f respectively. The number of leaders and followers in the system is denoted by $n_l = |N^l|$, $n_f = |N^f|$ respectively. The sum $n = n_f + n_l$ is the total number of agents. The agents are labeled $1, ..., n$.

1.2   The Dynamics of the Agents

In our model, the followers apply a local gathering control based on the relative position of all their neighbors and the leaders apply *the same local control* (1) *with the addition of the exogenous input* u. Since the agents have unlimited visibility, all nodes are neighbors of each other. Thus, we have:

– for each $i \in N^f$

$$\dot{p}_i(t) = \sum_{j=1}^{n}(p_j(t) - p_i(t)) \tag{1}$$

where p_i is the position of agent i.
– for $i \in N^l$

$$\dot{p}_i(t) = \sum_{j=1}^{n}(p_j(t) - p_i(t)) + u(t) \tag{2}$$

As shown in the sequel, this is an innovative model for controlling collective behavior, leading to new results.

Since $p_i(t) = [x_i(t) \quad y_i(t)]^T$ and $u = [u_x \quad u_y]^T$ and assuming that $x_i(t)$ and $y_i(t)$ are decoupled, we can consider $x_i(t)$ and $y_i(t)$ separately, as one dimensional dynamics (cf. Sect. 2).

1.3   Preliminaries

Since the dynamics of gathering is determined by a linear system described by the visibility graph of the agents in the swarm, we shall need in the sequel several well known properties of the matrix L - the graph Laplacian.

– L is real, symmetric and positive semi-definite.
– L has a single zero eigenvalue $\lambda_1 = 0$ and remaining eigenvalues $\lambda_i = n$; $i = 2, .., n$.
– The eigenvector associated with $\lambda_1 = 0$ is a vector of ones, denoted by $\mathbf{1}_n$.
– Each eigenvalue has equal geometric and algebraic multiplicity, i.e. there exist n independent eigenvectors that form an orthonormal basis.

– L can be diagonalized as $L = V\Lambda V^T$, where V is the matrix of orthonormal eigenvectors and Λ is a diagonal matrix of eigenvalues. This is known as the *the spectral theorem*.

1.4 Tina at mm survey and Original Contribution

Many ways of controlling the collective behavior of self-organized multi-agent systems by means of one or more **special agents**, referred to as *leaders* or *shills*, have been investigated in recent years. However, none of them follows our paradigm. A detailed literature survey and comparison to our paradigm appears in [10]. Tanner, Rahmani, Mesbahi and others in [8,9,11] etc. consider leaders that are pre-designated, with a fixed state value, and do not abide by the agreement protocol and show conditions on the topology that will ensure the controllability of the group. Demarogonas et al. in [3,4] consider pre-defined leaders that combine the consensus protocol with a goal attraction term. Han et al. [5], followed by Wang, [6] introduce the notions of shill and soft control. Shills are intelligent agents, with on-line state information about regular units, added to the swarm with the purpose of controlling the collective behavior. Recently Azuma et al. [1] have proposed a broadcast control framework for multi-agent coordination, but in their model a signal is sent by the controller, based on the observed performance, to each agent which in turn designs its local control.

1.5 Paper Outline

We derive the collective swarm behavior for a *time-independent system* over an interval $[0, t)$, the extension to piecewise constant systems being immediate. Section 2 presents the one dimensional case which is readily extended to two dimensions in Sect. 3. We conclude in Sect. 4 with a short summary and directions for future research.

Detailed proofs for the Lemmas and Theorems in this paper can be found in [10].

2 One Dimensional Group Dynamics

In this Section we consider agents evolving in a one dimensional space. The position of agent i is denoted by x_i. Each agent moves according to

$$\dot{x}_i(t) = \sum_{j=1}^{n}(x_j(t) - x_i(t)) + b_i(t)u(t) \tag{3}$$

where

– $u(t)$ is the detected exogenous control
– $b_i(t) = 1$ if agent i detects the exogenous control $u(t)$, 0 otherwise

The collective dynamics can be formulated by writing Eq. (3) in vector form as:

$$\dot{x}(t) = -Lx(t) + B(t)u(t) \tag{4}$$

where L is the Laplacian associated with the time independent interaction graph and $B(t)$ is the leaders indicator vector at time t, i.e. $B_i(t) = 1$ if agent i is a leader and 0 otherwise.

If we consider now a piecewise constant system, where $u(t), B(t)$ change at discrete times t_k, then for $t \in [t_k \quad t_{k+1})$ we have

$$\dot{x}(t) = -L \cdot x(t) + B_k u_k; \quad t \in [t_k \quad t_{k+1}) \tag{5}$$

where

- B_k is the leaders indicator vector in the interval $[t_k \quad t_{k+1})$
- u_k is the one dimensional exogenous control in the interval $[t_k \quad t_{k+1})$

In each interval $[t_k \quad t_{k+1})$, B_k, u_k are constant and thus the system evolves as a time-independent dynamic linear system. In the sequel we treat each such interval separately, and thus it is convenient to suppress the subscript k. Moreover, it is convenient to refer to the relative time since the beginning of the interval ($t = 0$) and to the state of the system at this time and denote them by t and $x(0)$ respectively.

Thus, we can write in each interval

$$\dot{x}(t) = -L \cdot x(t) + Bu \tag{6}$$

where L is the Laplacian associated with the complete pairwise interactions graph. Equation (6) has the well known solution (ref. [7])

$$x(t) = e^{-Lt}x(0) + \int_0^t e^{-L(t-\tau)} Bu d\tau \tag{7}$$

Equation (7) can be rewritten as

$$x(t) = x^{(h)}(t) + x^{(u)}(t) \tag{8}$$

where

- $x^{(h)}(t) = e^{-Lt}x(0)$ represents the zero input solution
- $x^{(u)}(t) = \int_0^t e^{-L(t-\tau)} Bu d\tau$ represents the contribution of the exogenous input to the group dynamics

2.1   Zero Input Group Dynamics

The zero input group dynamics is given by

$$\dot{x}^{(h)}(t) = -L \cdot x^{(h)}(t) \tag{9}$$

Lemma 1. *When there is no exogenous input, the states of the agents converge asymptotically to the average of the initial states.*

Proof. For proof see Lemma 1 in [10]

$$x_\infty^{(h)} = \lim_{t\to\infty} x^{(h)}(t) = \alpha 1_n \tag{10}$$

where $\alpha = \frac{1}{n}\sum_{i=1}^{n} x_i(0)$ is the average of the initial states

2.2   Input Induced Group Dynamics

The input-related part of the group dynamics, $x^{(u)}(t)$, given by Eq. (11)

$$x^{(u)}(t) = \int_0^t e^{-L(t-\tau)} Bu d\tau \tag{11}$$

Using again the properties of L we can write, after some algebra

$$x^{(u)}(t) = x^{(a)}(t) + x^{(b)}(t) \tag{12}$$

where

- $x^{(a)}(t)$ is the zero eigenvalue dependent term, representing the movement in the agreement space
- $x^{(b)}(t)$ is the remainder, representing the deviation from the agreement space

Movement Along the Agreement Subspace. We have

$$x^{(a)}(t) = \int_0^t e^{-\lambda_1\nu} V_1 V_1^T Bu d\nu = V_1 V_1^T But = \frac{n_l}{n} ut 1_n \tag{13}$$

where n_l is the number of leaders and we have used $V_1 = \frac{1}{\sqrt{n}}1$ and $1^T B = n_l$. Therefore:

Lemma 2. *Consider a group of n agents, forming a connected interactions graph, and moving according to (3). If there are n_l agents that detect an exogenous velocity control u, the entire group will move collectively with a velocity $\frac{n_l}{n}u$.*

Deviations from the Agreement Subspace. Consider now the remainder $x^{(b)}(t)$ of the input-related part, representing the agents' state deviation from the agreement subspace.

The geometric meaning of deviations is elaborated in Sect. 3.2.
We have

$$x^{(b)}(t) = \left[\sum_{i=2}^{n} \int_0^t \left(e^{-\lambda_i \cdot \nu}\right) V_i V_i^T d\nu\right] Bu$$

$$= \frac{1}{n}\left[\sum_{i=2}^{n}(1 - e^{-nt})V_i V_i^T\right] Bu$$

Thus, $x^{(b)}(t)$ converges asymptotically to a time independent vector, the vector of asymptotic deviations from the agreement subspace, denoted by ϱ, given by:

$$\varrho = \frac{1}{n} \left[\sum_{i=2}^{n} V_i V_i^T \right] Bu \tag{14}$$

Theorem 1. *The asymptotic deviations of all agents sum to zero*

$$\sum_{i=1}^{n} \varrho_i = 0 \tag{15}$$

where ϱ_i is the deviation of agent i.

Proof. See proof of Theorem 2 in [10]

Theorem 2. *1. In a network of n agents with unlimited visibility, all followers have the same asymptotic deviation and all leaders have the same asymptotic deviation, with opposite sign to the followers' deviation.*
2. If all agents are leaders, i.e. $n_l = n$, then all asymptotic deviations are zero, i.e. $\varrho_i = 0$, $\forall i$

Proof. See proof of Theorem 3 in [10], recalling that a network of n agents with unlimited visibility has a fully connected visibility graph.

3   Two Dimensional Group Dynamics

Since the two dimensions were assumed to be decoupled, applying the results derived in Sect. 2, we have

$$p(t) = p^{(h)}(t) + p^{(a)}(t) + p^{(b)}(t) = \begin{bmatrix} x^{(h)}(t) + x^{(a)}(t) + x^{(b)}(t) \\ y^{(h)}(t) + y^{(a)}(t) + y^{(b)}(t) \end{bmatrix} \tag{16}$$

3.1   Asymptotic Position of Agent i

The asymptotic positions of agent i, in the two-dimensional space, when an external control $\mathbf{u} = (u_x \quad u_y)^T$ is detected by n_l agents, is

$$p_i(t \to \infty) = \begin{bmatrix} \alpha_x + \beta u_x t + \gamma_i u_x \\ \alpha_y + \beta u_y t + \gamma_i u_y \end{bmatrix} \tag{17}$$

where

- $\alpha = (\alpha_x \ \alpha_y)^T$ is the agreement, or gathering, point when there is no external input, such that

$$\alpha_x = \frac{1}{n} \sum_{i=1}^{n} x_i(0)$$

$$\alpha_y = \frac{1}{n} \sum_{i=1}^{n} y_i(0)$$

- $\beta(u_x\ u_y)^T$ is the collective velocity, $\beta = \frac{n_l}{n}$.
- $\gamma_i(u_x\ u_y)^T$ are the components of the asymptotic deviation of agent i

3.2 Interpretation of the Asymptotic Deviations in the Euclidean Space

The vector of asymptotic deviations, s.t. $\varrho_i = \gamma_i \mathbf{u}$ is the deviation of agent i, in the (x, y) space, from the (moving) consensus $\alpha + \frac{n_l}{n} \mathbf{u}t$, where $\alpha = (\alpha_x, \alpha_y)$. The agents align along a line in the direction of $\mathbf{u}$. The line is anchored at the zero-input gathering, or consensus, point α. Since γ is time independent, the asymptotic dispersion of agents along this line is time independent, as illustrated in Fig. 1, where γ_l represents $(\gamma_i; i \in N^l)$; γ_f represents $(\gamma_i; i \in N^f)$ and $n_f\gamma_f + n_l\gamma_l = 0$. The swarm moves with velocity $\beta\mathbf{u}$, where $\beta = \frac{n_l}{n}$.

4 Summary and Directions for Future Research

This paper is the first in a series of papers, to be published, on the subject of stochastic broadcast control of multi-agent swarms. In this paper we introduced a model for swarms of identical simple agents with unlimited visibility and broadcast velocity control that is received by a random set of agents in the swarm and have shown the emergent behavior. In future research, we intend to extend the dynamic model to double integrators, i.e. acceleration controlled agents. Also, we are currently considering the same paradigm of stochastic broadcast control in conjunction with limited visibility, non-linear gathering processes, as for example [2].

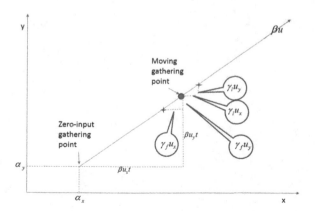

Fig. 1. Asymptotic dispersion of agents along the direction of u

References

1. Azuma, S., Yoshimura, R., Sugie, T.: Broadcast control of multi-agent systems. Automatica **49**, 2307–2316 (2013)
2. Bellaiche, L.I., Bruckstein, A.: Continuous time gathering of agents with limited visibility and bearing-only sensing. arXiv (2015)
3. Dimarogonas, D.V., Gustavi, T., Egerstedt, M., Hui, X.: On the number of leaders needed to ensure connectivity. In: Proceedings of the 47th IEEE Conference on Decision and Control (2008)
4. Gustavi, T., Dimarogonas, D.V., Egerstedt, M., Hui, X.: On the number of leaders needed to ensure connectivity in arbitrary dimensions. In: 17th Mediteranean Conference on Control and Automation (2009)
5. Han, J., Li, M., Guo, L.: Soft control on collective behavior of a group of autonomous agents by a shill agent. J. Syst. Sci. Compexity **19**, 54–62 (2006)
6. Han, J., Wang, L.: Nondestructive intervention to multiagent systems through an inteligent agent. PLoS ONE **8**(5), e61542 (2013)
7. Kailath, T.: Linear Systems. Prentice Hall, Upper Saddle River (1980)
8. Rahmani, A., Mesbahi, M.: On the controlled agreement problem. In: Proceedings of the American control Conference (2006)
9. Rahmani, A., Mesbahi, M.: Pulling the strings on agreement: anchoring, controllability, and graph automorphisms. In: Proceedings of the 2007 American Control Conference (2007)
10. Segall, I., Bruckstein, A.: On stochastic broadcast control of multi-agent swarms. arXiv (2016)
11. Tanneri, H.G.: On the controllability of nearest neighbor interconnections. In: 43rd Conference on Decision and Control (2004)

Route Assignment for Autonomous Vehicles

Nick Moran[✉] and Jordan Pollack

Brandeis University, Waltham, MA, USA
{nemtiax,pollack}@brandeis.edu

Abstract. We demonstrate a self-organizing, multi-agent system to generate approximate solutions to the route assignment problem for a large number of vehicles across many origins and destinations. Our algorithm produces a set of mixed strategies over the set of paths through the network, which are suitable for use by autonomous vehicles in the absence of centralized control or coordination. Our approach combines ideas from co-evolutionary dynamics in which many species coordinate and compete for efficient navigation, and ideas from swarm intelligence in which many simple agents self-organize into successful behavior using limited inter-agent communication. Experiments demonstrate a marked improvement of both individual and total travel times as compared to greedy uncoordinated strategies, and we analyze the differences in outcomes for various routes as the simulation progresses.

Keywords: Swarm intelligence · Vehicle routing · Autonomous vehicles · Multi-agent systems · Co-evolution · Coordination games

1 Introduction

As autonomous vehicles become a significant portion of road traffic, the routing decisions made by those vehicles will have a strong impact on the congestion and efficiency of the road network. At present, it is acceptable for any autonomous or autonomously-routed vehicle to simply greedily select the most efficient route from its origin to its destination. However, once these vehicles represent the majority (or even a large minority) of traffic, a problem with this greedy approach arises: if all vehicles take the apparent shortest route, that route will quickly become overloaded and travel will slow to a crawl. Such a situation could be avoided by more intelligent coordination between the vehicles - if they were to spread themselves out across a variety of routes, congestion could be avoided and travel times improved. This problem falls into the class of coordination games, in which players must simultaneously select a strategy, and the utility of a strategy decreases as more players select it. The solution to such problems is for each player to adopt an equilibrium mixed strategy over the set of possible choices, such that no one player can improve their expected utility by unilaterally deviating from that mixed strategy.

The problem of vehicle route selection is further complicated by the fact that travel time depends not only on the route selection of other vehicles traveling from the same origin to the same destination, but is also affected by the

© Springer International Publishing Switzerland 2016
M. Dorigo et al. (Eds.): ANTS 2016, LNCS 9882, pp. 265–272, 2016.
DOI: 10.1007/978-3-319-44427-7_24

choices made by vehicles traveling between other origin/destination pairs, even those which share neither the origin nor destination. Additionally, the domain of autonomous vehicles gives particular importance to the requirement that strategies be in equilibrium. If a particular traveler believed that a better route choice was available, he or she would simply direct the vehicle to use that route instead. This prevents arrangements in which a small subset of vehicles are assigned poor routes with the goal of alleviating congestion for the majority of vehicles. This concept of equilibrium is based on early work by Wardrop in which he defines "user equilibrium" on a travel network as a state in which every individual agent is acting in the way which minimizes its own travel time [16].

In this paper, we present a multi-agent simulation from which a set of equilibrium mixed strategies for route selection may be gleaned. Our algorithm begins from the greedy assignment of vehicles to the shortest route, and uses a combination of exploration of alternative routes, and reinforcement of successful, faster routes, to arrive at a set of routing strategies which are more efficient, and from which no individual agent can profitably deviate.

The study of route selection for vehicles and its effect on traffic congestion is not new. It has been studied since at least the 1950s to assist in the planning of extensions to the road network and the prediction of their effects on traffic flow. The problem has traditionally been modeled as optimization under constraints, in which a variety of simplifying assumptions are made about traffic dynamics to reduce the problem to an instance of convex non-linear programming which can be approximated through gradient descent methods such as the Frank-Wolfe Algorithm [6]. Further work has found an assortment of improvements [7] and alternative algorithms [4,10] within this paradigm.

More recently, there have been a variety of attempts to apply both evolutionary algorithms and swarm intelligence [2] algorithms to various traffic problems, including signal control [11,15], network layout [12], and scheduling [14]. There have also been efforts to adopt ant colony optimization [5] approaches to both the signal control [3] and vehicle routing problems.

2   Algorithm

Our algorithm works by modeling the road network as a graph of edges (also called links) and nodes, a set of vehicles, and a set of origin-destination pairs of nodes in the graph between which vehicles travel. Each vehicle is assigned an origin node and a destination node, and has a path of edges which leads from its origin node to its destination node. The number of vehicles travelling between a particular origin-destination pair remains constant throughout the simulation. For simplicity, the set of all vehicles traveling between a particular origin-destination pair is referred to as a *species*.

The algorithm proceeds by simulating the flow of these vehicles across the network. When a vehicle reaches its destination, it returns to its origin and begins another journey. It also informs another randomly selected vehicle of the same species of the route it took. The second vehicle will then adopt that strategy for its next trip, with a small chance of alteration through the addition of a detour. In this way, successful strategies spread throughout the population, and new strategies are explored through the occasional addition of detours.

The time it takes for a particular vehicle to pass through an edge is determined by a congestion equation, which calculates the delay due to the number of vehicles on the route. Each edge has a length which defines the base travel time t, and a capacity c, which defines the number of vehicles an edge can carry before congestion effects take over. The number of vehicles currently travelling on a link is denoted by v. In this work, we use a slight modification of the standard Bureau of Public Roads congestion equation [1]. The travel time on a link, S, is determined by the equation:

$$S = t * (1 + 0.15 * (v/c)^4)$$

A known difficulty with this equation is that the exponential form predicts unrealistic travel times in the case of severe congestion [13]. To avoid this, we model congestion with queuing once the traffic load passes a certain threshold (in our experiments, 2.5 times the capacity of the link). If a vehicle attempts to enter a link which is at the specified threshold, it instead enters the back of the queue for that link. Whenever a vehicle exits a link, if its queue is not empty, the vehicle at the front of the queue is removed and enters the link.

2.1 Spread of Strategies

When a vehicle reaches its designated destination, it has the potential to either spread its current path to another vehicle of its species (that is, a vehicle with the same origin and destination), or to replace its own path with one it has received from another vehicle. Upon reaching its destination, a vehicle returns to its starting node, and checks whether it has received a replacement path. If so, it adopts that path, and follows it through the network. If that vehicle has not received a replacement path, then it instead communicates its current path to another vehicle of the same species.

The exact procedure for communicating the path of a successful vehicle is as follows. Let v be the vehicle that has just successfully completed its route. Randomly select another vehicle w of the same species as v. Mark w as having received a replacement path, and set its replacement path to the path of v. With a small random chance (in our experiments, a chance of 5 % was used), modify the w's new replacement path with a detour, as explained in the next section. If w has previously received a replacement route, that route is overwritten with the new route from v. The vehicle w will continue on its current route, and will not adopt the new replacement route until it reaches its destination and begins a new journey. Note that w is selected at random, without consideration for the efficiency of its current path - the frequency of a path is modulated by its rate of reproduction, not by its rate of removal.

The result of this system of spreading successful strategies is that the average rate at which a particular path increases its share of the population is dependent on the speed at which vehicles following that path complete their route as compared to the average speed across all vehicles of that species. A path which allows vehicles to complete their journeys faster than this average speed will tend to increase its share of the population. As its share of the population increases, congestion effects will slow it, until eventually vehicles traveling along it are no longer faster than the average, and its share of the population levels off. Eventually, all paths used by a particular species will take roughly the same amount of time. In this case, each will spread at the same rate, and population will be stable (the random nature of path replacement and detours will of course allow some amount of variation to remain). Thus, the population will have found a set of equilibrium strategies for navigating the network - no vehicle could improve its time by switching, because the feasible paths all take approximately equal time.

2.2   Detours

It is not sufficient to only increase the frequency of efficient paths within the population. We also must explore new routes that are not currently in use. It may be that one of those is more efficient than any route being currently taken. To accomplish this exploration, we apply a detour (with a small random chance) to paths that are passed from one vehicle to another.

A detour is formed by randomly selecting two nodes from the current path to serve as the start and end of the detour, D_s and D_e such that D_s occurs before D_e in the path. Next, a random node is selected from the set of all nodes in the graph to serve as the midpoint of the detour, D_m. We then replace the section of the original path from D_s to D_e with the concatenation of the shortest (in distance, not apparent travel time) route from D_s to D_m followed by the shortest route from D_m to D_e. If this would result in any loops in the new route, those loops are removed.

Despite the name, the detour operator does not create only more circuitous routes. Because the paths between the start, midpoint and end of the detour are the shortest paths available, a detour operator can also make a path more direct. If D_m lies on the shortest path from D_s to D_e (or even a shorter path than is currently being taken), then the effect of this detour will actually be to simplify the route.

2.3   Initialization and Termination

It is necessary to select a starting set of routes for the vehicles in the simulation. In our experiments, we have each vehicle begin by taking the shortest path from its origin to its destination. Once this is done, simulation begins with a winding-up period in which no mutation and reproduction occurs - vehicles simply travel along their paths, and return to the start once complete. This allows any initial congestion due to the simultaneous start of many vehicles to dissipate before evolution begins. Once travel times along routes have roughly stabilized (or a pre-determined number of iterations have been performed), evolution can begin as described above.

Once sufficient evolution has occurred (as determined by a lack of further improvement across the simulation), a short period of simulation without further evolution is useful to allow the traffic patterns to stabilize before observing the final results. From these results, the routes taken for each origin-destination pair can be read off to create a mixed strategy for travel between that pair. Each route is assigned a probability equal to its relative frequency in the population.

3   Experiments

This algorithm was tested on a randomly-generated network consisting of 20 nodes and 98 edges, which was embedded in 2D space. The layout of the experiment network can be seen in Fig. 1. The base free-flow travel times for links were determined by the distance between the start and end of that link. The capacity of a link is proportional to its length. The origin-destination pairs used were all pairs of non-adjacent nodes on the convex hull of the network, giving 40 different origin-destination pairs. Adjacent nodes were omitted because they tend to lack feasible alternative routes, and therefore are not subject to meaningful evolution. Each origin-destination pair was loaded with a number of vehicles equal to the total capacity of the shortest path between those nodes. This would allow relatively uncongested travel for a single pair, but creates significant congestion when applied across all pairs. In total, over 1,100 vehicles were simulated.

Each experiment ran for five million iterations (that is, five million simulated edge traversals), with an additional five hundred thousand iterations each of initialization and termination periods to ensure stable starting and ending conditions. Data points about the current travel times in the network were collected every ten thousand iterations. Travel times were calculated based on the length of each vehicle's last completed trip. We conducted ten experiments in which we measured the total average travel time experienced across the network, and the average travel times experienced for each individual origin-destination pair. Additionally, we examined the average time of each individual path between a single origin-destination pair to determine whether travel times were approximately equal, which would be the expected outcome if the simulation had reached equilibrium.

4   Results

Over the course of the simulation, the average total travel time fell from roughly 310,000 simulation ticks to roughly 158,000 ticks, a reduction of nearly half, as seen in Fig. 1. A steep initial improvement occurs as the most severely congested routes clear out, followed by a period of slowing, somewhat unsteady improvement as vehicles settle into efficient equilibria.

Figure 2 shows two representative graphs which demonstrate the different types of behavior an origin-destination pair can display. On the left we have the data for vehicles traveling from Node 12, in the upper left corner of the network, to Node 4, near the lower left. Here we see the same steep initial improvement

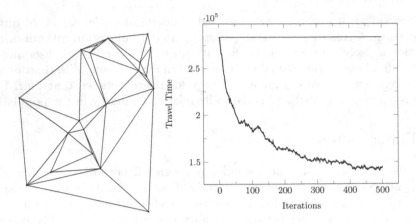

Fig. 1. The experiment network, and total travel time across all routes as the simulation progresses.

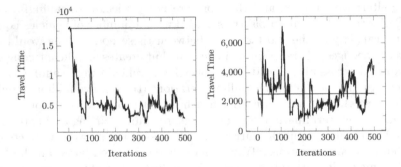

Fig. 2. Average travel times for two different origin-destination pairs. The horizontal lines represent the baseline travel time.

as in the overall average, followed by slower improvement marked by significant spikes in travel time. This occurs when the vehicles on other origin-destination pairs make an adjustment to their route choices such that more vehicles occupy the links being used to travel from 12 to 4. Once the congestion becomes severe, alternative routes are found to once again lower travel times.

On the right side of Fig. 2, we have the data for vehicles traveling from Node 4 to Node 3, both in the lower left corner of the network, separated by only two links. Here, instead of a sharp initial improvement, we see a brief, small improvement followed by a severe spike. Fluctuations occur throughout the rest of the simulation, but the travel time ultimately ends up worse than how it started. This is because the links along the initial path between these nodes were not used by the initial paths for other species. As evolution progressed, those other species discovered these little-used links, and congestion increased. We thus see that an overall improvement in travel time does not indicate uniform improvement across all origin-destination pairs.

$3 \Rightarrow 14 \Rightarrow 8 \Rightarrow 17 \Rightarrow 1 \Rightarrow 11 \Rightarrow 15$	39.4%	6025 ticks
$3 \Rightarrow 14 \Rightarrow 8 \Rightarrow 5 \Rightarrow 1 \Rightarrow 10 \Rightarrow 15$	36.4%	6266 ticks
$3 \Rightarrow 13 \Rightarrow 4 \Rightarrow 11 \Rightarrow 15$	18.2%	6205 ticks
$3 \Rightarrow 0 \Rightarrow 8 \Rightarrow 1 \Rightarrow 10 \Rightarrow 6 \Rightarrow 12 \Rightarrow 15$	6.1%	7320 ticks

Fig. 3. Routes from Node 3 to Node 15 at the end of an experiment run, showing the relative frequency of each route and the time taken in simulation ticks.

As an example of the routes generated for a particular origin-destination pair, consider the set of routes from Node 3 to Node 15 seen in Fig. 3. The first two routes are similar, passing through several common nodes. The third route uses an almost entirely different set of nodes, and passes around the outer edge of the graph, but still requires roughly the same amount of travel time. Only the fourth strategy, which has a very low share of the population, takes significantly longer due to its use of congested links (the direct $8 \Rightarrow 1$ link in particular, which is avoided by the other routes) and a circuitous detour to Node 12 near the end. This strategy likely represents a relatively recent mutation which has not yet been competed out of the population.

The fact that the travel times are roughly equal (aside from the small outlier) is to be expected - this represents an equilibrium state in which all three strategies will reproduce at approximately the same rate. The equality is only approximate, however, because of the discrete nature of the simulation and ongoing changes in the co-evolutionary fitness landscape up until the end of the simulation.

5   Future Work and Conclusion

Our algorithm offers several directions for potentially fruitful future work. In this paper we use a standard model for congestion, the BPR equation. This model is ultimately a simplification of real traffic behavior, made in order to allow efficient computation and provide mathematically convenient properties (in particular, a nicely concave shape for gradient descent approaches as well as full independence of delays along different links). Our algorithm does not rely on these properties of congestion modeling, and any desired model could be used instead, including those which account for interdependence between the congestion on links (such as models which account for the delay at intersections caused by cross-traffic [8], or cascading congestion across multiple links [9]). Further work is needed, however, to determine the performance of our algorithm under these more detailed congestion models.

Our experiments in this paper demonstrate the effectiveness on a moderately-sized, randomly-generated network, but more work is needed to study the behavior of this approach on a real-life road network. It may be necessary to alter the method of generating detours when working on a very large-scale network - perhaps by favoring local detours over distant ones.

We have demonstrated an algorithm by which a large number of autonomous agents can arrive at a set of equilibrium strategies for navigating a network. Our algorithm significantly outperforms a baseline greedy approach in which each agent independently selects its apparent fastest route. Further work is needed to adapt this approach to real-world road networks and vehicle behavior.

References

1. Traffic Assignment Manual. US Bureau of Public Roads (1964)
2. Beni, G., Wang, J.: Swarm intelligence in cellular robotic systems. In: Dario, P., Sandini, G., Aebischer, P. (eds.) Robots and Biological Systems: Towards a New Bionics? NATO ASI Series, vol. 102, pp. 703–712. Springer, Heidelberg (1993)
3. D'Acierno, L., Gallo, M., Montella, B.: An ant colony optimisation algorithm for solving the asymmetric traffic assignment problem. Eur. J. Oper. Res. **217**(2), 459–469 (2012)
4. Dafermos, S., Sparrow, F.: The traffic assignment problem for a general network. J. Res. Natl. Bur. Stan. B **73**, 91–118 (1969)
5. Dorigo, M.: Optimization, Learning and Natural Algorithms (in Italian). Ph.D. thesis, Dipartimento di Elettronica, Politecnico di Milano, Milan, Italy (1992)
6. Frank, M., Wolfe, P.: An algorithm for quadratic programming. Nav. Res. Logist. Q. **3**, 95–110 (1956)
7. Fukushima, M.: A modified frank-wolfe algorithm for solving the traffic assignment problem. Transp. Res. Part B: Methodol. **18**, 169–177 (1984)
8. Jeihani, M., Lawe, S., Connolly, J.: Improving traffic assignment model using intersection delay function. In: 47th Annual Transportation Research Forum, March 2006
9. Ji, Y., Geroliminis, N.: Modelling congestion propagation in urban transportation networks. In: Swiss Transport Research Conference (2012)
10. Larsson, T., Patriksson, M.: Simplicial decomposition with disaggregated representation for the traffic assignment problem. Transp. Sci. **26**, 4–17 (1994)
11. Medina, J.S., Moreno, M.G., Royo, E.R.: Evolutionary computation applied to urban traffic optimization. In: Advances in Evolutionary Algorithms (2008)
12. Schweitzer, F., Ebeling, W., Rosé, H., Weiss, O.: Optimization of road networks using evolutionary strategies. Evol. Comput. **5**(4), 419–438 (1997)
13. Spiess, H.: Conical volume-delay functions. Transp. Sci. **24**, 153–158 (1990)
14. Teodorovic, D., Lucic, P.: Schedule synchronization in public transit by fuzzy ant system. Transp. Plan. Technol. **28**, 47–76 (2005)
15. Turky, A.M., Ahmad, M.S., Yusoff, M.Z.M., Sabar, N.R.: Genetic algorithm application for traffic light control. In: Yang, J., Ginige, A., Mayr, H.C., Kutsche, R.-D. (eds.) Information Systems: Modeling, Development, and Integration. LNBIP, vol. 20, pp. 115–120. Springer, Heidelberg (2009)
16. Wardrop, J.G.: Some theoretical aspects of road traffic research. Proc. ICE **1**(3), 325–362 (1952)

Stealing Items More Efficiently with Ants: A Swarm Intelligence Approach to the Travelling Thief Problem

Markus Wagner[✉]

Optimisation and Logistics, The University of Adelaide, Adelaide, Australia
markus.wagner@adelaide.edu.au

Abstract. The travelling thief problem (TTP) is an academic combinatorial optimisation problem in which its two components, namely the travelling salesperson problem (TSP) and the knapsack problem, interact. The goal is to provide to a thief a tour across all given cities and a packing plan that defines which items should be taken in which city. The combining elements are the knapsack's renting rate that is to be paid for the travel time, and the thief's slowdown with increasing knapsack use. Previously, successful algorithms focussed almost exclusively on constructing packing plans for near-optimal TSP tours. Even though additional hill-climbers are used at times, this strong initial bias prevents them from finding better solutions that require longer tours that can give rise to more profitable packing plans. Our swarm intelligence approach shifts the focus away from good TSP tours to good TTP tours. In our study we observe that this is effective and computationally efficient, as we outperform state-of-the-art approaches on instances with up to 250 cities and 2000 items, sometimes by more than 10 %.

Keywords: MAX-MIN ant system · Travelling thief problem

1 Introduction

The travelling thief problem (TTP, [2]) is fast gaining attention for being a challenging combinatorial optimisation problem. This NP-hard optimisation problem combines two well-known combinatorial optimisation problems, namely the travelling salesperson problem (TSP) and the knapsack problem. The two components have been merged in such a way that the optimal solution for each of them does not necessarily correspond to an optimal TTP solution. The motivation for the TTP is to have a problem where the interactions of interdependent problem components can be investigated systematically.

So far, constructive heuristics, simple and complex hill-climbers, and also more sophisticated co-evolutionary approaches have been applied to the TTP. The drawbacks of these approaches are that they either focus almost exclusively on good TSP tours, or that they cannot navigate the search space neither

© Springer International Publishing Switzerland 2016
M. Dorigo et al. (Eds.): ANTS 2016, LNCS 9882, pp. 273–281, 2016.
DOI: 10.1007/978-3-319-44427-7_25

effectively nor efficiently. So far, minimally problem-specific local searches that alternate between solving the TSP and KP components appear to perform best.

In this article, we propose the use of swarm intelligence based on ant colony optimisation in order to solve the TTP's tour part. The packing part is then computed heuristically for each tour, and after each iteration the best solution is improved further using additional hill-climbers. Even though the local search in the tour generation still focusses on the TSP part, the individuals in the swarm are assessed based on the solution's TTP objective score. The use of swarm intelligence allows us to explore different tours in a collaborative fashion, and we are no longer limited by a single "current" tour. As we shall see later, this added flexibility and shift from good TSP tours to good TTP tours is very beneficial.

2   Traveling Thief Problem

2.1   Problem Description

We use the definition of the TTP by Polyakovskiy et al. [10]. Given is a set of cities $N = \{1, \ldots, n\}$ and a set of items $M = \{1, \ldots, m\}$ distributed among the cities. For any pair of cities $i, j \in N$, we know the distance d_{ij} between them. Every city i, except the first one, contains a set of items $M_i = \{1, \ldots, m_i\}$, $M = \bigcup_{i \in N} M_i$. Each item k positioned in the city i is characterised by its profit p_{ik} and weight w_{ik}, thus the item $I_{ik} \sim (p_{ik}, w_{ik})$. The thief must visit all cities exactly once starting from the first city and returning back to it in the end. Any item may be selected in any city as long as the total weight of collected items does not exceed the specified capacity W. A renting rate R is to be paid per each time unit taken to complete the tour. v_{max} and v_{min} denote the maximal and minimum speeds that the thief can move. The goal is to find a tour, along with a packing plan, that results in the maximal profit.

The objective function uses a binary variable $y_{ik} \in \{0, 1\}$ that is equal to one when the item k is selected in the city i, and zero otherwise. Also, let W_i denote the total weight of collected items when the thief leaves the city i. Then, the objective function for a tour $\Pi = (x_1, \ldots, x_n)$, $x_i \in N$ and a packing plan $P = (y_{21}, \ldots, y_{nm_i})$ has the following form:

$$Z(\Pi, P) = \sum_{i=1}^{n} \sum_{k=1}^{m_i} p_{ik} y_{ik} - R \left(\frac{d_{x_n x_1}}{v_{max} - \nu W_{x_n}} + \sum_{i=1}^{n-1} \frac{d_{x_i x_{i+1}}}{v_{max} - \nu W_{x_i}} \right)$$

where $\nu = \frac{v_{max} - v_{min}}{W}$ is a constant value defined by input parameters. The minuend is the sum of all packed items' profits and the subtrahend is the amount that the thief pays for the knapsack's rent equal to the total traveling time along Π multiplied by R.

2.2   Current State-of-the-Art

Polyakovskiy *et al.* [10] proposed the first set of heuristics for solving the TTP. Their approach was to solve the problem using two steps. The first step involved generating a good TSP tour by using the classical Chained Lin-Kernighan heuristic [1]. The second step involved keeping the tour fixed and applying a packing heuristic for improving the solution.

Bonyadi et al. [3] and Mei et al. [8] investigated experimentally and theoretically the interdependency between the TSP and knapsack components of the TTP. They proposed heuristic approaches including coevolutionary ones and a memetic algorithm. The latter called MATLS considered the interdependencies in more depth and outperformed cooperative coevolution.

Faulkner et al. [6] investigated multiple operators and did a comprehensive comparison with existing approaches. They proposed a number of operators, such as BITFLIP and PACKITERATIVE, for optimising the packing plan given a particular tour. They also proposed INSERTION for iteratively optimising the tour given a particular packing. They combined these operators in a number of simple and complex heuristics that outperformed existing approaches.

Recently, a relaxed version of the TTP was presented by [4] as reaction to the criticism that the TTP is not realistic. In the new version of the problem multiple thieves are allowed to travel across different cities (not necessarily across all) with the aim of maximising the group's collective profit.

Note that even when the tour is kept fixed, packing is NP-hard [11].

3   Using Ants to Steal Items

While swarm intelligence does not easily offer provable performance guarantees, it does give us a means of working on the tour part of the TTP, on top of which we can run other heuristics. Effectively, our approach is a bi-level one, where the ants are assessed based on the TTP solution for which they created the tour.

The packing heuristic of our choice is the fast and effective PACKITERATIVE [6]. It considers the items' profits and weight, and also their distances to the final city based on the provided tour. Its characteristic feature is that it performs a binary search on an internal parameter in order to fine-tune the packing.

Our implementation is built upon Adrian Wilke's ACOTSPjava 1.0.1,[1] which is based on Thomas Stützle's ACOTSP 1.0.3. The overall logic of the used swarm intelligence package remains unchanged, and our modifications are minimal.

In Algorithm 1 we show the simplified overview of our swarm intelligence approach. The TTP-specific injections are mainly in two places:

1. Whenever a tour is generated, a packing plan for it is generated using PACK-ITERATIVE. The tour's objective score, which is normally the total distance travelled, is replaced by the TTP solution's objective score.
2. At the end of each iteration, we run hill-climbers on the best solutions in order to achieve further improvements. We call this "boosting".

---

[1] ACOTSPjava: http://adibaba.github.io/ACOTSPJava/, last accessed 28 Feb 2016.

Algorithm 1. ACOTSP for the Travelling Thief Problem (injections in italics)

1:	**while (termination condition not met)**
2:	Construct tours using ants.
3:	*Construct for each tour a packing plan using* PACKITERATIVE, *resulting in a TTP objective score. If the tour has been assessed before, we skip the packing step and retrieve the score from a cache.*
4:	Perform local search on tours (if activated).
5:	Update ACO statistics.
6:	*Boost solutions using* (1+1)-EA, INSERTION, BITFLIP *(if activated).*
7:	Pheromone trail update.

Note that we make a rather strong assumption in the first injection: as the ants' tours are assessed using PACKITERATIVE, we assume that the packing heuristic is optimal. While this is not the case, we have observed in [6] that PACKITERATIVE quickly produces very good approximations of the optimal packing across a wide range of instances.

We improve the runtime of the first modification by caching <tour, objective score> tuples, as PACKITERATIVE is deterministic. Also, we rotate the tours so that they always start and end in the first city.

4   Experimental Study

4.1   Experimental Setup

For our investigations, we use the set of TTP instances defined by [10].[2] In these instances, the two components of the problem have been balanced in such a way that the near-optimal solution of one sub-problem does not dominate over the optimal solution of another sub-problem.

The characteristics of the original 9,720 instances vary widely. For our experiments, we use 108 instances with the following characteristics:

- nine different numbers of cities (spread out roughly logarithmically): 51, 76, 100, 159, 225, 280, 574, 724, 1000;
- two different numbers of items per city: 3 and 10;
- all three different types of knapsacks: uncorrelated, uncorrelated with similar weights, bounded strongly correlated;
- two different sizes of knapsacks (capacities): 3 and 7 times the size of the smallest knapsack.

We run all algorithms for a maximum of 10 min per instance. Due to their randomised nature, we perform 30 independent repetitions of the algorithms on each instance. All computations are performed on machines with Intel Xeon E5430 CPUs (2.66 GHz) and Java 1.8. Note that our code and results are available online: http://cs.adelaide.edu.au/~optlog/research/ttp.php.

---

[2] As available at http://cs.adelaide.edu.au/~optlog/research/ttp.php.

We assess the quality of the algorithms using the following approach. For each instance, we consider the best solution found to be a lower bound on the achievable objective value. Then, we take the average of the 30 results produced by an algorithm and then compute the ratio between that average and the best objective value found, which gives us the approximation ratio. This ratio allows us to compare the performances across the chosen set of instances, since the objective values vary across several orders of magnitude.

4.2 MMAS Configurations

The ACOTSPjava package allows us to set a large number of different parameters. One of them is the choice of the actual ant colony optimisation approach. To prevent pheromones from dropping to arbitrarily small values, we use the MAX-MIN ant system by Stützle and Hoos [12], which restricts all pheromones to a bounded interval. The MMAS parameters that we employ are the default ones in ACOTSPjava: $\rho = 0.5$, $\alpha = 1$, $\beta = 2$, ants=25, max_tours=100, tries=1, elitist_ants=100, ras_ranks=6.

In preliminary experiments, we noticed that the use of TSP-specific local search (see line 4 of Algorithm 1) was crucial for achieving good TSP tours, which is a commonly made observation (see for example [5,12]). In our study, we employ the following two variants of local search: *ls3* runs 3-opt on a tour generated by ants, and *ls4* randomly picks for each tour either 2-opt, 2-h-opt, or 3-opt. With the latter, we allow for slightly more varied exploitations of tours.

For the boosting that we perform, we use the operators described in [6]. If boosting is performed, then we first run (1+1)-EA on the packing plan for 10,000 iterations as a hill-climber. Then we perform one pass of INSERTION, which means that for each city we attempt once to relocate it to each position in the travel sequence. Lastly, we perform one pass of BITFLIP, where for each item we check once whether changing its packing status increases the objective score. The overall computational complexity of this boosting is quadratic in the number of cities and linear in the number of item.

In summary, we investigate the following four MMAS configurations, depending on the chosen local search and depending on whether or not boosting is activated: MMASls3, MMASls3boost, MMASls4, MMASls4boost.

In our opinion, our MMAS approaches are natural successors of the approaches S5 and C3–C6 from [6]. S5 resamples new routes independently, whereas our approach resamples new routes based on the previous ones. With boosting activated, our MMAS approaches are somewhat similar to the heuristics C3–C6, which employ hill-climbers on top of single tours as well. In contrast to C3–C6, our algorithms search with distributions of tours. With this change in focus we expect performance gains, as longer tours are investigated systematically.

4.3 Comparison with State-of-the-Art

We compare our MMAS-based approaches with recent ones from the literature. In particular, these are S1/S5 and C3/C4/C5/C6 [6] and MATLS [7].

In Fig. 1 we show a summary of the over 1100 average approximation ratios as trend lines. We can make the following observations.

1. The baseline approach S1, where PackIterative is run only once on top of a single ChainedLinKernighan tour, is clearly outperformed by all others.
2. Our MMAS-approaches (blue) are the best performing ones for TTP instances with up to 250 cities and 2000 items. Previously, the more holistic approach MATLS (red) performed best one these.
3. Our boosting of solutions and also the variation in the TSP local search prove helpful for instances with up to 200–250 cities and 800 items. For larger instances, MMASls3 is the best performing swarm intelligence approach.
4. For instances with 250–500 cities, the complex approaches C3–C6 with their local search routines achieve the top ranks. On even larger instances, the simple resampling heuristic S5 (black) dominates, as observed in [6].

Let us briefly look into the impact that the MMAS search has on the tours of the final solutions. In Table 1 we show details of different *best* solutions found.

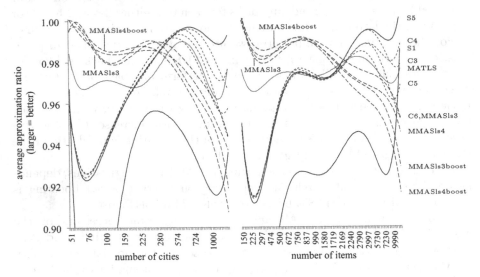

Fig. 1. Summary of results shown as trend lines. The curves are polynomials of degree six. Similar approaches are coloured identically to allow us to focus on the different types of the approaches: S1/S5 are solid black lines, C3–C6 are green short dashes, MATLS is a red solid line, and the MMAS-approaches are blue long dashes. Our MMAS-based approaches are the best performing ones for TTP instances with up to 250 cities and 2000 items, on which previously MATLS and C3–C6 performed best. (Colour figure online)

Table 1. For two instances, we show details of the best solutions (in terms of "objective score") found by different approaches for two instances. For example, MMASls3boost found an outstanding solution for the second instance, however, it is outperformed on average by S5 (0.871 vs 0.931). The shaded cells highlight the best objective scores and best average approximation ratios.

approach	used knapsack capacity	unused knapsack capacity	total profit of items	travel distance	travel time	objective score	average approx. ratio
eil51_n150_uncorr_07							
MMASls4	36538	11671	53368	467.00	652.11	11763	0.997
S1/C6	34622	13587	52145	459.00	659.35	10079	0.856/0.857
dsj1000_n2997_uncorr-similar-weights_03							
MMASls4	758385	62635	590594	19286106	27205708	46480	0.832
MMASls3boost	774523	46497	595519	19290271	26699765	61524	0.871
S1	758408	62612	584276	18705228	26709155	50093	0.622
S5	758364	62656	590515	18750512	26599551	58524	0.931
C6	761602	59418	587164	18750975	26376923	59626	0.876

While most solutions might look quite similar at first glance, they differ in some fundamental aspects, of which we highlight a few in the following.

For the first instance, which is one of the smallest investigated ones, our MMASls4 was the best performing approach on average, and it also found the best solution. For both S1 and C6, their best solution is >10 % worse. Even the local search routines in C6 are not sufficient to escape the local optima.

For the second instance, which is one of the largest investigated ones, the best solutions by S1, S5, and C6 are again the ones with the shortest travelled distances. S1's best solution actually has the shortest tour, but the resulting objective score is the second-worst. S1's resampling variant S5 investigates many tours, which can be longer and which can offer different ways of constructing the packing plans. MMASls4 now performs poorly as it lacks hillclimbers to optimise the packing plans. MMASls3boost performs significantly better on average, and even found an oustanding solution once. Interestingly, this solution has the longest travel distance *and* the highest knapsack use among all five shown solutions.

In summary, we can see that exploring longer tours can be very beneficial, if done efficiently. This is exactly what we expect to see in the TTP, as it is the combination of the travelling salesperson problems and the knapsack problem.

5   Concluding Remarks

While our MMAS approach is most definitely not "one approach to rule them all", it outperforms existing approaches on instances with up to 250 cities and

2000 items, sometimes by over 10 %. It achieves this because it focusses less than existing approaches on good TSP tours, but more on good TTP tours.

We investigated the boosting of solutions in the form of TTP-specific local search. This was effective in general, however, it is too time-consuming on larger instances and thus detrimental to the performance, as it reduces the number of tours the algorithms can consider given the fixed time budget. This brings us back to the general problem. Currently, the TTP's search space seems to be incredibly hard to navigate. We understand that it can be tempting for researchers to focus on large instances using construction heuristics and hill-climbers. However, we suggest to focus on small instances instead, because large performance gains are still possible there as our investigations show. By creating good approximation algorithms that are effective in considering the interaction of the problem components, but that are not necessarily computationally efficient, we should be able to gain additional insights into the actual interaction.

In the future, maybe instance analysis where the influence of the different components is varied may help to understand how the interactions influence algorithm performance. A first step towards this has recently been taken by [9], who systematically analysed the difficulty of TSP instances for MMAS with different parameter settings.

It is interesting to note that no parameter tuning on the MMAS side of our approaches has been performed. We have made all code and all results publicly available: http://cs.adelaide.edu.au/~optlog/research/ttp.php. On this project website, we also have an extended version of this article with additional insights.

References

1. Applegate, D., Cook, W.J., Rohe, A.: Chained Lin-Kernighan for large traveling salesman problems. J. Comput. **15**(1), 82–92 (2003)
2. Bonyadi, M.R., Michalewicz, Z., Barone, L.: The travelling thief problem: the first step in the transition from theoretical problems to realistic problems. In: Congress on Evolutionary Computation, pp. 1037–1044. IEEE (2013)
3. Bonyadi, M.R., Michalewicz, Z., Przybylek, M.R., Wierzbicki, A.: Socially inspired algorithms for the TTP. In: Genetic and Evolutionary Computation Conference, pp. 421–428. ACM (2014)
4. Chand, S., Wagner, M.: Fast heuristics for the multiple traveling thieves problem. In: Genetic and Evolutionary Computation Conference. ACM (2016). Accepted for publication
5. Dorigo, M., Stützle, T.: Ant Colony Optimization. MIT Press, Cambridge (2004)
6. Faulkner, H., Polyakovskiy, S., Schultz, T., Wagner, M.: Approximate approaches to the traveling thief problem. In: Genetic and Evolutionary Computation Conference, pp. 385–392. ACM (2015)
7. Mei, Y., Li, X., Yao, X.: Improving efficiency of heuristics for the large scale traveling thief problem. In: Dick, G., et al. (eds.) SEAL 2014. LNCS, vol. 8886, pp. 631–643. Springer, Heidelberg (2014)
8. Mei, Y., Li, X., Yao, X.: On investigation of interdependence between sub-problems of the TTP. Soft Comput. **20**(1), 157–172 (2014)

9. Nallaperuma, S., Wagner, M., Neumann, F.: Analyzing the effects of instance features and algorithm parameters for max min ant system and the traveling salesperson problem. Front. Robot. AI **2**, 18 (2015)

10. Polyakovskiy, S., Bonyadi, M.R., Wagner, M., Michalewicz, Z., Neumann, F.: A comprehensive benchmark set and heuristics for the traveling thief problem. In: Genetic and Evolutionary Computation Conference, pp. 477–484. ACM (2014)

11. Polyakovskiy, S., Neumann, F.: Packing while traveling: mixed integer programming for a class of nonlinear knapsack problems. In: Michel, L. (ed.) CPAIOR 2015. LNCS, vol. 9075, pp. 332–346. Springer, Heidelberg (2015)

12. Stützle, T., Hoos, H.H.: MAX-MIN ant system. J. Future Gener. Comput. Syst. **16**, 889–914 (2000)

Extended Abstracts

Achieving Synchronisation in Swarm Robotics: Applying Networked Q-Learning to Production Line Automata

Christopher Deeks[✉]

Centre for Complexity Science, The University of Warwick, Coventry, UK
`c.r.deeks@warwick.ac.uk`

This paper describes a novel approach to the control of production line automata that aims to enable a pattern of complex synchronised behaviour to emerge from a number of independent automata that are not aware of or coordinated with each other. The motivating application is to enable greater concurrency and co-location of production line automata.

It is supposed that there is cause to co-locate a potentially large number of robots in a physically constrained area, with a high degree of concurrent tasking, where the robots have no awareness of the overall state or purpose of the collective. As the number of robots grows, complexity is introduced to the planning and initiation of the production line due to the need to carefully synchronise the behaviours of the robots. The goal is to be able to conduct many tasks in tightly choreographed synchrony without prohibitive ramp-up times.

Q-learners are a class of reinforcement learning agent that associate earned rewards to observed states and actions, thereby enumerating the value of different control actions. Adapting the standard formulation of Q-learning has been considered to enable autonomy within systems featuring concurrent subsystems by [1]. Q-learning has been considered as an approach to improve production line ramp-up times by [2]. These ideas combine to motivate a network of Q-learners controlling each automaton in a collective, to learn appropriate responses to situations when the automata impede each other, without the need for communication or pre-programmed mitigation.

For initial experimentation, ten agents must learn to trace out specified arcs on a lattice. The complication is that arcs overlap thus forcing collisions. The mathematical formulation used for this problem is Q-learners following the Markov Decision Process as discussed in [3]. Q-learners calculate not just an optimal policy, but a whole family of candidate policies. To avoid a collision, the Q-learner can be compelled to switch to a next best policy without any additional calculation. Figure 1 displays a snapshot of the ten agents tracing out their specific arcs featuring several examples of clear deviation to avoid collision.

The work reported in this paper has demonstrated that networked Q-learning is a viable approach to the synchronised autonomy problem. Next steps will be to incorporate random or aperiodic obstructions that cannot be learned by habit, and scaling up the number of agents by an order of magnitude and investigating emergent effects in particular clustered areas of the state space, for it is in configuring large collectives that big savings in ramp-up time can be expected.

© Springer International Publishing Switzerland 2016
M. Dorigo et al. (Eds.): ANTS 2016, LNCS 9882, pp. 285–286, 2016.
DOI: 10.1007/978-3-319-44427-7

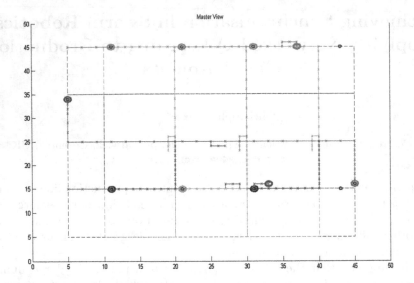

Fig. 1. Ten agents tracing learned paths with deviation to avoid collision.

Acknowledgements. The research reported in this paper was funded by the Engineering and Physical Sciences Research Council under the supervision of Prof. R. Mackay of the Centre for Complexity Science and Prof D. Ceglarek of the Warwick Manufacturing Group, University of Warwick.

References

1. Deeks, C., Vitanov, I., Williams, B.: Safety critical autonomy: bounding the behaviour of autonomous systems with hierarchical adaptive controllers (2008)
2. Doltsinis, S., Ferreira, P., Lohse, N.: An MDP model-based reinforcement learning approach for production station ramp-up optimization: Q-learning analysis (2014)
3. Sutton, R.S., Barto, A.G.: Reinforcement learning: an introduction (2012)

Autonomous Task Allocation for Swarm Robotic Systems Using Hierarchical Strategy

Yuki Wei[1]($^{\boxtimes}$), Toshiyuki Yasuda[1], and Kazuhiro Ohkura[1,2]

[1] Graduate School of Engineering, Hiroshima University, Higashi-Hiroshima, Hiroshima, Japan
wei@ohk.hiroshima-u.ac.jp
[2] Institute of Engineering, Hiroshima University, Higashi-Hiroshima, Hiroshima, Japan
{yasu,kohkura}@hiroshima-u.ac.jp

Autonomous task allocation in swarm robotic systems refers to the behavior resulting in robots being distributed over different sub-tasks dynamically while dealing with a complex task. The goal is to maximize the performance of the robot swarm [1]. However, the design of robot controller for generating autonomous task allocation behavior is difficult when the communication is limited, that is, each robot has to make decisions through its local observation.

In this study, we used a variation of the classic foraging task as our testbed, where two types of food: large and small, are in the field to be foraged by robots. Large foods must be moved to a split-up area first to be decomposed into small foods, and the small foods need to be transported to the nest, where the robots start.

To synthesize the controller for solving the given task, we adopted a hierarchical strategy based evolutionary robotics approach in which the controller is composed of several sub-controllers. The hierarchical strategy is based on the divide-and-conquer thinking: if a task is too complex to be solved directly, one can decompose it into relatively simple sub-tasks and achieve them respectively.

To apply the hierarchical strategy, the designer decomposes the original task into sub-tasks in a hierarchical and recursive way until all sub-tasks are solvable. The original task can be therefore represented by a tree-like graph. Importantly, the decomposition is based on the analysis of task specification rather than the robot individuals' abilities, which allows the designer to devise task structure by top-to-down schemes. In our task, we decomposed the original task into three sub-tasks: explore the field, decompose large foods by moving them to the split-up area, and, transport small foods to the nest.

In order to achieve those sub-tasks respectively, the controller is also organized in a hierarchical way similar to the sub-tasks, in which sub-controllers have two types: behavior primitive and arbitrator [3]. A behavior primitive is used to solve the corresponding sub-task, and a arbitrator combines several primitives together for generating relatively complex behaviors. In this study, we have three primitives and one arbitrator, all represented by artificial neural networks, receiving a part or all of the sensory inputs of the robot respectively. The outputs of primitives have direct control of the robot, while the outputs

© Springer International Publishing Switzerland 2016
M. Dorigo et al. (Eds.): ANTS 2016, LNCS 9882, pp. 287–288, 2016.
DOI: 10.1007/978-3-319-44427-7

of arbitrators are used to activate or restrain their primitives dynamically. The controller architecture is illustrated in Fig. 1.

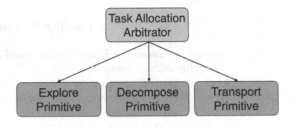

Fig. 1. Hierarchical Controller

The development of the controller is a hierarchical evolution process following a bottom-to-top procedure, that lower sub-controllers are evolved first, and then they are combined together through the artificial evolution of its upper arbitrator. This process is repeated until all controllers are developed. In addition, proper fitness functions for primitives are easy to find after the manual decomposition in our task, but it is not straightforward for the arbitrator. In this case, the arbitrator could derive the fitness functions from its sub-controllers [2].

We performed simulation experiments to compare the results obtained by the proposed approach with the ones by the original evolutionary robotics approach in which the robot controller is represented by a single artificial neural network. The results show that the hierarchical strategy based evolutionary robotics approach is effective: working controllers that generate autonomous task allocation behavior are obtained in eight of ten runs. On the contrary side, with the original evolutionary robotics approach, controllers with the highest fitnesses have resolved only one sub-task: move large foods to the split-up area, or transport existing small foods back to the nest while ignoring large foods, that is, they failed to change their roles performing different sub-tasks to achieve the original overall task.

References

1. Brambilla, M., Ferrante, E., Birattari, M., Dorigo, M.: Swarm robotics: a review from the swarm engineering perspective. Swarm Intell. **7**(1), 1–41 (2013)
2. Duarte, M., Oliveira, S., Christensen, A.L.: Hierarchical evolution of robotic controllers for complex tasks. In: Development and Learning and Epigenetic Robotics (ICDL), pp. 1–6 (2012)
3. Lee, W.P., Hallam, J., Lund, H.H.: Learning complex robot behaviours by evolutionary computing with task decomposition. In: Birk, A., Demiris, J. (eds.) EWLR-6. LNCS, vol. 1545, pp. 155–172. Springer, Heidelberg (1998)

Avoidance Strategies for Particle Swarm Optimisation in Power Generation Scheduling

Karl Mason[✉], Jim Duggan[✉], and Enda Howley[✉]

Discipline of Information Technology,
National University of Ireland Galway, Galway, Ireland
{k.mason2,james.duggan,ehowley}@nuigalway.ie

Particle swarm optimisation (PSO) is a swarm intelligence algorithm that consists of particles traversing a problem space, moving towards the best known locations [3]. This paper will apply multiple PSO variants to the problem of power generation. In power generator scheduling, it is crucial that electricity is produced in a cost-effective and environmentally friendly manner [1].

The **Standard PSO (SPSO)** has the following equations of motion [2]:

$$v_{t+1} = \chi(v_t + r_1 c_1(pb_t - x_t) + r_2 c_2(gb_t - x_t) \tag{1}$$

$$x_{t+1} = x_t + v_t \tag{2}$$

The **PSO with Avoidance of Worst Locations (PSO AWL)** incorporates a negative stimulus on the motion of the particles as follows [6]:

$$v_{t+1} = \chi(v_t + r_1 c_1(pb_t - x_t) + r_2 c_2(gb_t - x_t)$$
$$+ r_3 c_3 \left(\frac{t_1}{(1 + |x_t - pw_t|)}\right) + r_4 c_4 \left(\frac{t_2}{(1 + |x_t - gw_t|)}\right)) \tag{3}$$

Four topologies, Global, Ring, von Neumann and Gradually Increasing Directed Neighbourhood (PSO GIDN) will be evaluated [4].

The DEED problem consists of optimising the power P from $N = 10$ generators over $M = 24$ h to minimise both cost and emissions [1]. The cost function f_1 and emissions function f_2 are:

$$f_1 = \sum_{m=1}^{M} \sum_{i=1}^{N} [a_i + b_i P_{im} + c_i P_{im}^2 + |d_i sin\{e_i(P_i^{min} - P_{im})\}|] \tag{4}$$

$$f_2 = \sum_{m=1}^{M} \sum_{i=1}^{N} [\alpha_i + \beta_i P_{im} + \gamma_i P_{im}^2 + \eta \exp \delta P_{im}] \tag{5}$$

Where a_i, b_i, c_i, d_i, e_i, α_i, β_i, γ_i, η_i and δ_i are operation coefficients. Solutions are constrained by the power demand, generator operation limits and ramp limits [1].

© Springer International Publishing Switzerland 2016
M. Dorigo et al. (Eds.): ANTS 2016, LNCS 9882, pp. 289–290, 2016.
DOI: 10.1007/978-3-319-44427-7

Table 1. Average performance

Algorithm	Topology	Cost 10^6 \$	Emissions 10^5 lb
SPSO	global	2.6229	3.1858
SPSO	ring	2.6044	3.1075
SPSO	vn	2.6139	3.1565
SPSO	gidn	2.6406	3.2378
PSOAWL	global	2.5618	2.9923
PSOAWL	ring	2.5673	3.0020
PSOAWL	vn	2.5521	2.9559
PSOAWL	gidn	2.5463	2.9455
NSGA-II [1]	-	2.5226	3.0994
MARL [5]	-	2.6641	3.3255

Each PSO variant was averaged over 10 statistical runs, each run consisting of 100,000 iterations. The Wilcoxon Signed Sum Rank test (p-value of 0.05) was used to determine statistical significance. Table 1 shows that every topology variation of the PSO AWL performs statistically better than its SPSO equivalent. The PSO AWL with GIDN topology performed best overall, consistent with previous results [7]. Every variant of PSO AWL performs equally well when compared to the NSGA-II [1]. All PSO variants outperform MARL [5].

References

1. Basu, M.: Dynamic economic emission dispatch using nondominated sorting genetic algorithm-ii. Int. J. Electr. Power Energy Syst. **30**(2), 140–149 (2008)
2. Bratton, D., Kennedy, J.: Defining a standard for particle swarm optimization. In: IEEE Swarm Intelligence Symposium, SIS 2007, pp. 120–127. IEEE (2007)
3. Kennedy, J., Eberhart, R.: Particle swarm optimization. In: Proceedings of the IEEE International Conference on Neural Networks, vol. 4, pp. 1942–1948, November 1995
4. Liu, H., Howley, E., Duggan, J.: Particle swarm optimisation with gradually increasing directed neighbourhoods. In: Proceedings of the 13th Annual Conference on Genetic and Evolutionary Computation, pp. 29–36. ACM (2011)
5. Mannion, P., Mason, K., Duggan, J., Howley, E.: Dynamic economic emissions dispatch optimisation using multi-agent reinforcement learning. In: Proceedings of the Adaptive and Learning Agents Workshop (at AAMAS 2016) (2016)
6. Mason, K., Howley, E.: Avoidance strategies in particle swarm optimisation. In: Matousek, R. (ed.) Mendel 2015. Advances in Intelligent Systems and Computing, vol. 378, pp. 3–15. Springer International Publishing (2015). http://dx.doi.org/10.1007/978-3-319-19824-8_1
7. Mason, K., Howley, E.: Exploring avoidance strategies and neighbourhood topologies in particle swarm optimisation. Int. J. Swarm Intell. (2016, In Press) (Special Issue on Advances in Evolutionary Computation, Fuzzy Logic and Swarm Intelligence)

Clustering with the ACOℝ Algorithm

Ashraf M. Abdelbar[1](✉) and Khalid M. Salama[2]

[1] Department of Mathematics and Computer Science, Brandon University,
Manitoba, Canada
abdelbara@brandonu.ca
[2] School of Computing, University of Kent, Canterbury, UK
kms39@kent.ac.uk

The ACOℝ algorithm [2] is an Ant Colony Optimization (ACO) algorithm for continuous variable optimization. Given a set of continuous-domain random variables $V_1, \ldots, V_n$, and an objective function $Q(V_1, \ldots, V_n)$, ACOℝ seeks to find the values of the n variables that optimize the objective function.

Although a large number of approaches to clustering have been investigated [3], including several ACO approaches [1], ACOℝ has not previously been applied to the clustering problem, to our knowledge. In the present work, we use ACOℝ to optimize the cluster centres, where the number of clusters C is externally prescribed by the user. We restrict our attention to dataset with only numeric attributes, although our approach can be extended to categorical attributes.

Let t denote the number of (numeric) attributes in the problem of interest. Then, clustering can be viewed as a continuous optimization problem where we are optimizing a real-valued vector of $n = tC$ dimensions. In other words, we are optimizing the centres of C clusters where each centre is specified by a t-dimensional vector. We refer to the C t dimensional vectors, collectively, as a n-dimensional candidate solution vector $V = (V_1, \ldots, V_n)$.

To compute the quality of a candidate solution vector V, we consider its constituent C t-dimensional cluster centre vectors, denoted $u_1, \ldots, u_C$, where each u_k consists of $u_k = (u_{k1}, u_{k2}, \ldots, u_{kC})$. Let $\mathcal{T}$ denote the dataset to be clustered; $\mathcal{T}$ is partitioned into C disjoint clusters $\mathcal{T}_1, \mathcal{T}_2, \ldots, \mathcal{T}_C$ as follows. For each instance $x \in \mathcal{T}$, we find the nearest cluster centre $\phi(x)$:

$$\phi(x) = \operatorname*{argmin}_{k}\{\|x - u_k\|\} \tag{1}$$

and assign x to the cluster $\mathcal{T}_{\phi(x)}$.

We then compute Q as a measure of the cohesion of each cluster as follows:

$$Q(V) = \sum_{x \in \mathcal{T}} \|x - u_{\phi(x)}\|^2 \tag{2}$$

Note that $\|\cdot\|$ in Eqs. (1) and (2) can be an arbitrary distance measure, but in the present work we use Euclidean distance.

We evaluated our approach using 20 benchmark datasets, containing only numeric attributes, obtained from the UCI repository, comparing to the classical c-means algorithm. For each datasets, we carried out three experiments, with 3 different values for the prescribed number of clusters (2, 3, and 4). In each

© Springer International Publishing Switzerland 2016
M. Dorigo et al. (Eds.): ANTS 2016, LNCS 9882, pp. 291–293, 2016.
DOI: 10.1007/978-3-319-44427-7

Table 1. Experimental results: the cohesion index for each number of clusters is reported, for each dataset. The better (smaller) value in each case is shown in boldface.

	$C=2$		$C=3$		$C=4$	
	ACO_R	c-means	ACO_R	c-means	ACO_R	c-means
breast-p	**148.1**	148.1	126.5	**126.4**	124.5	**117.0**
breast-tissue	**17.3**	**17.3**	**13.6**	13.6	**10.1**	11.2
breast-w	**215.8**	**215.8**	196.7	**187.1**	183.3	**171.4**
cmc	**939.5**	965.3	**768.9**	778.5	**650.2**	683.0
credit-a	**655.3**	671.5	**561.3**	582.5	**492.1**	513.1
credit-g	**1,614.9**	1,648.7	**1,523.5**	1,526.4	**1,450.7**	1,461.2
dermatology	792.5	**787.0**	**564.8**	633.5	**509.0**	562.6
ecoli	**49.7**	50.3	**35.4**	36.4	**30.1**	30.6
glass	**34.1**	37.7	**28.8**	30.0	**23.7**	26.7
hay	**59.0**	64.0	**48.6**	51.0	**40.0**	41.8
iris	**12.1**	**12.1**	**7.0**	8.2	5.8	**5.8**
liver-disorders	**30.0**	30.0	**25.3**	25.5	**22.2**	22.5
monks	**492.6**	523.7	**426.4**	449.8	**353.5**	380.8
parkinsons	**98.7**	98.7	**78.5**	78.5	**66.3**	66.9
pima	121.3	**121.3**	**107.2**	107.5	**96.3**	97.5
pop	**71.1**	76.0	**59.4**	60.9	**47.8**	54.8
thyroid	**16.4**	17.2	**10.7**	**10.7**	8.9	**8.9**
vertebral-column-2c	**24.2**	24.2	**19.3**	19.6	**17.4**	17.5
voting	**1,717.4**	3,453.0	**1,618.6**	3,430.2	**1,516.7**	3,430.2
wine	**64.5**	64.5	**49.0**	49.0	**45.3**	45.5
wins	**18**	5	**18**	3	**16**	4
rank (avg)	**1.18**	1.83	**1.13**	1.88	**1.20**	1.80

experiment, we applied each of our approach and c-means 10 times, and took the average performance as representative of each algorithm. Table 1 shows these results reporting the value of cohesion as calculated according to Eq. (2) in each case. The final two rows show the average rank, and the number of "wins", of each algorithm in each experiment. We can see that our approach performed better in all three experiments.

We applied a Wilcoxon signed-ranks test, at the conservative 0.01 threshold, to compare the two algorithms for each of the three experiments. The p-values were determined to be 0.002 for 2 clusters, 0.001 for 3 clusters, and 0.005 for 4 clusters, indicating that the difference is statistically significant for all cases.

References

1. Jafar, M., Sivakumar, R.: Ant-based clustering algorithms: a brief survey. Int. J. Comput. Theory Eng. **2**, 787–796 (2010)
2. Liao, T., Socha, K., Montes de Oca, M., Stützle, T., Dorigo, M.: Ant colony optimization for mixed variable optimization problems. IEEE Trans. Evol. Comput. **18**(4), 503–518 (2014)
3. Xu, R., Wunsch, D.: Clustering. IEEE Press, Piscataway (2009)

Consideration Regarding the Reduction of Reality Gap in Evolutionary Swarm Robotics

Toshiyuki Yasuda[✉], Motoaki Hiraga, Akitoshi Adachi, and Kazuhiro Ohkura

Graduate School of Engineering, Hiroshima University, Higashi-Hiroshima, Japan
{yasu,kohkura}@hiroshima-u.ac.jp, {hiraga,adachi}@ohk.hiroshima-u.ac.jp

The design methodology for swarm robotic systems can be classified into two approaches [1] behavior-based and automatic design methods. To date, relatively few automatic design methods have been developed; however, one widely used principled approach is evolutionary robotics (ER), in which robot controllers are represented by evolving artificial neural networks (EANN).

Since ER approach on real robots might be time-consuming, results obtained in simulations are often implemented in real robots. This implementation, however, causes another issue: the reality gap—it is hard to build simulations that transfer relatively smoothly to real robots. Typical approaches for this issue are modeling as accurately as possible the robot-environment interactions [4] or modeling only real world characteristics relevant for the emergence of a desired behavior [3].

An alternative approach, especially for swarm robotics, was proposed by Gauci et al. [2]. The optimal controller was designed by a behavior-based method in an aggregation task. Gauci et al. anticipated that the ease of porting the synthesized controller onto a system of physical robots would carry forward to other platforms. With inspiration stemming from their approach, this paper investigates how the individual-level simplicity affects swarm-level behavior in ER approach. The performance is evaluated in a box-pushing task, relatively complex one compared with that tackled by Gauci et al.

The arena used for the experiments is a rectangle of size 600 cm × 400 cm surrounded by walls as is shown in Fig. 1. Three circular boxes, each of which needs two or more robots to be moved, are located in the field. The task for the robots is pushing the boxes in the right direction.

Figure 2 shows the two-wheeled mobile robot. The robot is 28 cm tall and 18 cm in diameter. It is equipped with seven distance sensors and an omnidirectional camera. In the experiments, how the quantity of information from the camera affects the reality gap is investigated. The computer simulation is developed using Box2D, a two-dimensional physics engine.

In the experiments, 20 mobile robots are employed. A robot has the same artificial neural network (ANN) as its controller and has a sensory system consisting of eight infrared (IR) sensors and an omnidirectional camera. The camera images are equiangularly segmented into $p(= 2, 3, 4, 8, 12, 24)$ partitions. The synaptic weights are evolved by using (30, 200) evolution strategies. The swarm performance is evaluated by means of the moving distance of the boxes.

M. Dorigo et al. (Eds.): ANTS 2016, LNCS 9882, pp. 294–295, 2016.
DOI: 10.1007/978-3-319-44427-7

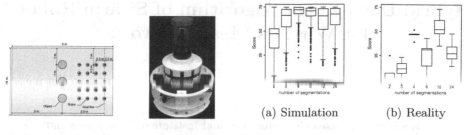

(a) Simulation   (b) Reality

Fig. 1. Experimental   **Fig. 2.** Robot.   **Fig. 3.** Moving distance of
environment: top view   boxes

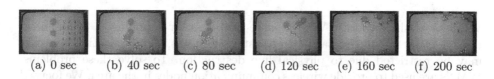

(a) 0 sec   (b) 40 sec   (c) 80 sec   (d) 120 sec   (e) 160 sec   (f) 200 sec

Fig. 4. Generated behavior ($p = 4$)

Figure 3(a) shows the fitness values of all the simulated run and Fig. 3(b) shows those obtained by implementing the best individual to the real robots. Although the performance in the real robot experiments degrades compared with computer simulations, the similar tendency can be observed: the robots with $p = 4$ generate the best results. The behavior observed in the real robot experiments are shown in Fig. 4.

Conclusions: This paper focused on the reality gap in evolutionary swarm robotics approach and conducted physical experiments. The results obtained suggested that the simplicity of individuals can mitigate the reality gap. In future, we plan to examine the reality gap of robots with simply designed motor outputs and neural controllers. In addition, we plan to conduct physical experiments in other scenarios such as foraging and pursuit.

References

1. Brambilla, M., Ferrante, E., Birattari, M., Dorigo, M.: Swarm robotics: a review from the swarm engineering perspective. Swarm Intell. **7**(1), 141 (2013)
2. Gauci, M., Chen, J., Li, W., Dodd, T.J., Groß, R.: Self-organized aggregation without computation. Int. J. Robot. Res. doi:10.1177/0278364914525244 (2014)
3. Jakobi, N.: Half-baked, ad-hoc and noisy: minimal simulations for evolutionary robotics. In: Fourth European Conference on Artificial Life, p. 348–357. MIT press (1997)
4. Miglino, O., Lund, H.H., Nolfi, S.: Evolving mobile robots in simulated and real environments. Artif. Life **2**(4), 417–434 (1995)

Hybrid Deployment Algorithm of Swarm Robots for Wireless Mesh Network

Kiyohiko Hattori[1]([✉]), Naoki Tatebe[2], Toshinori Kagawa[1], Yasunori Owada[1], and Kiyoshi Hamaguchi[1]

[1] Resilient ICT Research Center, National Institute of Information and Communications Technology, Miyagi, Japan
{hattori,kagawa,yowada,hamaguchi}@nict.go.jp
[2] So-net Corporation, Tokyo, Japan
pasmpd1024@gmail.com

Wireless Mesh Networks (WMNs) were proposed for supplying a communications network in a huge disaster. In disaster situations, communication networks may be restricted due to physical line destruction. To solve these problems, WMNs are used to provide wireless communication nodes in the area. We focused on the use of many swarm robots as communication node, and employed a RSSI to estimate positions. Our objective was to develop a method for deploying swarm robots for a WMN.

There are two approaches to deploy WMNs: (1) stationary nodes, and (2) mobile nodes approaches. Here, we review previous studies on mobile nodes (robots) approaches. In this approach, mobile robots placed at initial positions. A particular mobile robot estimates the positions of the other robots and decides on a course of action. Correll et al. [1] proposed a method for deploying robots based on the variation of the RSSI with the distance between the transmitter and the receiver. The method involves rough estimation of the distance between the robots and was improved by Shibata et al. [2]. In these studies, the robots moved randomly when the stipulated condition was not fulfilled.

We propose a algorithm that allows robots equipped with transceivers to expand over the target area based on the RSSI. In the proposed method, a robot moves based on the RSSIs between itself and other robots. Because the RSSI is inversely proportional to the square of the distance between the transmitter and the receiver, a decrease in the RSSI between two robots indicates increasing distance between the transmitter and receiver of the robots. This feature was effectively used to increase the distances among all the robots. The spreading out of the robots enables a larger area to be covered by the WMN that they form.

To spread out the robots by RSSI to a environment that includes some obstacles, we used three algorithms for (1) dynamic role allocation involving moving, referencing, and waiting; (2) direction update for move-ment of robots by RSSI, and (3) detouring obstacle by movement function along walls, respectively. Here, we explain a detail of (3). We understood that our direction update algorithm has a weak point for detouring obstacles, because RSSI based direction control only be able to control direction roughly. This idea well performed in no obstacles

© Springer International Publishing Switzerland 2016
M. Dorigo et al. (Eds.): ANTS 2016, LNCS 9882, pp. 296–297, 2016.
DOI: 10.1007/978-3-319-44427-7

flat area, however, is not good at many obstacles no flat area. To overcome this problem, we added new function for detouring obstacle by movement function along walls. The idea is very simple that all robots move for deploying area based on RSSI based control by touching obstacles. If a robot touches an obstacle, its mode changed to along wall moving mode and try to along wall using touch sensor by predefined certain seconds.

We understood that our direction update algorithm has a weak point for detouring obstacles, because RSSI based direction control only be able to control direction roughly. This idea well performed in no obstacles area, however, is not good at many obstacles area. To overcome this problem, we added new function for detouring obstacle by movement function along walls. The idea is very simple that all robots move for deploying area based on RSSI control by touching obstacles. If a robot touch an obstacle, its mode changed to along wall moving mode, and try to along wall using touch sensor by predefined certain seconds.

In this study, we developed a WMNs for facilitating intervention in a major disaster. We employed the method of deploying mobile robots using RSSI and detouring obstacles by movement function along walls to deploy robots effectively. The proposed method and a conventional method were examined by simulations. It was found that the proposed method required less time than the conventional method for the deployment of a network with nearly the same coverage.

References

1. Correll, N., Bachrach, J., Vickery, D., Rus, D.: Ad-hoc wireless network coverage with networked robots that cannot localize. In: IEEE International Conference on Robotics and Automation, ICRA 2009, pp. 3878–3885 (2009)
2. Shibata, Y., Mori, S., Yono, H.: B-6-66 mobility control algorithm considering distance among neighboring robots for mobile mesh networks. In: Proceedings of the Society Conference of IEICE 2011, vol. 66 (2011)

On the Definition of Self-organizing Systems: Relevance of Positive/Negative Feedback and Fluctuations

Yara Khaluf[1(✉)] and Heiko Hamann[2]

[1] Department of Information Technology-iMinds, Ghent University, Ghent, Belgium
ykhaluf@Ugent.be
[2] Department of Computer Science, Heinz Nixdorf Institute, University of
Paderborn, Paderborn, Germany
heiko.hamann@uni-paderborn.de

Self-organization is a foundational feature in collective systems. It is one of the building blocks of swarm intelligence and occurs in both natural and artificial systems. There are several relevant definitions of self-organization but most of them agree in listing the following three main components: positive feedback, negative feedback, and fluctuations [1, 2]. The occurrence of fluctuations combined with amplification effects of positive feedback allow a system to explore new alternatives and to switch between stable states. That way a decision-making process is implemented. Negative feedback, in turn, stabilizes the system. The conflictive effects of positive and negative feedback combined with fluctuations keep the system in a dynamic state. The evolution of the system, hence, is a sequence of exploitative and explorative phases. Our objective is to test whether each of these three components is required to define self-organizing systems. We investigate all possible combinations of keeping and leaving out components. Then we check the respective systems for self-organization by testing their ability to make collective decisions. We model the collective systems on a global level and make innovative use of methods from different fields. While we find the expected result that the definitions of self-organization in collective systems are probably concise and appropriate, our main result is that non-self-organizing systems with interesting collective behaviors exist.

We use population models in our study to represent infinite systems that have no fluctuations. They are described by deterministic ordinary differential equations (ODE). We investigate the dynamics of systems that have either positive or negative feedback by modeling two interdependent subpopulations. We study the domination of one population over the other as a result of the feedback. We also use the logistic growth model [3, 5] to study the dynamics of systems with both positive and negative feedback in the absence of fluctuations. Due to the interplay between positive and negative feedback, the system stabilizes when its so-called 'carrying capacity' is reached. We test the process of reaching the carrying capacity starting from population sizes below and above the carrying capacity. This way we observe the inverted effects of the interactions between positive and negative feedback.

Urn models can represent both infinite and finite systems and they also implement stochastic processes, that is, they model fluctuations. We use specific

© Springer International Publishing Switzerland 2016
M. Dorigo et al. (Eds.): ANTS 2016, LNCS 9882, pp. 298–299, 2016.
DOI: 10.1007/978-3-319-44427-7

urn models, such as the Pólya urn model [4, 6]. This model is used to analyze systems that are either based only on fluctuations or on positive feedback in combination with fluctuations. An interesting result is that tuning the strength of the positive feedback can provide the system with the ability of making collective decisions. This effect was observed in systems that grow in size and it relies on a random initial steep increase in the number of marbles belonging to a particular color. Furthermore, we have defined several other variants of the urn model such as the 'inverted' Pólya urn model in which the rule of adding marbles is inverted compared to the original model (drawing one color increases the number of marbles of the other color). This urn model was used for systems with negative feedback and fluctuations. In these systems, we find that the stabilizing effect of negative feedback keeps the system away from situations with big majorities of either color and hence keeps it undecided. In addition, we use a finite urn model for systems with finite sizes and find that these systems lose their ability to explore alternative options.

With our results we confirm that the definition of self-organizing systems in the context of collective systems is probably minimal and complete, that is, all three main components are required. However, our study also shows that there is a set of systems that needs to be labeled as non-self-organizing according to the definition but which shares key features with self-organizing systems. For example, we found non-self-organizing systems with the ability to make decisions. That result could be used in the future to design collective decision-making systems with even more limited requirements compared to self-organizing systems.

References

1. Bonabeau, E., Dorigo, M., Theraulaz, G.: Swarm Intelligence: from Natural to Artificial Systems. Oxford University Press, New York (1999)
2. Camazine, S., Deneubourg, J., Franks, N., Sneyd, J., Theraulaz, G., Bonabeau, E.: Self-Organizing Biological Systems. Princeton University Press, Princeton (2001)
3. DeAngelis, D., Post, W.M., Travis, C.C.: Positive Feedback in Natural Systems. Springer, Berlin (1986)
4. Drinea, E., Frieze, A., Mitzenmacher, M.: Balls and bins models with feedback. In: Proceedings of the 13th ACM-SIAM Symposium on Discrete Algorithms. pp. 308–315. Society for Industrial and Applied Mathematics, Philadelphia, PA (2002)
5. Malthus, T.: An Essay on the Principle of Population, as it Affects the Future Improvement of Society, vol. 2. J. Johnson, London (1809)
6. Pólya, G., Eggenberger, F.: Über die Statistik verketteter Vorgänge. Zeitschrift für Angewandte Mathematik und Mechanik **3**(4), 279–289 (1923)

Particle Swarm Optimisation with Diversity Influenced Gradually Increasing Neighbourhoods

Karl Mason[(✉)], Caitriona Kellehan[(✉)], Jim Duggan[(✉)], and Enda Howley[(✉)]

Discipline of Information Technology,
National University of Ireland Galway, Galway, Ireland
{k.mason2,c.kellehan2,james.duggan,ehowley}@nuigalway.ie

Particle swarm optimisation (PSO) is a nature inspired approach to solving optimisation problems. The algorithm was initially developed by Eberhart and Kennedy in 1995 [1]. There have been many variations to PSO since its first proposal [3, 5] and many real world applications [4]. This paper will focus on the area of particle neighbourhoods by extending the PSO with Gradually Increasing Directed Neighbourhood (PSO-GIDN) [2]. The proposed PSO variation will use particle diversity as an indicator of when to increase neighbourhood size. Particle diversity is a measure of how spread out the particles are throughout the problem space and is a popular area of research [5, 6]. This paper will answer the following research question: Can the performance of the PSO algorithm be improved by incorporating a diversity based dynamic topology?

The drawback with the PSO GIDN is that new neighbours are added at a fixed rate regardless of the problem space [2]. This is a problem which the proposed the PSO Diversity Influenced Gradually Increasing Neighbourhoods (PSO-DIGIN) aims to address. The PSO-DIGIN will incorporate a diversity measure, based on the ARPSO, to indicate when the addition of neighbours should be performed [5]:

$$D(S) = \frac{1}{|S||L|} \sum_{i=1}^{|S|} \sqrt{\sum_{j=1}^{D}(x_{ij} - \bar{x}_j)^2} \tag{1}$$

Where $|S|$ is the size of the swarm, $|L|$ is the length of the longest dimension, D is the number of dimensions, x_{ij} is the particle position and $\bar{x}_j$ is the average position in the jth dimension. To increase the neighbourhood size, the following neighbourhood expansion function m_t is proposed:

$$m_t = \lfloor (D_o - D_t) \times (\frac{t}{max_t})^{\rho} \times |S| \rfloor \tag{2}$$

Where t is the current iteration, max_t is the maximum iteration, and $\rho = 0.5$ is the time step influence coefficient, i.e the parameter which determines the influence that the current iteration has on the diversity measure. If $m_t > m_{t-1}$ a new neighbour is added to each particle. To ensure that convergence occurs in the later stages, the swarm becomes fully connected at $0.9 * max_t$.

In order to evaluate the performance of the proposed PSO DIGIN, a suite of 32 benchmark functions will be used as a test bed [7]. Table 1 outlines the

© Springer International Publishing Switzerland 2016
M. Dorigo et al. (Eds.): ANTS 2016, LNCS 9882, pp. 300–302, 2016.
DOI: 10.1007/978-3-319-44427-7

Table 1. Average Performance

Function	DIGIN Mean (STD)	GIDN Mean (STD)
Sphere	**7.00E-04 (1.83E-04)**	8.07E-04 (2.00E-00)
Rosenbrock	**2.08E+01 (1.61E+00)**	2.28E+01 (2.25E+00)
Ackley	**9.38E-15 (3.86E-15)**	5.58E-14 (4.05E-14)
Griewank	7.39E-03 (1.01E-02)	**5.32E-03 (1.00E-02)**
Rastrigin	**4.76E+01 (9.94E+00)**	6.34E+01 (1.52E+01)
Schaffer	**0.00E+00 (0.00E+00)**	**0.00E+00 (0.00E+00)**
Griewank10	4.36E-02 (2.43E-02)	**2.59E-02 (1.97E-02)**
f_1	**−4.50E+02 (3.54E-13)**	−4.50E+02 (2.53E-13)
f_2	**−4.50E+02 (3.54E-13)**	−4.50E+02 (3.10E-13)
f_3	**9.73E+06 (2.02E+07)**	1.45E+07 (1.33E+07)
f_4	−4.50E+02 (1.01E-08)	**−4.50E+02 (6.99E-13)**
f_5	**5.07E+03 (9.58E+02)**	5.41E+03 (1.64E+03)
f_6	**4.24E+02 (3.50E+01)**	4.51E+02 (6.05E+01)
f_7	−1.78E+02 (4.13E+00)	**− 1.79E+02 (1.59E+00)**
f_8	−1.19E+02 (6.43E-02)	**−1.19E+02 (4.73E-02)**
f_9	**−2.91E+02 (1.16E+01)**	−2.76E+02 (1.34E+01)
f_{10}	**−2.93E+02 (8.98E+00)**	−2.80E+02 (1.34E+01)
f_{11}	**1.19E+02 (3.17E+00)**	1.21E+02 (2.28E+00)
f_{12}	**3.34E+04 (2.80E+04)**	4.05E+04 (3.09E+04)
f_{13}	**−1.26E+02 (7.59E-01)**	−1.25E+02 (1.50E+00)
f_{14}	−2.87E+02 (3.22E-01)	**−2.87E+02 (2.84E-01)**
f_{15}	**4.67E+02 (7.02E+01)**	4.80E+02 (7.01E+01)
f_{16}	**2.29E+02 (2.37E+01)**	2.81E+02 (5.07E+01)
f_{17}	**2.51E+02 (5.22E+01)**	3.29E+02 (5.45E+01)
f_{18}	2.28E+02 (1.13E+02)	**1.89E+02 (1.13E+02)**
f_{19}	**1.70E+02 (8.10E+01)**	1.81E+02 (1.10E+02)
f_{20}	2.08E+02 (1.37E+02)	**1.60E+02 (8.77E+01)**
f_{21}	1.04E+03 (2.27E+02)	**9.30E+02 (2.77E+02)**
f_{22}	**1.43E+03 (2.47E+01)**	1.43E+03 (2.22E+01)
f_{23}	1.08E+03 (1.78E+02)	**8.74E+02 (3.64E+02)**
f_{24}	7.20E+02 (4.26E+02)	**5.89E+02 (3.59E+02)**
f_{25}	8.98E+02 (4.41E+02)	**6.27E+02 (3.74E+02)**
Statistically		
Better	14	8
Equal	10	10

performance of the PSO DIGIN and PSO GIDN. The performance of each PSO was averaged over 25 statistical runs, each run consisting of 60 particles.

Table 1 illustrates that the PSO-DIGIN algorithm performs best on the highest number of functions and never performs the worst. With a significance level $\alpha - 0.05$, the Wilcoxon test reveals that PSO-DIGIN statistically outperforms or performs statistically equal to the PSO-GIDN on 24 functions. The results clearly demonstrate that a dynamic topology based on diversity can improve the performance of the PSO algorithm.

References

1. Kennedy, J., Eberhart, R.: Particle swarm optimization. In: Proceedings of the IEEE International Conference on Neural Networks, 1995, vol. 4, pp. 1942–1948, November 1995
2. Liu, H., Howley, E., Duggan, J.: Particle swarm optimisation with gradually increasing directed neighbourhoods. In: Proceedings of the 13th Annual Conference on Genetic and Evolutionary Computation, pp. 29–36. ACM (2011)
3. Mason, K., Howley, E.: Exploring avoidance strategies and neighbourhood topologies in particle swarm optimisation. Int. J. Swarm Intell. (2016, in press) (Special Issue on Advances in Evolutionary Computation, Fuzzy Logic and Swarm Intelligence)
4. Mason, K., Mannion, P., Duggan, J., Howley, E.: Applying multi-agent reinforcement learning to watershed management. In: Proceedings of the Adaptive and Learning Agents Workshop (at AAMAS 2016) (2016)
5. Riget, J., Vesterstrøm, J.S.: A diversity-guided particle swarm optimizer-the arpso. Department of Computer Science, University of Aarhus, Aarhus, Denmark, Technical report 2, 2002 (2002)
6. Shi, Y., Eberhart, R.C.: Monitoring of particle swarm optimization. Fronti. Comput. Sci. China **3**(1), 31–37 (2009). doi:10.1007/s11704-009-0008-4
7. Suganthan, P.N., Hansen, N., Liang, J.J., Deb, K., Chen, Y.P., Auger, A., Tiwari, S.: Problem definitions and evaluation criteria for the CEC 2005 special session on real-parameter optimization. KanGAL Report 2005005 (2005)

Author Index